D0713049

The Decline of Popular Politics

THE AMERICAN NORTH, 1865 - 1928

Michael E. McGerr

REPLICA BOOKS
A DIVISION OF BAKER & TAYLOR
BRIDGEWATER, NJ

FIRST REPLICA BOOKS EDITION MAY, 2000

Published by Replica Books, a division of Baker & Taylor,
1200 Route 22 East, Bridgewater, NJ 08807

Replica Books is a trademark of Baker & Taylor

Biographical Note

This Replica books edition, first published in 2000, is an
unabridged republication of the work first published by
Oxford University Press, New York in 1986

Baker & Taylor Cataloging-in-Publication Data

McGerr, Michael E.
The decline of popular politics :
the American North, 1865-1928 / Michael E. McGerr.
1st Replica Books ed.
p. cm..
Originally published: New York :
Oxford University Press, 1986.
Includes bibliographical references and index.
ISBN 0-7351-0359-3
1. United States--Politics and government--1865-1933.
2. Political participation--United States--History.
3. Voting--United States--History.
I. Title.
E661 .M4 2000
324.973'08--dc21

Manufactured in the United States of America

THE DECLINE OF
POPULAR POLITICS

THE DECLINE OF POPULAR POLITICS

The American North, 1865–1928

MICHAEL E. McGERR

New York   Oxford
OXFORD UNIVERSITY PRESS
1986

Oxford University Press

Oxford   New York   Toronto
Delhi   Bombay   Calcutta   Madras   Karachi
Petaling Jaya   Singapore   Hong Kong   Tokyo
Nairobi   Dar es Salaam   Cape Town
Melbourne   Auckland

and associated companies in
Berlin   Ibadan

Copyright © 1986 by Michael E. McGerr

Published by Oxford University Press, Inc.,
200 Madison Avenue, New York, New York 10016

Oxford is the registered trademark of Oxford University Press

Library of Congress Cataloging-in-Publication Data
McGerr, Michael E.
The decline of popular politics.
Bibliography: p.
Includes index.
1. United States—Politics and government—1865–1933.
2. Political participation—United States—History.
3. Voting—United States—History.   I. title.
E661.M4   1986   324.973'08   85-21535
ISBN 0-19-503682-4
ISBN 0-19-505424-5 (PBK)

Printing (last digit): 9 8 7 6 5 4

Printed in the United States of America

FOR MY PARENTS

PREFACE

Put simply, this book seeks to explain why politics no longer excites many Americans. The chapters that follow trace the political withdrawal of Northerners after the turn of the twentieth century, not primarily to changes in election laws or the intrinsic interest of public issues, but rather to transformations in the style of politics. Over time, I believe, the customary language and behavior of public life have played a critically important role in determining whether Americans have participated in their government. In the mid-nineteenth century an intense partisanship, embodied in the party press, and spectacular election campaigns helped to sustain a popular politics embracing all social classes. Under attack from above after the Civil War, the partisan style gave way in the twentieth century to a mix of styles, educational and advertised, that made political participation difficult for millions of Northerners. By the 1920s the inclusive popular politics of the nineteenth century had largely disappeared; in its place was a more constricted public life, much like our own, characterized by low voter turnout, skepticism about parties and partisanship, and a curious emphasis on both objective discussion of issues and emotional identification with charismatic leaders.

This study is not another example of the quantitative "new" political history; others have counted turnout far better than I can. The problem now is not to refine the statistics but instead to interpret what they mean. The voting data here are a jumping-off point for a broader inquiry, necessarily speculative at some places, into the sources and significance of the transformation of style and the decline of popular politics.

I came to the matter of political style and participation because some years ago I was fortunate enough to encounter the work of Walter Dean Burnham, Richard Jensen, Paul Kleppner, and Robert Marcus. My debt to them should be apparent throughout the following pages.

I have incurred many other debts in the course of my work. Fellowships from the Graduate School of Yale University left me free to pursue my research at the beginning of this study. Later, the generosity of the Mrs. Giles Whiting Foundation enabled me to concentrate on research and writing for a year.

The help of numerous archivists and librarians speeded my labor. I am particularly grateful to staff members at the Connecticut State Library, the Harvard University libraries, the Library of Congress, the New York Public Library, and the Yale University libraries.

My fellow writer Celia Regan helped gather the statistics on newspapers. More than once, Ben and Erika Potz showed me their fine hospitality.

At Oxford University Press, Sheldon Meyer offered encouragement at several important points. Leona Capeless meticulously supervised the preparation of the manuscript.

Over the last several years, I have profited from the chance to exchange work and ideas with Edward Ayers, Iver Bernstein, and David Ward. Paul Bushkovitch, George Miles, and Frank M. Turner contributed to this study in ways I hope each will recognize. Early on, Michael F. Holt and David Montgomery asked hard questions that I still have not answered. David B. Davis, Lewis L. Gould, Melvyn Hammarberg, Pauline Maier, Gaddis Smith, and R. Hal Williams offered important criticism of various drafts of my ideas. For several years Professor Gould has generously shared with me his good humor and the fruits of his labor in far-flung archives. I have learned much political history from Richard L. McCormick; his criticism and his example inspired me to make this a better book.

When I was about to write a study that no longer fulfilled my original intentions, C. Vann Woodward encouraged me to follow my instincts and broaden the focus of my work to the entire

North. As on other occasions, I have not regretted his advice. For some time now, John M. Blum has labored to make me into an historian of the twentieth century. He has saved me from more than one mistake in these pages and improved my prose throughout. Since Howard R. Lamar took a chance by admitting a junior to his graduate seminar ten years ago, I have benefited from his scholarship, enthusiasm, and advice. Despite the demands of his position as Dean of Yale College, he guided me throughout my graduate career and patiently supervised this study.

In so many ways, Rosemarie McGerr made this book possible. She had help towards the end from Katherine McGerr, who made sure I finished the job.

Cambridge, Massachusetts   M.E.M.
May 1985

CONTENTS

THE DECLINE OF
POPULAR POLITICS

1

POPULAR POLITICS

Early one evening in October 1876 groups of young men wearing military-style caps and capes and carrying kerosene torches in the shape of rifles gathered in the sixth ward of the city of New Haven, Connecticut. The men were members of the "York Escort," the "Shelton Escort," the "Bradley Guard," and the "H. G. Lewis Guard," marching companies formed for the presidential campaign that year and named in honor of four of the city's leading Democrats. Samuel A. York and Levi B. Bradley were judges; William R. Shelton and Henry G. Lewis, wealthy manufacturers. Lewis had served as mayor of New Haven since 1870; now Shelton hoped to succeed him. All four of these successful, middle-aged men belonged to the city's Protestant, Yankee upper class. The members of the marching companies, mostly Irish immigrants and the sons of immigrants, lived and worked as day-laborers and factory operatives in the poorest sections of New Haven's fifth, sixth, and eighth wards.

By seven o'clock, the companies had formed into line and lit their torches. On orders from the commanding officers, the men set off, a brass band at their head, through the darkening streets of the city. Several blocks away, in the first ward, the procession was joined by the "Deutsche Feger" or "German Sweepers," carrying brooms "symbolical of the coming sweeping clean of corruption from the land." In the third ward, the parade met two more companies of the "Shelton Escort" and the "Young Democracy," the latter with a banner that read "A clean sweep for our next Mayor—William R. Shelton." At city Democratic headquarters, the procession, now numbering about five hundred uniformed, torch-bearing marchers, offered an escort to several politicians, the orators for the evening.

Returning to the sixth ward at eight o'clock, the companies found three or four thousand people filling the streets around a temporary platform at a main intersection in a working-class neighborhood. Gas lights and Chinese lanterns brilliantly illuminated the surrounding buildings. As the companies marched and counter-marched, the band played and fireworks lit the sky. "The windows near," a reporter noted, "were filled with the fair faces of ladies, who smiled down upon the enthusiastic crowd below their sympathy with the meeting and its objects." While the band blared "The Star-Spangled Banner," a huge flag bearing the names and portraits of Samuel J. Tilden and Thomas A. Hendricks, the Democratic presidential ticket, was "flung to the breeze" from the roof of a building. "The cheering and applause . . . was deafening and continued," the reporter wrote, "the audience being so worked up by the occasion that it was with great difficulty that they could be called to sufficient order to allow the speakers to proceed." From the platform, six orators in turn denounced the corruption of the Republican party, praised Tilden and the American flag, and urged men to vote a straight Democratic ticket. Because the audience was so large, politicians also left the stand to speak from two points in the crowd. After more music and fireworks, the meeting ended at 10:30 "with cheers for Tilden and Hendricks, and William R. Shelton for Mayor."[1]

The "flag-raising" in the sixth ward, typical of thousands of public demonstrations across the United States in 1876, epitomized a popular politics that had flourished for nearly half a century. Popular politics had its roots in the eighteenth-century mobs who took to the streets to put pressure on governments in England and America. Slowly, out of the Revolution's proclamation of American independence and freedom grew an unprecedented politics of the people, increasingly sure of their power, increasingly heeded by political leaders.[2] In the early nineteenth century, popular politics was still largely an extra-legal affair. All men could not yet legally participate in government because the new states, like the colonies before them, restricted the right to vote. But restraints on the suffrage gradually eased after 1800. State legislatures repealed property qualifications for suffrage and gave most white men the vote. Politics was not yet fully inclusive: "universal suffrage" excluded women and, until the ratification of the Fifteenth Amendment in 1870, most blacks as well. But by the 1840s the nation had generally accepted the notion that white men of all classes should participate in politics by voting. More and more of them did just that. An average of 48 percent of eligible Americans cast ballots at the presidential elections from 1824 to 1836. From 1840 to 1872, the average turnout for presidential contests reached 69 percent; from 1876 to 1900, a record 77 percent.[3]

Popular politics involved more than suffrage rights and record turnouts. As the flag-raising in the sixth ward made clear, elections in the mid-nineteenth century required the visible endorsement of the people. Politics in the American colonies and the early republic mainly took place indoors among elites. To be sure, most of the important political decisions of the nineteenth century occurred in private as well. But much of political life was necessarily acted out in the streets. However undemocratic the results, American politics from roughly the 'thirties to the 'nineties demanded the legitimacy conferred by all classes of the people through parades and rallies and huge turnouts.

The political world of that rally in New Haven's sixth ward in 1876 has long since disappeared. The popular politics of street parades and record turnouts is gone. By now, Americans realize that they have lost interest in politics. Low voter turnouts, down almost to 50 percent at presidential elections, measure that loss in much-publicized statistics. Politicians and editorial writers often bemoan the drop in turnout. But by and large, we have come to terms with our disengagement from politics.

Americans accept the contemporary political world partly because they no longer have a sense of any alternative. The world of popular politics is remote. For the most part, social-scientific discussions treat falling interest and turnout as contemporary phenomena, perhaps traceable as far back as the 1950s.[4] Yet the origins of declining political participation lie much farther back. The matter is a problem of history as much as of social science. Voting first began to fall off around the turn of the century. After reaching the record levels of the late nineteenth century, turnout at presidential elections fell to 65 percent during 1900 to 1916 and then to 52 percent from 1920 to 1928. The Great Depression and the New Deal sparked a partial recovery, up to an average turnout of 60 percent at the presidential elections from 1932 to 1960, but voting has fallen back since then to the nadir of the 'twenties.[5] The political withdrawal of contemporary America cannot be understood without comprehending the decrease in turnout at the turn of the century.

Neither can that withdrawal be understood without explaining the disappearance of rallies like the one in New Haven's sixth ward in 1876. High voter turnouts were only one facet of the complex world of popular politics. Historians and social scientists have tended to forget the vital democratic theater that accompanied elections. We need to do more than explain falling turnout; we must also account for the demise of a politics that depended so clearly on the visible assent of the governed.

Part of the story of the decline of popular politics is well known. In the South during the 1890s, the prospect of an inter-racial coalition of the poor, marching under the banner of the People's party, frightened conservative white leaders. Those powerful men struck back with intimidation, fraud, and restrictive election laws to disfranchise blacks and many whites. Turnout in the South fell off sharply, from 64 percent at the presidential elections from 1876 to 1892 down to 50 percent at the elections of 1896 and

1900, 32 percent during the elections from 1900 to 1916, and finally just 20 percent in the contests of 1920 and 1924. The Southern upper class carried out disfranchisement with a candor that left few questions about the process and its causes. To be sure, there are disagreements over disfranchisement, but they center on a question of means: whether or not election laws only ratified a situation already brought about by force. The intentions of the disfranchisers and the results of their work are not in doubt.[6]

In contrast, the decline of voting in the North was slow and enigmatic. Average presidential turnout, 82 percent from 1876 to 1892, actually edged upward to 84 percent in 1896 and 1900 before sliding down to 75 percent from 1900 to 1916 and then 58 percent in 1920 and 1924.[7] New registration laws made voting a bit more difficult in some areas of the North, but there were no dramatic episodes of violent or legalized disfranchisement.[8]

As scholars have recognized for some time, the transformation of political parties played an important role in the drop in voting across the North. Falling turnout seems to have followed the succession of so-called "party systems"—distinct eras of relatively stable competition between major political parties, each drawing on a roughly unchanging constituency. Voting reached a peak during the third party system, a period from the mid–1850s to the early 'nineties in which Republicans and Democrats battled almost evenly in national elections. In the late 'nineties, turnout began to decline just after the creation of the fourth system, dominated by the Republicans. Competition between the major parties seemed to affect turnout as well. The close contests of the third party system spurred voting in the late nineteenth century; the fourth system, with its solidly Republican North and still more solidly Democratic South, offered less competitive elections. In some way, too, the hegemony of the Northern Republican business class that characterized the fourth system may have cut into popular political interest and involvement. Apparently, after the conservative William McKinley, aided by his canny manager Mark Hanna, won the presidential election of 1896, politics lost much of its democratic character and no longer engaged many of the people. Voting also seemed tied to decreasing loyalty to parties. During the record votes of the late nineteenth century, nearly all men cast straight tickets for a single party. As turnout started to fall in the fourth system, more and more voters split their tickets among candidates of different parties.[9]

Changes in the function of parties may have affected turnout. In the mid-nineteenth century the parties articulated the ethnic and religious loyalties and hostilities of Northern society. From the fourth party system on, the Democrats and Republicans did not draw so clearly on these social identifications and divisions; presumably as a consequence, Northern voters lost some of their interest in politics.[10] For much of the nineteenth century, political parties also served as the principal means of influencing the distribution of economic resources and privileges by government. When interest and pressure groups developed late in the century as a new vehicle for affecting governments increasingly involved in regulation of the economy, voting for party candidates in elections became less important.[11]

All these points are important and suggestive, but they leave the essential problem of the decline of popular politics in the North unresolved. We do not know why a decrease in party loyalty among some Northerners who cast ballots should have affected others who did not bother to vote. Competition and turnout were not perfectly linked: uncompetitive contests have often led to large votes; tight elections have sometimes produced small votes.[12] In any case, why should party competition have been so important to Northerners' decision to vote?

The connection between classes and turnout, so obvious in the South at the turn of the century, remains puzzling to the north. Was the triumph in the 1890s of McKinley and Hanna, and the businessmen they represented, truly so portentous for political participation? It is unclear, too, that the waning of ethno-religious politics, hardly absolute, can explain why some groups—women, the poor, the young—have voted less readily than others in the twentieth century. Neither is it immediately apparent why the emergence of pressure groups and government regulation should have kept many of the poor—ironically enough, the people least involved with interest-group politics—from casting ballots. In short, we know that changes in party affected political participation in the North, but we do not know precisely why or how. Equally important, we do not understand how parties and voting were linked to the disappearance of the ritual of popular politics. What did the end of torchlight parades and rallies mean for the parties and political participation in the North?

To explain the decline of popular politics, we must first explore how party, as an idea expressed in Northern culture and institutions, helped people to translate their political concerns into the act of voting in the mid-nineteenth century. The next chapter describes how popular politics was entwined in a subjective, demonstrative kind of partisanship. Supported by the party press and spectacular election campaigns, that partisanship made political participation easier than before or since.

The balance of this study recounts the collapse of popular politics. Chapter 3 analyzes the first decisive blow against that order, delivered, not in 1896 with the triumph of McKinley, but thirty years earlier. It was in the late 1860s and 1870s that liberal, upper-class reformers rejected popular politics and formulated a new, less partisan, and less democratic conception of political life. Chapter 4 describes how politicians, adopting the liberal style, replaced spectacular electioneering with the "campaign of education" in the 'seventies, 'eighties, and 'nineties. Chapter 5 continues the story of the spread of liberal ideas in these years, this time through the press in the form of "independent journalism." But the chapter also introduces a competing political vision, alike anti-partisan and anti-liberal, that emerged from sensationalist newspapers by the turn of the century. The sixth chapter describes how the electoral counterpart of sensationalism, the advertised campaign, challenged the supremacy of educational electioneering after 1896. In the twentieth century, turnout began to fall: the seventh chapter considers the explanations Americans gave for the drop in voting. The chapter also recounts the failure of the "Get-Out-the-Vote" movement, well-to-do America's effort to lure men and women to the polls in the 1920s. All five chapters consider how, in different ways, the transformation of ideas and institutions made it increasingly difficult for many Northerners to link their political impulses with political action.

This study largely concerns political style, the different fashions in which people perceive, discuss, and act in politics. The following chapters focus on the trappings—partisan headlines, parades, and advertisements—that scholars usually consider useful only for adding a dash of color to history.[13] Political style deserves more serious attention. Without an understanding of the transformation of political style, we cannot account for the decline of popular politics in the North.

"Style" is a purposely narrow notion. Historians often speak of "political culture," by which they mean the whole complex of issues, ideologies, institutions, and social relationships that define politics. Style, as I intend it, is one part of political culture—the manner in which people think and behave politically. The history of political style embraces, not the reasons men voted Democratic or Republican, but only why it was natural for them to vote and to vote only for the candidates of a single party. The study of style does not explain why being Roman Catholic made a man Democratic, but rather how he could make the connection between his religion and political action. Neither does the history of style tell us why William McKinley ran for president in 1896 on a platform promising prosperity and the gold standard, but rather how Mark Hanna chose to present the candidate and his policies to the people.

Narrowly defined, political style leads nonetheless to critical issues of American history. Style does not exist apart from the concerns of power and policy that historians consider the substance of the past. My hope here is to demonstrate that changes in political style flowed from the needs and experiences of different classes in the North after the Civil War. The connection between style and class experience became most apparent in the liberal reformers, whose sense of social and political peril in the 1860s and 'seventies led them to recast the rules governing the conduct of public life. Sensational journalism and advertised campaigns grew out of a more complex situation in which several segments of Northern society—not just the big businessmen represented by McKinley and Hanna—responded to the diminishing cultural authority of partisanship, the alteration of class relations and communal life, and the evident failure of liberal politics.The evolution of political style brings us to the heart of social change in the North and to the origins of the decline of popular politics.

This study presents a certain paradox. Concerned with the demise of a "popular" form of politics, I have nonetheless devoted most of the following pages to the political strategies of the rich. That is because, after the Civil War, the different elements of the upper class placed their mark on the dominant styles of Northern politics more clearly than anyone else. I do not mean to neglect the radical alternatives of Greenbackers, Knights of Labor, Populists, and Socialists that glimmered at certain times and places after the Civil War: one of my principal aims is to explain why radical politics emerged more easily from the exuberant partisanship of the nineteenth century than from the educational, advertised public life of the twentieth.

At many points, this study treats participation as a matter of voting because turnout serves as a rough but acceptable gauge of political interest and because elections represent the sole form of political influence available to many Americans. Certainly voting is not the only form of political participation.[14] Between 1865 and 1928, Americans tried to influence government through new devices—above all, the non-partisan pressure group. As I hope to show, the early history of extra-partisan devices is critical to an understanding of the decline of voter turnout. Still, in the early twentieth century, just as today, the majority of Americans had nothing to do with pressure groups; the vote was their only political weapon. The last chapter considers whether decreases in voter turnout have made any difference in American society. For now, it is sufficient to note that the decline of voting between 1900 and 1928 meant that many Northerners lost or yielded their only opportunity to affect the state.

The history of Northern political style and participation from the 1860s to the 1920s is important because it provides an essential clue to the character of American politics in the 1980s. Commentators tend to treat contemporary political style, with its emphasis on candidates' personalities and media campaigns rather than on parties, as a revolutionary departure from the past. Yet by the 'twenties, the mix of educational and advertised styles in the North had produced a politics different in degree, not kind, from public life today. In many respects, though of course not all, Northern politics in the 1920s anticipated much of contemporary politics, North and South, in which so many fail to participate by choice rather than by law. The decline of popular politics in the North is also the origin of modern American politics.

2

PARTISANSHIP

From the start, parties were bound up in popular politics. The second party system, comprising the emerging Whig and Democratic organizations, developed as turnout increased across the North through the late 'twenties, 'thirties, and 'forties. In the mid-'fifties, the break-up of the Whig party, the founding of the Republican party, and the consequent formation of the third party system of Republicans and Democrats boosted turnout again. The parties stimulated political participation in several ways. Most plainly, party leaders fighting for the presidency and lesser electoral prizes needed votes; accordingly, the Democrats, Whigs, and Republicans built cadres of party workers to encourage men to go to the polls. Close elections, hotly contested by the parties, naturally spurred popular interest in politics and elections. Further, the parties, imperfectly and often reluctantly, articulated differences among people over economic and social issues, over tariffs, internal improvements, temperance, and slavery.[1]

The parties could serve as instruments of popular politics only because partisanship, the idea of loyalty to a party, was so deeply imbedded in Northern society. Partisanship won cultural acceptance slowly. The founders of the republic deplored parties and "party spirit." A man pledged to a faction or party could not be loyal to his country, the Revolutionary generation believed. They feared that conflicts between self-serving partisans might well topple the new nation. These ideas lost their hold in the nineteenth century as parties developed and men took sides in the battles of Federalists and Jeffersonian Republicans and then in the contests of Whigs and Democrats. By the 1830s and 1840s, many men agreed with politicians like Martin Van Buren that unswerving allegiance to a party was the first commandment of politics.[2]

An undercurrent of anti-party sentiment did persist, bubbling to the surface briefly during the collapse of the second party system during the 'fifties.[3] But by then nearly all men voted regularly for one party, almost always cast a straight party ticket, and threw their allegiance to another party only after much soul-searching.[4] "Fifty years ago, in times of peace, and twenty years ago, in time of war," the *Philadelphia Inquirer* recalled in 1884, "party lines were as strictly drawn as were the lines of religious sects. A man belonged to either the Democratic or the Whig party, to the Republican or the Democratic. He did not merely entertain opinions, he had convictions. A national political canvass was like a warlike campaign, both in its bitterness and the distinctness with which partisans were ranged upon sides." The editor of the *Inquirer* wrote at a time when party spirit had again come under attack. Yet for the last half-century, partisanship had been the touchstone of Northern politics, the common language of public life.[5]

Party was an essentially simple creed, but one woven deeply and intricately into the pattern of Northern society. Partisanship entailed more than attachment to a particular political organization. For mid-nineteenth-century Northerners, party became a natural lens through which to view the world. Most men found it second nature to perceive events from a partisan perspective and to imagine a black-and-white world of absolutes, of political friends and enemies. Party encouraged an intense, dogmatic cast of mind. Men made little distinction between fact and opinion: one's beliefs, Northerners assumed, rightly conditioned one's perception. This was a subjective way of apprehending the world, with party at the center, the basic principle of public life. Mid-nineteenth-century partisanship was aggressive, demonstrative, contentious, and often vicious. Party membership was a part of men's identity; as such, their partisanship had to be paraded and asserted in public.

Like most deeply held beliefs, partisanship remained largely unexamined. No important academic treatise appeared in the mid-nineteenth century to lay bare the workings of party in America.[6] Despite the tradition of anti-partyism, few men chose to reject partisanship and stand as independents. Those who did were excoriated, their manhood questioned. Not until after the Civil War would their dissent begin to have an effect on popular thinking.[7] The contours of partisanship emerged, not from textbooks and tracts, but from the institutions of public life, from the columns of the press and the rituals of election campaigns. At once product and cause of partisanship, newspapers and campaigns sustained popular politics in the mid-nineteenth century.

By the end of the Civil War, the press had become the principal medium of mass communication in the North. Newspapers set the tone of public life and established its language. In their columns, they created a world dominated by politics and partisanship. The political role of the press was hardly surprising. Newspapers and parties had developed in tandem in the nineteenth century. Beginning with the quarrels of Federalists and Jeffersonian Republicans, party leaders had founded papers to champion their causes. Other journals had chosen one side or another in partisan contests. At first, many papers were little more than "organs"—semiofficial mouthpieces of parties and factions in Washington and state capitals. As the number of papers increased, the era of near total party domination of the press soon ended. The last "organ" of an administration in Washington expired in 1861. But the press, more free from direct party control, still remained overwhelmingly partisan. In 1850, 95 percent of the daily and weekly papers in America claimed loyalty to some party. The few independent papers included the cheap "penny press" whose sensational style was significant for the future but whose political stance had little influence.[8] For virtually all editors, partisan affiliation came naturally and necessarily. "No political paper in the United States can be independent and live," a journalist wrote in 1871. "It may, in some cases, be independent of persons, but never of party principles and party fealty."[9]

Such fealty was usually eager and voluntary. Occasionally an editor bridled at the "party managers and heelers" who "put their feet on our tables, smoked our cigars," and tried to give orders. But such outbursts were exceptional. On the whole, newspapers gave themselves quite willingly to the support of one party or another.[10]

The press and the parties worked well together because they needed each other. Papers provided the communication necessary for a politics that depended on the participation of the people. Before the Civil War, politicians had been so desperate to reach the voters that the parties even published their own temporary papers to supplement the regular press during elections.[11] The campaign paper became less important by the 'sixties because the increasing number of outspokenly partisan papers gave the parties such an excellent forum.

Editors, for their part, needed the capital and business the parties could provide. Newspapers were not a large or very profitable enterprise for most of the nineteenth century. Rural "country" weeklies, limited to a few hundred, often delinquent, subscribers, usually had to keep up a job-printing business on the side in order to survive. "There are many comfortably rich men in the country, but few of them are editors," a writer observed as late as 1891. "Running a newspaper is like rowing a boat up-stream." The same was true even of urban dailies with circulations in the thousands. "Making newspapers," a city newspaperman lamented in 1881, "is not usually a primrose path to wealth."[12]

Parties boosted the income of journalists in several ways. In control of the White House, the Republicans or the Democrats could give valuable official advertising to several papers in each state and territory. The party in power often rewarded faithful editors with Federal patronage positions, particularly local postmasterships.[13] Senators and congressmen provided local papers with

printing contracts and out-of-town correspondents with unde-
manding extra jobs as clerks and secretaries of congressional committees.[14] Across the country, loyal journals could count on receiving a contract for official county and city advertising when their
party held local office.[15] Parties gave favored newspapers the contracts for printing ballots and campaign documents.[16] During elections the leading papers in large cities could expect to sell editions
in bulk lots to party clubs and committees for distribution to voters.[17] Politicians regularly paid subsidies to papers, particularly at
election time. Unscrupulous editors dangled their support of a
candidate or policy in return for payoffs: "Blackmail," snapped
Simon Cameron, a candidate for the Republican presidential
nomination in 1860.[18]

The relationship of parties and newspapers was not simply that
of business partners. Particularly up to the Civil War, press and
party often became one in the person of the editor-publisher.
Most papers were small establishments easily dominated by the
editor, who, in many cases, owned his paper in whole or in part.
On country weeklies, he did the work of writing and producing a
journal with help from only one or two assistants. City papers were
more elaborate affairs, but even the largest had only a small staff
of several editors and reporters. The urban dailies, for that matter,
produced the leading figures of this era of "personal journalism."
Such editors as Horace Greeley of the *New York Tribune,* William
Cullen Bryant of the *New York Evening Post,* and James Gordon
Bennett, Sr., of the *New York Herald* became famous for the indel-
ible personal stamp each placed on his paper.[19]

The mid-nineteenth-century editor often made his mark as a
politician as well. Typically, he sat on his party's county or city
committee and served a term or two in the legislature. Many leading national politicians had experience as the editors and publishers of newspapers. Schuyler Colfax, vice president in the first
Grant administration, had been an editor; so, too, had the speaker
of the house in those years, James G. Blaine. Although an editor
might bridle sometimes at the politicians who put their feet on his
desk, most often he considered these men associates, not intrud-
ers. Newspapers and parties of the mid-nineteenth century were
not a single entity, but they had overlapping business interests and
personnel.[20]

The press served the parties well. The ante-bellum editor, recalled Beman Brockway, a newspaperman from upstate New York, "used all of his talents to build up and strengthen his party, and to weaken and undermine the one to which he was opposed. His party and the measures it advocated were wholly right, those of his opponent wholly wrong."[21] Papers provided several tangible services to the parties. They publicized meetings and rallies for free and even collected campaign contributions on occasion.[22] Far more important was the papers' creation of a political, intensely partisan world for their readers.

The pages of the press made partisanship seem essential to men's identity. Party faith was the foundation of a journal, something to declare on inaugurating the paper, to reaffirm after a change of publishing partners or at the start of a new year. "We publish a Republican paper because we are Republicans, and have faith in Republican principles," the *Chicago Inter Ocean* told readers the week it began publishing in 1872.[23] Party papers also proclaimed their partisan convictions each day in a motto below the nameplate on the front page or atop the editorial masthead. The LaCrosse, Wisconsin, *Democrat,* remained proudly "Democratic at all times and under all circumstances." The *Chicago Inter Ocean* stood "Republican in everything, independent in nothing." Sometimes a paper clarified its ideological convictions with a motto. Each week during the sectional crisis, the *Independent Democrat,* a Republican sheet in Elyria, Ohio, invoked Daniel Webster on its masthead: "Liberty and the Union—the End and the Means." Year after year, the Democratic *Register* of New Haven featured a line from Jefferson under the nameplate on page one: "Equal and Exact Justice to All Men, Of Whatever State or Persuasion, Religious or Political."[24] During elections, papers demonstrated their loyalty to their party by running the names of its candidates each day on the masthead.[25] A paper failing to do so risked immediate censure from party members.[26] Through declarations, mottoes, and masthead tickets, the press conveyed the idea that fundamental loyalties and beliefs should naturally dictate people's view of the world.

Newspapers' editorial voice reinforced the sense of party as the basic guide to men and events. The editor presented a landscape starkly divided into friends and foes. Readers belonging to his party were admitted to an intimate discourse. When he used "we," the word referred not only to himself but also to fellow party members. The opposition party was "our enemies."[27] The editor explained his party's position on the issues and urged readers to work harder for party victory. "REPUBLICANS," asked the Ashtabula, Ohio, *Sentinel* before the election of 1860, "ARE YOU READY?" The editor cautioned readers to ignore propaganda from the opposition and to watch for tricks at the polls. On election day, he sprinkled his pages with injunctions to "Pay No Attention to Campaign Lies and Liars" and to "Guard the Polls" and "Vote Early!"[28]

Always ready to expose the opposing party's "lies" and "roorbacks," the editor set an example of militant, combative partisanship for his readers. "ANOTHER DEMOCRATIC SHAM" ran a typical heading in the Republican *New York Tribune* in 1880. Democratic papers took the same tack. In 1876, the *New York World* could head a news story about a Republican leader "HOW BLAINE KEEPS UP HIS LYING STATEMENTS."[29] Party papers saved their harshest fire for the opposition press. Privately, opposing editors often enjoyed warm friendships, but in public they cultivated a style of thrust and parry.[30] "Editors assailed their opponents as if they were villains of the most depraved stamp," Beman Brockway noted. "They did not appear to consider that there could be such a thing as an honest difference of opinion." Papers routinely accused one another of "twaddle," "inferior ability," "feeble malignity," lying, and, during and after the Civil War, treason.[31]

In much of the press, partisan opinion seemed almost to overwhelm the news. The mid-nineteenth-century paper, Beman Brockway insisted, "was not a newspaper at all. It contained little news of a general character, and almost no local intelligence. It was simply the organ of a party."[32] Many editors did not pursue news stories aggressively. Even after the advent of the telegraph in the 1840s, papers were content to await the arrival of papers from New York City or Chicago for full accounts of important stories. The journals of Davenport, Iowa, typified the party press on the eve of the Civil War. "They had no telegraph news save such as came at second-hand from the then limited supply of the Chicago newspapers," a journalist remembered. "Devotion to party was the test of the value of the journal. All else was subordinated to this feature."[33] Readers did not seem to mind. The novelist William Dean Howells conjured up the thinking of the subscribers to his father's weekly paper, the *Ashtabula Sentinel*, in the Western Reserve of Ohio. Even at election time, Howells wrote, "there was nothing very burning or seething in the eagerness of our subscribers. They could wait; their knowledge of the event would not change it, or add or take away one vote either way."[34]

Consequently there were only a few columns of news in papers, mostly limited by slow presses and high costs to just four pages an issue. Politics predominated. During campaigns, political stories flooded the papers and drove out other features, particularly those intended for women. "Now that the battle is over we shall have more time to devote to matters of general interest . . . ," the editor of the *New Haven Journal and Courier* promised after the spring elections of 1872. "The ladies, who are not generally fierce politicians, will be glad that the papers are able to devote more attention to other topics."[35]

Not surprisingly, the party press treated the news in partisan terms. Editors drew no clear line between fact and opinion, between reportage and editorial. The editorial page, as an entity separate from news stories, developed slowly before the Civil War. In the 'seventies and 'eighties, papers still did not distinguish consistently between story and editorial. Throughout the first three-quarters of the nineteenth century, editors and reporters considered both fit places for partisan opinion and distortion.[36] "Election returns were persistently falsified," wrote a veteran of ante-bellum editorial rooms, "political questions were elaborately misrepresented."[37] Outright falsification had no doubt diminished by the end of the Civil War, but party papers continued to distort the news. Their side's meetings and rallies always drew huge, enthusiastic crowds; the other party's were uniformly dismissed as a "fizzle" and "a dull affair," "Feeble," "tame," "despondent," and "forced," a "dead failure" and "a funeral."[38]

Accordingly, in towns and cities with both Republican and Democratic papers, readers confronted puzzling contradictions. Reporting on the Connecticut Republican state convention of 1876, the Democratic *New Haven Register* found the convention floor "half full, while the galleries were almost empty." The keynote address "fell flat on delegates and audience alike. Even the mention of the name of the republican candidate for the presidency created no enthusiasm." A second speaker was "long and rambling"; a third, "long and tiresome." In contrast, the Republican *Journal-Courier's* reporter discovered that "every available seat in the body of the hall was filled, while a large number of citizens occupied seats in the galleries." The keynote speaker "was loudly applauded," the second orator spoke "impassioned words exciting tumultuous applause," and the third delivered "an able and telling speech which excited renewed enthusiasm." Democratic and Republican papers offered conflicting realities in the mid-nineteenth century.[39]

The party press rooted in the news as well as twisted it. Papers habitually reported victories for their party as "Good News" and "GLORIOUS NEWS." "BOYS, WE'VE GOT 'EM!," the *New York Tribune* exulted over a report of state elections in 1860. "PENNSYLVANIA HAS DONE IT!"[40] Naturally, party editors played down defeat. Usually, they tucked bad news away with small, undemonstrative headlines. Sometimes, an editor tried to snatch victory out of defeat. When, as usual, the Democrats lost the Maine elections in 1876, the *New York World* rejoiced, "THE DEMOCRATIC VOTE 3,500 LARGER THAN EVER BEFORE." Most party papers tried to ignore bad news as much as possible. The day after a defeat, an editor might suddenly find fascination in the weather and "SIGNS OF SPRING."[41]

Papers emphasized the importance of politics and partisanship through their use of illustrations and headlines. Expensive and time-consuming to produce, wood-cut drawings seldom appeared in mid-nineteenth-century papers. Multi-column headlines in large type were unknown; single-column headlines were usually small and seldom lavish. But party victory in an election upset convention. Papers used a wealth of headlines and illustrations to mark political triumphs. Common victory wood-cuts included a firing cannon, a waving American flag, an eagle, an applauding raccoon, a crowing rooster, and a dead possum on its back symbolizing the vanquished opposition. Typically, an editor chose one or two of these symbols. Sometimes, giddy with triumph, he unleashed a flood of them. In 1876, the *Commercial* of Bangor, Maine, mistakenly certain that the Democratic candidate, Samuel

Tilden, had won the presidency, greeted the event with "HAL-
LELUJAH!," "THE REPUBLIC SAVED," "VOX POPULI! VOX
DEI!," woodcuts of an eagle, two large crowing roosters, two
smaller roosters, the Goddess of Liberty, two more eagles, the
names of the states casting electoral votes for Tilden arranged in
the "Democratic Pyramid," the names of the other states in the
"Republican Pyramid," and a wet, downcast rooster representing
a Republican leader "After the Shower!" For good measure, the
paper threw in "The Millions Have Spoken and Liberty Is Proclaimed Throughout the Land," "The Golden Age Begins," and
"The Republic Given a New Lease of Life." The editor liked the
display so much he ran it on the front page two more days.[42]

Day after day in the mid-nineteenth century, newspapers presented a political world and encouraged readers to view it in partisan terms. By reducing politics to black-and-white absolutes, the
press made partisanship enticing. The committed Republican or
Democrat did not need to puzzle over conflicting facts and arguments; in his paper he could find ready-made positions on any candidate and every issue. Undeviating loyalty to a party became the
key to simplifying and comprehending society. With their mottoes
and masthead tickets, party papers made such loyalty seem fundamental to personal identity. The press also legitimized a subjective partisanship grounded in the notion that a man's political
affiliation should color, and even distort, his perception of men
and events. Further, the press set an example of exuberant and
demonstrative party spirit. Through combative editorials and lavish victory displays, newspapermen declared that one's partisan
attachment must be publicly asserted, defended, and celebrated.

Of course, the press alone did not make men into partisans. But
newspapers had a subtle influence on Northern society. They reinforced patterns of popular thought and provided the common language of politics. Confronting the politically apathetic with the
worldview of the partisan majority, the press imposed a coercive
cultural uniformity on Northern public life. Editors could not
manipulate the outcome of a particular election or change opinion
on a given issue at will, but they did establish a partisan context
for politics in the mid-nineteenth century.

Northerners were not simply unknowing pawns of journalists.
Certainly people realized that the press distorted the news. They

often saw and doubtless heard of the accounts of the opposition's papers. Because no local paper supported their party, many men had to read an opposing sheet. This was particularly the case for Democrats, because Republican journals outnumbered the Democratic press by nearly two to one throughout the third party system.[43] A few readers liked to buy an opposition paper for the latest news.[44] But most Northerners preferred a paper devoted to their own party. The editor Richard Watson Gilder, recalling his days as a journalist in Newark, New Jersey, in the 1860s, noted that "men and women were common who swore by one paper, and they'd no more think of taking some other paper of a different stripe of politics than they would of drinking milk on lobster."[45]

Nevertheless, readers had to come to terms in some fashion with the obvious distortions of the partisan press. James Bryce, the perceptive English student of the United States in the Gilded Age, found Americans quite content with party journalism and altogether caught up in its slanted view of the world. Bryce observed the effect of the accusations of corruption levelled against the Republican nominee for president, James G. Blaine, during the campaign of 1884. "The immense majority of his supporters did not believe these charges," Bryce wrote. "They read their own newspapers chiefly, which pooh-poohed the charges. They could not be at the trouble of sifting the evidence, against which their own newspapers offered counterarguments, so they quietly ignored them. I do not say that they disbelieved. Between belief and disbelief there is an intermediate state of mind."[46] Although mid-nineteenth-century readers realized the press twisted the news, they seemed to believe that distortion was natural and proper. Republicans and Democrats knew their party's press sometimes lied, but they remained willing to live, as Bryce so astutely recognized, in that "intermediate state of mind." Readers themselves shared the newspapers' subjective, demonstrative partisanship. The stronghold of party on Northern society became dramatically apparent in presidential elections.

By the end of the Civil War, Northerners had turned political campaigns into spectacular displays of exuberant partisanship. Through participation in torchlight parades, mass rallies, and campaign clubs and marching companies, men gave expression to the partisan outlook of the newspaper press. The product of a constellation of social forces, spectacular campaigning powerfully influenced Northern political life. Along with the party press, the partisan display of elections made it easier than before or since for Northerners to act politically. Both cause and result of political participation, spectacular campaigns helped to push voter turnout upwards toward the record highs of the late nineteenth century.

The elements of spectacle first appeared at different times around the North: as early as 1802 in Maryland; as late as 1844 in conservative Connecticut, the "land of steady habits." Struggling to win presidential elections in the 'twenties and 'thirties, politicians formed campaign clubs, held rallies, delivered stump speeches, led the singing of campaign songs, and staged torchlight parades. In many states, the Whigs' exciting campaign for William Henry Harrison in 1840 established spectacle as an essential feature of political life.[47] During the third party system, Republicans and Democrats perfected the art of spectacular campaigning. For presidential contests, and occasionally those state contests charged with national issues, Democrats and Republicans used the traditional elements of political display more extensively than ever before and added the uniformed marching company to create an intense, enveloping partisan experience.

Spectacular electioneering in the third party system depended on the activities of clubs and marching companies usually formed for the duration of a campaign. Soon after the major parties' presidential nominations, often as early as June and July, the clubs gathered hundreds of voters, and sometimes men between eighteen and twenty-one as well, around a nucleus of party workers.[48] Most clubs organized along the geographical boundary lines of politics. In the countryside, there were school district and township clubs; in the cities, ward and election district organizations. Many clubs named themselves for their party's presidential ticket, as in the case of the Democratic "Hancock and English" clubs and the Republican "Garfield and Arthur" clubs of 1880.[49] Some clubs, such as the New York City Democrats' "John A. Gallagher Association" and "James A. Stauf Association" in 1876, paid tribute to local party leaders and candidates.[50] In towns and cities, many clubs represented social groups rather than election districts. Immigrants, set apart by language and culture, had their own organizations during campaigns; so, too, did blacks, isolated by color and prejudice.[51] Clubs also formed in the workplace. In 1880, employees of the "Plough Works" in Yonkers, New York, organized a Republican campaign club. Workers from different shops and trades joined together in the "Workingmen's Free Labor Club" of Chicago in 1860 and in the "Republican Mechanics' Club" of New Haven twenty years later. In New York City, employers had their own clubs, too, such as the "Merchants' and Manufacturers' Republican Association" and the "Produce Exchange Republican Association" of 1880.[52] Cities, in fact, found every constituency imaginable—old men, veterans, even deaf mutes—banded together for presidential campaigns.[53]

At its first meeting, a campaign club chose officers from president to corresponding secretary and drafted a constitution and "rules of order." Members joined by signing the constitution or club rolls as an affirmation of party loyalty.[54] Each club usually met at its "headquarters"—rented rooms with newspapers and campaign literature available for the public.[55] Occasionally, a club erected a temporary building, known as "Liberty Hall" or, perhaps more accurately, "the Wigwam."[56]

Formed alongside the clubs, and often sponsored by them, were uniformed marching companies. Men may have paraded in uniform occasionally during Jacksonian elections, but the military company became the trademark of spectacle in the third party system. In 1856, some Republicans formed companies of "Wide Awakes" to march in parades.[57] Four years later, Wide Awake companies led the Republican ranks across the North. The Wide Awakes and other companies of "Lincoln Guards," "Lincoln Rangers," "Lincoln Continentals," "Rail-Splitters," and "Young Americans" attracted mainly late-teenage boys and young men, who chose captains, lieutenants, and sergeants to lead them. The Wide Awakes wore military-style caps and oil-cloth capes to keep off the oil that dripped from the torches and lanterns they carried in parades.[58] At first scornful of the Republicans' organizations of young voters and minors, the opposition soon had to concede their popularity. Stephen Douglas's followers raised troops of "Little Dougs," "Little Giants," and "Ever Readies." The Constitutional Unionists had "Minute Men" and, playing on the surname of their presidential candidate, "Bell Ringers." More sober, the supporters of John C. Breckinridge fielded "National Democratic Volunteers."[59]

With so many men in real military uniforms, neither the Republicans nor the re-united Democrats raised uniformed companies in 1864. But after the Civil War, the marching company became a fixture of Northern presidential elections. Some Republicans still called their companies "Wide Awakes." Party leaders, however, preferred to remind voters of Republican prosecution of the war to save the Union by naming companies the "Boys in Blue." In 1884, perhaps as war memories faded, the Republican companies became the "Plumed Knights" in honor of presidential nominee James G. Blaine, Maine's "Plumed Knight."[60]

Some Democrats, emphasizing the presence of enfranchised blacks in the Republican party, founded companies of "White Boys in Blue" in 1868. Other Democrats paid tribute that year to their old leader with the "Jackson Guards." In the 'seventies and 'eighties, the Democracy usually honored the presidential ticket with companies like the "Tilden and Hendricks Guards" of 1876.[61] Both Republicans and Democrats also enlisted thousands of companies called "Zouaves," "Escorts," "Batteries," "Phalanxes," "Legions," "Hussars," "Minute Men," and "Continentals." Many of these, like New Haven's "Shelton Escort" and "H. G. Lewis Guard" in 1876 took their name from some local party leader.[62]

While most companies marched on foot and carried torches, others equipped themselves as "Engineer Corps" or as "Pioneer Corps" with battle axes to clear the way—symbolically—for parades. Some companies borrowed a cannon or two and became "Artillery"; some brandished fireworks as "Flambeau Corps"; many rode on horseback as "Cavalry."[63] Most companies, like the Wide Awakes of 1860, attracted young men ranging in age from the mid-teens to the mid-thirties. Sometimes, local leaders raised entire companies of minors, such as the "Blaine and Logan Cadets" of 1884. As veterans of the Civil War aged, the parties organized the old soldiers in companies of their own.[64]

Like the clubs, campaign military organizations gathered in towns and city wards under the leadership of party workers. Soon after their formation, the companies elected officers[65] and spent hours choosing just the right uniforms from campaign supply companies or a local clothier. Most political footsoldiers carried kerosene torches shaped like guns and simply wore a military cap and a shirt or oil-cloth cape, bought for about a dollar-and-a-half or two dollars, over their street clothes. Many companies went in for more expensive and elaborate ensembles. During the campaign of 1884, the "Michael C. Murphy Cleveland and Hendricks Legion" of New York City's first assembly district "wore jaunty uniforms of light gray, white leggings and white navy caps, each carrying a cane, with numerous colored lantern-bearers." In Augusta, Maine, the Republicans' "Zouaves" turned out for parades in 1880 dressed in "red trousers, white gaiters, white jackets trimmed with scarlet, and scarlet fezes with long yellow tassels." Naturally, the "Plumed Knights" of 1884 wore "helmets of ancient shape" with "white plumes" and carried battle axes "surmounted by torches."[66] As proud of their marching as of their new uniforms, the political soldiers then spent the rest of the summer and early fall drilling in preparation for appearances at parades and rallies.[67]

By September and October, clubs and companies marched and counter-marched across the North. In small towns each party typically had a campaign club, a marching company or two, and perhaps companies of veterans, boys, and blacks.[68] There were so many marchers in cities that the parties grouped the companies together in battalions, legions, regiments, brigades, and armies, whose colonels and generals issued "battle orders" to the troops on the eve of parades.[69] The companies and clubs absorbed the energies of millions of Northerners. During the campaign of 1880, New Haven, a city of 62,000 people living in thirteen wards, produced 42 clubs and 68 companies for the two major parties. Perhaps 5000 out of 16,000 eligible voters signed club constitutions or marched in the city's campaign army.[70] New Haven was not unique: more than a fifth of Northern voters probably played an active part in the campaign organizations of each presidential contest during the 'seventies and 'eighties.

Together the clubs and companies created a partisan spectacle that engulfed Northern communities for the three months before election day. When the national conventions chose the presidential candidates, local party members "ratified" the ticket with speeches, parades, bell-ringing, and cannon fire.[71] The campaign clubs held weekly open meetings in their rooms and wigwams to hear speeches.[72] "Pole-raisings" were popular events, particularly in rural areas. In 1828, Democrats had raised hickory poles in honor of "Old Hickory," Andrew Jackson. During campaigns in the third party system, men spent the better part of a day straining to erect Democratic "Hickory" poles or Republican "Liberty" poles, topped off with American flags or even "two sets of bucks horns." Spliced together from two tall trees, a pole could reach as much as 150 feet high.[73] In small towns and city wards, Democrats and Republicans held flag-raisings and banner-raisings much like the New Haven Democrats' affair in October 1876.[74] A keen sense of party rivalry animated the raisers of poles and banners. Republicans and Democrats competed to erect the highest pole in town or to obscure the opposition's banners with larger ones.[75]

In cities, the appearance of a party hero from another state, with an escort of local marching companies, filled halls and "opera houses." Unable to find seats inside, thousands of people often stood in the streets to hear orators speak from make-shift platforms.[76] Away from the cities, all-day rallies highlighted the campaign. In the morning, farmers formed their wagons in procession and drove to the county seat to watch a parade, perhaps eat a free lunch, listen to an afternoon of speeches from visiting party leaders, and then applaud a torchlight parade at night.[77]

In country and city alike, music accompanied campaign meetings and processions. The parties hired brass bands to lead parades and entertain at meetings and rallies. Republicans and Democrats often formed their own glee clubs during elections.[78] At rallies, audiences joined the clubs in singing songs written especially for the campaign. The songs, usually new lyrics set to familiar tunes, were collected in campaign songbooks issued by state and national party campaign committees and even by enthusiastic local party members. In 1876, Republicans sang such songs as "We will not vote for Tilden" and "Once more, ye true Republicans."[79]

Everywhere, parades marked the climax of the spectacular campaign.[80] In small towns, a company or two marched down the main street. In New York, as many as 50,000 local and out-of-town marchers might turn out for a parade. Across the North, the more elaborate processions included special attractions along with the usual uniformed marching companies. Sometimes men rolled a giant ball or wheel to symbolize the inexorable progress of party principles. Occasionally a live animal—a "coon" or a caged eagle—appeared in a procession. More often parades featured horse-drawn floats and giant wagons. The "ship of state," with girls and young women in white representing the states and the Goddess of Liberty, was particularly popular. Floats celebrated the varieties of labor, with men forging tools and making wheels. In 1860, Republicans underscored Abraham Lincoln's common origins with displays of rail-splitting. Eight years later, Republican floats portrayed the tanning of leather to remind people of Ulysses Grant's background.[81]

Republicans and Democrats held parades both day and night. The clubs and companies marched by day with banners proclaiming the ticket and party mottoes. By night they marched with torches and "transparencies"—more mottoes illuminated by oil lamps. Torchlight parades were the most popular. By the end of a campaign, communities were bathed in the glow of torches and transparencies. "You can hardly go out after dark without encountering a torchlight procession," a visitor to Maine wrote during the election of 1880. "In the larger places not a night passes without a demonstration of some sort. . . . Everything is at high tension." Cutting through the darkness of city streets or the black night of the prairie, the parades made a memorable sight. To one observer, a parade in Ohio looked "like the waves of a river on fire."[82]

Filling communities with politics, the spectacular campaign of rallies and parades drew people into the ritual of partisan display. Cheering crowds along parade routes set off roman candles and fireworks and burned chemical "red fire." Sympathetic businessmen lit up their stores and factories for parades. When a man's party marched by his home, his family turned on all the gas lamps. If he was well off, they decked the place with Chinese lanterns, bunting, and flags, and his daughters, dressed as Goddesses of Liberty, went out to stand on the lawn. When the opposition appeared in parade, his family hurried to turn off all the lights.[83] Voters wore increasingly elaborate campaign buttons and badges and ostentatiously made bets on the outcome of the election. Most bettors wagered money, dinners, hats, boots, or ties. More than one losing bettor had to push the winner or a pig around the town square in a wheelbarrow, shave off one side of his beard, or sit all day in a tree.[84] On election day, men cast distinctively printed or colored ballots that made their partisan choice clear to the crowd around the polling place.[85] If their party won, they turned out to cheer a victory parade.[86]

A celebration of partisan values, campaign pageantry was also popular because it offered people martial excitement and welcome diversion. Equally important, partisan display reflected the class relations and communal autonomy of Northern towns and cities in the mid-nineteenth century.

Marshaling their phalanxes of "Guards" and "Zouaves," spectacular campaigns catered to the popular fascination with the military brought to a peak by the Civil War. The vocabulary of war naturally provided the lexicon for nineteenth-century politicians and editors, who liked to portray elections as battles of contending armies.[87] Spectacular campaigns sometimes did seem like war. Parades of uniformed political soldiers often suffered attacks from opposition "roughs" armed with rocks, brickbats, guns, and knives.[88] In 1860 fearful Southerners believed the Wide Awakes would become an invading anti-slavery army.[89]

Spectacle clearly provided leisure activity for its actors and audiences. Yet partisan display was more than a diversion for an entertainment-starved people. In the countryside, men and women may have turned to spectacle for want of anything better to do. In cities and the larger towns, on the other hand, even the poor could choose between spectacle and such recreations as theaters, saloons, and fraternal organizations. During presidential elections, city-dwellers often preferred politics. "Now that the great political drama is played through . . . ," the New York Tribune reported after Lincoln's election in 1860, "a brighter era approaches for the theaters; and once more the benches, too often but scantily filled of late, will be crowded. . . ." Political spectacle, as a promoter of lectures in New Haven ruefully acknowledged in 1876, "keeps people away from amusements. . . ."[90]

Partisan display was not purely entertainment. Recalling the thousands who flocked to hear party orators in the campaign of 1860, a journalist noted years later, "People did not go to the stands for amusement. Everybody was intensely excited."[91] Spectacular campaigns mingled the intellectual stimulation of an open-air, hour-long oration on the tariff with the military nostalgia of the uniformed company. Partisan display combined the exertion of long marches with the delights of a fireworks show. Transforming communities into partisan tableaux, spectacle fused martial dreams, intellectual endeavor, leisure enjoyment, and hard labor in the service of politics.

Spectacular campaigns emerged from the pattern of class relations as well. Before the Civil War, partisan display had taken shape from the different needs of newly enfranchised workers and farmers, on the one side, and party leaders and local upper classes on the other. Spectacle, played out by these groups, became an intricate dance of accommodation between candidate and people, between rich men and poor men.

The ritual of campaign pageantry underscored the power of the North's workers and farmers. Nominated by a convention, candidates still had to receive the symbolic approval conferred by the thousands of ratification meetings around the region. This affirmation was hardly in doubt, but both candidates and voters believed a campaign could not begin until the people gave their assent. Pole-raisings also celebrated the significance of the people. Developing out of May-pole rituals in England, the "Liberty Tree" had become a symbol of popular rights and rebellion against authority in the eighteenth century. American colonists raised the tree in protest against the Stamp Act; French Jacobins erected poles in celebration of the end of the monarchy; Massachusetts farmers made them a sign of sympathy for the Whiskey Rebellion; and opponents of the Sedition Act raised the poles once again as an emblem of protest just before the turn of the century. The "Liberty Tree" lost some of its radical aura as it became absorbed into Democratic and Republican pageantry in the nineteenth century, but "Liberty" and "Hickory" poles still conveyed a message of popular rights.[92]

Political parades, with their demonstrations of different crafts, further instructed leaders in the importance of workers and farmers. So much like the processions of artisans in Europe and early nineteenth-century America, these partisan displays repeated age-old expressions of the pride and power of labor.[93] Craft demonstrations such as rail-splitting in 1860 and leather-tanning in 1868 also served a newer political purpose: they were a reminder that leaders and followers had common origins in the world of work. "Every farmer's wagon bore some emblem," a reporter noted at a Republican rally at Urbana, Illinois, in 1860; "a rail and a maul was a popular one with the sons of toil, as it showed that their gallant leader had sprung from their own ranks and occupations in life."[94] In this way farmers and workers paid tribute to Abraham Lincoln but also reminded the candidate, and the Republican party, of his ties and obligations to the working class. These demonstrations were double-edged, of course. Party leaders could use them as well to evoke among people a false community of interest with candidates who had long since left behind the realities and outlook of working-class life. In a sense, by taking up campaign pageantry, politicians and voters carried out a ritual struggle in which each side declared friendship and common origin in order to win the support of the other.

Partisan display served even more clearly as an expression of the relations between the classes of a particular township or city. Spectacular electioneering developed in the ante-bellum North while the wealthy still maintained direct control of local politics and government.[95] In nearly all cities and towns, members of the upper class continued to hold most of the important local elective offices. New industrialists, along with older commercial and professional elites, sought to use spectacle as a testament to their political and economic power, and as a symbol of their paternal regard for the lower orders. Parades stopped at the homes of the wealthy to serenade them and to hear their wisdom.[96] At rallies, the well-to-do sat on the speakers' platform as "presidents" and "vice presidents."[97]

The paternalist dimension of partisan display was particularly evident in the campaign clubs and companies. In return for money and other gifts, "a large Capitalist, at the head of general business enterprises" expected the members of a club or company to name their organization for him, serenade him, and march in his honor.[98]

During the campaign of 1880, some Democrats in New Haven, Connecticut, founded the "James E. English Phalanx" in tribute to the party's gubernatorial candidate. A millionaire manufac-

turer, English had already served terms as selectman and council-
man of New Haven, representative and senator in the state legislature, and United States congressman and senator, as well as
governor of Connecticut. One of the members of his Phalanx was
Michael Campbell, a twenty-year-old Irish-American factory
worker who had stood, enthralled, in the crowd at the Democrats'
flag-raising in the sixth ward four years before. Appointed a ser-
geant and member of the Phalanx's finance and uniform committee, Michael left his home one evening and walked to English's
imposing Spanish-style mansion a few blocks away. Michael,
apparently admitted as though there were nothing unusual in a
working-class Irishman calling on a rich Yankee, asked English for
money to pay for the Phalanx's uniforms. The former governor,
Michael wrote in his diary, "said to call again and bring the figures
of the lowest Manufacturers." A week later, Michael returned with
"Figures and estimates" and the former governor "promised to
give us $100.00." The Phalanx bought its uniforms and also a ban-
ner emblazoned with English's name and portrait.

At nightly drills, Michael and his friends learned to honor their
patron by marching in an E-shaped formation. After the Phalanx's
first parade, the company serenaded English at his home and listened to the former governor lecture on the duties of young citizens. Through his speeches and gifts, the manufacturer, who worried over workers no longer living under "the care and oversight
of responsible masters," tried to show himself as a concerned,
paternal figure providing for those loyal to him. Perhaps the lesson did not get across. Michael and the Phalanx marched night
after night, but English lost the election to another New Haven
manufacturer who had his own uniformed "battalion."[99]

Through marching companies, wealthy politicians hoped that
young men like Michael Campbell would give their loyalty, not
only to a candidate and a political party, but also to the local upper
class. More broadly, spectacle, by displaying the generosity of the
rich to the poor, could establish the upper class's right to rule. But
workers did not necessarily interpret partisan display in this way.
Once more, campaign spectacle showed itself a double-edged
sword of class relations. The wealthy, after all, could not count on
buying loyalty in return for money, drinks, food, and uniforms. In
making these gifts, the rich also paid tribute to enfranchised work-

ers and acknowledged their freedom and worth. By participating in spectacular campaigns, the upper class left itself open to exploitation. The mid-nineteenth century was the heyday of "political strikers," men who took advantage of leaders' needs, real and psychological, for popular support. In the working-class wards of cities, strikers held a rally or raised a pole for a candidate in order to force him to pay for drinks at a nearby "groggery." Campaign clubs sometimes formed simply to extract payments from the candidate. The more ingenious strikers organized an imaginary club, its members drawn from the pages of the city directory, and dedicated the organization to some hapless nominee. After the strikers had dunned the candidate for several hundred dollars in "campaign expenses," the club and its promoters disappeared. There was deception and coercion on both sides in popular politics.[100]

The relationship of candidates and voters, rich men and poor men, varied from place to place and from time to time. The political world of Michael Campbell and James English in industrial New Haven in 1880 surely differed from that of the farmers driving their decorated wagons to a Lincoln rally in rural Illinois in 1860. To be sure, we still know too little about the diverse local settings of mid-nineteenth-century politics. But across the North, partisan display seems to have emerged from a particular phase of class relations notable for its intimate quality. In the mid-nineteenth century, the members of different classes expected to confront one another face-to-face in the public ritual of clubs, companies, rallies, and serenades. Even on the vast stage of national poltics, candidates and voters used the ratification, the pole-raising, and other display to declare their worth and to diminish, symbolically, the social distance between them.

Campaign pageantry apparently also sprang from a powerful sense of local community. At mid-century, Northern cities and towns were not isolated enclaves sealed off from the rest of the country. Railroad and telegraph lines increasingly bound places together in regional and even national markets. National party labels and issues defined local partisan politics. There were no important and enduring local parties. Communities staged campaign pageantry, not for purely local elections, but for Federal elections and, occasionally, state contests fought over such national questions as slavery. Still, Northern towns and cities retained a certain autonomy in the mid-nineteenth century. Local newspapers provided residents with their news. For the most part, local capitalists, not distant trusts and corporations, appeared to make the important decisions affecting communities. Americans have been bound together by different forms of community over the centuries; in the mid-nineteenth, Northerners experienced a delicate balance of local and national community. Members of a nation reunited after civil war, they still felt strongly the bonds of a community defined by the geographical boundary lines of township, ward, and city.[101]

The conduct of presidential campaigns reflected the importance of local community in Northern life. Ostensibly in command of their parties, the Republican and Democratic national committees exercised imperfect control over spectacular presidential campaigns. Indeed, the committees were rather unimportant in the highly decentralized party structure of the mid-nineteenth century. The Democrats had not even bothered to create a permanent committee until 1848; the Whigs waited four more years before establishing one of their own. In the third party system, the Democratic and Republican committees seldom met between the quadrennial presidential contests, maintained headquarters only for the campaign, and wielded almost no power over the selection of candidates and platforms.[102]

Even after the selection of the party ticket, each national committee cut a rather small figure. The chairman and a few aides assessed the party's rich men and officeholders for contributions but found it difficult to raise enough money.[103] National headquarters in New York City was a small operation: in 1872, the Republican National Committee took up a mere three rooms in a Manhattan hotel.[104] In both major parties, the chairman did have help from the congressional campaign committee, a group in Washington charged with promoting the election of candidates for the House of Representatives. Typically, the national committee disbursed money, subsidized loyal editors, paid for the free distribution of newspapers, and assigned the party's leading orators to rallies around the country; the congressional committee took care of the production and shipment of campaign literature.[105] Not much of an operation either, the congressional committee scraped by on handouts from the national committee and compulsory contributions—"assessments"—from the party's officeholders. The committee usually turned out a rather uninspired set of pamphlets including speeches by party leaders, the party platform, and a biography of the presidential candidate. Most of this literature was in English, but a few publications appeared in German and even in French. Making use of its members' congressional mailing privileges, the committee usually furnished the pamphlets in bulk lots for free to local party workers.[106]

Campaign literature never drew too much attention in spectacular campaigns—and neither did the national committees.[107] From the 'fifties into the 'eighties, the press wrote little about the daily activities of the party headquarters. Campaigns focused instead on communities' spectacular partisan displays, which often began weeks before the national committees officially got down to business. While both national and state party committees provided some money for uniforms and occasionally organized rallies and other demonstrations, spectacular politics depended upon local activity. Party leaders in the communities formed the clubs and companies and put up most of the money for uniforms and torches.[108] More important, the voters themselves filled the ranks of the campaign armies and illuminated houses along parade routes. Communities, more than the national committees, created spectacular electioneering.

Like their national organizations, the presidential candidates also played a limited public role in campaigns. Speakers and editors endlessly publicized a candidate's virtues and defects, but the nominee himself withdrew as much as possible from the spotlight. The mid-nineteenth century inherited its notion of the proper behavior for a presidential aspirant from the early days of the United States. In a new nation imbued with a republican fear of politicians' grasp for power, first George Washington and then other candidates for president avoided public campaigning and adopted the pose of the "mute tribune," unambitious for himself, yielding reluctantly to the people's call to office. Briefly, during the factional struggles early in the formation of the second party system, candidates struck a different stance. Since coalitions of politicians and voters were forming around Andrew Jackson and other presidential hopefuls rather than around parties, a politics of personality, based on active campaigning by the nominees, began to emerge in the 'twenties and 'thirties. Most candidates, like Jackson, wrote political letters for publication; some, like William Henry Harrison in 1840, even made extensive speaking tours. But as the Whig and Democratic parties developed in the 'thirties and 'forties, politics started to turn on party organizations, labels, and loyalties. Faithful party men, the candidates wrapped themselves once more in the mantle of the "mute tribune."[109]

In the third party system, most candidates wrote a letter accepting the nomination and endorsing the platform and then retired for the duration. Although the vice presidential nominees sometimes made campaign tours, party managers refused to run the risk of letting presidential aspirants make a disastrous slip in public.[110] Observers noted what had happened to those few candidates who spent much time on the campaign trail: Stephen A. Douglas lost in 1860; Horace Greeley lost in 1872; James G. Blaine lost in 1884. Blaine's example, in particular, became a cautionary tale. Initially opposed to campaigning, the Republican nominee succumbed to temptation and went on a fatiguing tour through the Midwest. Returning to New York City, he stood silently in apparent agreement as a Protestant minister stigmatized the Democrats as the party of "Rum, Romanism, and Rebellion." The remark, many believed, cost Blaine the election.[111]

Still touched by republican values, most Northerners considered public campaigning by the nominees unseemly as well as risky. Into the 'seventies and 'eighties, few men questioned the logic of hiding the candidate and demanded that he give the people a chance to see him and hear his views.[112] Most commentators did not want such self-revelation from a nominee. Angered by Blaine's decision to campaign in 1884, the Republican *Philadelphia Inquirer* declared that "it is better that the country should make its choice between the two candidates from what they know of their public records rather than from what they may learn of their personal appearance." The tour seemed pointless to another observer: "To suppose," he wrote, "that any intelligent men who have made up their minds are going to change them after gazing at Mr. Blaine a few minutes seems to me absurd." A personal campaign by a presidential aspirant still seemed a breach of taste. "It is thought a dignified part in a lady or a candidate in so serious an affair as marriage or the Presidency, to wait till they are asked," the *Atlantic Monthly* noted in 1872, "and it is believed that they would hurt their cause by making advances."[113] The greater a politician's ambition, the more he had to conceal it. A candidate for governor and even vice president might publicly urge his own cause, but a candidate for the presidency must place himself, as the saying went, "in the hands of his friends."

The retiring behavior of the candidates established a relationship between nominee and voter peculiar to the era of popular politics. The former concealed himself, his personality, his ambitions, and his emotions, while the latter revealed his feelings through the ritual of partisan display. The emotional economy of candidate and voter in the nineteenth century fixed attention on events in communities across the North.

Dominated neither by national party committees nor candidates, spectacular campaigns became a process of communal self-revelation. In effect, men voted twice at an election—once at the polls by casting a ballot, and once in the streets by participating in campaign pageantry. For Northerners in the mid-nineteenth century, the campaign meant publicly revealing their political preferences. Underlying all aspects of spectacular electioneering, from uniformed companies and the signing of club constitutions to campaign buttons and humorous election bets, was the premise that how one thought and acted, and how one's neighbors thought and acted, meant a great deal. Through campaign pageantry, the people of a city or a rural township translated a national election into communal ritual. They did not sit passively at home reading about the activities of the candidates and the national party committees outside their community. For them, the city or township itself became the campaign. Political spectacle testified to Northerners' persisting sense of the local community as an important arena of experience formed, but not overwhelmed, by national events.[114]

Part leisure, part martial demonstration, part inter-class mediation, and part communal theater, campaign pageantry was above all a ritual of partisan display. The rise of spectacle marked the fullest acceptance of partisanship in popular culture. Through participation in spectacular campaigns, Northerners revealed their belief not merely in the legitimacy of party commitment, but also in the necessity of demonstrating that commitment in public before the community.[115] Like the party press, political spectacle made partisanship appear an integral element of men's identity and outlook.

This celebration of partisanship made spectacle useful to politicians. At a time when most men ardently and almost irrevocably identified with one party, the problem for political leaders was less to win over the small minority of undecided and independent voters than to bring out the party's regular supporters.[116] By legitimizing and reinforcing party loyalty, spectacle served the politicians admirably.

Party leaders were less certain about spectacle's role in persuading the undecided and independent. Some politicians, whose views would dominate the parties by the early 'nineties, preferred quieter forms of persuasion: newspapers, campaign literature, and personal appeals. For obvious reasons, newspaper editors considered the press more important than spectacle in reaching the people. "To put a good, efficient journal into the hands of every voter who will read it is the true mode of prosecuting a political canvass," Horace Greeley declared; "meetings and speeches are well enough, but this is indispensable." Even before the Civil War, politicians worried that the parties too often neglected the "serious work" of canvassing electors and bringing them out to vote for the excitement of parades and rallies. "We understand," the *Chicago Press and Tribune* lectured its Republican followers in 1860, "that it is infinitely more agreeable to make one of a large, an excited and enthusiastic crowd, in which the music is loud and sonorous, the speaking eloquent and persuasive, and the applause vehement, than to do school district drudgery in the organization of local and feeble clubs, the distribution of campaign documents to doubtful voters and the enumeration of electors." But the object of party organization, the paper concluded, "must be not so much the exciting of new enthusiasm in those who already profess the Republican faith, as the conviction of those whose prejudices and want of information have led them to oppose the grand movement in which Republicans are engaged."[117]

Yet many leaders believed that spectacle was well suited to winning over the "doubtful voters." "The effect of the demonstration was immediately and plainly manifest," a Republican claimed after a party rally in rural Illinois in 1860. "A friend of ours informed us that eight Douglasites, after hearing the speeches of the after-noon, had come square over into the Republican ranks. . . ."[118] Spectacle converted the undecided not only by the persuasiveness of its oratory, but by its grandeur as well. Huge parades and rallies testified to a party's deep popular appeal. "The maxim that noth-ing succeeds like success is nowhere so cordially and consistently accepted as in America," James Bryce wrote. "It is the corner-stone of all election work. The main effort of a candidate's orators and newspapers is to convince the people that their side is the win-ning one, for there are sure to be plenty of voters anxious to be on that side . . . because reverence for 'the People' makes them believe that the majority are right." In the closely contested state of Indiana, for instance, the parties closed their campaigns with "as imposing an affair as possible": competing rallies at the state capital. "The success or failure of the effort," a reporter noted, "makes considerable impression on the voters who are waiting to see which way the political current is setting."[119]

Although politicians disagreed on the usefulness of spectacle in wooing the uncommitted, most of them relied on partisan display to win elections. A party editor summed up the consensus in 1880: "As to how much political parties profit by these spectacular dem-onstrations is a matter upon which political leaders and managers have varying opinions, but whether they help or not they have come to be regarded as a necessary appendage to all exciting polit-ical contests when important issues and interests are at stake."[120]

Even though the appeal of partisan display to the undecided was debatable, its effect on voter turnout seemed clear. The wide-spread acceptance of a subjective, extroverted concept of parti-sanship, reflected in campaign spectacle and the party press, helped to make possible the record turnouts in the North during the nineteenth century. At once product and cause of political involvement, spectacle developed as voter turnout rose before the Civil War. Partisan display and turnout together reached their peak in the Gilded Age. The correlation of spectacular campaign-ing and turnout was hardly perfect; the impact of spectacle on vot-ing at a particular election remained uncertain and, in a sense, unimportant. Partisan display, along with the press, established the context for higher turnouts, a basic setting in which short-term influences such as a particular issue or the competitiveness of the parties could take effect. The significance of political spectacle and party journalism lay not so much in their effect on voting at this or that presidential election as in their influence on the habits of the generations of men voting at all elections, local as well as national, in the nineteenth century.

Spectacular campaigns and partisan newspapers increased turnout in several ways. The ritual of partisan display captivated young men in the nineteenth century and bonded them to a party and to politics. Michael Campbell admired uniformed companies as a boy, joined one of them as a young man, and became a regular voter as an adult. In the long run, the most important impact of electoral pageantry in a given campaign may not have been on men already old enough to vote, but on those boys and young men, like Michael Campbell in 1876 and 1880, still too young to cast a ballot. Later generations would not receive such an intense initiation into politics.

Spectacular campaigning touched adults deeply as well. For one thing, it helped to persuade a voter that his ballot, one among millions, was worth casting. Campaign pageantry did not convince a man his one vote would make a decisive difference in the outcome of an election. Instead, parades and rallies solved the problem of a ballot's insignificance by investing the act of voting with additional meanings. Partisan display presented politics as entertainment, military nostalgia, and class theater as well as the selection of candidates. Spectacular campaigning also encouraged the voter to see himself as a member of a well-defined community rather than as an unimportant figure lost in a sea of electors. Indeed, spectacle made membership in the community appear, in part, to be contingent on the revelation of one's partisan preferences, on the demonstration of one's political involvement. Playing heavily on people's sense of community, campaign pageantry pressured the uninvolved into politics. At the least, it brought out for presidential contests those men who avoided off-year elections. By parading the political enthusiasm of their neighbors, spectacle persuaded men that voting, if only once in four years, was the thing to do.

The intense partisanship embodied in the press and campaigns further stimulated the sustained high turnouts of the nineteenth century by presenting politics as a matter of enduring attachment

to party as much as the excitement of the moment. A man's decision to vote at a particular election did not depend solely on the
allure of a candidate, the interest of an issue, or the closeness of
an election; instead, his vote became a testament, regularly given,
to his persisting identification with one of the parties. By reinforcing that identification, a spectacular presidential campaign
encouraged him to vote in off-year elections as well.

Spectacular campaigns and partisan papers contributed to the
record turnout of the Gilded Age by simplifying politics. Along
with the party press, election ritual helped to reduce the complex,
daunting process of thinking through many issues and choosing
among hundreds of candidates to a matter of black-and-white
opposites. Newspapers and torchlight parades legitimized and
even necessitated partisan commitment. They encouraged men to
decide public questions merely on the basis of their partisan affiliation. Exalted by the press and spectacle, party emerged as the
first principle of public life by the mid-nineteenth century. Following the gospel of partisanship, men could conscientiously adopt
the Republican or Democratic line on an issue and drop a straight
ticket into the ballot box.

Spectacular display was not simply emotional oversimplifica-
tion. Mid-nineteenth-century campaigns tied parades and fireworks to long expositions of issues on the stump and in the press.
In a sense, the excitement of partisan display could lure men into
dealing with complex questions such as slavery. Popular politics
fused thought and emotion in a single style accessible to all—a
rich unity of reason and passion that would be alien to Americans
in the twentieth century.

Working through the party press and campaign spectacle, partisanship made it easier than before or since for people to act
politically. In a rousing communal setting, the ritual of partisan
display inspired them to make the connections between their political impulses and political action. That was why the nineteenth
century marked the highpoint of voter turnout in the North.

The record votes of the 'eighties and 'nineties were deceptive.
Even as turnout reached its zenith across the North, the foundation of popular politics had already begun to give way.

3

PARTISANSHIP REDEFINED

For many Northerners of wealth and education, the years following the Civil War seemed to unfold a myriad of evils. Radical
Reconstruction disrupted the South. The policy of high protective
tariffs, established during the war, continued to restrict international trade. Farmers and workers, seduced by demagogues,
threatened to replace the true, hard money of gold with a debased
currency of greenbacks and silver. Workers upset the harmonious
relations of capital and labor with strikes and demands for eight-
hour laws. Immigrants poured into cities no longer run by the
"best men" of the community but by bosses and party machines.
A Republican machine dominated the Federal government, too,
and at all levels of the polity there seemed to be corruption, fraud,
and waste. The public service belonged to incompetent party
workers rather than educated men. Elections fell into the hands

of party machines. Nominations went to mere politicians rather than "statesmen."

Thus ran the complaints of the "best men," the liberal reformers of the Gilded Age. Repeated over and over from the 'sixties to the 'nineties, the liberals' litany of evils produced the most fertile and significant reconsideration of popular politics by the Northern upper class in the late nineteenth century. Sometimes successful, often futile, the efforts of the liberal reformers redrew the boundaries of partisanship, fostered new political ideals and techniques, and helped start the decline of popular politics.[1]

The "best men" were a loosely knit, often divided group, whose different facets gave rise to several names: "liberals," "educated men," "reformers," "independents," "Scratchers," "Mugwumps," and other, less flattering epithets. Nineteenth-century liberals, the "best men" believed in laissez-faire, limited government, free trade, and hard money. Self-conscious reformers, they devoted their public lives to improving the tariff, the monetary system, the civil service, the ballot, and the parties. Primarily Republicans before 1884, they demonstrated their independence of party in the struggles against Ben Butler in 1868 and Boss Tweed in 1871, the Liberal Republican bolt from the renomination of Ulysses Grant in 1872, the "Young Scratcher" movement against the Republican machine of New York State in 1879, and the Mugwump rejection of the Republican nominee, James G. Blaine, in 1884. These liberal, independent reformers liked to call themselves "educated men," a label that stressed what set them apart from the rest of the Northern upper class. More than their opponents in the Republican party, the reformers had gone to college and earned advanced degrees. Strong in the universities, liberals prided themselves on their culture and their devotion to the new social science and its faith in empirical enquiry into public problems.

Reformers were set off from Northern society in other ways as well. Nearly all were born of English stock in the United States. For the most part, the reformers lived in the Northeast, in Massachusetts, Connecticut, and New York. Urban men in a still rural land, many spent their lives in Boston, New Haven, New York, and Chicago. In a country of new fortunes, some enjoyed old money.

Rather few ran factories; most built careers in mercantile houses and, especially, the professions. Virtually all the reformers were Protestants; many attended exclusive Congregational and Episcopal churches.[2]

The reformers occupied a distinctive place in the partisan system. After the Civil War, they followed their own leaders, at first, middle-aged men like Carl Schurz of Missouri and David Ames Wells of Connecticut. In the late 'seventies and 'eighties, the reformers turned to a younger generation of leaders typified by the New York publisher R. R. Bowker and the Massachusetts reformers Josiah Quincy and Moorfield Storey.[3]

Avoiding the party press, the reformers had their own network of journals. Newspapers like William Cullen Bryant's *New York Evening Post* and Samuel Bowles's Springfield, Massachusetts, *Republican* publicized the reform cause. But liberalism was best identified by its magazines: George William Curtis's *Harper's Weekly*, E. L. Godkin's *Nation*, the *North American Review* of Henry Adams and Allan T. Rice, and William Dean Howells's *Atlantic Monthly*. Like the liberals in the 'seventies and early 'eighties, these journals leaned toward the Republican party but avoided unswerving party loyalty. Most liberal publications had small circulations and seldom touched the general public directly. But they provided a responsive forum in which the liberals could nurture an alternative to traditional party politics. Linking together men around the North who shied away from the tight organization of party machines, these journals were the linchpin of liberal reform.[4]

Socially and politically distinctive, the liberals nonetheless were not outcasts. For all their struggles with the parties and their occasional pessimistic lamentations, they were not fighting a losing war with the Northern upper class. Certainly liberals and regulars often dealt harshly with one another. Voters who cast independent ballots could expect to lose business and friendships and to suffer attacks on their manhood. Party editors and politicians derided the Young Scratchers as "namby-pamby, goody-goody gentlemen" and doubted whether Mugwumps were Republicans "of the manly type."[5] But the reformers and party regulars did not differ fundamentally in important respects. The social distinctions among them were matters of degree, not absolutes. Wealthy and well-educated men also filled the hierarchy of the Republican party.[6]

In the late nineteenth century no impassable gulf separated liberal reform from partisan regularity. Instead, Northern journalists and politicians placed themselves at every point along a continuum ranging from complete independence to unquestioning partisanship. So, the reformers' influence reached the partisan public through such sympathetic party newspapers as the *Cincinnati Commercial* and the *New York Times*. Powerful party politicians such as the Democratic presidential nominee of 1876, Samuel J. Tilden, and the presidents Rutherford B. Hayes, James A. Garfield, and Grover Cleveland proved responsive to reform ideas. That was why the reformers' redefinition of partisanship could resound so clearly throughout the political system.[7]

In their quest for power, the reformers tried the usual political routes and tested some unused backroads as well. Questioning popular politics, liberal reformers began with its most basic element, the right to vote. For many of them, the evils of late nineteenth-century America sprang from universal suffrage. The liberals had acquiesced in the enfranchisement of black freedmen after the war but soon began to deplore the extension of the suffrage to all classes of men. "When the war closed," the liberal writer Jonathan Baxter Harrison explained in 1879, "the last class government in the United States had been swept away by the destruction of the slave power, and men found themselves face to face with a pure democracy from one end of the country to the other. Then it was that the change in public sentiment. . .began." At first privately and then more boldly in public, reformers assailed "pure democracy." "Thirty or forty years ago it was considered the rankest heresy to doubt that a government based on universal suffrage was the wisest and best that could be devised," Harrison observed. "Such is not now the case. Expressions of doubt and distrust in regard to universal suffrage are heard constantly in conversation, and in all parts of the country." The opposition to the right to vote, he concluded, had "begun at the top of our society, among some of the most intelligent, the most thoughtful, and the most patriotic men, and it is slowly and surely creeping downwards."[8]

Suffrage troubled the reformers primarily because of increasing immigration. In 1878, the historian Francis Parkman, perhaps the most outspoken liberal opponent of the right to vote, saw the United States beset by "an invasion of peasants . . . . an ignorant proletariat" who threatened the nation's democratic heritage. "A New England village of the olden time—that is to say, of some forty years ago—would have been safely and well governed by the votes of every man in it; but, now that the village has grown into a populous city, with its factories and workshops, its acres of tenement-houses, and thousands and ten thousands of restless workmen, foreigners for the most part, to whom liberty means license and politics means plunder, to whom the public good is nothing and their own most trivial interests everything, who love the country for what they can get out of it, and whose ears are open to the promptings of every rascally agitator, the case is completely changed, and universal suffrage becomes a questionable blessing."[9]

The Boston patrician, Charles Francis Adams, Jr., recognized the same threat in 1869 and cast it in the apocalyptic terms more typical of his brothers, Henry and Brooks. Lamenting "the irruption of those swarms of foreigners, who have within forty years landed on our shores," he foresaw a nightmare of domination by Irish, black, and Chinese immigrants: "Working upon such a mass as must result from the blending of all these incongruous elements, Universal Suffrage can only mean in plain English the government of ignorance and vice:—it means a European, and especially Celtic, proletariat on the Atlantic coast; an African proletariat on the shores of the Gulf, and a Chinese proletariat on the Pacific." Less melodramatically, the *Nation* summed up the implications of immigration for liberal reformers in "the severance of political power from intelligence and property."[10]

Frightened by this vision of the future, reformers tried to undermine universal suffrage. Rather than an honored, fundamental right of American citizenship, the vote seemed to them only "an experiment," a "new and vicious principle," "a kind of talisman or fetish."[11] Using the arguments of earlier American opponents of the right to vote, reformers denied the premise of universal suffrage that men were equal and equally worthy of power. Parkman decried "the flattering illusion that one man is essentially about as good as another." Attacking the creed of the democrats, the liberals charged that the ballot would not make men better. In immigrant communities, Parkman complained, the vote "educates only to mischief."[12]

Reformers also denied that men had the right to vote. "It would be a great gain," the *New York Times* wrote in 1878, "if our people could be made to understand distinctly that the right to life, liberty, and the pursuit of happiness involves, to be sure, the right to good government, but not the right to take part, either immediately or indirectly, in the management of the State." Dismissing the idea of natural rights, reformers treated the suffrage as a bargain or contract—"a trust," "simply a grant of power, existing and exercised by virtue of a contract, compact, or agreement between consenting parties." And like a contract, it could be modified and altered. In the 'sixties and 'seventies many reformers tried hard to change the terms of the deal.[13]

When liberals cast about for a standard to limit the right to vote, they naturally turned to the attributes that set the upper class apart from the rest of society: education and property. Most liberals favored an educational requirement for the suffrage. In the pages of the *Nation*, Godkin called repeatedly for the institution of an educational test for prospective voters. He and other liberals demanded not only proof men could read but also evidence that they could "vote intelligently" as well. But the reformers never devised a test that would reveal the ability to vote intelligently. Neither did they work up popular support for the educational requirement.[14] Some liberals themselves recognized its impracticality. Ante-bellum literacy requirements for suffrage in Massachusetts and Connecticut went unenforced and no effective new laws entered the books in the late nineteenth century. Sentiment for an educational requirement persisted into the twentieth century, but the plan never had a chance of adoption.[15]

Reformers made a more concerted effort to install property-holding as the basis of the right to vote. Realizing that a general property requirement would not succeed,[16] liberals tried to narrow and sharpen its focus to gather popular support. So they turned to municipal disfranchisement, which became a serious liberal goal in the late 1870s.

The city presented obvious problems as the home of immigrants, the worst political machines, and the most blatant corruption and misgovernment. "The cities are to be dreaded in modern times," wrote Theodore Dwight Woolsey, a liberal and former president of Yale, in 1878. "They take the lead in all commotions, they have less wisdom and stability, but more energy and political fanaticism than the thinly settled country, where men living apart act less on each other, and think for themselves." "It is in the cities," Parkman agreed, "that the diseases of the body politic are gathered to a head, and it is here that the need of attacking them is most urgent. Here the dangerous classes are most numerous and strong, and the effects of flinging the suffrage to the mob are most disastrous." Immigrants, of course, were the cause of the threat. "We all know what the source of the evil is," Godkin declared. He traced the woes of the cities to "foreigners. . .ignorant, credulous, newly emancipated, brutalized by oppression," who "learn to look on the suffrage as simply a means of getting jobs out of the public, and taxation as another name for the forced contributions of the rich to a fund for the poor man's relief."[17]

To justify municipal disfranchisement, liberals insisted on the difference between city government and the government of the nation and the states. While the Federal and state governments dealt with questions of politics and of personal and civil rights, the cities, liberals maintained, were only administrative bodies or corporations of property owners. "The true function of the Federal Congress and administration is governmental, and not merely administrative . . . ," argued Simon Sterne, a New York lawyer and reformer. "In municipalities, however, we cease almost entirely to deal with governmental functions proper, but . . . deal with and act upon private property interests. . . ."[18]

Since the city was a corporation, only its shareholders—taxpaying property owners—should participate in its government. Men without property had no right to vote on the corporation's affairs. "There is no denying," allowed another New York reformer, Dorman B. Eaton, "that the poorest have a common interest with the richest, in the greater subjects of human legislation,—life, liberty, religion, family, character, health,—for they are the whole of the poor man's fortune; but no voter has a right to participate in the care of funds to which he does not contribute, or in the fixing of expenditures of which he does not pay any part."[19]

The liberals made their greatest push for municipal disfranchisement in New York, a natural target as the nation's largest city and its leading symbol of misgovernment. In 1875, Governor Samuel J. Tilden created a bi-partisan commission to frame a plan for the governance of New York State's cities. The twelve-man body was dominated by liberal reformers, among them Simon Sterne and E. L. Godkin. Not surprisingly, the Tilden Commission's report, presented in March 1877, reflected the liberal critique of urban suffrage. To reform city government, the commission offered a constitutional amendment that included a provision placing power in the hands of a board of finance selected by taxpayers and rentpayers. The amendment applied to all cities but it aimed most clearly at the largest, New York. The commission set no property requirements for voters for the board of finance in cities of less than 25,000 population, stipulated $100 in property for voters in cities of 25,000 to 100,000 people, and demanded $500 in property or annual rental payments of $250 for voters in cities of more than 100,000.[20]

The proposed amendment received strong liberal support. Praise for the Tilden Commission's work came from *Harper's Weekly*, the *New York Evening Post*, and of course Godkin's *Nation*, which modestly described the plan as "the most important measure of municipal reform proposed by the present generation."[21] The amendment also received broad support from the New York City business community. The Chamber of Commerce, the Stock Exchange, the Produce Exchange, and the Cotton Exchange all passed resolutions endorsing the Tilden Commission's amendment. Many wealthy New Yorkers, including William E. Dodge, Jr., John Jacob Astor, Henry Havemeyer, Theodore Roosevelt, Sr., and Cornelius Vanderbilt, publicly endorsed the plan. Party leaders, particularly Republicans, proved quite willing to support a restricted suffrage. The chairman of the Tilden Commission was William M. Evarts, later a Republican United States senator and secretary of state. Advocates of the amendment included Whitelaw Reid, editor of the *New York Tribune* and Republican candidate for vice president in 1892, Levi P. Morton, later Republican vice president and governor of New York, Cornelius N. Bliss, longtime treasurer of the Republican National Committee, and Abram S. Hewitt, congressman, chairman of the Democratic presidential campaign of 1876, and later mayor of New York.[22]

For all this upper-class support, the amendment faced great opposition. The New York State constitution demanded that two different legislatures approve the measure before it could be submitted to the electorate for ratification. In the fall of 1877, the amendment passed on almost strict party lines. Republican legislators mostly favored the amendment, but the Democrats, their party's strength founded on the votes of New York City's poor, were not about to limit universal suffrage. During the fall elections, Tammany Hall led the opposition to the election of legislators supporting the amendment. Tammany orators, concentrating on the suffrage provision of the amendment, portrayed the Tilden Commission's proposal as a "menace to the rights of the people" and an effort to "set up an oligarchy of wealth." As it became clear that most voters did not favor suffrage restriction, the wealthy backers of the amendment seemed to lose heart. In the spring of 1878, the next session of the legislature refused to pass the amendment and the reformers' plan for city government quickly became forgotten.[23]

The Tilden Commission marked the high tide of the liberal attack on suffrage. Thereafter, public opposition to the right to vote diminished. Suffrage was not an issue in the North in the 1880s and 1890s. By then, politicians doubtless preferred not to recall their support for the Tilden Commission.

Divisions among the liberals themselves hastened the collapse of the anti-suffrage movement. A few reformers, such as the former abolitionist George Washington Julian, insisted that the suffrage was a natural right.[24] Others defended the vote as an expedient. To the poet James Russell Lowell, the ballot was "a safety-valve" for working-class discontent. "It may be conjectured," he said, "that it is cheaper in the long run to lift men up than to hold them down, and that the ballot in their hands is less dangerous to society than a sense of wrong in their heads."[25] Charles Dudley Warner, a Connecticut writer and liberal, saw the suffrage as a barrier to domination by the rich. Some liberals believed the ballot had not caused all of America's woes or at least had not prevented national prosperity.[26] Still others insisted the ballot would educate ignorant voters. "The activity of mind produced throughout all classes of society by an exciting election, the habit of considering public affairs, the occupation of the mind with matters of great scope, not having a merely selfish or local interest—these are educatory powers of immense value to the community," declared Thomas G. Shearman, a New York reformer. "No system of restriction offers any compensation for their loss."[27]

Still, most liberals turned away from suffrage restriction, not because it was wrong, but because it was impossible. Whether or not they favored disfranchisement, reformers recognized that argument over the suffrage would not produce legislation. "For strictly practical purposes," Shearman wrote as early as 1866, "as far as this country and the white race in it are concerned, the debate is scarcely more likely to have any effect than an argument in favor of abolishing railroads and going back to stagecoaches. Universal suffrage is established, and it would be little less easy to reduce the masses of voters to slavery than to deprive them of their votes." Jonathan Baxter Harrison drew the same conclusion thirteen years later. "There is no use in crying out against unlimited suffrage," he cautioned. "We cannot directly limit it, except possibly in a very small way, or retrace our steps, without a social convulsion." By 1890, even E. L. Godkin had to concede that universal suffrage "is so firmly lodged in the political arrangements of most civilized nations, that it is a mere waste of time to declaim against it."[28]

Anti-suffrage sentiment persisted quietly among the upper and middle classes in the 1890s and the new century, but few Northerners would speak openly about depriving poor white men of the vote. While the Southern upper class disfranchised blacks and even some poor whites in the 'eighties and 'nineties, the Northern elite largely abandoned talk of the suffrage.[29] Northern anti-suffrage agitation did not die away because the educated and powerful favored a broad extension of the right to vote; there was too much evidence that they did not. But the leaders of the North did not face the crisis of rule that confronted their counterparts in the post-bellum South. Never as desperate as the wealthy men of the South, the Northern elite could shape a more restrained and subtle response to popular politics. Neither did the upper class of the

North have an effective ideological justification for disfranchisement. The Southern upper class could play on white racism to deprive blacks of the vote. Education and property, the Northerners' justifications for disfranchisement, could never rival race as an ideological weapon in the United States. Although influential at certain times, nativist arguments were another inadequate instrument of disfranchisement. Further, the urban poor of the North had strong defenders in machines like Tammany Hall. For all these reasons, disfranchisement never provided the answer for the political crisis of the Northern liberal reformers.

Abandoning suffrage restriction, the liberals gradually found other solutions to their difficulties during the 'seventies and 'eighties. Not a few reformers enlisted in the movement for the restriction of immigration.[30] Most concentrated on three interrelated endeavors: education of the voters; rejuvenation of the upper class; and the limitation of party. Out of these liberals' efforts emerged a new style of politics.

As reformers acknowledged the inviolability of the right to vote, they began to consider how to make the best of the situation. Since all men could vote, educated men would have to remodel the voter in their own image. "If we cannot take the suffrage from the ignorant class," reasoned the *New York Times*, "can we not do still better by requiring that there shall be no ignorant class?" The Philadelphia reformer Henry C. Lea recognized the same imperative: "To render the verdict of the ballot-box worthy of respect we must train and educate the ignorant voter, and we must inspire the educated citizen with a higher ideal of public morality." "We must either raise the lowest classes in the state or they will drag us down," wrote Moorfield Storey. "If we would not be governed by the leaders of Tammany Hall, we must reach their followers and lead them ourselves. The more difficult the task, the more it demands the attention of educated men."[31]

Lea's and Storey's appeals to the educated pointed to the second element of the liberal program: the rejuvenation of the cultivated Northern upper class. The 'seventies and 'eighties resounded with calls to educated men to bestir themselves and take their rightful place in public life. Lectures and pamphlets such as George William Curtis's "The Public Duty of Educated

Men" and Storey's own *Politics as a Duty, and as a Career* urged the well-bred men of the North to lead and educate the mass of voters. The reformers traced their political predicament as much to their own inactivity as to the votes of immigrants. Godkin, for one, wrote that "the responsibility for our local misgovernment by no means rests on 'the ignorant foreigners': on the contrary, it rests very distinctly on the intelligent and well-to-do natives." "What is needed, above all else," George Washington Julian declared, "is a brave and honest leadership. The masses, with all their faults and shortcomings, are capable of responding to it, and the supply of this desideratum would be one of the surest means of their further political enlightenment." Julian decried the political apathy of the educated. "If 'the scholar in politics' and the declaimer against our fearful political debauchment will place their shoulders to the wheel, and bear witness to their interest in the work of reform by doing their share of the hard and disagreeable work which may be found necessary to accomplish it, they will earn a better right to moralize about the mischiefs of a brutalized suffrage, and feel less inclined to take refuge in doing it."[32]

Reformers were well aware that American society in the late nineteenth century did not value education highly; they knew that the "self-made man" won public favor in the Gilded Age. But the reformers had confidence in the power of their wealth and background. "The class of educated men. . .though comparatively small in numbers, is, in the inherent power to control the course of human affairs, immeasurably superior to all the rest combined," wrote a New York reformer. "That it is not distinctly felt to be the ruling class always and everywhere, in public and in private life, in the state as in society, is owing to the fact that it is not an organized class." Forging the educated into "an organized class" became one of the principal goals of liberal reform.[33]

What educated men had to organize against was the political party. This became the final conclusion of the reform analysis of popular politics. The evils of party ran through the whole reform litany. Recalcitrant parties thwarted reform goals, ignored issues or took the wrong side, controlled nominations, exploited public office for patronage, excluded good men, and fostered corruption. Party had grown out of proportion, the reformers believed, until it overshadowed the government itself. Henry Adams laid out the problem in 1876. "No serious impression can ever be made on those evils," he wrote, "until they are attacked at their source; not until the nation is ready to go back to the early practice of the government and to restore to the constitutional organs those powers which have been torn from them by the party organizations for purposes of party aggrandizement." Adams's analysis went to the heart of the reform agenda of the late nineteenth century: "The fabric of party must be reduced to a size that corresponds with its proper functions. The relation between the party system and the constitutional framework must be reversed."

Trimming "the fabric of party" became one of the central preoccupations of reformers. Virtually all of them acknowledged that parties were necessary and legitimate. "[W]hile it is common to hear very plain speaking as to the abuses of party organization, we all know that party is an indispensable feature of our political life," a Philadelphia liberal observed. "Without it, indeed, democracy is, to a certain extent, a fiction." R. R. Bowker, the New York independent leader, summed up the liberal attitude toward parties. "No one," he wrote in the *Atlantic Monthly* in 1880, "objects to organization: it is the abuse of organization which is stigmatized as 'the machine.' When a railroad train is wrecked by reckless driving, it is not proposed to abolish steam-engines, but to discharge drunken engineers."[34]

After the Civil War, the liberals quickly found out how difficult it was to discharge the engineers running the party machine. Fighting for power in primaries and conventions, reformers learned they could not win at politics as usual. The politicians, who devoted their working lives to politics, would always triumph.[35] Reformers had to take another tack. If they could not beat the party leadership at its own game, then they would change the rules. That resolve led the reformers to a new code of political conduct and new political techniques.

The reformers began with one of the politicians' main sources of power, party loyalty. Liberals had to pull free from the party harness, but they understood how hard that was in the partisan culture of the nineteenth century. Brooks Adams, the brother of Charles F. Adams, Jr., bemoaned "the singular American loyalty to party . . . [the] strange fear of breaking from old ties." Another liberal complained of the "grossly exaggerated view of the sacredness of party." R. R. Bowker observed how "the party state of mind" captured the liberals themselves. Over time, he explained, "party becomes a name, and the absence of purpose is forgotten: deceived by dead bones and living hucksters of them, educated voters are enslaved by a superstition."[36]

Almost as soon as the Civil War ended, liberals began to chip away at the concept of party loyalty. Their first efforts were uncertain. Should liberals make temporary independent stands against their party, or should they create an enduring third party of their own? At first, independency offered mixed results. In 1868, Massachusetts reformers tried to deny re-election to Republican congressman Benjamin Franklin Butler, whom they despised as a demagogue, unsound on currency and labor issues. When the Republicans renominated him, the reformers put up one of their own, Richard Henry Dana, author of *Two Years Before the Mast*, and lost miserably.[37] More promisingly, a bi-partisan coalition of wealthy New Yorkers defeated William M. Tweed's organization in 1871 and for a brief, heady time seemed to have subdued the Tammany tiger.[38] A year later, liberals experimented with a third party. After the Republicans renominated Ulysses Grant for president, reformers met as "Liberal Republicans" at Cincinnati and selected Horace Greeley, editor of the *New York Tribune,* as their own candidate. Eccentric, strongly identified with the Republican party, and opposed to tariff reform, he was a disastrous choice for the Liberal Republicans. Although the Democrats endorsed him, Greeley lost badly to Grant.[39] Reformers ruled out the possibility of a third party thereafter.[40]

Turning back to the major parties, the liberals evolved by trial and error a strategy of independence within the party system. Most of them remained members of a party but claimed the right to bolt it when necessary. Theodore Dwight Woolsey set down the liberals' "ethical rules" of party membership in 1878: "No person ought to sustain a party or a representative of a party when either of them, as he has reason to believe, will advocate any positively wrong measure. . . . In voting for representatives and public officers, the character of the candidate or nominee ought to be regarded as of great importance." Woolsey unfolded the central premise of the independent strategy. "Parties ought to be kept up to their promises and pledges by the fear of disaffecting independent men," he urged. "If it were well understood that such men watched the movements of parties, and withdrew confidence from them for defection from their own principles . . . the leaders of parties . . . would not venture . . . to commit acts inconsistent with their professions." Independence, Woolsey concluded, "is the great purifying agency in politics."[41]

In the 'seventies and 'eighties, most reformers shared Woolsey's faith. Henry Adams viewed the liberals as the "party of the centre," which would use the threat of defection or support to bend the parties to its will. "There is no one whose views and preferences are so utterly unimportant . . . as the man who 'belongs to the party,' and whose vote is a dead certainty anyway," a Connecticut reformer declared. "Let it be understood that he, with his friends, has once bolted . . . and that there is a serious danger of his bolting again, and he will have his full share of influence in the party councils."[42]

Likening independency to "political Protestantism," R. R. Bowker described the independents' reformation as an effort to reshape popular thought: "It strives to produce a habit of mind in the community differing from the present habit of mind in political matters, and indeed reversing it. A voter is now called upon to show why he should *not* vote with 'his party,' whereas the party ought to show why he *should* vote with it." Bowker, too, envisioned the independents as the "balance-of-power vote" in American politics. "It is by the free flux of independent votes on the edge of party lines, the fluidity of parties, so to speak, that politicians can most practically be controlled and politics be most effectually reformed," he wrote. "The independent voter is the strong man." James Russell Lowell captured the excitement of the reformers as they grasped the possibilities of independency. "A moral purpose multiplies us by ten, as it multiplied the early Abolitionists," he proclaimed in a well-known address. "They emancipated the negro; and we mean to emancipate the respectable white man."[43]

The emancipation began in 1876. A conference of reformers, spurred by Carl Schurz, met at the Fifth Avenue Hotel in New York in May to try to influence the Republicans' presidential nomination that year. Most of the reformers hoped to win the top place on the ticket for Benjamin Bristow, who had earned their admiration for his opposition to corruption as secretary of the treasury in the Grant administration. The Republican convention did not choose Bristow, but the eventual nominee, Rutherford B. Hayes, was far less offensive to the reformers than the likely alternative, the renowned spoilsman James G. Blaine.[44]

During Hayes's administration, the independent movement took a step forward in its battle against the New York State Republican machine of Roscoe Conkling. Opposed to civil service reform and hostile to Hayes and the liberals, Conkling soon forced independent Republicans into rebellion. When the machine renominated a governor opposed by reformers and also put up a corrupt candidate for state engineer in 1879, the independents struck back with the "Young Scratcher" movement led by R. R. Bowker. The Scratchers resolved to delete—to "scratch"—the name of each offensive Republican nominee from their ballots. The difference between the votes for the two candidates and for the other Republican nominees would be a measure of the independents' strength. To the delight of reformers, the candidate for engineer lost and the governor, although re-elected, ran 5 percent behind his ticket—a sobering margin for the Conkling machine in an era of close elections. The following year, the Young Scratchers sparked a national drive for an acceptable presidential candidate. They failed to secure the choice of their favorite, Senator George Edmunds of Vermont, but they did help to defeat Conkling's presidential aspirations and to nominate James A. Garfield, a congressman long sympathetic to reform. In 1882 the Young Scratchers turned against the Republican nominee for governor and watched him run behind his ticket to defeat.[45]

Bowker and his followers had added a potent new technique to the independent strategy. Dubbing the Scratcher "the minuteman of politics," George William Curtis saw the independent movement in New York as the beginning of a new Revolutionary War against the party system. The Scratcher, secretly marking his ticket, was as hidden and as powerful as the men who fought in 1776. "It is like that withering fire of the Concord and Lexington minute-men from behind walls and trees and fences upon the appalled English red-coats," wrote Curtis, making the history lesson plain. "The red-coats were the regulars, but the irregulars won the day."[46]

The independent movement reached its culmination in 1884. When the Republicans nominated James G. Blaine, whose shady business dealings made him the symbol of the corrupt machine politician, many Republican independents bolted the party and supported the Democrats' Grover Cleveland. The closely contested election seemed to turn on the electoral votes of New York, where the bolting "Mugwumps" were strongest. To contemporary observers, the Mugwumps' votes gave the Empire State to Cleveland and put him in the White House.[47]

The Mugwump movement was the highpoint of organized independency on the national level. Many reformers, admiring Cleveland, became Democrats after 1884. Other liberals, remaining Republican, found their party somewhat more responsive than in the past. After Blaine's defeat, party politicians had to pay attention to the reformers' claims to be the "balance of power" in politics. "The position of the independents is a recognized one . . . ," *Harper's Weekly* declared proudly in 1892, "for they constitute the very element to which, in election times, both parties address their appeals, in order to win the votes with which to make up their majorities."[48]

By the 1890s the reformers had created a new style of limited partisanship. They had broken down the doctrine of absolute party loyalty, established the principle of independency, and forged a potent political force.

Reformers asserted their power and further developed the politics of limited partisanship through their extra-party organizations. From the 'sixties to the 'nineties, liberals used an array of clubs and associations to pressure politicians and to educate the public. These organizations emerged as a way for men who did not make politics a business to influence the legislature and the people. The clubs and associations reflected the liberals' faith in empirical social science and their hopes for a less emotional, more intellectual public life. The Massachusetts reformer Moorfield Storey expressed the ideals animating reform organizations. "The complex problems of modern life require constant study from him who would master them, and this study is much facilitated by clubs or associations meeting at regular intervals throughout the year," Storey contended. "Political conclusions must be the result of cool and deliberate reflection, if they are to bear the test of discussion." The liberal, having made up his mind, should then engage in "an earnest effort to educate and arouse public opinion." According to Storey, a handful of liberals banded together could use the press and platform to win over the people. "Through articles in newspapers and magazines the facts can be published, the arguments presented, and the fullest light poured upon any subject. Public meetings, addresses, lectures, and a hundred other methods of creating public opinion may be used with great effect by organizations which are numerically small." "Political progress . . . ," he concluded, "is the result of educating the whole community."[49]

The liberal writer Jonathan Baxter Harrison also expressed the reformers' dream of popular education. "The people who believe in culture, in property, and in order, that is in civilization, must establish the necessary agencies for the diffusion of a new culture," he wrote. "Capital must protect itself by organized activities for a new object,—the education of the people." Harrison envisioned an organization which would provide articles and broadsides for the press, "setting forth . . . in ever-varying forms the few great simple truths and facts which explain our present national condition . . . ." A newspaper, books on political economy, and the "persuasive power of public speaking, lecturing, and preaching" would all serve in "the education of the people."[50]

Here was the vision of the power of educated men. Instead of a liability, the reformers' background would become a source of political authority. There were precedents for this vision. Reformers drew on the example of the English liberals Richard Cobden and John Bright, who founded the Anti-Corn-Law Leagues in 1839 to agitate against protective tariffs.[51] The American liberals also benefited from their own experience during the Civil War. They learned about propaganda from the Loyal Publication Society, which supported the Republicans' prosecution of the war by distributing pamphlets, and from the Society for the Diffusion of Political Knowledge, which served the Democratic opposition with its own barrage of tracts. The Sanitary Commission, a private group for the relief of wartime suffering, introduced the liberals to the possibilities of scientific, non-partisan organizations staffed by the "best men."[52] But the post-war reform organizations brought the educational, extra-partisan approach to a more self-conscious, articulated level. A main reliance of reform, these organizations signified an effort to replace spectacular partisanship with a didactic, elitist kind of politics.

The tariff issue fostered most of the first liberal organizations after the war. In Chicago, the editor Horace White and other reformers founded a Free Trade League in 1866. Three years later, the Chicago liberals joined with tariff reformers elsewhere to form a national tariff reform organization. The American Free Trade League sponsored lectures, pamphlets, tracts, and a periodical, the *American Free Trader*. Like many reform groups, the Free Trade League had an up-and-down existence. After an early burst of activity, it languished in the mid-'seventies and then revived for a time in the early 'eighties.[53] Another liberal group founded in 1875, the Free Trade Alliance, demanded pure free trade more stridently but pursued much the same educational strategy. The alliance produced a journal called the *New Century*, pamphlets, press appeals, lectures, local chapters, and two satellite organizations, the New York Free Trade Club and the Council for Tariff Reform.[54] In Chicago, reformers set up another Free Trade League in 1876, with similar educational activities and grandiose, unfulfilled plans for organization on a nation-wide basis.[55] Back in the East, the Massachusetts Tariff Reform League did educational work in the 'eighties and expanded into the New England Tariff Reform League in 1890.[56] Massachusetts tariff reformers also created a variant on the educational approach with their Question Clubs, founded in 1886. These were small groups in towns and cities around the state who collaborated in posing questions on tariff policy to legislators and then publishing the responses in the press.[57]

Reformers used much the same extra-party strategy of education and pressure in their drive for civil service reform. In 1877, they set up the New York Civil Service Reform Association under the former head of the Sanitary Commission. The association did not prosper, but George William Curtis and others revived it in 1880. The next year the association became the basis for the National Civil Service Reform League, a prime example of the strategy of education and pressure outside the party. The league publicized reform through local branches, speakers, and its periodicals, the *Civil Service Record* and *Good Government*.[58]

The liberals also brought extra-party organization to bear in municipal politics. In New York, Theodore Roosevelt and young friends from Harvard created the City Reform Club in 1882 to secure good elective officials "irrespective of party." As part of its attempts to publicize the conditions of local government, the club began the practice of publishing the voting records of New York City's legislators. Small, elite, and ineffective, the club gave way in the 'nineties to the less exclusive City Club.[59] The new organization went into neighborhoods to form Good Government Clubs among the working and middle classes and helped to form a non-partisan coalition that elected a Republican mayor in 1894. By then, municipal reform clubs devoted to the non-partisan exposure of city problems and the election of candidates on a non-partisan basis had appeared all over the North. An umbrella organization, the National Municipal Reform League, coordinated the movement through conferences and publications.[60]

The tariff, civil service, and municipal reform organizations pursued the liberals' educational ideal by publicizing a single issue. Groups devoted to a range of reform concerns gave still fuller expression to the liberal dream of an educational, extra-party politics. The first liberal organization of the post-war, the American Social Science Association (ASSA), largely avoided overt political action for the study and discussion of problems in "Education, Health, Economy and Jurisprudence," among them tariff, civil service, municipal, and monetary reform. Founded in 1865, the association embodied the liberal faith in an all-embracing social science that would provide authoritative solutions to questions of public policy. Through national and local meetings and a journal, the ASSA tried to teach the Northern upper class about liberal reform.[61]

Other reform organizations took a more active role in politics. In 1867 and 1868, reformers inspired by the Loyal Publication Society used the facilities of the *Nation* to publish "broadsides" on economic questions. In 1869, some of the same men organized the Boston and the New York Reform League, the first of which published weekly news-sheets on tariff and monetary reform.[62] During the 'eighties, new organizations reasserted the idea of education.

The Massachusetts Reform Club, founded in 1882, agitated a variety of reform issues for over twenty years.[63] In New York, the Reform Club, established in 1888 by R. R. Bowker, E. L. Godkin, and other liberals, worked for tariff, civil service, currency, municipal, and ballot reform by publishing and distributing political literature. Organized at the height of interest in the tariff issue, the club made a particular effort to teach the public about the evils of protection through a semi-monthly named *Tariff Reform*, a compilation called the *Red-Book*, and pamphlets.[64]

The purest expression of the liberal educational ideal was R. R. Bowker's Society for Political Education. Established in 1880, the society reflected Bowker's faith in social science and his belief in educating the people. Dedicated to ballot, civil service, municipal, monetary, and tariff reform, the society published a series of *Economic Tracts* and a *Library of Political Education*. Through auxiliary societies, the group disseminated tracts and bibliographies and sponsored reading groups, lectures, and political forums. Bowker's organization worked fairly well for a time but ran out of members and money in 1891.[65]

Most of the liberal groups were not notably successful. They struggled through brief lives with small memberships, little money, and rarely much to show for their efforts. But the reform organizations helped to transform political style. Along with the strategy of independence, they represented an attempt to transcend partisan politics. Like the Young Scratchers and the Mugwumps, organizations such as the American Free Trade League and the New York Reform Club tried to whip the parties into line. And like those independent movements, the liberal educational groups offered a vision of a new kind of political conduct.

The final liberal attempt to reshape politics was through the legal limitation of parties. Unable to fight the politicians on their own ground, reformers turned to the law to change the rules governing patronage, elections, and municipal government. In each case, the struggle for tangible restriction of party produced concomitant ideological innovation—competing ideals to the doctrine of partisanship.

As in the evolution of independent strategy and reform organizations, the liberal effort to redraw the legal boundaries of party did not develop smoothly and easily. Along the way, liberals tried unsuccessful reforms later forgotten. Some reformers urged permanent tenure in office for well-behaved elected officials as the means of breaking party control of government and elections. Others promoted "self-nomination" by individual candidates to circumvent the parties' monopoly of primaries and conventions. Still others suggested allowing extra-local candidacy: a district hungering for reform could then elect non-resident "best men" to office.[66] Minority or proportional representation proved especially popular among reformers for many years. In this plan, complicated voting procedures would guarantee seats in legislatures to the upper-class minority and by means never quite clear would break down party control of the nominating process.[67] A few liberals even backed compulsory voting to boost upper-class power by forcing laggard reformers to the polls. But this plan seemed a dubious proposition, particularly because such foes of liberalism as Benjamin Butler also endorsed compulsion as a way of swelling their own vote.[68]

Along with these proposals, the liberals offered more enduring and successful measures to limit the parties. The best known was civil service reform. Promising to allot government offices on the basis of merit rather than party favor, civil service reform had obvious attractions for liberals. Educated men, of course, would do well on the written tests that would be prescribed for job candidates. More important, the reform would free the government from party politics to return to matters of state. The battle for a non-partisan civil service did not end with the passage of the first Federal civil service law, the Pendleton Act, in 1883. But by 1900, reformers had some success in reducing the parties' hold on Federal and local offices. In urging reform, the liberals established as well the idea that government should be run on "business principles" rather than party needs.[69]

Reformers also made effective use of ballot reform. By the 'eighties, they recognized the evils of leaving election machinery unregulated in the hands of the parties. Because party leaders chose election officials, the parties secured a windfall of patronage places useful in maintaining a cadre of loyal workers. Because the parties printed and distributed ballots, the party leadership controlled nominations. Reformers, on the other hand, did not have the money to circulate ballots and so could not put their candidates before the voters. Because it printed the ballots, each party naturally produced tickets listing only its own nominees. Thus it was difficult for citizens to vote independently by splitting their votes among candidates of different parties. Finally, because the parties were free to print distinctive and therefore non-secret ballots, they could bribe voters with the certainty that the right ticket had been dropped into the public ballot box.[70]

Liberals came slowly to ballot reform. In the 1870s many even opposed the idea of a secret ballot. A true man, they believed, should be willing to reveal his political preferences.[71] But the rigors of independency soon taught reformers otherwise. In the 'eighties, they practiced "vest-pocket" voting by making up their tickets privately at home and carrying them concealed in their pockets to the polls in order to confuse party workers.[72] By then, liberals had become firm advocates of a secret ballot regulated by the government. Along with labor reformers such as Henry George, the liberals urged the adoption of the Australian system for the secret voting of government-printed ballots listing all parties' candidates. Battles with party leaders forced compromises, particularly in the layout of the ballot: often, party emblems and lists of candidates by party rather than office helped voters cast the straight ticket of old. But by 1892, nearly every Northern state used some version of the Australian ballot system.[73]

As with civil service reform, ballot legislation brought with it an ideal antagonistic to traditional party politics. In place of the display of spectacular partisanship, liberals advanced the notion of restrained, secret behavior. Political preferences, they suggested, were a private matter and not the stuff of communal ritual.

Liberals tried, too, to limit the role of party in municipal government. In city after city the "best men," with business and middle-class allies, offered a variety of schemes such as the strong mayor to weaken the parties' hold on urban administration.[74] Municipal reform had two key ideological components. The reformers insisted that city government had nothing to do with party. Just as they tried to separate the right to vote in municipal elections from state and national suffrage, so too they tried to divide municipal politics from state and national partisanship. Party considerations should not affect the voter, the reformers believed. He should cast his ballot for the best local candidates regardless of his party affiliation. In the reformers' view, city politics could never produce the differences over principle which naturally and properly spawned the national parties. "Party divisions. . .properly arise, only when men differ in respect to some general principles or methods of state policy," the Tilden Commission claimed in its *Report.* "Good men cannot and do not differ as to whether municipal debt ought to be restricted, extravagance checked, and municipal affairs lodged in the hands of competent and faithful officers. There is no more just reason why the control of the public works of a great city should be lodged in the hands of a democrat or a republican, than there is why an adherent of one or the other of the great parties should be made the superintendent of a business corporation."[75]

The Tilden Commission's invocation of the corporation pointed the way to the second ideological underpinning of municipal reform. As with the civil service, reformers tried to replace the ideal of party with the ideal of business practice. Like the Federal government, cities should be run on business principles. "[C]ity government is a sphere for personal honesty and business capacity, rather than for political policy or party principles," wrote Dorman B. Eaton. "It is in the region of business, and must be provided for and conducted on business methods."[76]

Like other liberal endeavors, municipal reform movements met with mixed success. By 1900, they had achieved some tangible reduction of party control of the government, but much more significant for the party system was their establishment of ideas competing with partisanship.

By the mid-'nineties, the heyday of liberal reform had passed. The second generation of reformers was growing old; the first was retired or gone. Many reform organizations had folded; the national independent crusades for reform-minded presidents had ended. Liberalism was slowed in part by failure, in part by the acceptance of its ideas. Some liberal aims had been realized—hard money, an improved civil service, a secret ballot. Others, like suffrage restriction, minority representation, and free trade, never succeeded. In the twentieth century some of the reformers still active enlisted in the progressive drives for municipal reform and

honest government, but liberal reform as an identifiable movement ceased to exist.[77]

Despite its disappointments, liberal reform made a critical
impact on the politics of the nineteenth century. The reformers
presented three important challenges to the system of popular
political participation based on mass partisanship. First, and least
momentous, was the tangible, legal change in the rules of politics.
Civil service, ballot, and municipal reform hurt the parties but did
not destroy them or end their control of politics and government.

More significant, perhaps, liberal reform struck at the party system by nurturing and publicizing a group of voters who rejected
demonstrative partisanship. Reserving the right to abandon their
party if it offended them, the independents were impervious to the
old appeals to party spirit and loyalty. Henceforth, the parties
would have to shape new appeals to win these voters.

Most damaging of all to the parties and to popular politics was
the liberals' creation of an alternative political style grounded in
ideals hostile to the old party politics. Liberal reform narrowed
the cultural authority of partisanship. Through their campaigns,
liberals raised doubts about the propriety of party involvement in
the management of state and Federal bureaucracies, the administration of elections, and the government of cities. The reformers
also offered an alternative to the partisan political style. In place
of the self-revelation of demonstrative partisanship, they urged
the secrecy of vest-pocket voting and the Australian ballot. In
place of emotional party spirit, they offered a cool, social scientific
politics of education. In place of parades and rallies, they relied
on factual pamphlets and tracts. In place of the doctrine of party
loyalty, they elevated the ideals of individual conscience, independency, and business methods. In place of the loyal partisan, they
substituted the independent man who tamed his party with bolts
and scratches and educational pressure groups.

No other political group did so much to discredit the rationale
of nineteenth-century partisanship. Certainly other men broke
from the major parties in the Gilded Age. Workers and farmers
offered important third-party challenges to the Republicans and
Democrats. But the major parties could buy off third-party competitors with partial recognition of their demands, as the Populists
discovered in the 'nineties.[78] More significant, third parties did not

pose a direct threat to the legitimacy of party, even if their leaders criticized the Republicans and Democrats. After all, many third-party politicians themselves hoped to capitalize on the loyalty of their followers.

In contrast, the liberal reformers, with their strategy of independence, wounded the party system more deeply and served as the harbinger of twentieth-century politics. The reform style would foreswear third parties and retain the two-party framework, but it rejected the unquestioning partisanship that had forged the party into such an effective political instrument. To put further pressure on the Republicans and Democrats, reform turned to extra-party organizations to educate the public and lobby for legislation. To be sure, there were other pressure groups in the late nineteenth century. Manufacturers in particular made use of trade organizations like the American Iron and Steel Association to lobby for high protective tariffs. Yet the liberals did more to make the educational pressure group a centerpiece of political strategy. They recognized most clearly the usefulness of appearing to be outside the party system and above politics. They had the most self-conscious appreciation of the possibilities of a less-partisan politics of propaganda and publicity.

Increasingly, the middle and upper classes would recognize the liberal style as the best way of achieving their political goals. Abandoning the party as their sole means of political expression, well-to-do Americans would accept weakened party organizations and diminished party spirit and take up the pressure group and independent voting. Never quite the "organized class" they hoped to become, the liberals nonetheless set the example for the politics of the twentieth century.

The reformers' political style had fateful implications for popular politics. Class concerns underlay the liberals' reconsideration of partisanship and gave it bite. As their interest in suffrage restriction made plain, liberals were not sympathetic to popular political participation. Unable to keep the poor and the uneducated out of politics, they tried to reshape the political world in which these voters lived. The reformers' political style rested on an elitist dream of cultured and enlightened leaders educating a receptive electorate. This was a politics with the educated man once more at the center, his principles the yardstick of public life, his pamphlets the means of shaping the people to his will. The exuberant, subjective partisanship of the party press and the spectacular campaign had no place in the reformers' political vision. Never attentive to the role of the parties, however corrupt and boss-ridden, in stimulating voter turnout, the liberals cut away the partisan basis of mass political participation. Through sympathetic editors and party leaders, their political style began to remake popular politics.

4

EDUCATIONAL POLITICS

In the 'seventies and 'eighties, Republican and Democratic leaders confronted new political realities. Issues such as tariff and civil service reform were capturing public attention. More and more Northerners worried over the power of party machines and bosses. Most troubling of all, increasing numbers of voters had rejected undeviating partisan loyalty. To win elections, party leaders needed to find ways of coping with new issues and attracting the votes of the independent-minded. For politicians sympathetic to liberal reform, the solution was evident: the parties could appeal to reformers by adopting a version of their own style. By the mid-'eighties even party leaders hostile to reform recognized the uses of the liberals' educational brand of politics. Both Republicans and Democrats began to replace the demonstrative partisanship of torchlight parades with a more deliberative and intellectual canvass of pamphlets and documents. By the presidential election of 1892, the two parties had almost entirely abandoned spectacular display for the less partisan and emotional "campaign of education."

As early as the 1850s and 'sixties, politicians had questioned whether spectacle persuaded the uncommitted to vote for a party's ticket. Some leaders favored more systematic campaign methods; editors offered their newspapers as the best means of reaching the voters.[1] Nevertheless, partisan display remained the mainstay of campaign managers. But in the 'seventies, party leaders influenced by liberal reform began to break free from the chains of spectacular partisanship and create a new political style.

No single party manager invented the campaign of education. Yet, to a remarkable degree, educational politics owed its ascendancy in the 'eighties and 'nineties to one man, Governor Samuel J. Tilden of New York. Tilden exemplified those politicians who bridged the worlds of party politics and liberal reform in the 'seventies. A protégé of Martin Van Buren, Tilden was an ardent Democrat who reveled in the party struggles that liberals deplored. But he also shared much of the liberal outlook. A man of wealth and social position, he belonged to New York City's upper class and reflected its prejudices and experience. Despite a long career in politics, Tilden, the "Sage of Gramercy Park," was a withdrawn, cultivated man who preferred the quiet of his study to the give-and-take of the stump. Like so many reformers, he believed in social science, in disciplined scientific enquiry conducted by educated men. He, too, had faith in the persuasive power of pamphlets and tracts. During the Civil War, he helped found the Society for the Diffusion of Political Knowledge, the Democratic propaganda agency that had influenced the liberals. Tilden had a passion for statistics, order, and organization. Along with other well-to-do reformers, he doubtless drew political lessons from his experience with the nation's developing economy. As an attorney for railroads, then the most elaborate and successful business hierarchies in America, he saw at firsthand the possibilities of tightly controlled, highly centralized organization. A party man, Tilden still displayed some of the antipathy to corrupt political machines and universal suffrage so typical of the reformers. Belatedly and reluctantly, he led the movement against the Tweed Ring in 1871 and 1872; as governor, in 1875, he established the commission that advocated limiting the right of suffrage in New York State's municipal elections.

Tilden owed his political success in the 'seventies and 'eighties to his appeal to reformers. In an era still largely ruled by strict partisanship, he cultivated support among independents and Republicans as well as Democrats. It was a bi-partisan coalition that overthrew William Tweed, a bi-partisan commission that proposed to limit the vote in New York's cities. Tilden's reputation as a reformer made him attractive to Democratic leaders handicapped for a decade by the party's opposition to the Civil War. In 1874 they nominated him for governor. Two years later, his reform credentials bolstered by attacks on the state's corrupt Canal Ring, he received the Democrats' presidential nomination.[2]

Tilden's political style, perfected over the years, grew out of his liberal disposition and his dependence on independent and Republican votes. Although Tilden, secretive and laconic, never publicized his methods, admiring contemporaries realized his departure from traditional electioneering. "He never believed in the skyrocket and Roman candle system . . . ," a journalist recalled. "[As] a rule he considered brass bands and orators a waste of money and time." Instead of using spectacular devices to arouse the party faithful, he preferred to concentrate on the uncommitted with quiet appeals. Tilden, *Harper's Weekly* noted, "introduced the cold business methods . . . in political campaigns. Before his time much energy was wasted in hurrahs. He, however, was nothing if not businesslike, and believed that a systematic canvass quietly made would be much more effective than the old noisy method." Running for governor in 1874, Tilden directed a tightly knit organization that used circular letters to reach down to loyal personal representatives in each township across New York. Through polls of the entire electorate, these men identified the undecided and independent. To capture their votes, the organization tried to cultivate a sense of personal contact with the candidate. Party workers visited each wavering voter and left behind pamphlets on Tilden, copies of his speeches, and issues of Democratic newspapers. The technique worked: Tilden, the champion of reform, was elected governor of the North's most populous state.[3]

The campaign of 1874 became the model for Tilden's presidential canvass two years later. Retreating to the governor's mansion in Albany, Tilden left the details of the contest to Congressman Abram S. Hewitt, the Democratic national chairman. Like Tilden, Hewitt was a party man deeply affected by liberal ideas. He, too, was a wealthy New Yorker interested in municipal reform, social science, and organization. His political success also depended on bi-partisan support. Republican votes had sent him to Congress; later, they would help him to defeat Henry George and Theodore Roosevelt in the tumultuous mayoral election of 1886. Hewitt flirted with limiting the suffrage as a proponent of the Tilden Commission's constitutional amendment on municipal government. But Hewitt, like other liberals, accepted universal suffrage as an unalterable fact of life in state and national elections. He saw in a reformed partisan politics, dominated by the men of his class, the opportunity to educate the enfranchised poor.

Hewitt's public philosophy emerged with stunning clarity in his speech at the dedication of Brooklyn Bridge in 1883. Celebrating the span as a product of "organized intelligence," he urged his audience to apply "the lesson of the bridge" to public life. "Instead of attempting to restrict suffrage," he said, "let us try to educate the voters; instead of disbanding parties, let each citizen within the party always vote, but never for a man who is unfit to hold office. Thus parties, as well as voters, will be organized on the basis of intelligence." No one ever put more clearly the aims of the men who tried to reshape partisanship in the late nineteenth century. Hewitt made an ideal choice for the head of the first national campaign of education.[4]

Tilden and Hewitt, despite some personal friction, responded creatively to the challenge of recasting presidential electioneering. Unlike past managers, they did not intend to leave the production and distribution of campaign literature to the party's congressional committee. At the outset, Hewitt began to prepare "all the necessary documents to show the fraud & corruption of the Administration." He also assembled the *Campaign Textbook,* a compendium designed to indoctrinate party speakers and writers and give them facts with which to educate the voters. The parties had put out textbooks before: Hewitt was surely influenced by the *Hand-Book of the Democracy for 1863 & '64,* a collection of the pamphlets from Tilden's Society for the Diffusion of Political Knowledge, and by the Republicans' own *Textbook* for the campaign of 1868. But Hewitt's 754 pages of densely printed argument and statistics, almost four times the length of the Republican volume, made an unrivaled educational tool.[5]

In New York, meanwhile, Hewitt's lieutenants expanded the "Literary Bureau" that had publicized Tilden's drive for the nomination. A campaign operation of unprecedented size, the bureau employed a staff of perhaps forty writers, editors, and clerks, and took up much of the second floor of a Manhattan office building. Following Tilden's model, the bureau used circular letters instructing Democratic politicians to form campaign clubs and take polls of the voters. In typical Tilden fashion, one circular letter, sent under Hewitt's name, told Democratic county chairmen, "The work to be done should be done *carefully* and *silently*." William S. Andrews, a lawyer, journalist, and secretary of the bureau, boasted that "he . . . would be enabled to give the name of each voter throughout the United States, his politics, and the way he voted at the last election. . . ." The bureau wrote, printed, and mailed out 27,000,000 pieces of literature, undoubtedly the most campaign documents used in an American election to that time.[6] The literature ranged from long speeches by Tilden and other Democratic leaders to simple leaflets the size of railroad timetables. One leaflet told *WHAT TILDEN HAS DONE. IN BREAKING RINGS. THE TWEED RING;* another promised *REFORM. FACTS FOR INDEPENDENT VOTERS.* A section of the Manhattan office drafted articles and editorials which it offered to 2000 Democratic and independent newspapers. Another section sent out speakers to Democratic meetings around the country.[7]

The bureau represented, in Andrews's opinion, "the first systematized effort . . . to organize public opinion by attempting to reach the voters directly through the party press, and by the distribution of documents specially prepared and designed to direct thought and discussion within the lines upon which it was intended that the contest should be made." Andrews may have exaggerated, but the Literary Bureau had gone far toward substituting seemingly reasoned, objective argument for the emotional, irrational appeal of spectacular partisanship.[8]

Despite the innovations of the *Textbook* and the Literary Bureau, Tilden and Hewitt faced a difficult task in 1876. It was one thing to mount an educational campaign in the candidate's home state, quite another to harness the entire Democratic party to the new politics. Tilden could not convert the Democracy to his political style in a single campaign. Some state committees were too weak and inefficient to be of much help; others did not care for the literature and instructions from New York. It is highly unlikely that W. S. Andrews ever received all the comprehensive reports on individual voters that Hewitt had requested. Leading Democrats "sneered" at the Literary Bureau, which Tilden and Hewitt carefully kept separate from the headquarters of the national committee. State and local Democratic organizations, inundated with the products of the bureau, often failed to accept the literature or distribute it to the voters. Some of the pamphlets did not address important local issues or took an inconvenient stance on national questions. "The documents sent out from New York are, with two or three exceptions, almost useless here," an Ohio Democrat complained. "The canvass is lumbering along without much method or direction." Tilden and Hewitt had set an educational apparatus atop a traditional spectacular campaign. The voters, caught up in the excitement of events like the flag-raising in the sixth ward of New Haven, did not know what the candidate and his chairman had hoped to accomplish. While educational politics took shape on the second floor of a Manhattan office building, spectacular display went on as usual in the streets below.[9]

Little of Tilden's approach was brand new by the mid-'seventies. His campaign resembled the old "still hunt" in which a weak party tried to lull the opposition by dropping public electioneering for quiet work among the undecided and the purchasable. But the still hunt had always been a desperate resort; no politician had made secrecy and outward calm into the essence of his electioneering before. Polls, literature, personal appeals, and organization were familiar elements in politics.[10] But Tilden fashioned these devices into a fresh, coherent whole coupled with a rejection of spectacular display. He offered a sober, rather intellectual approach aimed at uncommitted voters in place of emotional appeals intended for committed partisans.

Although Tilden won the popular vote and probably the electoral vote as well, Congress and its Electoral Commission took the presidency away from him in 1877. In defeat, he left two important legacies. Tilden's campaigns in 1874 and 1876 adapted the political style of the reformers to party politics. Even those politicians who had "sneered" at the Literary Bureau had to acknowledge the effectiveness of his technique. In 1876, he ran the best race by a Democratic presidential candidate in a generation. His canvass set an example that party leaders would find increasingly compelling. In later years, Tilden's name and methods seemed to awe some politicians. During the campaign of 1888, thieves tried to make off with his blank polling sheets and lists of voters, then more than a decade out of date![11] Tilden also left a group of followers, veterans of 'seventy-four and 'seventy-six, who understood and accepted his ideas. As these men grew powerful in the 'eighties and early 'nineties, they would convert the Democratic party to educational politics.

Tilden's ideas did not triumph immediately. Winfield Scott Hancock, the Democratic presidential nominee in 1880, kept the Literary Bureau alive under William Andrews, but it played a minor role in an otherwise typical spectacular campaign. Four years later, the nomination of Grover Cleveland signalled better fortunes for Tilden's ideas and disciples. Cleveland, like Tilden, had made his national reputation as a New York governor devoted to political reform. As age and ill-health brought Tilden's career to a close, Cleveland inherited the older man's advisers and his place in the party. In 1884, former Tilden lieutenants managed Cleveland's campaign and ran another Literary Bureau. But key members of the Democratic National Committee, particularly Chairman William H. Barnum of Connecticut and Senator Arthur Pue Gorman of Maryland, still had no interest in the educational style.[12]

The Republicans, meanwhile, clung even more tightly to spectacular campaigning. In 1876, the party ran a traditional canvass for its nominee, Rutherford B. Hayes of Ohio. Without much money, system, or careful procedure, the national committee allowed state party organizations almost free rein. As before the national headquarters in New York left the preparation of nearly all campaign literature to the congressional committee. Unlike the Democrats, the Republicans had no educational textbook. Their documents were unimaginatively produced and distributed. "Many of them are upon old issues and others are too long and heavy for popular use," the secretary of the national committee complained, "and they have been distributed with no particular system, while Gov. Tilden's pamphlets are circulated with a most perfect system."[13]

Four years later, the national committee staged much the same kind of campaign for James A. Garfield. Headquarters in New York concentrated on raising money, sending speakers to rallies, and mailing out documents. Most of the Republican literature was still prepared by the congressional committee. But the Republicans did produce a textbook this time. There were more signs of change in the campaign for the ticket of James G. Blaine and John A. Logan in 1884. Copying Tilden and Hewitt, the national committee prepared many of its own documents, some of them even in Swedish and Welsh. But the party still had nothing like Tilden's highly developed organizational scheme or his superb Literary Bureau. The Republicans' canvass was most memorable for Blaine's disastrous campaign swing. Conducted mainly in spectacular fashion by both sides, the election degenerated into emotional exchanges about Cleveland's illegitimate child and Blaine's corrupt business dealings.[14]

Despite its spectacular qualities, the campaign of 1884 marked a turning point in the political style of the Republicans and Democrats. Some state leaders, following Tilden's example, paid more attention to organization, polls, subdued appeals, and documents. In Pennsylvania the headquarters of the Republican State Committee in Philadelphia organized like "the management of some business enterprise." The committee printed documents of its own and mailed them out to local party organizations along with literature provided by the national committee in New York. The Republicans' literature included "useful abstracts of the State and National election laws, the speeches of acceptance of Blaine and Logan, histories showing the results of protective and free trade legislation, together with some of the formidable arguments of eminent statesmen on the beneficial workings of the tariff, and an abstract of the foreign policy during Mr. Blaine's administration of the department of State."[15]

The Democratic canvass in Pennsylvania even more closely resembled Tilden's design. "The outline of the campaign in the State is to have less noise and more solid work, contrary to the policy of the Hancock campaign," announced William U. Hensel, the Democratic chairman. "We will depend more on a complete organization of the party in every election district of Pennsylvania than on clubs, brass bands and torchlight processions." Hensel used a poll to identify "all Democrats and doubtful voters." Party workers were assigned "to look after" these voters "to see that they are registered . . . and that they are supplied first with the local Democratic paper, and with other sound political literature." To reach voters in towns without a Democratic journal, Hensel produced his own campaign weekly with a circulation of perhaps twenty thousand. "The Democratic cardinal principle . . . ," a reporter concluded, "is to supply its voters with the 'right kind' of literature."[16]

By 1884, politicians had become more critical of spectacular display. Not unexpectedly, much of the criticism came from men sympathetic to reform. The *Philadelphia Record*, an independent paper edited by Alexander K. McClure, deplored the "MIL-LIONS WASTED" on uniformed companies and torchlight parades. McClure, the manager of the Republican campaign in Pennsylvania in 1860, had become a municipal reformer, a Liberal Republican, and an independent candidate for state senator and mayor after the Civil War. He now rejected partisan display as an expensive travesty that failed to win votes and led to "lost love of industry" and "lost sobriety." Through the *Record*, McClure called on "the better men of every faith" to "close their purse strings and retire partisan profligates from every party direction."[17]

In New York, Whitelaw Reid, editor of the influential *Tribune*, attacked campaign spectacle throughout the 'eighties. Once a reformer himself, Reid had backed Horace Greeley, his chief on the *Tribune*, for president in 1872 and explored independence before returning permanently to the Republican party late in the decade. Although Reid supported the Republican ticket in 1876, he was perhaps the only newspaperman in New York to publicize the Literary Bureau of his friend Samuel Tilden. At each presidential election in the 'eighties, Reid demanded the Republican party place less emphasis on spectacle and more on "the dry diet of public education."[18]

Party spokesmen seldom friendly to independent reform also criticized traditional campaign methods in 1884. The Republican *Inquirer* of Philadelphia pointed out "that party ties are no longer as binding as they were, and that the old battle cry of the leaders, 'Vote the Regular Ticket,' has lost its controlling force." The paper scored Republican managers who tried to win votes by staging a parade for the arrival of the party's vice-presidential candidate, John A. Logan. "A torchlight procession is, at the very best, a silly sort of show," the *Inquirer* insisted. "It is exceedingly costly and the chances are as a million to nothing that it does not make Democrats vote the Republican ticket." In New Haven, the Democratic *Union* lamented the money "flung away on torches, uniforms and outside demonstrations that have no other result than noise and hurrah." "We do not believe that the Republicans make votes by it, and we are sure the Democrats do not," the paper declared. "In our opinion the money would be much better spent in circulating judiciously prepared documents that would enlighten the voters by appealing to their intelligence."[19]

Cleveland's victory accelerated the parties' conversion to educational politics. His election, achieved with the help of the Mugwumps, demonstrated that reformers were a political power no party could ignore any longer. In office, Cleveland publicized the liberal issues of civil service and tariff reform. At the periphery of national politics since the sectional crisis of the 1850s, the question of protective duties on imports divided both the Democratic and Republican parties. The issue figured more prominently in the elections of 1880 and 1884 as the Democrats slowly adopted a low-tariff stand and the Republicans rallied around high protective rates. In December 1887, Cleveland gladdened the liberals by devoting his entire annual message to the necessity of tariff reform. On the eve of the campaign of 1888, the reformers were a critical factor; one of their main issues, the tariff, commanded the political stage.[20]

During Cleveland's administration, party leaders tried to accommodate the changed conditions of national politics. Republicans and Democrats contemptuous of independence and reform now took up the liberals' techniques. James S. Clarkson, an editor and businessman from Iowa, led the Republicans' conversion to the educational style. The prosperous owner of Des Moines' leading Republican paper, Clarkson yearned for success in the metropolis: someday, he might have the chance to buy into a daily in New York or Chicago. A veteran of Iowa's Republican party, he dreamed of bigger things in national politics. Earnest and purposeful, Clarkson had a confident swagger; his nickname was "Ret." Yet an aura of disappointment, of unfulfilled expectations, seemed to hang over him. An intense, reflective man, Clarkson was energetic and full of ideas yet often burdened by ill-health. Rumors swirled continuously around him: he was about to become a cabinet officer, postmaster general, publisher of this or that big-city paper, owner of a literary magazine, even a presidential candidate. None of the rumors ever came true. But Clarkson was a man of solid political achievement. In the late 'eighties, he produced the first substantial refinement and extension of Tilden's ideas. More than any other man, James Clarkson revolutionized the political style of the Republican party in the late 'eighties and early 'nineties.[21]

Clarkson first broke from convention after the campaign of 1884. That year he had watched the Mugwump bolt as a member of the executive committee running Blaine's canvass from Republican national headquarters in New York. A staunch partisan, Clarkson despised the independents, whom he called "Pharisees." But his party, wounded by the Mugwumps' defection, had lost the White House for the first time in a quarter of a century. Clarkson, above all a practical politician, knew when to compromise. He would never lose his distaste for liberals, but he did admire Samuel Tilden. Like the New Yorker, Clarkson saw the need to steer a middle course between traditional politics and reform. He realized, too, that voters absorbed in new issues such as the tariff could not be won over with spectacular appeals. "The need for the new and more universal form of party method and work was first shown in the campaign of 1884, and the first campaign since the War fought fairly on the economical issues," he recalled a few years later:

All men who were active in that campaign will remember the sur-
prise that came when the brass band, the red light, and the mass
meeting seemed suddenly to have lost their power. That was the
beginning of the change of political discussion from the open field,
as in Lincoln's day, to the private home where each family began to
examine and discuss for itself the policy of the parties to find which
party promised the most for the elevation and comfort of that special home. It was an evolutionary result, arising from the demand
of changing conditions from sentimental to economic issues, - the
evolution into education as the superior force in American politics.

So Clarkson set about transforming the Republican party into a
weapon of political education.[22]

Influenced by Tilden, he did not intend simply to match the
Democrat's style. Instead, Clarkson sought to give educational
politics a wider appeal. Sober education, he realized, had to be
made more accessible to voters raised on spectacle. Accordingly,
Clarkson helped create the National League of Republican Clubs
in 1887. The league marked the culmination of efforts to replace
the temporary clubs and marching companies of spectacular campaigns with permanent organizations that would educate voters
during and after elections. In the early 'eighties, Republicans in
Northern towns and cities had established "Young Men's Republican Clubs," many of which lasted through the decade. "Lincoln
Leagues" appeared in some states during the mid-'eighties. In
New York, New Jersey, and Ohio, permanent political clubs
formed state organizations in 1886 and 1887. In December 1887,
ten days after Cleveland's tariff message, these state organizations
joined delegates from clubs in other states to inaugurate the
national league.

The convention of the clubs dramatized the merging of the liberal style into regular Republicanism. Senator William M. Evarts,
chairman of the Tilden Commission, presided. Working side by
side with him were such veterans of the Republican National Committee as Senator William E. Chandler of New Hampshire, chairman of the league's rules committee, and Clarkson, chairman of
the executive committee that controlled the new organization.[23]

Many of the reformers envisioned the league as another
weapon in the attack on party bosses and machines. One New
York Republican hoped the organization would "interest in such

clubs the best men in the community" and "become the relentless champion of good government." Robert M. La Follette of Wisconsin, a member of the executive committee, typified the optimism of the reformers in the league. "Such clubs cannot be used as machines for individuals or factions," he declared. "Wherever they are actively maintained, political slates will be shattered and political bargains fail of consummation. Cliques and rings thrive upon the citizens' indifference to the plain duties of representative government. They cannot co-exist with the persistent, continuous, intelligent personal interest of the individual voter." Other leaders of the league shared La Follette's faith. "I see in the well directed maintenance of political clubs in the large cities a very powerful means for municipal reform," wrote Daniel J. Ryan, chairman of the convention. "No organization properly managed can afford to lend its aid to the election and perpetuation in power of a dishonest ring; the very nature of the club forbids it."[24]

Clarkson, Chandler, and the other Republican regulars had no intention of allowing the league to threaten their management of the Republican Party. They planned the network of clubs as a supplement, not a rival, to the party's dominant local, state, and national committees. For the regulars, the league offered a means of winning back the Mugwumps, preventing future bolts, and explaining the protective tariff.

Clarkson was not the only leader who recognized the new realities. "Party ties have gradually weakened," wrote a Kansas Republican soon after the convention. "These clubs will revive interest, adjust differences, and by the exchange of opinion show the wavering person that while he differs from the party on some points, he can find no other party from which he does not differ more, and he will again act with the party which most nearly represents him."[25] W. W. Phelps, a wealthy New Jersey Republican and associate of James G. Blaine, underscored the league's value in promoting the tariff and other new issues. "The old kind of questions—slavery and disunion, for example—are so nearly questions of right and wrong, that any man could answer them, so soon as put," Phelps noted. "But the questions of to-day, protection and free trade, universal or restricted immigration, and the like, can be answered only after investigation. The citizen must first inform himself, or be informed." Phelps believed the temporary clubs of spectacular campaigns were inadequate to this task. "With the old-time questions it was enough to give notice that they were at issue, and then to kindle the zeal of the voter to settle them," Phelps wrote. "But it is useless to try to stir men's souls to enthusiasm for economic truths, until you have convinced men of the value of them. This is the function of the permanent club. It gathers facts and draws conclusions from them."[26]

Differing in their goals, the regulars and reformers both viewed the permanent clubs of the league as instruments of "education," that liberal word which politicians now used freely. "The political club of the present and future, under organization, means more than mere display," exclaimed Daniel Ryan. "They are directed toward work and education in the interests of party politics." Joseph H. Manley of Maine, another associate of Blaine, wrote, "The permanent club will occupy to the Republican party the relative position that the Sunday-School does to the Church. . . . The club will have this field to cultivate in disseminating proper literature upon all economic and political questions, by the circulation of newspapers, the distribution of public speeches, and the encouragement of public discussion; work in the broad field of educating the people on the great questions which should absorb their interest." Robert La Follette foresaw the same educational function for the league. "Clubs can only sustain a continuing interest in politics by studying present political issues, reviewing political history, holding regular discussions on pending and proposed legislation," he argued. "If permanent, they must become centres of political education and exchange. . . . They will do much to substitute intelligent interest for unthinking enthusiasm, the lamp of reason for the torchlight, earnest conviction and wise leadership for the party whip and the party boss." The liberal reformers' vision had conquered much of the Republican party.[27]

The Democrats immediately copied the Republicans' innovation. In April 1888 the New York Young Men's Democratic Club, wealthy supporters of Cleveland, municipal reform, and a low tariff, founded the National Association of Democratic Clubs. Like the National League of Republican Clubs, the association blended reformers and regulars. Its president, Chauncey F. Black of Pennsylvania, was a liberal and a sharp critic of traditional partisanship. In 1882, Black had become lieutenant governor of his staunchly Republican home state through skillful appeals to independents and Republicans. He realized how campaign clubs and companies served the old style of politics. "The trouble has been that men were accustomed to 'clubs'—to shouting and marching and not to associations intended for deliberation," he wrote. "The *better* class of people . . . will not join 'clubs' either social or political." Like Clarkson and the leaders of the league, Black hoped to reshape the clubs into an instrument of education.[28]

Cleveland's message and the organization of the Republican and Democratic clubs set the tone of the campaign of 1888. Both parties moved closer than before to the educational style. Accepting Cleveland's challenge, the Republicans took up the tariff issue and nominated a committed protectionist, Benjamin Harrison, for president. Still, the Republicans did not run quite the sort of canvass Clarkson would have preferred. The party installed him as vice-chairman of the campaign but gave the chairmanship to a traditional politician, the Pennsylvania boss Matthew S. Quay.[29] Quite unlike Clarkson in temperament, Quay did not share the Iowan's concern about political style. Clarkson, a newsman wrote, was a "sentimentalist" in politics; but Quay "is not a sentimentalist. He does not believe, or pretend to believe, as Clarkson does, that education may be a force in elections." Quay seemed more interested in distributing money liberally to party workers. With a large campaign fund on hand, the committee bought off newspapers and subsidized traveling orators. Clarkson was appalled at the pandering to "mercenary newspapers & greedy speakers": here was the beginning of what he later called "the party's modern vicious habit of paying millions of dollars to Repn papers & Repn speakers to support the party."[30]

Quay had no aversion to partisan display either. Across the North, Republicans dressed up in uniform and paraded much as before. The prospect of another spectacular campaign alarmed some influential Republicans. Whitelaw Reid's *Tribune* warned early in the campaign that "the one thing uncertain in this great contest is . . . whether the Republican party is going to fight Chinese fashion, at some points—with loud noises and a dreadful beating of gongs—or at every vital point in a civilized and effective way. . . . There are some symptoms of a desire to convert this into a shouting campaign at the outset; to rely upon many bands and numerous torches. . . ."[31]

The national committee was ready to provide some of the education that Clarkson and the *Tribune* wanted. To meet the strong demand for information on the tariff, Quay set up a large headquarters in Manhattan with as many as seventy-five clerks and writers. For the first time, apparently, the Republicans had their own "literary bureau." Another department at headquarters provided stories and editorials to the press. Quay's payoffs did have an educational purpose: the committee bought up quantities of a New York daily committed to high protection and distributed it free around the the country.[32] Headquarters had help from protectionist propaganda agencies. Liberally endowed by manufacturers frightened by Cleveland's low-tariff message, the American Protective Tariff League, the Home Market Club, and the American Iron and Steel Association sent out at least a million pamphlets of their own. The tariff league provided 3,500 papers with a newsletter on protection.[33]

In a way, Quay's reliance on the tariff agencies was a measure of his limited commitment to education. The chairman did not think literature important enough to produce all the necessary documents at his own headquarters. Similarly, instead of distributing the campaign textbook for free as in the past, the committee had a New York bookdealer put copies up for sale. Clarkson's educational machine, the Republican League of Clubs, received scant recognition from Quay. Some veteran politicians did not take the "nice young" advocates of education very seriously; other party leaders, with some reason, feared the clubs were loyal to James G. Blaine. As a result, the league was "sat down upon" and "absolutely ignored by the Republican National Committee."[34] In the end, Quay just did not seem to think that educational efforts were vital to the campaign. "The committee," a reporter noted, "is not issuing so many bulletins or sending out so many million tracts as its Democratic rivals, who keep a corps of men at work now preparing copy for the press. . . ." Education had not yet found a home in the Republican party.[35]

The educational style had much more support in the Democratic party. Cleveland delegated the management of the canvass to his private secretary Daniel S. Lamont, a former Tilden aide and party secretary in the gubernatorial campaign of 1874.[36] Once again, William Andrews would supervise the literary operation. In

February 1888, Andrews drew up for his chiefs a blueprint of "The work of a Presidential Campaign." Seizing the opportunity, he described his experience in past elections and called for the adoption of Tilden's style. "There, perhaps, never was a time in our history when party allegiance was more unsettled than now," Andrews wrote. "There is to be more of thought and less of passion than usual in the approaching contest; and, consequently, it was never more important than now to place before the voters full and plain statements of the real issues of the Campaign."

Andrews urged Cleveland and Lamont to prepare the campaign textbook and other literature earlier than ever, well before the national convention. Meanwhile, the national committee should collect addresses and personal data for a million-and-a-half Democrats and independents—"active and intelligent voters"—around the country. Then, when necessary, the committee could mail a pamphlet on an important issue to representatives of an ethnic or occupational group in two days' time. Distribution of documents by mail would flatter the voter and draw him close to the national leaders, Andrews believed: "It is as if he were personally known to the sender, and he unconsciously feels that his importance as a voter is recognized."

Use of the mails would free the national committee from reliance on the local party committees whose waste and inefficiency had plagued the Tilden campaign in 1876. By appealing directly to independent and "intelligent" men, the national committee would also avoid rousing these local politicians into old-fashioned partisan excess. Andrews cautioned that "partisan feeling in the heat of a contest drives men apart, makes them antagonistic, and not easy to be influenced by argument." His plan, suggestive of direct-mail campaigns a century later, would preserve the calm needed to educate the people about tariff reform.[37]

"The work of a Presidential Campaign" offered the apotheosis of Tilden's approach to politics. Here was the dream of a centrally controlled canvass: the national committee, bypassing local politicians, influenced the electorate directly. Like Tilden, Andrews would cater to the independent and "intelligent" rather than the partisan. He substituted literature for parades, reason for emotion. In Andrews's vision, leaders no longer indulged the spectacular tastes of the people; instead, a national elite, aided by polls and pamphlets, played schoolmaster to the electorate.

The dream of "The work of a Presidential Campaign" outran the reality of 1888. Cleveland and Lamont, doubtless aware of the cost in dollars and alienated local leaders, did not take up Andrews's plan for direct mailings to voters. Nor had it been practical to write and print campaign literature before the president's renomination in June. More ominously, the disciples of Samuel Tilden still confronted Democratic leaders hostile to tariff reform and unsympathetic to educational politics. Aided by Arthur Pue Gorman, the protectionist and old-school partisan William H. Barnum returned as chairman of the national committee. With Cleveland's misguided assent, Gorman, Barnum, and the committee chose Calvin S. Brice, a wealthy Ohio railroad investor and high-tariff man, to handle the day-to-day management of the canvass at party headquarters in New York. Brice promised "a campaign of intellect" with "an educational effect which will be felt for many years," but supporters of tariff reform and educational electioneering doubted his sincerity.[38]

The course of the campaign confirmed their fears. Party headquarters now occupied three floors of a Manhattan office building. The "department of oratory" assigned speakers to rallies; the "telegraphic bureau" sent out "proper Democratic news" to the press; Andrews's Literary Bureau wrote articles and pamphlets; another bureau prepared documents for the printer; yet another mailed out Andrews's productions to newspapers and local party committees. A dazzled reporter claimed that "never before, even in 1876, under Mr. Tilden, were there such facilities for the spread of Democratic literature through the country."[39]

Brice made poor use of the facilities. Facing an uphill fight to educate workers and farmers about the controversial issue of tariff reform, the national committee organized slowly in June and July. Headquarters, beset by incompetence, inefficiency, and jealousy, could not meet the huge demand for literature. More than once, the mailing of documents stopped altogether. Brice, new to educational electioneering, chose campaign literature poorly. He sent out too many long Congressional speeches and tied up the presses with 500,000 copies of the Democratic tariff bill, a maze of schedules comprehensible only to experts. Brice also had difficulty raising the large sums necessary for an educational campaign. Worse, he failed to spend enough of what he collected on the headquarters and on the four "doubtful" states—Connecticut, New York, Indiana, and Ohio—that would determine the election. Tilden's method concentrated on the undecided; Brice wasted money on the certain.[40]

Watching from Washington, Daniel Lamont intervened to save the election. In August he turned the Literary Bureau over to George F. Parker, a journalist who had edited the new campaign textbook. Given free rein, Parker cut off production of as many old documents as possible, commissioned clear explanations of the tariff bill and Cleveland's record, and sent out more short pamphlets and leaflets. But Parker could not cure the headquarters' inefficiency or make Brice and Barnum into loyal tariff reformers. In the end, the national committee, for all its facilities, did not match the record of 27,000,000 documents turned out by Abram Hewitt in 1876.[41]

The campaign did have its encouraging aspects. From an office in the headquarters of the Democratic National Committee, the National Association of Democratic Clubs distributed pamphlets and leaflets through its 3000 member organizations.[42] Liberal propaganda agencies such as the Reform Club of New York and the the Connecticut Tariff Reform Club held rallies and distributed literature for Cleveland and a low tariff.[43]

There were signs, too, that the educational style had filtered down through the Democratic ranks. Around the country, local leaders organized fewer marching companies than in the previous presidential election and devoted more time and resources to the dissemination of documents. Caught up in the spirit of educational politics, one Connecticut club formed "for the purpose of doing hard and honest work and not to enjoy themselves in torch light parades and banquets." In Racine, Wisconsin, the president of the local Democratic club promised "to abstain from such methods of campaigning as address themselves to the excitement of the emotions rather than educating or convincing the intelligence of our citizens." He resolutely turned away from spectacle: "Torchlight processions, bonfires and all appeals to the emotions rather than to the judgment of men are to be barred."[44]

The new style failed to sweep away the old entirely. Educational politics never took hold firmly enough in the "doubtful" states critical to Cleveland's re-election. In Connecticut, home state of William H. Barnum, the chairman's hostility to tariff reform and education doomed the canvass. Democrats loyal to Cleveland protested that the state campaign began late and remained uninspired.[45] In Indiana, Democratic leaders refused to adopt Tilden's approach. "They all think they know a great deal about politics," George Parker bitterly complained. "And so they do from one point of view and that, is the holding of meetings, the organization of parades and processions . . . and the persistent making of speeches. But in the matters of perfecting organization by way of classifying the voters . . . and the intelligent use of newspapers and documents, they are lamentably deficient." [46]

New York, Cleveland's own state, proved even more troublesome. There, Tammany Hall in New York City and Governor David B. Hill in Albany gave the president lukewarm support at best. The inefficient state Democratic committee in New York City, oblivious to the aims of the educational campaign, failed to distribute literature effectively. The committee chose documents poorly, mailed them slowly, and sent too few to some places and too many to others. As at national headquarters, Lamont intervened to rescue the election; once more, the results were disappointing.[47]

The campaign revealed as well some of the flaws in the conception of educational politics. Tilden and his followers hoped to bypass local party organization and bring the party leadership and the voters into close contact. Yet the cultivated schoolmasters at headquarters did not always know how to speak to their working-class students. George Parker and others recognized the need for "lighter documents" to capture the attention of farmers and workers. But the men commissioned to write the documents had trouble understanding their audience. "The difficulty, of course, is that what might seem to us forcible might not seem so to those addressed," one editor confided to Lamont. "Our relations with those people are not close enough to ascertain what is in their minds."[48]

Some supporters of the educational campaign worried that papers and pamphlets did not reach the voters as effectively as partisan display. "Farmers will not read the political papers, because they have not the time, and if they do they only hear one side," the editor of a Kansas City agricultural paper reported to Lamont, "but they will turn out to a barbecue . . . ." Urban workers also seemed to prefer spectacular display. "In New York," a Cleveland lieutenant explained, "people do not read documents, and in any event a documentary campaign is always a chilly one." Accordingly, he asked Lamont to begin the local campaign with outdoor rallies.[49]

Democratic leaders also pondered the best means of using the printed word to educate the voters. Some politicians, considering pamphlets and leaflets redundant, advised Lamont to rely on the party press. "A newspaper is read & has its effect," a journalist insisted, "when 'public documents' and special campaign literature are thrown away." But another newspaperman believed that documents appealed to unskilled workers, "a stratum of ignorance that no newspaper can reach."[50]

At least one Democrat wondered whether the campaign of education, by concentrating on the distribution of literature to undecided voters, neglected to arouse the party faithful. "Political meetings . . . are the effective means of incitement within party lines, of party adherents, to activity & enthusiasm," declared John Cochrane, an older Tammany leader. In vain, he asked the president's support for "a collossal Torch Light Parade" to stir up the Democrats of New York and to bring out party loyalists around the country. Cochrane had touched on a critical flaw in educational politics, one that would become more apparent in later years. By tailoring campaigns to attract the non-partisan and undecided minority, party managers lost the power to rouse the partisan majority.[51]

The problems of the educational campaign went unsolved in 1888: Cleveland lost his bid for re-election. Yet even in defeat, advocates of Tilden's method felt hopeful. Around them, they saw signs of a new politics. The *New York Times* praised Cleveland's introduction of the tariff issue: "It has . . . this great difference from and advantage over the issues upon which past campaigns have been fought . . . that it makes no appeal to the emotions." Applauding the campaign's "thoroughly rationalistic spirit," the *Times* believed it made the voter "a better and more trustworthy citizen." Chauncey Black also admired the Democracy's "straight, constant and manly appeal to the intelligence of the voter." The president of the National Association of Democratic Clubs marked the decrease in marching companies and parades and took pleasure in the financial losses of the "campaign supply companies." He prophesied that the Democrats' rejection of spectacle would force the Republicans—the "Federalists," as he called them—to change their political style. "It takes two to make a bargain, and to make a nonsensical rivalry in the streets," Black wrote. "The Democrats, in large measure, declining such folly, the Federalists could not very profitably pursue it alone."[52]

Although he did not give the "Federalists" enough credit for their use of education, Black was right about the future. James Clarkson, rewarded with the patronage plum of the First Assistant Postmaster Generalship, became a key figure in Harrison's administration. On the one hand, Clarkson played the role of the traditional partisan to the hilt. He earned notoriety among liberals by denouncing civil service reform and replacing Democratic postmasters with loyal Republicans.[53] On the other hand, Clarkson played a more innovative role as a party manager. During the Harrison years he developed a fresh, elaborate strategy to transform the Republican party into an educational machine. Continuing his efforts to make education more palatable to the voters, he also began emphasizing new means of publicizing the party, particularly through the press.

As Clarkson had no doubt learned in 1888, his new ideas meant nothing if he did not hold power. Matt Quay, so unsympathetic to education, was still national chairman. To make over the party's style, Clarkson would have to displace the boss from Pennsylvania. In the early days of the new administration, the First Assistant Postmaster General set about winning the President's favor. Clarkson soon became the indispensable man: in 1890, Harrison chose him to oversee the congressional campaign.[54]

The canvass showed off Clarkson's light-handed use of education. Under his direction, the Republican Congressional Committee in Washington dispatched not only speakers and the usual printed speeches but also "a lot of lighter and more catchy cards, dodgers, circulars, and the like, printed in bright colors, most of them adorned with the American flag and all designed to attract the eye. . . ." Here was a less somber education, simpler and more accessible.[55]

Despite Clarkson's work, the election was an unprecedented disaster for the Republicans. The party's high protection policy, enshrined that year in the McKinley Tariff, proved unpopular. In the West, the Farmers' Alliance and its political offshoot, the new People's party, twin expressions of economic discontent among farmers and workers, cut into the Republican vote. In several states the party repelled some ethnic and religious groups with its sympathy for temperance and other evangelical Protestant reforms. Buried in a landslide, the Republicans lost control of the next Congress.[56]

Defeated, Clarkson redoubled his efforts to pull the Republican party away from the old spectacular style. The election had increased his respect for the Democrats' educational apparatus. "One thing . . . far more than all others insured the result," he told the White House shortly after the election, "& it was that these people had been reading since 1888 Revenue Reform newspapers & literature where we had no protection papers & gospel." A majority of the press in the cities, he noted, was either Democratic or hostile to protection. He realized, too, the inadequacy of protectionist propaganda agencies, so inferior to liberal organizations like the Reform Club. "The Reform Bureau of New York has done this sort of work ever since the campaign of 1888, and it has told very powerfully against us," Clarkson reported to Harrison. "We must do the same thing now. We cannot rely on such agencies as the American Protective Tariff League, which *sells* its documents, and whose documents show on their face special pleading, and therefore prejudice the reader at the start."[57]

To Clarkson one remedy was obvious: "Our newspaper circulation must be increased very greatly, & we must employ more than ever before all possible agencies for reaching the people on all the lines of literature." Significantly, he listed newspapers, not documents, first. Here Clarkson broke with Tilden, whose Literary Bureau had relied mainly on literature. "I had seen," Clarkson later explained, "the uselessness and the waste of the old form of campaign documents, branded as partisan on the face, discounted by everyone who read them at all, not read by one in a thousand to whom they were sent, and therefore useless alike to the party and the country." Clarkson considered stories in the press superior to the obvious propaganda of the parties' own literature. "This," he wrote, "is the most effectual sort of literature—that which the reader casually encounters, and which has not the appearance of a set of campaign documents."[58]

To carry out his ideas, Clarkson proposed a detailed, ambitious plan to Harrison late in November 1890. The Iowan called for increased circulation of Republican newspapers around the country and for the start of loyal new dailies in Boston, Chicago, and New York. A longtime newspaperman, Clarkson knew how much small weekly journals depended on companies supplying stereotyped metal plates of stories called "plate matter" and sheets of paper, blank on one side and printed on the other, known as "patent insides." If he could make deals with those companies to carry Republican propaganda, the party could build support in the countryside. Aiming at important constituencies, he would cultivate agricultural, labor, and foreign-language publications and break the liberals' monopoly of genteel magazines like *Harper's Weekly* that "go into the intelligent homes of the land, to the controlling minds of each neighborhood." As another means of influencing the press, Clarkson proposed "bureaus of correspondence, to furnish letters of all kinds, illustrated and otherwise, giving news and gossip, with Republican color, to all papers that will take them." Finally, he suggested "a bureau to prepare and circulate literature of attractive and efficient kind directly to the homes of the country." [59]

With Harrison's support, Clarkson struggled to win Matt Quay and the national committee over to his strategy.[60] Publicly, Clarkson underscored the need for a more active, assertive Republican press committed to protection. He also started talking with newspapermen and dickering with the plate matter and patent insides companies.[61]

At the same time, Clarkson turned to the second part of his plan, the Republican League of Clubs. He paid particular attention to the league as an antidote to the Mugwumps and the Farmers' Alliance. As before, Clarkson believed the clubs could keep liberal reformers in line. "I find universal response to the League plan of work, not only among ardent Republicans but among thinking men and scientific people," he wrote Harrison in 1891. "I have had letters and interviews with several Mugwumps, who say that in this sort of campaign they will join heartily."[62]

Blind, like so many of the middle and upper classes, to the economic roots of the Farmers' Alliance, Clarkson saw this agrarian protest movement as one more sign of the need for organization in modern society. The alliance, he believed, sprang from the "social habit" already evident in big business, labor, and ethnic organizations. "The Farmers' Alliance is in itself more the product of social hunger than political thought or action," he declared. "The farm neighborhood has little social life, has none of the secret societies, nothing of clubs, scarcely a church sociable." Filling that void, the league of clubs would become "rivals of the Alliance as social organizations." Clarkson aimed to make each club "the social centre of power in nearly every farm neghborhood and small village"—a place for debate, a library of economics and politics, a meetingplace for party workers, and simply a sponsor for "entertainments." Above all, the club coordinated a cycle of Republican political activity leading up to campaigns. "We expect," he said, "to use the clubs for literary, social, and political purposes and discussion through the winter, educating them up to the development of glee clubs, and campaign songs, using them for the distribution of campaign literature, and having them ready to turn into campaign or marching clubs in the spring."[63] Clarkson worked into the spring of 1891 to build up the league in states where it was weak. In April he accepted the presidency of the organization. Full of optimism, he hoped to have 30,000 clubs with 3,000,000 members.[64]

By the spring of 1891 Clarkson's star was rising rapidly. Matt Quay, long on the outs with Harrison, resigned the chairmanship of the national committee at the end of July. Returning from a European trip, Clarkson took over the job. In control of the two principal Republican organizations, Clarkson was now in the perfect position to reshape the party's style.[65]

Looking ahead to the presidential campaign of 1892, the new national chairman tested his plans in the fall elections in Massachusetts, New York, Ohio, and Iowa. He put the league of clubs to work early in each of these important states. Although Clarkson could not raise the money for his ideal literary bureau, he did manage to distribute documents and send out plate matter to newspapers. The Democrats, meanwhile, had their own educational drive in these states using plate matter, documents, and the association of clubs. But Clarkson's work paid off with impressive showings in all four states.[66]

Buoyed by the results of the elections, Clarkson pressed on with his plans. He urged the party to get an early start on the presidential campaign. By January 1892, he had a permanent literary office—"our Bureau of Information"—operating in Washington. The office would not churn out the usual partisan pamphlets. "In order to avoid the party imprint, or the imprint making everything a campaign or partisan doctrine," Clarkson recalled, "I devised . . . the method of a publication society called the Ben Franklin Publishing Company, and began the printing of papers and articles signed or verified by the names of their own writers under the general name of The American Voters' Library." Clarkson also planned to tailor his pamphlets to individual constituencies. "I had the further idea of protecting the party against the useless waste always in practise before, of printing one kind of literature for all kinds of people," he explained. "Instead of this I had intended to have prepared evolutionary or scientific or practical articles dealing with each special question . . . separating all branches of industry and giving to each class literature of its own, as prepared by some eminent authority or patient investigator who had made a special study of each especial interest."

The Bureau of Information would reach these voters directly, as well as through the Republican League of Clubs. Apparently, Clarkson had succeeded where Tilden and William Andrews had failed: the bureau had complete mailing lists of voters. "[I] had with two years of hard work," Clarkson boasted, "secured a list of the names of all the voters in all the important States of the North, in 20 or more States, and lists which gave the age, occupation, nativity, residence and all the other facts in each voter's life, and had them arranged alphabetically, so that literature could be sent constantly to every voter directly, dealing with every public question and issue from the standpoint of his personal interest."[67]

Clarkson's plans and achievements added up to an original recasting of Tilden's style. Through the league of clubs and the catchy flyers of the 1890 campaign, Clarkson tried to make education less somber, more accessible. He substituted the press for literature as the primary medium of education. With his plans for newspapers and the Ben Franklin Publishing Company, he went further than Tilden in abandoning the appearance of overt partisanship. For all his hatred of the Mugwumps, Clarkson revealed himself as a liberal man devoted to scientific discussion, careful organization, and the suppression of spectacular partisanship—all, of course, in the interest of party victory. Samuel Tilden introduced education into party politics; James Clarkson gave that liberal notion its fullest partisan expression in the late nineteenth century.

The opening of the Bureau of Information marked the highpoint of Clarkson's political career. Then, with surprising suddenness, his fortunes unraveled. By the spring of 1892, his recurring health problems had finally forced him into an Arkansas sanitarium. Released in mid-May, he found his place in the administration in doubt. Clarkson had been a booster of James G. Blaine in the 'eighties. Now Blaine, once Harrison's secretary of state, appeared to challenge the President for the Republican nomination. Clarkson did not back Blaine in 1892, but Harrison seemed to lose confidence in his national chairman. Perhaps the President took seriously rumors that Clarkson had tried to get the league of clubs to endorse Blaine. Perhaps, too, Harrison had begun to listen to the politicians who disliked Clarkson and his league. The sequence of events was murky, but its effect on Clarkson and his plans was emphatically clear. After Harrison won renomination in June, Clarkson stepped down as national chairman.

Out of power, Clarkson could not save his educational projects from Harrison's men. Two years later, he bitterly summed up what had happened: "The severe illness that overtook me in 1891, my inability to carry out the details of the organizations I had begun, in order to secure such literature and to print and circulate it, and the manner in which the friends of President Harrison, then in power in the party, in failing to go ahead with these plans to touch every neighborhood and every voter, and the diversion of all the energy of such a powerful element in the party toward securing the President's renomination, made the whole program miscarry." Harrison had backed him, Clarkson believed: "It was the men who took charge of his campaign for renomination, and who, while I was in the South very ill for many months and unable to attend to business at all, took charge of the executive management of the party, and being out of sympathy with the sort of methods I had set up, stopped all the work, disorganized all the organization, practically stopping every wheel of national work in the party so far as the National Committee and the National League of Clubs were concerned . . . ."[68]

Despite Clarkson's personal disappointment and the frustration of his most ambitious plans, the Republican party had finally come around to the kind of educational politics practiced by Samuel Tilden. The presidential election of 1892 revealed a bi-partisan consensus on campaign methods. In a rematch of 1888, Cleveland squared off against Harrison on the tariff issue. This time, both sides fought the same way. Clarkson's advanced ideas did not guide the Republican campaign, but the new powers in the party copied the educational campaign staged by the Democrats in 1888. Fittingly, the Republicans marked their conversion by giving the vice-presidential nomination to *New York Tribune* editor Whitelaw Reid, the former liberal and apostle of education. Succeeding Clarkson as chairman, Thomas H. Carter of Montana, a rather obscure young politician who had been secretary of the congressional committee in 1890, promised "a campaign of education."

Carter kept his word. The national committee lavished more resources than ever on the New York headquarters, which included literary and speakers' bureaus, and also an elaborate newspaper office. Refusing to give money to state leaders for spectacular displays, the committee planned to spend its funds on orators, pamphlets, and newspaper propaganda. "Whatever money is needed for organizing clubs and associations and paying the expenses of local rallies," reported a visitor to headquarters, "will be raised by the Republicans of the district where the money is to be spent." Although the committee dismantled or ignored much of Clarkson's preparations, it did take advantage of his work to print documents early in the campaign. The newspaper office clipped articles from several thousand papers, telegraphed stories to the Republican press, distributed a weekly sheet called *Protection and Reciprocity,* and sent out stereotyped plates of propaganda "disguised as news matter" ready for use by almost two thousand papers.[69]

Not quite as extensive as the Republicans' operation, Democratic headquarters in New York organized along the same lines. Cleveland, out of office, had reaffirmed his commitment to "The Campaign of Education." Having learned his lesson in 1888, he collected for the first time a party leadership wholly loyal to his ideas. The national chairman, William Harrity, nominally directed the canvass, but the real authority went to William C. Whitney of New York. A millionaire, former Tilden adherent, and longtime opponent of Tammany Hall, the elegant Whitney typified the elite reformers of party in New York City. He fell easily in step with the educational campaign. Under Whitney and Harrity, the New York headquarters concentrated on explaining the tariff to the electorate through pamphlets and plate matter. George Parker remained in the Literary Bureau, but overall direction of that department fell to Josiah Quincy, scion of the Massachusetts political family and a veteran of reform politics. Although Quincy sometimes ran short of money, the bureau functioned more efficiently than in 1888. "Its motive power," Parker wrote of the Democratic campaign, "was not new: it was merely the application to the country at large . . . of the methods so successfully employed in New York a few years earlier by Samuel J. Tilden."[70]

The educational efforts of the Republicans and Democrats received extensive, admiring treatment from newspapers increasingly receptive to the new, restrained partisanship. Journals of both parties praised the national committees and described their headquarters at length. The Democratic *New York Sun* neatly expressed the committees' fusion of the liberals' thoughtful, rather academic manner with the hard-headed business mentality of the regulars: "The big political leaders say that this is a campaign of education, and they have established foundries and are turning out education in great hunks and wads—by the yard, mile, or ton, in any quantity that may be desired."[71]

The press understood quite well the transformation in party styles. "The old method in this country was that of noise, clash and enthusiasm," noted the *Review of Reviews*. "All that was desired was to play upon party feeling in such a way as to get everybody magnetized or gravitated into one or other of two hostile camps."

Newspapers recognized that bolts and independence had forced a change in the parties' campaigns. "In the close States in the North . . . which determine national elections," the *Philadelphia Inquirer* observed, "it is the doubtful voter who decides the battle, and these men are reached through the mails and by personal approach." The Democrats' campaign, stated the *Cleveland Plain Dealer,* a loyal Democratic paper, "does not depend so much on stump speeches, on bands of music, on processions and fireworks as it does on thorough organization to bring out every Democratic vote. This is not a campaign of noise and dazzle, but of reading, of thinking and of work." The Republican *Minneapolis Journal* dismissed "noisy demonstrations" as ineffective "political flim-flam." "Voters," the *Journal* concluded, "are influenced less by noise and more by facts."[72] Journalists bestowed on the national committees the highest compliments of late nineteenth-century America. Campaigning, the press concluded, had become a "science"; now the parties "organized after the manner of . . . the greater corporations in New York."[73]

The educational style also won over most local party leaders. In Philadelphia, the Republican campaign chairman opposed uniformed companies as "an unnecessary expense."[74] In Connecticut, leaders of both parties refused to subsidize spectacular demonstrations. "The political organizations throughout the state will not spend any money in band-and-torchlight-and-uniformed enthusiasm," a paper reported. "Political pamphlets on the tariff, free silver, free trade and protection will be scattered by the local clubs and will be on their club house tables."[75] "The Shelby county democrats are hard at work . . . ," noted a visitor to rural Iowa. "Tariff reform literature is being distributed all over the county. . . . and while you will not see any torchlight processions or hear any brass bands, you will find hosts of earnest democrats who have dedicated their efforts to the good cause for 1892." Even in Indiana, a stronghold of spectacle, party leaders cut down on display and distributed more newspapers to voters than in the past. "The dealers in campaign goods," wrote an observer of the Indiana election, "have, it is said, gone off the road utterly disgusted with politics."[76]

Everywhere, politicians emphasized polls, organization, and literature.[77] Republican leaders were even a bit more willing to let the league of clubs carry out its educational work.[78] The other instruments of education—the National Association of Democratic Clubs, the Reform Club, the American Protective Tariff League—played their part in the campaign as well.[79] Surveying the nation, the *New York Commercial* found that "effervescent enthusiasm and brass band features have yielded to serious reflection." The "battle" of the campaign, the *New York Sun* decided, was being fought "at close quarters, and by individual appeals to voters, instead of by the old and now disapproved tom-tom methods."[80]

Educational politics still had its critics in 1892. As four years earlier, some journalists considered the parties' campaign literature redundant. Newspapers, their editors believed, did the real work of educating the voters. A few politicians, too, longed for the old methods. "The average man in the country has neither time nor inclination to read long, dry articles upon the tariff question . . . ," a Michigan Democrat told William C. Whitney. "In the country districts a ringing campaign speech is considered to be worth two tons of literature," wrote a reporter about New York State. "With the crops all in, the farmers ache to attend a campaign round-up and listen to a rattling speaker. The voters in interior towns and cities enthuse over torchlight processions and bands, especially if there is a corking stump speaker on hand." After attending a Democratic barbecue in Indiana, a Republican begged Harrison's private secretary to arrange a rally. "It is idle to say that these big demonstrations are of no value to a party," he declared. "I know personally a considerable number of men who have been wavering who from today will be reliably democratic unless we can bring a counter-demonstration to unsettle them again."[81]

Partisan spectacle, despite the plans of the national leaders, did not disappear in 1892. Companies like the Republicans' "Lincoln Pioneer Corps" of New York City's eighth assembly district turned out for parades "in all the glory of their bearskin shakos and gorgeous uniforms." Around the North, local leaders of both parties, often after some debate, put up the money for companies and torchlight processions.[82] But there were fewer spectacular events and far fewer uniformed companies than in years past. New Haven, Connecticut, with a population of 62,000, had raised sixty-eight marching organizations in 1880. Twelve years later, the city, now more than eighty-six thousand people, fielded only eight companies.[83] Some Northerners began to find the remaining companies rather old-fashioned. When the Republican clubs of Chester County, Pennsylvania, "declaring the glory of partisanship," marched in 1892, the scene now reminded a reporter of "an old-time rally."[84]

Certain that torchlight parades belonged to the past, the national leadership of the two parties confidently went on teaching the nation about the tariff. But the politicians shortly discovered a shocking fact: bi-partisan education alienated many people. What would have struck twentieth-century Americans as a gaudy, demonstrative campaign seemed a flat bore to Northerners raised on the spectacular campaigns of the nineteenth. There were still companies, parades, and rallies, but the campaign, clearly different from what had come before, upset the expectations of men used to lavish partisan display.[85] From all over the North, leaders of both parties reported "lethargy," "astonishing lethargy," "extraordinary calmness," "Political lassitude," "a great lack of enthusiasm or even of interest," "no enthusiasm, no activity, rather a feeling of indifference," "a great indifference."[86] Above all, politicians spoke of "apathy"—"general apathy," "listless apathy," "astonishing . . . apathy," "a most unexpected and discouraging apathy," "so much *apathy.*"[87]

The voters did not seem to pay attention to their tariff lessons. Connecticut had "the deadest Presidential campaign for many a year." Sophisticated New York City found no time for the election: "Many political meetings are occurring nightly, yet the theatres are crowded as if there were no such distraction of the people from them. In no past campaign for President was the regular course of business and pleasure so little disturbed as it is now by political excitement." The Midwest, famous for its intense partisanship, remained calm as well. "I remember when people used to stop work for three months to devote themselves to politics," one Ohio politician told an interviewer. "Now they are not even talking politics." It was the same in Indiana. "At this time four years ago their enthusiasm seemed to be without bounds," an Indiana Republican wrote of the voters in his state. "Now they scarcely speak of the election—when they meet they talk of almost every-thing else."[88]

The situation puzzled some politicians.[89] Occasionally, in the 'eighties, observers had detected signs of "a gradual but steady increase in political apathy." Such comments were infrequent and seemed to apply mainly to the genteel middle and upper classes troubled by traditional party politics.[90] Nothing had prepared most party leaders for the lack of political interest displayed by all classes across the North in 1892.

Editors and politicians traced some of the apathy to the people's familiarity with the presidential candidates and the tariff issue.[91] Other observers blamed the "Political lassitude" on the distractions of a cholera scare, the Sullivan-Corbett boxing match, an encampment of the Grand Army of the Republic, and the Columbian Exposition in Chicago. This explanation was only partially satisfactory. Sports and other events had competed with elections before without cutting so deeply into political interest. In 1892, the public's fascination with boxing and the Grand Army of the Republic was a result, as well as a cause, of waning involvement in politics.[92]

Confronted by so much boredom, some politicians predicted a low turnout for election day.[93] A few men blamed the situation on the parties' abandonment of spectacle. "It seems to me," a Democrat wrote William C. Whitney, "that those who are in control of the campaign are promoting the very apathy they deprecate by failing to afford the people an opportunity of coming out and demonstrating their enthusiasm . . . . " Wondering the same thing, the managers tried "to infuse a little more vim" into the canvass by allowing a bit more spectacular display than originally planned.[94]

Most party leaders and editors remained confident of a heavy turnout. These men read the public mood as a vindication of the educational campaign. The people, they believed, had not lost interest in politics; men had simply given up extroverted emotionalism for deliberative partisanship. Thomas Carter, the Republican chairman, attributed "the quietness of the campaign . . . to the careful study on the part of the people of the issues at stake. . . ." After interviewing the leaders in New York, a correspondent wrote, "[The] suggestion is that while the political interest is not so noisy as it has been in times past, it is intense, and is directed rather to private study of political questions than to exciting campaigns. . . ." The *Minneapolis Journal* repeated the political orthodoxy of 1892. "People who have been calling this campaign 'slow,' 'quiet' and 'uninteresting' are beginning to realize that campaign methods are changing with the development of the life of the people," the *Journal* insisted. "The voters have been reading, not shouting; but their ballots will be just as numerous and far more intelligent in the aggregate."[95]

Charles Dana's *New York Sun* agreed on the likelihood of a large vote, but disputed its cause. Hostile to tariff reform and only moderately supportive of Cleveland, the *Sun* had no use for educational politics and its quiet, less partisan style. To ensure a strong turnout, the Democratic leadership "must learn what really interests the Democratic people," the *Sun* declared. "A 'campaign of education,' about which we have heard so much, does not interest them. They do not want to go to a political school to learn tariff statistics, and to hear the harangues of professors of the so-called science of political economy." Traditional partisanship, the paper reminded Democratic leaders, was what made men vote:

> The great mass of the people will go into this political campaign as into a contest, a battle, in which they range themselves on opposing sides from pure partisan passion, or they will not enter into it with any spirit. . . . The Democratic people must be aroused by an appeal to party spirit. They must be stirred up by appealing to their devotion to Democratic principle. They must feel that they are battling for the life of their party, not merely for a disputed theory of political economy.

Enduring party spirit, not the year's educational campaign, would bring men to vote in 1892, the *Sun* believed. "They are fired by party spirit . . . ," the paper concluded. "In the end, we doubt not, it will send men to the polls so generally that the vote cast at the election will comprise as great a part of the voting population as have ever before been counted in an election for President."[96]

The turnout of 1892 set no record after all. By a narrow margin, Cleveland reclaimed the White House from Harrison. Only 75 percent of eligible Northerners, the smallest percentage since 1872, cast ballots—a large turnout by twentieth-century standards but a disappointing one in the late nineteenth century. The vote came as a relief to some observers. "It has been the most quiet and thoughtful campaign of the past fifty years," said an editor; "yet a great vote has been polled. . . ."[97] Both the *Sun* and the celebrants of the educational campaign had been wrong about the vote. Yet Dana's paper understood the electorate rather well. As the *Sun* realized, party spirit persisted. Men brought up on spectacular partisanship could not quickly abandon old habits of thought and feeling. Northern voters found the well-publicized campaign of education, with its denigration of emotional party spirit, confusing and boring. They did not turn, as the advocates of education argued, to "private study." There was too much evidence that, instead, Northerners lost interest and refused to talk of politics. Without the old partisan calls demanded by the *Sun*, the voters' attention wandered from the tariff to boxing, the Columbian Exposition, and cholera. Still, as the *Sun* understood, Northerners remained partisan. They voted on memory, out of longstanding habit, in 1892. Despite the educational campaign, the old partisanship, not the new, brought men to the polls. In this respect, the *Sun* came closest to the truth of the matter.

Most party leaders paid little attention to the low turnout of 1892. Politicians worried more about victory than the size of the vote. For them, the educational style was the best means of attracting the critical support of liberals, members of the Farmers' Alliance, and other increasingly independent voters. Education had special appeal for national party leaders. The campaign of education strengthened their power as community-based spectacular canvasses had not. When the propaganda of documents and plate matter became the focus of elections, the producers of the propaganda—the national committees—grew in importance. The big New York dailies acknowledged the greater significance of party headquarters in 1892 when, for the first time, they assigned reporters on a daily basis to cover the Republican and Democratic committees.[98] A fall in voting meant little to national leaders newly clothed in power and bathed in the light of publicity.

Those Republicans and Democrats who did note the drop in turnout could plausibly attribute it to distracting events and the familiarity of the candidates. Perhaps, too, the politicians had a certain blindness, the product of class bias. Educational politics originated in the needs of upper-class critics of party and reflected their outlook. More broadly, the campaign of education rested on a material and ideological base provided by the Northern upper class.

After the Civil War, the development of businesses like the railroads with national rather than narrowly local concerns raised new possibilities for party structure. Intimately associated with large-scale business enterprise, politicians like Tilden, Hewitt, and Whitney applied the example of centralized organization to their parties. The success of huge businesses also offered legitimacy for the campaign of education. Drawing on the cultural cachet of business, the national committees organized in 1892 like "the greater corporations" and turned out literature like "foundries" producing ingots.

The campaign of education sprang from the wealth as well as the example of big business. Educational electioneering, with its large literary bureaus, cost the national committees much more than spectacular canvasses. Northern capitalists, anxious for power and legislative favors, gave the money that made expensive educational campaigns possible. In 1856, the Democratic National Committee raised only $100,000 and the fledgling Republican National Committee less than $50,000. As late as 1872, the Republicans, firmly in command of Congress and the White House, could muster only $200,000 for their headquarters. The Democratic National Committee managed to collect twice that figure for the first attempt at a campaign of education in 1876. Tilden was the first rich man to run for the presidency in many years; much of the Democratic campaign fund came from his personal fortune and from the bank accounts of his wealthy associates, Abram Hewitt and the Cooper family. By 1892 the Republican and Democratic committees could each spend between one and two million dollars for the bi-partisan educational canvass. Corporate, rather than private, political contributions had not yet become commonplace, but by the early 'nineties business had given the parties enough to establish the campaign of education.[99]

From the beginning, an elitist vision inspired educational politics. While spectacular electioneering exalted the grass roots, the campaign of education emphasized the high command in New York. Tilden's method focused on undecided and independent voters, men fixed in the public mind as representatives of upper-class gentility. Educational politics valued William Andrews's "intelligent" voter more than the ordinary emotional partisan. It assumed that the electorate needed enlightenment—"education"—from more knowledgeable experts.

An edge of contempt often crept into the tone of the advocates of education. "Banners are fine," the *New York Tribune* allowed, "but the man who votes for the best-looking face on the costliest banner is not fit to vote at all." "Political managers tell us that the brass band and the sky-rocket have their effect and are necessary to secure a certain class of votes," a liberal reformer wrote in the spring of 1888; "to which the proper answer is, that it would be better to let such votes go where they will, and expend the effort in winning votes that carry with them the power of intelligence and the weight of character. Any fool can buy a sky-rocket, and put a match to it; but sky-rocket votes have never determined a question so that it remained settled." The wealthy members of the Young Men's Republican Club of New Haven, Connecticut, debating whether to parade in 1892, deplored "trudging through the mud for the sake of instructing the mind of the grex vulgaris. . . ."[100] Two generations younger than James E. English, these well-to-do Republicans rejected the political style that had brought the Connecticut governor together with Michael Campbell and the English Phalanx in the spectacular campaign of 1880.

Like Tilden and Hewitt, the young Republicans of New Haven expressed a new class sensibility, one that demanded a reshaping of political styles. Undemonstrative and intellectual, the campaign of education enabled the Northern upper class to appeal to the "grex vulgaris" more comfortably. Despite the effort to establish a sense of personal contact between candidate and voter, the educational campaign was a decisive step away from the intimate class relations of popular politics. In an era of strikes and confrontations, of the railroad walkout in 1877, the Haymarket Massacre in 1886, and the Homestead Strike in 1892, the classes drew apart. Less concerned with eliciting the visible popular assent of spectacle, the upper class wanted to deal with the poor at arm's length, through pamphlets, polls, and propaganda agencies. Education suited the needs of the well-to-do; they had little reason to lament its failure to bring out the "sky-rocket" vote. Here was the first sign of a shift away from popular politics that would become quite plain in the early twentieth century. So long as turnout did not fall too much, Northern leaders would not worry over those who did not vote. Silently, one of the central assumptions of popular politics—that all men would participate—was giving way.

With the election of 1892, education displaced demonstrative partisanship as the dominant political style of the North. Jubilant reformers celebrated the triumph of their candidate, issue, and style. The canvass, concluded *Harper's Weekly*, "has shown how unnecessary spectacular campaign displays and noisy demonstrations are to excite the popular interest if the questions at issue are discussed with thoughtful argument."[101] A generation after the Civil War, the reformers' attack on popular politics had borne fruit.

5

THE PRESS TRANSFORMED

From the 1860s to the 1920s, the newspaper served less and less well as a medium of traditional, exuberant partisanship. The changing material conditions of publishing served to free editors and publishers from dependence on the parties. A growing popular demand for news suggested new ways for papers to address the public. Journalists caught up in liberal reform were the first to take advantage of this opportunity and challenge the party press. In the 1870s and 'eighties, they established "independent journalism," a less partisan, more restrained and factual style, akin to the educational campaign. The party press also gave ground in the 'eighties and 'nineties to the sensational and somewhat anti-political journalism of Joseph Pulitzer and William Randolph Hearst. Under attack from two sides, party papers diluted their traditional partisanship. At the turn of the century, Northern journalism had fractured into three styles offering competing modes of comprehending political life: partisan, independent, and sensational.

By the end of the Civil War the newspaper business had begun to change. In the cities, particularly the largest, journalism outgrew its dependence on the parties and became a more lucrative enterprise. Improved, high-speed presses and cheaper newsprint allowed papers to print more copies and reach more readers. Railroads widened the boundaries of circulation. As a result, the average circulation of daily papers climbed from 2,200 a day in 1840 to 8,007 in 1904 and 16,684 in 1925. In 1870, only two papers had over 100,000 circulation; by 1890, there were eight. By the 'nineties, the leading papers of New York City sold over 300,000 copies a day. In an expanding economy, businesses sought advertising outlets for their products. The newspapers' revenue from advertising doubled from 1870 to 1880, nearly doubled again over the next decade, and then continued to expand in the twentieth century. As early as the 'seventies, the press had taken on the aspects of big business. The metropolitan daily, noted Whitelaw Reid, publisher of the *New York Tribune,* in 1879, had become "a great business enterprise, as legitimate as a railroad or a line of steamships, and as rigidly demanding the best business management." Urban dailies required large capital and hundreds, sometimes thousands, of employees. The press even shared in the trend toward consolidation of businesses, as old papers merged and "chains" like Scripps-Howard, Hearst, and Munsey appeared.[1]

With the growth and prosperity of the press, observers detected a new motivation among newspaper proprietors, once mainly editors and politicians. "Newspapers are run as the miller runs his mill, the miner his mine, the farmer his farm," a journalist declared in 1891. "Hence, they are worked as other money-making corporations are worked—for all the profit they can be made to yield." Looking back in 1911, another journalist, Will Irwin, caught the same transformation taking place by the 'nineties. "Now," he said, "was the spirit of journalism become mostly commercial, and the typical publisher was a business man, running a million-dollar property for money—not an editor."[2]

The growth of the press also brought with it the end of personal journalism, the old single-handed control of every aspect of his paper by the editor-publisher. Even the most dynamic proprietor found it hard to impose his will on a staff of hundreds. "It used to be Bryant's paper, or Greeley's paper, or Raymond's, or Bennett's," a New York editor attested in 1906. "Now it is simply *Times, Herald, Tribune,* and so on. No single personality can stamp itself upon the whole organism. It is too vast." The increased size of newspaper establishments meant party considerations could not guide hiring, even at the top. "[In] the United States," wrote one observer in 1898, "a man's politics have nothing to do with the politics of the paper which he edits. The editor of the leading Republican paper in the country is quite likely to be a Democrat, and *vice versa.*"[3]

After the Civil War, journalism became a profession as well as a business. Reporters, a rarity before 1860, filled the ranks of the press. The lives of these men, relatively uninvolved in the business and political management of their newspapers, revolved around the gathering and writing of the news. The reporters and their editors came to consider journalism as a vocation, with its own standards and special training. Both editors and reporters were more likely than their ante-bellum predecessors to have gone to college. Some journalists spoke of establishing college courses and even professional schools devoted to journalism. In this respect, newspapers reflected the increasing specialization of American life and particularly the heightened self-awareness of the professions around the turn of the century. The professional consciousness of the press isolated journalism from politics as a career in its own right. The days of the editor-politician were ending. A newspaper demanded too much of its proprietor's time for him to devote himself to party management and public office. Politics and government, in turn, had become too complex for many politicians to spend time running papers on the side.[4]

The Federal government no longer provided pecuniary benefits for most of the press after the Civil War. The era of semi-official presidential organs had come to an end in 1861, when James Buchanan severed his ties with the *Washington Constitution.* The year before, Congress ended its printing arrangements with newspapers by establishing the Government Printing Office. In 1875, the House and Senate halted the practice of printing new laws in several papers in each state and territory. By then, Federal patronage for a few hundred papers had little impact on a Northern press numbering nearly 6000 journals.[5]

By themselves, the material changes in the newspaper business did not destroy partisan journalism. Ante-bellum editors had been willing partners, not slaves, of party. Freed by their profits, they did not necessarily want to run away. The newspapers and the parties were partners in thought and outlook as well as business. Certainly publishers and editors, conscious of the business and professional possibilities of journalism, had a new awareness of the newspaper as an instrument independent of party. They revealed that awareness symbolically by substituting boasts about their circulation for the old ideological slogans on their papers' nameplate and masthead.[6] More significantly, publishers and editors emphasized their autonomy and power through the self-promotion of stunts and crusades. James Gordon Bennett, Jr., earned publicity for the *New York Herald* by sending his reporter Henry M. Stanley to Africa in search of the explorer David Livingston from 1869 to 1872. Other papers used series of articles to expose various evils. One of the first and most famous of these crusades was the campaign of the *New York Times* against the Tweed Ring in 1870 and 1871.[7]

Although crusades and circulation boasts underscored the financial strength and self-confidence of the press after the Civil War, they did not necessarily signify a revolt against party journalism. Publishers, eager for circulation, might be tempted to aim for a broader audience than the members of one party, but no one was certain that readers wanted a non-partisan paper. The business and professional development of the press after the 1860s established a context for new kinds of journalism, but it did not determine their nature or even demand their creation.

Changing public expectations did place new constraints on party journalists after the Civil War. Americans, in part because of their eagerness for reports of battles during the war, began to demand up-to-the-minute news. More of them picked up the habit of reading papers. The news, Will Irwin observed in 1911, "has come to be a crying primal want of the mind, like hunger of the body." The press had to feed that hunger. Improved techniques of newsgathering and transmission made it possible to meet the demand. The telegraph sped news over the wires. By the 1870s and 'eighties, news organizations such as the New York Associated Press and the United Press improved the collection of news and sent stories quickly to papers around the country. "It is pretty generally recognized now that a newspaper has to print the news," commented the journalist Lincoln Steffens in 1897. "[Even] the old organs of class and political prejudices, which rely for their standing upon their editorial and literary articles, find it necessary to keep up a news service. They did not always do so."[8]

The demand for news upset the balance of editorials and reportage. A paper had to give greater space to news stories, which now seemed more important than the editorial for many readers. Some of them, in order to get the news, were willing to buy a journal whose editorial policy they disliked. "That a paper supports a political faith opposed to his own doesn't count with the modern reader," the editor Richard Watson Gilder noted in 1899. "The editorial opinion on political movements as expressed in the papers doesn't have the weight with readers it once did. Journalism's greatest power to-day lies in the dissemination of fact rather than in the advocacy of policy."[9]

Like the business and professional development of the press, the "news revolution" had less significance for partisan journalism than first appeared. To a degree, the availability of the news gave a reader the data with which to draw his own conclusions about events. He could view the world more directly, without having to look through the filtering lens of partisanship. "Since the telegraph came into use newspapers publish the news to a much greater extent than formerly; hence people see a good deal of both sides and form their own conclusions," a veteran editor argued in 1891. "They read what the editor has to say, and weigh it in the light of known facts, and sometimes reach conclusions exactly opposite to those he arrives at. People are more enlightened than they once were."[10]

Their enlightenment did not necessarily turn them against partisan coloring of the news. "In our thirst for news," a journalist put it in 1871, "we do not object to a little prematureness or imagination on the part of the writer." Neither did the news revolution deprive the editor of his power to shape the world for his audience. As early as 1881, Charles Dudley Warner, editor of the Hartford, Connecticut, *Courant*, recognized the opportunity for the journalist to maintain his political influence by manipulating the news columns. "The editor," he said, "does not expect to form public opinion so much by arguments and appeals as by the news he presents and his manner of presenting it, by the iteration of an idea until it becomes familiar, by the reading-matter selected, and by the quotation of opinions as news, and not professedly to influence the reader. And this influence is all the more potent because it is indirect, and not perceived by the reader."[11]

Even the rise of the standardized news services like the Associated Press did not thwart the political aims of party journalists. Although the press associations promised impartial news, they were sometimes managed in the late nineteenth century by editors sensitive to the needs of party. Even more impartial managers had to depend on biased reports from local representatives who were partisan journalists. As a result, politicians frequently complained about distorted wire-service copy. Their complaints were too numerous to dismiss entirely.[12]

In any case, an editor could bend even straightforward accounts from the press associations to suit the needs of partisanship. "If he aims at political partisans the manager sees that the colorless reports of political news that come into the office from the Associated Press are interpreted in the heading," Lincoln Steffens explained. "Another means . . . is to 'edit' the Press despatches, and the managing editor of a metropolitan journal has a staff of 'copy readers' and telegraph editors who do this work. . . . These skilful men also 'cut down' or 'spread' a piece of news according to its value for the particular purposes of the paper." Readers wanted more and more news, but their "hunger" and "thirst" did not dictate less-partisan treatment of the news.[13]

The long development of the press as a business, a profession, and a source of news from the Civil War into the twentieth century did not by itself transform partisan journalism. These changes emancipated the press from direct financial dependence on one party or another. But they did not prevent the publisher from affiliating with a party or the editor from shaping his editorials and news stories for partisan effect. The fate of party journalism still rested in the hands of these men, now freer to make their papers as they wished. "The truth is," Charles Dudley Warner concluded in 1881, "that the development of the modern journal has been so sudden and marvelous that its conductors find themselves in possession of a machine that they scarcely know how to manage or direct." Warner exaggerated the situation. There were already newspapermen who knew quite well what to do with their papers.[14]

During the late 'sixties and early 'seventies, a group of news-papermen, mostly Republicans, began to reconsider their relation-ship to the parties. Even in 1869, an editor could point to the "many journals, especially of late, which seem to be breaking loose from partisan shackles and inclined to judge of facts and measures according to principles, nor of party, but of right."[15] Some of the foremost Republican papers in the country led the reconsidera-tion of party ties: the *New York Tribune* of Horace Greeley and Whitelaw Reid, the *New York Evening Post* of William Cullen Bryant and later Horace White, E. L. Godkin, and Carl Schurz, Samuel Bowles's *Springfield Republican*, Horace White's *Chicago Tribune*, and the *Cincinnati Commercial* of Murat Halstead. Along with God-kin's *Nation* and George William Curtis's *Harper's Weekly*, these dailies formed the communications network that nurtured liberal reform within the Republican party.[16]

Like the majority of reformers, most of the liberal editors were cultured, well-educated men. Here was the significance of the growing number of college-trained journalists: they brought the press more firmly within that upper-class social group most trou-bled by traditional partisan politics after the Civil War. Along with other well-to-do urban Republicans, the liberal editors worried over radical Reconstruction, the high protective tariff, govern-mental corruption, and the party machine. They, too, looked approvingly on suffrage restriction for a time in the 'seventies. Horace White attacked universal suffrage in the columns of the *Chicago Tribune* in 1874; Bryant and Reid publicly urged the adop-tion of the Tilden Commission's plan of city government in 1877.[17] Under Reid's editorship, the *New York Tribune* admired Tilden's educational campaign in 1876 and called on the Republican party to take up the new style of electioneering in the 'eighties.[18]

In addition to publicizing the concerns of reformers, these newspapermen applied liberal ideas to journalism. Together, Reid, Halstead, White, and the others established a new kind of paper, more independent of the parties and devoted to the impartial reporting of the news.

Rejection of the newspapers' partisan role was not without precedent. In the 1830s, much of the "penny press"—cheap one-cent papers aimed at a largely working-class audience not yet reached by party journals—had claimed independence from party. The most famous representative of the independent penny papers was James Gordon Bennett, Sr., editor and publisher of the *New York Herald.* Later brands of journalism all owed something to his breezy, sensational style and his broad conception of a news that embraced stories of sex and crime as well as politics. Bennett rejected a party affiliation for the *Herald* not so much out of a reasoned anti-partisan philosophy as out of personal bitterness over his rejection by Democratic leaders. Other journalists admired the success of the Herald, but few copied Bennett's political stance. Only 5 percent of American newspapers claimed independence in 1860. Bennett and the penny press signaled the possibility of successful independent journalism, but they had hardly established independency as a powerful political presence by the Civil War. Neither had they linked independence from party with a significant critique of partisan journalism.[19]

The liberal journalists of the 'seventies and 'eighties did both. Re-examining the relationship of the press and the parties, these men promulgated a new code known as "independent journalism." Unhappy with their party, the liberal editors criticized the constraints of party loyalty and deplored the twisting of the news for partisan purpose. "Independent Journalism!—that is the watchword of the future in the profession," exclaimed Whitelaw Reid, perhaps the leading spokesman of the movement. "An end of concealments because the truth would hurt the party; an end of one-sided expositions, because damaging things must only be allowed against our antagonists; an end of assaults that are not believed fully just, but must be made because the exigency of party warfare demands them . . . an end of hesitation to print the news in a newspaper because it may hurt the party . . . that is the boon to which every perplexed conscientious member of the profession a new and beneficent Declaration of Independence affords." Truthful, independent journalism, Reid promised, would make the newspaper "the master, not the tool, of party."[20]

Chafing under restraints of loyalty to a party they could not entirely support, liberal newspapermen discovered a conflict between the callings of politics and journalism. "The methods of the politician and of the journalist," said David Croly, editor of the *New York Graphic,* "are radically different—that of the former is secretiveness; the editorial function, on the contrary, is to publish everything to the world. Editors always come to grief when they are influenced by leaders of parties. The great object of the politician is to be secret, to work out his plans in the dark; the aim of the journal is to open things, to let in light, to tell the truth." George William Curtis recognized the same contradiction. "Party spirit . . . commands its newspaper to equivocate, to pervert, to deny the truth," he told a convention of editors in 1881. "This servility to party spirit is the abdication of that moral leadership of opinion which is the great function of the political press."[21]

Accordingly, the independent journalists proceeded to redraw the relationship between the editor and his party. They pondered whether an editor might properly hold public office. Too ambitious to renounce place and power altogether, the independent editors never came down on the question one way or the other. Greeley settled the matter for himself by running for president in 1872.[22] The independent journalists were more united on government advertising. An editor, they believed, should reject ads with party strings attached so that he might remain free from improper influence.[23]

The independents agreed as well on the broad question of the newspaper's stance on parties and partisanship. "I think the greatest service a public journal can to render to its readers is to encourage them to form independent opinions," Horace White declared. "This can only be done by holding out to them an example of independence."[24] But like other liberals, the leaders of independent journalism did not deny the legitimacy of party or the propriety of party membership. They deplored the notion of political neutrality: men must have principles after all. As early as 1841, when he founded the *New York Tribune,* Greeley contemplated a journalism "removed alike from servile partisanship on the one hand and from gagged, mincing neutrality on the other."[25] "Hitherto," wrote George William Curtis after the war, with the *New York Herald* clearly in mind, "the newspapers calling themselves independent have been too often merely the meanest trimmers and panders. They have apparently thought independence consisted in abusing one party to-day and another party to-morrow." Curtis would have none of that. For him, membership in one of the two major parties was natural and necessary. "The man who thinks that both are equally bad, and who does not care which prevails, is a man without opinions, or without principle, or without perception, and in either case is wholly unfit to be an editor," Curtis insisted. "But the more deeply an independent journal sympathizes with the principle and purpose of a party, the more strenuously will it censure its follies and errors, the more bravely will it criticise its candidates and leaders, for the purpose of keeping the principle pure, and of making the success of the party a real blessing."[26]

William Cullen Bryant summed up the independent journalists' conception of the partisan role of the newspaper more succinctly: "The success of a party—for all newspapers will naturally support one party or another—should be rigidly subordinated to the good of the community, and when the party to which the journal belongs makes a wrong step it should be boldly rebuked." In short, Bryant and his colleagues sought for the press the same right claimed by other liberal reformers—non-binding party membership.[27]

The independent journalists put their creed into practice in 1872. That year editors took the lead in the Liberal Republican rejection of Ulysses S. Grant. Halstead, Bowles, and White, along with Henry Watterson of the *Louisville Courier-Journal,* formed the "Quadrilateral," which tried to maneuver the nomination of Charles Francis Adams, Sr., or some other suitable candidate at the Liberal Republicans' convention in Cincinnati. The Quadrilateral lost out, of course, to Whitelaw Reid, who helped capture the nomination for his chief on the *Tribune,* Horace Greeley.[28] Despite the abysmal failure of Greeley's candidacy, the Liberal Republican bolt widely publicized the rise of independent journalism. For the first time, newspaper readers could watch such pillars of the G.O.P. as the *New York Tribune,* the *Chicago Tribune,* and the *Cincinnati Commercial* give a demonstration of independence from party.

It was difficult for the liberal editors, raised in an era of intense partisanship and bound to the Republican party in the crucible of the Civil War, to maintain their independent stand. The cost of the Liberal Republican bolt in lost readers and lines of advertising also had its effect. Taking over the *New York Tribune* when Greeley died shortly after the election, Reid gradually returned the paper to the Republican fold. Halstead, too, beat a retreat to more profitable old-fashioned Republican journalism. Horace White found himself forced out by his partners on the *Chicago Tribune*, which also returned to the party fold.[29]

As the first generation of independent journalists died or lost heart in the 'seventies, it gave way, like the liberal movement in general, to a second generation ready to explore fresh ideas and tactics. In cities around the North, new papers appeared, avowedly independent of any permanent party affiliation. The most famous of them included the *Chicago Daily News*, started by Melville E. Stone in 1875, and the *Kansas City Evening Star*, first published by William R. Nelson in 1880. Others typical of the group included the *New Haven Morning News*, founded in 1882, and the *Newark Evening News*, which began the next year.[30] These papers' rejection of enduring party attachment shocked some of the early leaders of the independent press. "I may claim to have been one of the apostles of independent journalism, but the zeal of the new converts has quite left me among the old fogies," Whitelaw Reid conceded in 1879. "It never occurred to me that in refusing to obey blindly every behest of a party it was necessary to keep entirely aloof from party—to shut off one's self from the sole agency through which, among a free people, lasting political results can be attained."[31]

Reid, by then more of a regular Republican than perhaps he cared to admit, overstated the case. The second generation of independent journalists neither denied the legitimacy of the party system nor rejected temporary alliance with a party. They, too, deplored the political withdrawal of "neutrality." But, as Reid realized, these men set a new example of political conduct before the public. Through their columns, Stone, Nelson, and the other editors of independent journals encouraged readers to cast off the blinders of political partisanship. "The only happy voter . . . ," the *Newark Evening News* announced in its first edition, "is the independent voter." "The most sensible appeal that can be made to young voters," Nelson declared, "would be directed to their manhood, and would urge them not to surrender their consciences and their judgments to the keeping of party bosses, but to maintain their independence and exercise the suffrage according to their own convictions." These papers initiated readers in the political style of independency. In good liberal, educational fashion, the *New Haven Morning News* promised "it will always place fact before opinion, proof before inference, principle before partisanship" and "discuss political matters with clearness, directness and impartiality." The *Morning News* and the other new independent papers assessed each candidate at each election in the light of his commitment to municipal, tariff, and civil service reform. They could back Grover Cleveland for president one year and a Republican for Congress the next. No wonder the increasingly partisan Whitelaw Reid was offended.[32]

The first and second generations of independent journalists did share a commitment to the accurate and impartial presentation of the news. They responded much more readily to the growing popular demand for news after the Civil War than did the party press. The independents' emphasis on impartial news reflected the empiricist cast of the liberal mind, confident that social science laid bare the truth about human life and that a written examination revealed a man's fitness for the civil service. Their concern for the news also flowed naturally from the liberal notion of the educated man in politics: newspapers had to provide the factual information men needed for informed, independent judgments about public life. Maintaining a clearer distinction between fact and opinion than did party journalists, the independent editors tried to confine subjective judgments to the editorial page. Their papers largely dispensed with masthead tickets, cheering headlines, and victory displays. "The essence, the life-blood of the daily paper of to-day, is the *news,*" Reid argued in his more independent days. "The ambition of the director of every great political journal should be to make his reports, his election returns, every article and item of *news,* so impartial and truthful that his political opponents will accept them as unquestioningly as his political friends." Samuel Bowles set the same goal for his paper. "The honest reader may take our opinion on trust, if he chooses," Bowles promised in the *Springfield Republican.* "But if he prefers, as he ought, we are bound to furnish him the raw material. And that is the philosophy of independent journalism in a nut-shell."[33]

The second wave of independent papers recognized the same imperative. Amid uncertainty over the outcome of the presidential election of 1884, the *Newark Evening News* reminded other journals, "The duty of all newspapers at such a time as this is to give the people the latest news without coloring or bias. It is the truth that the people craves." "The epoch in which the editor imagined that he must do all the thinking for the people is about past," the *New Haven Morning News* observed in 1882. "The people now think for themselves and what they ask of the editor is simply a text of fact." The independent papers did not always live up to their promises. Some of them, most notably the *Kansas City Star,* used their news columns to crusade for municipal reform. Committed to accurate reporting, the crusading independent papers were quite willing to choose stories to serve their political goals. Still, the independent press did far more than the party papers to promote the fair presentation of the news.[34]

By the mid-'eighties, independent journalism was well established. The presidential election of 1884 helped to ensure its legitimacy and publicize its apparent power. Affronted by the nomination of James G. Blaine, many Republican papers, including such leading journals as the *New York Times,* the *New York Evening Post,* the *Boston Herald,* the *Boston Transcript,* the *Springfield Republican,* and the *Philadelphia Record* bolted the party ticket. The ranks of the Republican press in the major cities were so depleted that the party's national committee had to resort to the ante-bellum device of establishing a temporary paper in New York for the duration of the campaign. Fittingly enough, the apostate independent editor Murat Halstead received the dubious honor of running the paper. After the 1884 election, party journalism, particularly in the country's newspaper capital, New York, was never quite the same.[35]

Profits accompanied the new prestige of independent journalism. With the increasing legitimacy of independency and other liberal ideas, the second generation of independent papers found the going easier than their predecessors had. "The journals which pay best in this country are those which are absolutely free from all external influences, and which are conducted as legitimate business enterprises on strict business principles," the *Kansas City Star* happily insisted in 1884. "Such papers, and only such, can afford to print all the news without fear or favor, and express their honest opinions upon all occasions. It is only for such papers that the public really cares." The *Star* exaggerated, of course, but the growing number of papers acknowledging no party affiliation attested to the appeal of independent journalism. By 1890, 25 percent of the more than 9000 Northern weeklies stood before the public as independent papers; 24 percent of the region's 1300 dailies claimed independence as well. Not surprisingly, independent journalism was strongest in and around the centers of liberal reform. Thirty-three percent of Northeastern weeklies called themselves independents. Of the 144 Northern urban papers whose sales reached at least 10,000 copies a day, 56—39 percent—had declared their independence. So, too, had 19 of the 28 metropolitan journals with circulations of 50,000 or over—a striking 68 percent.[36]

Contemporary observers recognized the emergence of independent journalism. "We have behind us the past—a partizan, unscrupulous, dependent, frequently an inane journalism—and have begun a new era," wrote the manager of the Associated Press in 1891. "A newspaper organ is a thing of the past," an editor agreed the same year. "A newspaper today is what the name imports. It gives the news, with such comments as its conductor may see fit to offer."[37] Some students of the press were not so sure the independent utopia had arrived. The majority of newspapers, they noted, still claimed affiliation with a party. Many papers, partisan and independent alike, twisted the news. "The most obvious faults of the daily newspaper of the present day are its inaccuracy and its partisan unfairness," one writer complained in 1890. "Almost all the daily newspapers are political newspapers. They are bitterly partisan, the so-called independent journals being as unfair as any of the brood."[38]

Certainly independent papers did not always live up to their principles and did not outnumber the party press. But they had established a significant presence, especially in the cities, and had broken the partisan monopoly on public discourse. Each day the independent press offered readers the example of a journalistic counterpart of the educational campaign, deliberative and only mutedly partisan. The traditional party press could survive but only by accommodating this new style. "Party and personal journalism, in an offensive sense, will before long be things of the past," a writer confidently predicted in 1891. "The journal of the future, almost of the present, is independent of the party whip."[39]

The implications of independent journalism for popular politics were portentous. Like the educational campaign, the independent press gave broader expression to an essentially elitist political style. "Independent journalism" had its roots in the post-war political crisis of the educated upper and middle classes; its first exponents championed the remedies of liberalism—municipal, civil service, and tariff reform, and, even for a time, suffrage restriction. Later independent editors did not share all these goals but they had much the same upper- and middle-class orientation. By the 'nineties, they had broadcast the liberal political message far beyond the confines of the first small network of reform journals.

The spread of the independent press represented a considerable victory for the educational politics of reform. The independent journals' successful emphasis on giving the news marked another important achievement. They had tied the "news revolution" in the public mind with independence from party, with the cool, deliberative politics of education. Thus, independent journalism reinforced the effect of liberal reform and educational campaigns on popular political participation. Like educational electioneering, independent papers made politics less accessible for many people, particularly those without much education. Undemonstrative papers without cheering headlines and victory displays, the independent journals offered a less exciting political world than the one created by the old party sheets. Although some of the independent editors carried on crusades, the majority never offered particularly scintillating papers. Independent journalism was, as Whitelaw Reid lovingly described it in 1872, a "passionless ether."[40]

Like the campaign of education, the independent press offered a more complex political world. Independent papers presented politics without the easy guides of masthead tickets and ideological mottoes. The independent editor urged his readers to abandon dogmatic adherence to party and think for themselves. By attacking the old black-and-white simplicity of party journalism, the independent press made political involvement more difficult. "Of course this printing of all the news and giving both sides a fair hearing is apt at times to rather bewilder the reader," Samuel Bowles conceded. "He finds in his paper opposite statements, assertions and contradictions, charges and countercharges, a conflict of plausible arguments. He doesn't know what to think, nor which version to believe."[41] With the rise of the independent press and the educational campaign, politics became less simple and accessible and the partisanship that sustained high voter turnouts lost its cultural hegemony.

For all the optimism of its creators, independent journalism never achieved the virtual monopoly of public discourse that the party press had enjoyed until after the Civil War. By the mid-'eighties, another group of journalists had already begun to challenge both traditional partisanship and liberal independence. Sensational journalism, established by Joseph Pulitzer, developed by William Randolph Hearst in the 'nineties, and reduced to caricature by the tabloids of the 1920s, offered readers a new political orientation. Often as partisan as the old party press, sensationalism nevertheless shifted public attention away from political events. Reaching out to an immigrant, working-class audience, Pulitzer, Hearst, and the tabloids rejected the middle- and upper-class style of educational campaigns and independent journals. But like these expressions of liberal reform, sensationalism weakened popular involvement in politics.

Presaged by James Gordon Bennett, Sr., and others, sensationalism took the national stage with the phenomenal success of Joseph Pulitzer. In May 1883, Pulitzer arrived in New York to rescue the nearly moribund *New York World.* He might have been expected to make the paper into yet another example of independent journalism. After all, as an immigrant to America in the 1860s, Pulitzer had become a protégé of his countryman, the liberal leader Carl Schurz. Pulitzer began his journalistic career on Schurz's German-language paper in St. Louis, the *Westliche Post;* he began his political career by following Schurz from the Republican party into the Liberal Republican movement. In 1872,

Pulitzer took the stump for Horace Greeley. Four years later, along with many liberals, he became a Democrat and campaigned for Samuel Tilden. Like the pioneers of independent journalism, he despised the partisan press. With so many of them, he opposed Radical Reconstruction and favored municipal and tariff reform.[42]

For all that, Pulitzer differed in important respects from the independent journalists he met in New York in the 'eighties. Friendly to the revolutionary spirit of the European '48ers, Pulitzer had more popular sympathies than most liberals born in America. As did other Western reformers in Missouri and Ohio, he had a strong fear of corporate and monopoly power. He even favored an income tax—an evil notion in the eyes of most liberals. An educated, intellectual man, Pulitzer was nonetheless suspicious of the upper-class elitism that permeated liberal reform. Chiding Whitelaw Reid only half-jokingly in 1884, Pulitzer contrasted "poor Democrats, like myself" with "your aristocratic class." Almost alone among civil service reformers, he deplored merit examinations for government office as an unfair advantage for the well educated and a threat to the poor.[43]

As a newspaperman in St. Louis, Pulitzer deviated from the commandments of independent journalism. In 1878, he bought the bankrupt *Dispatch,* merged it with the independent *Post,* and pledged the new *Post-Dispatch* to "principles and ideas rather than prejudices and partisanship." But the paper soon became a vehicle for Pulitzer's partisan ambitions. Hoping to play kingmaker for the Democratic party in state and national politics, Pulitzer indulged in the biased, black-and-white journalism of the party press. When the local Democratic leadership denied him a nomination for Congress in 1880, he remembered his commitment to independent journalism and launched crusades against corruption, monopoly, and machine politics. Still, he hoped to elect a Democrat to the White House.[44]

Pulitzer's ambivalence toward liberalism and partisanship followed him to New York. Like a good independent journalist, he insisted on accurate, factual reporting and likened "the ideal editor" to "a Judge upon the bench, without private ambition, with but one law before him and that the public good."[45] Yet he did not make the *World* into an independent journal for the educated classes. Instead he offered a party paper to the Democratic voters of New York. Laying down the principles of the *World* in 1883, Pulitzer listed the demands of more radical Democrats for taxes on incomes, luxuries, and corporations, as well as the liberal goals of tariff and civil service reform. Pulitzer still wanted public office and the role of kingmaker. In 1884, he ran for Congress as a Democrat and backed Grover Cleveland for the presidency. Eager for Democratic victory, he used most of the weapons from the arsenal of party journalism. News stories in the *World* attacked James G. Blaine, portrayed a dispirited Republican party, and proclaimed the certainty of Cleveland's election. The paper, like most New York journals, did not run the party ticket on the editorial masthead because, as an editorial explained, "it is not necessary. Every column of our paper tells the story of our devotion to the principles of the Democratic party." But the *World* did celebrate Cleveland's triumph with a traditional display: three roosters crowed "VICTORY" on the front page.[46]

This conventional partisanship was a basic element of Pulitzer's journalism. He used the *World* to sell his politics, and he believed his politics sold the *World*. Like other partisan journalists, Pulitzer addressed his editorials to the members of his party. He offered the *World* as a paper primarily for Democrats. During the campaign of 1884, he advertised the weekly edition of the *World* as "indispensable to the Democratic voter . . . one of the best 'campaign documents' that can be circulated." Pulitzer, as a partisan editor, expected to make money off the election. He watched happily as circulation, only 15,000 a day when he took over, climbed past 100,000 during the campaign. "We . . . believe the success of THE WORLD is largely due to the sound principles of the paper rather than to its news features or its price," he wrote. The journal's circulation, he added another day, "should cheer the supporters of CLEVELAND and the friends of honest government generally." For Pulitzer, journalism, business, and partisanship were bound together.[47]

Despite the *World*'s role in the campaign of 1884, Pulitzer never allowed the paper to remain simply a party journal. Trying to reach as broad an audience as possible, he changed the way the *World* presented the news in its pages. Just as important, he broadened the paper's definition of the news.[48] More anxious to communicate with the poor than most independent journalists,

Pulitzer wanted a paper accessible to working-class men and women, many of them unfamiliar with newspapers and uneasy with English. He made certain that stories in the *World* were cast in simple language easy to understand. To clarify and dramatize those stories, he added more and more illustrations—zinc cuts in the 'eighties, then halftone reproductions of photographs in the 'nineties. Along with line drawings and halftones, he printed cartoons. By the 'nineties, his illustrators had developed the single panel of the cartoon into the short story of the comic strip. The most famous of these, featuring "The Yellow Kid," spurred the sales of the *World*'s Sunday edition and inspired the phrase "yellow journalism."[49]

The cartoons and illustrations accompanied a fresh approach to the news. Drawing on the example of the penny press, Pulitzer supplemented the traditional political news of the party journal with sensational stories of sex and crime. He favored gossipy "human interest" stories focussing on personalities and the details of private life. To appeal to men, Pulitzer established the first sports department and gradually consolidated sports news on a single page. He also tried to attract women readers, increasingly valued as consumers by his advertisers. The columns of the *World*, once a masculine preserve of politics and business, now featured stories on fashion, cooking, and etiquette as well.[50]

Pulitzer also used promotions to establish the *World* as something more than the advocate of a party or the passive bearer of the news. He was one of the first newspapermen to boast about his paper's accomplishments on the masthead and on "ears" of text around the nameplate on page one. More significantly, he went in for stunts and crusades. In the 'eighties and 'nineties, the *World* collected donations to build a pedestal for the Statue of Liberty, sent Nelly Bly out to beat the fictional speed record set in Jules Verne's *Around the World in Eighty Days*, exposed the squalor of life in New York's tenement houses, and attacked Standard Oil. Other journalists had already used the crusade, but none did more to make it, in the words of one reporter, "the means of fighting popular causes by the news."[51]

Pulitzer's remaking of the *World* proved an extraordinary success. Within a few years, the paper had more advertisers and more readers than any other paper in New York. By 1892, daily circulation had climbed to an unprecedented 374,000. Abandoning both independent and pure partisan journalism, Pulitzer had created the most profitable newspaper in history. Soon after his arrival in New York, the publisher was a figure of criticism, envy, and imitation.[52]

The political implications of Pulitzer's success were epochal but oddly contradictory. Pulitzer, the onetime liberal reformer, created the anti-type of liberal, independent journalism.[53] Liberals glorified the "educated man"; the *World,* openly anti-intellectual, derided scholarship and the pretensions of college men. Independent editors wrote for the educated and well-to-do; Pulitzer, for the poor and semi-literate. Independent journalism stressed the impartial presentation of essentially political news; sensationalism, the exciting, graphic portrayal of crime and sex.

Despite his sympathy for the poor, Pulitzer was no radical. He made the *World* into a Democratic paper friendly to labor, not a tribune of class war addressed solely to workers. Pulitzer rejected exclusive, "class" journalism in any form, liberal or working-class. "Generally speaking, always remember the difference between a paper made for the million, for the masses, and a paper made for the classes," he lectured a subordinate in 1910. "In using the word masses I do not exclude anybody. I should make a paper that the judges of the Supreme Court of the United States would read with enjoyment, everybody, but I would not make a paper that only the judges of the Supreme Court and their class can read." Observers, impressed by Pulitzer's appeal to the poor, tended to forget his desire to speak to the middle and upper classes as well. Through the *World,* Pulitzer offered a reply to the narrow class politics of liberalism, not by creating a working-class political style, but by rehabilitating the old inclusive style of the party press.[54]

He did so at some cost. Crafting a new appeal to a broad audience, Pulitzer helped to depoliticize the poor even as he tried to stir them to action. Except during the excitement of a presidential election, he was reluctant to feature political news, particularly on the front page.[55] Once the centerpiece of party journalism, politics became engulfed in a sea of sports, gossip, murder, and scandal. The sense that elections held a special place in public life ebbed away: the three-rooster victory display hardly stood out among so many other illustrations and cartoons.

To a degree, Pulitzer made politics more accessible. In 1884 he used facsimile drawings of Blaine's correspondence and devastating cartoons to damage the Republican candidate.[56] But these illustrations were part of a subtle shift in emphasis away from partisanship and politics. The paper's drawings and cartoons focussed on the candidate and his personality rather than his party. A similar shift appeared in some of the paper's stories. One piece on "CLEVELAND'S INSIDE LIFE," revealed that the Democratic nominee "is full of the milk of human kindness and his heart is big enough to take in all mankind." After the election, the *World* devoted a piece to speculation on who would be the lady of the bachelor president's White House. As early as 1884, Pulitzer had begun to turn politics into "human interest," a matter of gossip about personalities.[57]

What was only hinted and implied in the *World* was writ large—literally—in the yellow journalism of William Randolph Hearst. Coming to New York from San Francisco to compete with the *World* in 1895, Hearst transformed the old *Journal* into a lurid, simpler, often rather dishonest expression of Pulitzer's sensationalism. Even more clearly than Pulitzer, Hearst intended the *Journal* and the other papers of his growing national chain for those people, primarily workers and immigrants, alienated by the dry intellectualism of the independent press. Will Irwin noted that Arthur Brisbane, Hearst's editor on the *Journal*, "reaches that class least infused with the modern intellectual spirit of inquiry, least apt to study their facts before forming their theories. . . ." For this audience, Hearst and Brisbane downplayed politics still further in favor of sensational, frequently insubstantial stories simply presented. Banner headlines, breaking the column rule in big block letters of black and red, often misrepresented sensational and insignificant stories. Illustration played an even bigger role than in the *World*: halftone pictures, freely employed, filled the Hearst press. Many of them bore no relation to the stories they accompanied; some were even faked. Cartoons adorned the editorial page; comic strips sold the Sunday edition.[58]

Hearst, imitating Pulitzer, cast himself as a champion of the people. The Hearst papers, Arthur Brisbane insisted, defended the poor and spurred them to participate in politics. "Yellow journalism is war," Brisbane wrote, "war on hypocrisy, war against class privilege, especially war against the foolishness of the crowd that will not think and will not use the weapon that it holds—the invincible ballot." But Hearst's journals did not live up to these promises. For one thing, he and his yellow journalism were hardly radical. Hearst began his journalistic career as a Democrat, the son of a millionaire senator from California. He used his papers to back the Democratic party, William Jennings Bryan, and his own quixotic quests for public office. The Hearst press, as Brisbane himself conceded, served as an outlet for frustration and discontent rather than a conduit of radical change. "Yellow Journalism is important to the peaceful stability of society, *BECAUSE IT ACTS AS A SAFETY VALVE FOR PUBLIC INDIGNATION,*" he maintained. "While the great majority feel that they have a yellow journal to speak for them, while they see each other reading with approval the opinions of an editor who fights their battles, they know that their side is heard."[59]

Despite Brisbane's claims about the ballot, yellow journalism hindered the development of a politically active working class. Carrying further Pulitzer's de-emphasis of political news, Hearst often kept politics off the front page, even during election campaigns. More important, his papers reduced politics to a new level of triviality. Political stories in the *Journal* frequently turned on the personalities and private lives of public men. "Year by year," Will Irwin wrote of the yellow press, "public affairs had sunken in importance, and gossip about public characters had correspondingly risen." In 1911, during the administration of William Howard Taft, a Washington correspondent summed up the revolution in political news since the days of legislative fights over the tariff in 1890 and 1909: "The debate on the McKinley tariff . . . drew four or five columns—mostly literal transcriptions from the speeches," he said. "The report of the Payne tariff bill drew half-columns of condensation. But if Taft puts on a sweater and walks around the Washington Monument, *that's* worth a half-column."[60]

Hearst also undermined popular political involvement by his use of stunts and crusades to create sensation. The *Journal* prided itself on "THE JOURNALISM THAT ACTS," a series of crusades on behalf of the public. To be sure, Hearst often turned to politics for sensational effect. He earned perhaps his greatest fame for his papers' jingoistic role in stirring up the country before the Spanish-American War. But Hearst offered readers no sustained perspective on political life comparable to the viewpoint provided by the old party press. After all, as Lincoln Steffens pointed out, yellow journalism could not afford to dwell for long on any topic. "Care must be exercised not to overdo one subject," he reported, "for the theory of sensationalism includes the belief that the average newspaper reader's mind is as fickle as it is shallow, so the managing editor has to be always on the lookout for fresh material or novel ideas." Yellow journalism could concentrate public attention on politics for a moment, but at the cost of a more enduring interest in public affairs.[61]

Hugely successful for about a decade, yellow journalism itself succumbed to the "fickle" public's taste for novelty. Hearst's virulent hatred for William McKinley put off readers when the president fell victim to an assassin in 1901. But the heyday of the yellow journals came to an end around 1910 largely because people had simply grown tired of them.[62] By then, Hearst had deeply influenced the American press.

Sensationalism attained its simplest, crudest expression in the tabloid dailies of the 'twenties. Such papers as the *New York Daily News*, the *New York Graphic*, and Hearst's own *New York Daily Mirror* featured more pictures, more sex, more crime, and still less politics. Accommodating barely literate readers, the tabloids used as simple language as possible. Billing itself as "NEW YORK'S PICTURE NEWSPAPER," the *Daily News* covered page one with pictures and a banner headline and reduced most stories inside to a few sentences accompanying halftones. In 1924, the paper set an example of independence by backing a Republican, Calvin Coolidge, for president and a Democrat for governor of New York. But politics hardly mattered in the *Daily News* and the other tabloids. Through several different editions each day over the last two weeks of the presidential campaign of 1924, the *News* put politics on the front page in only two editions. The rest of the time, the paper's headlines offered a sensational world of sports, sex, and scandal: "COACH HAUGHTON DROPS DEAD," "DEMPSEY ROMANCE SMASHED," "RUM RUNNERS SHANGHAI CREW," "CHARGES DOCTOR BEAT BOY." Like the *World* and the *Journal* before it, the *Daily News* was a great success. In the mid-'twenties, the paper could claim "THE LARGEST DAILY

CIRCULATION IN AMERICA." By then, the tabloids had brought Americans one step closer to an apolitical view of the world.[63]

Well established at the turn of the twentieth century, independent journalism and sensationalism did not monopolize the newspaper business. Instead they represented two poles, positive and negative, that charged the mass of papers between them. Much of the press drew on the two styles to create a middle-of-the-road journalism. "Between them is a regiment of conscientious editors whose idea of news-publication is to blend what the public wants and what it *should* want," Will Irwin noted in 1911. "They publish enough sensation, enough highly seasoned matter, to keep up circulation; but they publish also more than the public really wants of 'uplift' matter, of news touching on intellectual affairs. The mere, passing, human news of the day is the sugar on the pill."[64] Country weeklies, in particular, continued much as before, printing local news and gossip in lieu of sensation.[65] Most of this mid-road press remained partisan. As late as 1931, some 34 percent of the 1500 and 42 percent of the 8300 weeklies in the North declared loyalty to either the Republicans or the Democrats. Another 18 percent of the dailies and 9 percent of the weeklies maintained party ties as "Independent Republican" or "Independent Democratic" papers.[66] Partisan journalism was far from dead.

Much of the party press continued to maintain financial ties with the Republicans and Democrats after 1900. Small papers still depended on the patronage of county printing contracts and on direct subsidies from the parties. "Ever since I have been in the newspaper business it has been considered that a political campaign was a legitimate source of extra revenue to a party newspaper, and I do not think the custom has staled," wrote an owner of the *Daily Yellowstone Journal,* one of Montana's Republican papers, in 1908. "There never has been a campaign in which the paper has not been paid something . . . . For 1902 we received $400.; for 1904, $600.; for 1906, $500., and I recall that in 1906 I was thanked by the committee for being so reasonable."[67] Such small sums were important mostly to country papers, increasingly the bastion of traditional party journalism. The editors of these papers found the going rough. Old-time partisanship was gravely weakened by liberal reform, educational campaigns, independent journalism, and the yellow press. By the turn of the century, the party editor found it difficult to please his readers. "What a blessed relief it is to the party newspapers that the campaign is over," sighed John Kautz, editor of the Republican *Tribune* of Kokomo, Indiana, after the presidential election of 1900. "No other line of business suffers so much as a result of strenuous political campaigning as the party press." Forced to uphold the Republican line, the paper alienated its Democratic and independent readers. Compelled to concentrate on politics, the *Tribune* drove away "the women, God bless 'em, . . . the chief reliance of the local newspaper." "Thus it is," the disgruntled editor concluded, "that the party paper must disappoint its best friends and alienate all but its strictly partisan support, throughout the campaign. . . ."[68]

Party editors like Kautz found themselves isolated in the twentieth century as more and more papers succumbed to "cold commercialism." "The newspapers of the great cities seldom acknowledge allegiance to any political party," Kautz observed in 1904. "They make of themselves chiefly commercial enterprises, buying and selling news, with money-getting their only purpose. The mercenary spirit is in and through and over everything they do." Party journalism, insisted the editor of the *Tribune*, depended on the papers of the towns in the hinterlands. "It is only the country newspapers," Kautz declared, "that are willing always to make their party's cause their own, to fight under its standard, to stand or fall with it in the fiercest contests. Such a Republican paper is the *Kokomo Tribune* and such it has been for more than fifty years."[69]

Party journalism lasted longer in the cities than John Kautz allowed, but Republican and Democratic editors had watered it down by the twentieth century. As Will Irwin realized, they now paid homage to independent and yellow gods. In 1924, the Independent Republican *Des Moines Register,* observing "the futility of the old-fashioned kind of 'political organ,' which was political organ first and newspaper only incidentally," dismissed "this obsolete method." By then, the party press recognized an ideal much closer to the creed of independent journalism in the 1870s and 'eighties. An editorial in the newly merged, loyally Republican, *New York Herald Tribune* painted a highminded picture of the modern party editor: "Partisan, as he is certain to be, so long as the party system endures and politics are inseparable from the heartbeats of journalism, he nevertheless maintains in the essential governance of his functions a freedom from partisan bias which transcends the mere word 'independence.'" Journalism, the paper concluded, "is the most objective of all the professions save surgery. How could it be otherwise?"[70]

Party journalists began remaking their papers in response to these new commandments as early as the 1870s. By the turn of the century, editors were less likely to attack each other in print or in the streets.[71] Republican and Democratic papers alike gradually stopped parading their partisan loyalty. By the 'eighties, the press of New York City, at the center of independent journalism, had largely abandoned the daily printing of their party's ticket on the editorial masthead. By 1892, most city papers around the North had also given up what one of them called an "antedeluvian scheme." Masthead tickets became a rarity even in country weeklies after the turn of the century.[72] The old party mottoes disappeared as well. When twentieth-century journals used a motto, it typically proclaimed their worth as a purveyor of news rather than partisanship. "If It's News And True, It's Here," the *New Haven Journal Courier* promised its readers. In New York, the *Herald Tribune* offered "FIRST TO LAST—THE TRUTH!" Other papers boldly advertised their own brilliance. The *Des Moines Register* proclaimed itself "The Newspaper Iowa Depends Upon." Less modestly, the *Chicago Tribune* called itself "The World's Greatest Newspaper."[73]

Influenced by the independent press, Republican and Democratic papers became more willing to print the news whether it advanced party prospects or not. In 1892 the papers of both parties applauded the campaign of education and its emphasis on "facts."[74] The *New Haven Palladium* mocked fellow Republicans who criticized the paper's even-handed writing during the presidential campaign that year. "We hadn't insulted anybody. We hadn't foamed at the mouth," the *Palladium* conceded. "Still, we are narrow-minded enough to believe that the average American citizen ranks fairness above partisanship." Disappointed by the

G.O.P.'s defeat that year, the staunchly Republican *Philadelphia Inquirer* proudly declared, "*THE INQUIRER* gave the news in spite of the fact that that news defeated its candidate. It was the first on the street. It led all its contemporaries in getting before the people and in the correctness of its returns, and while it deplores the Republican defeat, it is satisfied that it has done its full duty by the people in placing before them the exact facts and in concealing nothing." By 1920 the paper could announce that "the idea that news relating to one political party must be printed at length, while news relating to another political party must be ignored, is as extinct as the dodo."[75] With the rise of such attitudes, partisan ebullience diminished. After 1900, few papers trotted out the old cuts of roosters and cannon for victory displays.

Although party journals promised impartial reporting, they did not always provide it. The Democrats, still commanding the support of only a fraction of the press, considered themselves mistreated by Republican journals and hostile newspaper chains. "One trouble about the newspapers today," complained the Democratic leader William Gibbs McAdoo in 1923, "is that they have become so partisan in their news columns that real news is not disseminated any more."[76]

Such charges had some foundation. Although at least one observer considered the newspapers' treatment of the 1924 presidential election notably fair, signs of the old biased reporting surfaced during the campaign.[77] Republican papers highlighted stories forecasting the certainty of Calvin Coolidge's victory and resorted to nineteenth-century tricks to attack his opponents, John W. Davis and the Progressive, Robert La Follette. The *Los Angeles Times* ran news stories under such headlines as "DAVIS STRADDLES ISSUE" and "LA FOLLETTE A MENACE TO EVERY CALIFORNIAN." Over a story about La Follette's running mate, the Times blared "ANOTHER LIE EXPOSED." Democratic papers used the same techniques. The *Cleveland Plain Dealer* sounded like an old-time party paper as it reported "DAVIS' SPEECHES PUTTING FIRE INTO PARTY CAMPAIGN." In the 1920s, the Northern press had yet to reach Whitelaw Reid's "passionless ether."[78]

Nevertheless, by the twentieth century, traditional party journalism was crippled. The remaining party papers had largely abandoned their old role of creating for readers an essentially political world comprehensible in partisan terms. No longer dominating journalism, the party press had to compete with the independent and sensational styles. Like the independent press, Republican and Democratic papers downplayed partisanship, promised fair reporting, and generally produced it. Like the sensational press, they de-emphasized politics and turned to sports, women's features, and cartoons. By the 'twenties, the party papers also filled their pages with the advertisements for a wealth of consumer goods. Politics lost its old prominence as papers grew longer. Technical advances enabled editors to replace the four-page paper of the mid-nineteenth century with editions of eight, twelve, and sixteen pages by the 'nineties. Twentieth-century papers, particularly on Sundays, offered even longer editions divided into separate sections. Even in party journals, politics could not monopolize all that space. In short, the partisan press of the twentieth century offered a less political world, one in which numerous attractive diversions competed with politics.

The message of the partisan papers was further diluted after the 'nineties as new mediums of communication competed with the press. Magazines, previously the modestly rewarding province of genteel liberals like George William Curtis and Henry Adams, became a profitable enterprise by 1900. The most successful of the new magazines, such glossy productions as *Collier's, McClure's,* and *Munsey's,* were never affiliated with a political party. These journals often wrote about politics; their muckraking articles on party bosses and big business owed an obvious debt to the crusading techniques of the press. Like the sensationalist papers, the muckrakers did not dwell for long on any topic. The muckraking vogue, again like sensationalism, was over by World War One. The magazines promoted sporadic rather than sustained attention to politics. Along with the press, they buried political stories among ads for clothes and cars. The development of movies in the 'teens and radio in the 'twenties continued the dilution of partisanship. There were, after all, no Republican movie theaters, no Democratic radio stations.[79]

In ways their publishers and editors perhaps did not understand, the independent, sensational, and party papers helped to diminish popular political involvement after the Civil War. Traditional party journalism before the war had eased readers' participation in politics by creating an accessible political world. Party papers made politics seem important, simplified issues, encouraged the public to judge men and measures with the yardstick of partisanship, and urged voters to display their political beliefs. The independent and sensational styles shattered this partisan political world. It was as though the different aspects of men's experience were pulled apart and the unity of their thought and feeling destroyed.[80]

Independent journalism separated reportage and editorial, fact and opinion, thought and emotion. The independent papers denied the validity of partisan subjectivity, the belief that one's values and prejudices should condition one's perception. For many people independence was an uninspiring, confusing guide to the world. Sensational journalism, the anti-type of the independent style, represented the other half of the split of thought and feeling. As its name emphasized, sensationalism offered a world of excitement and emotion rather than intellect. While the independents depicted a confusing, complex world of contradictions and ambiguities, the sensational editors offered a much simpler, more straightforward one. In this respect, sensationalism resembled old partisan journalism; both distorted events in order to make them comprehensible. But Pulitzer and Hearst directed people's emotions from party politics to personalities, to vicarious involvement in other people's lives.

The unified language and consciousness of nineteenth-century partisan politics had split into two modes of expression, both of which presented obstacles to political understanding and involvement. The independent press made politics complicated and unexciting; sensationalism made it unimportant. The party press, caught between the conflicting styles of its competitors, provided only a weak alternative, a kind of lukewarm partisanship that had long since lost its power. By 1900, the party spirit that sustained popular politics was gone.

The press did not simply foist a less political vision of the world on an unwilling public. Newspapers responded to their readers; the current of influence ran both ways. Yet the press did not respond to all readers alike. The province of men with money, the newspaper business generally represented their interests. That was why a region whose voters were roughly half Democrats and half Republicans had an overwhelmingly Republican press. The men who put up the capital, the Northern business class, were predominantly Republican. To be sure, the press could not shape the public at will. An editor could not count on overcoming popular opinion on a particular issue or election. Obviously, the Republican press did not always compel the election of Republican candidates. But the publishers and editors of newspapers had an undeniable power to set the tone of public life and to influence popular thinking in subtle ways. Through the press, the well-to-do had the opportunity, largely unavailable to any other social group, to disseminate their conception of politics and partisanship and set the agenda of public life.

Class concerns permeated the transformation of the Northern press. As journalism grew into a profitable enterprise, many publishers became wealthy men sympathetic, if not always to big business, then to the preservation of a stable capitalist social order. Independent and sensational journalism reflected the different styles and strategies of the Northern upper classes as they rejected popular politics with its ritual accommodation of both sides, workers and wealthy.

Independent journalism was the creature of the liberal reformers. Intellectual and restrained, the independent press sponsored a narrow class politics attractive mainly to the educated middle and upper classes. Sensationalism, so simply laid out on newsprint, was a much more complicated product of class development in the late nineteenth century. For all their attacks on the wealthy, Pulitzer and Hearst, rich men themselves, were never radicals building a class-based politics of the poor. The *World* and the *Journal* represented an effort to establish once more a safe popular form of politics embracing all classes within the old party conflict of Democrats and Republicans. Pulitzer and Hearst, acknowledging class tensions, funnelled them in other directions. The sensational and yellow papers were an indication that the intellectualism of liberal reform and independent journalism could not provide the common public language of Northern society. No newspaper could any longer. The emergence of sensationalism and the persistence of both independent and diluted partisan journalism were a sign that no single brand of discourse, no single political style, could inherit the old monopoly of the party press.

The varieties of journalism were closely linked with the different kinds of campaigning. The party press and spectacular electioneering both drew on exuberant, demonstrative partisanship; independent journalism and educational campaigns alike reflected the dispassionate, deliberative politics of liberal reform. The sensational papers had their electoral counterpart as well. Like Pulitzer and Hearst, it posed a challenge to educational politics.

6

ADVERTISED POLITICS

So confidently celebrated in 1892, educational politics soon lost its hold on Northern public life. A deep depression, brought on by the Panic of 1893, overwhelmed the Cleveland Democrats and nearly eclipsed their political style. Blamed for the hard times, the Democracy suffered heavy defeats in the elections of 1894 and 1895. In 1896, Cleveland's followers watched their enemy, William Jennings Bryan, take control of the party and win its presidential nomination. The election that year promised a new political alignment in America; it also established a new political style to challenge education.[1]

At first glance, the presidential election of 1896 seemed a vindication of educational politics. The contest turned on monetary policy, a new issue more highly charged than the tariff and made to order for an educating war of pamphlets. The most exciting

campaign in years, the election pitted Bryan's advocacy of a bi-
metallic currency of "free silver" and gold, anathema to Cleveland
Democrats and most Republicans, against McKinley's defense of
an essentially gold-based "sound money" system. Across the country, voters bored by the tariff campaign four years before clam-
ored for pamphlets explaining the "battle of the standards" over
the currency.[2]

Bryan's nomination and the silver issue placed unprecedented
demands on party managers. Each national committee had to
build a canvass around a new issue. Moreover, the parties had to
campaign intensively in more states than before. Bryan's sudden
rise turned much of the North into a sharply contested battle-
ground. "The middle west, the great west and the Pacific coast
were all in doubt," a Republican leader later recalled. "Consequently . . . the number of people to be reached, educated and
convinced was much larger than in any National campaign in the
history of the country. That demanded a greater number of speakers to argue the question, greater quantities of literature for distribution and greater efforts to reach the educational influence of
the press. . . . It was the greatest campaign in history, so far as
political management was concerned, because we had to meet an
entirely new issue, and because we had to expand our efforts over
a much greater territory."[3]

The Democratic National Committee, wounded by the defection of many Cleveland men, lacked the money and organization
to rise to the challenge. The committee did have one advantage—
the groundwork laid by the silver propagandists and Populists who
had given speeches and spread tracts across the country for the
past several years. But the Bryan campaign built a flimsy educational structure on that foundation. The new national chairman,
Senator James K. Jones of Arkansas, moved too slowly to set up
headquarters in Chicago, near the most fiercely contested states,
and to get out literature. The delay hurt all the more because
Bryan could not rely on a hostile Democratic press, especially the
urban dailies, to publicize his cause. Still, the national committee
found loyal papers, mostly rural sheets, willing to accept its stereo-
plated stories and editorials. In addition, the well-run Democratic
Congressional Campaign Committee in Washington mailed out

House and Senate speeches and even entire articles and pamphlets that had been read into the *Congressional Record*.[4]

Despite their press service and congressional committee, the Democrats could not compete with the Republican campaign managed by national chairman Marcus A. Hanna. A wealthy coal magnate from Cleveland, Hanna had given up business in 1894 to make his friend William McKinley president. Bluff and self-confident, Hanna seemed a conventional figure, one more big businessman caught up in the excitement of politics. At the outset, he appeared to be planning a conventional campaign. Anxious to win back Republican farmers and workers lured by silver propaganda, Hanna spent July and early August preparing an educational counteroffensive of pamphlets and speeches. Hanna's plans called for nothing new in the way of literature, but their scale was truly original.[5] Because Bryan's nomination horrified wealthy Democrats as well as rich Republicans, the G.O.P. could draw for the first time on corporations whose directors agreed politically as never before. The national committee's huge campaign fund of $3,500,000 gave Hanna the chance to construct an unprecedented educational apparatus.[6]

He made the most of his opportunity. Shuttling back and forth between twin national headquarters in New York and Chicago, Hanna received almost as much notice as McKinley. Hanna's tight control over the campaign and his frequent interviews in the press epitomized the shift of attention from communities to centralized leadership demanded by educational politics.[7] At Hanna's direction, the New York headquarters, in the center of corporate wealth, served as the campaign's fund-raising center. Much of the money collected in New York went west to Chicago, where Hanna established a vast educational organization.[8] Along with a large Speakers' Bureau, the Chicago headquarters included departments for relations with a variety of constituencies including labor, blacks, Germans, Scandinavians, traveling salesmen, college students, and Republican clubs.[9] Naturally, the manager of the headquarters, the Chicago businessman Charles G. Dawes, borrowed the practices of railroads and utility companies in order to make the departments as much like a business as possible.[10]

The heart of the Chicago headquarters was the Literary Bureau run by Perry Heath, a newspaperman and veteran of the educational campaign of 1892. Funded with over half a million dollars, Heath's operation dwarfed the literary bureaus of Tilden and Cleveland. A large staff, including a "statistical department," prepared stories and editorials for shipment to country and urban newspapers. The bureau also produced over two hundred different pamphlets, printed in twenty-one languages, on money, the tariff, and other issues. By the end of July, the demand for pamphlets and their sheer variety forced Heath to prepare a catalog. As the campaign wore on, Heath's operation poured out more than a hundred million documents, measured in good business fashion by the ton and the carload.[11]

The Literary Bureau embodied the restrained partisanship of the educational style. In his pamphlets Heath tried to appear above the bias of old-fashioned party spirit. "Our printed matter will be so non-partisan in character that no one will be able from reading it to tell by whom it was prepared, beyond the fact that it comes from somebody interested in sound money," he promised. "All party epithets, all words generally used in campaign abuse, will be carefully eliminated from our printed matter, whether it pertains to the money, the tariff, or any other question under discussion."[12]

For all his resources, Heath could not keep up with the tremendous demand for literature. Some state committees, unable to secure enough documents from headquarters, began printing their own. In August the New York headquarters, with the aid of the American Protective Tariff League, had to begin producing documents. New York did not match Heath's output in Chicago, but the joint effort with the tariff league yielded perhaps twenty million copies of various pamphlets.[13] Heath had help, too, from the Republican Congressional Campaign Committee in Washington. Surpassing previous efforts, the committee gave congressional speeches and other documents to special state committees for mailing direct to voters.[14] Other groups, most notably the Non-Partisan Sound Money League, an organization run by anti-Bryan Democrats, also contributed to the tidal wave of Republican literature.[15]

Across the North, state and local organizations of the two parties labored to distribute the productions of the national committees. Party workers and voters seemed more comfortable with the educational style than in 1892. "It is affirmed by veteran political campaigners on both sides that never before has the instinct of partisanship been so clearly subrogated to the process of intellectual conviction," the *Newark Evening News* observed. "Never before. . . . has there been such an incessant bombardment of the public mind and conscience by leaflets, pamphlets and reprints of arguments by public men and economic authorities." Northerners seemed to welcome the bombardment. "The people display an amount of interest in pending questions which is astonishing," a man reported from Kansas. "They listen to long and tedious discussions with extraordinary patience. They even bear the reading of coinage acts and quantities of dry statistics."[16]

After the dull campaign of 1892, the battle of the standards seemed a culmination of the promise of educational politics. The party with the better literary operation, the Republicans, won a campaign of great excitement and record turnout. But McKinley's victory was not a triumph of pure educational politics. In 1896 the three great political styles of the century from the 1830s to the 1920s stood side by side. Education alone did not win the battle for McKinley or lose it for Bryan.

Both parties still used spectacle in 1896. The Democrats, divided and impoverished, could not produce much campaign pageantry.[17] The Republicans, on the other hand, made effective use of spectacle. Pragmatic above all, Mark Hanna had no fervent commitment to education or to any single political style; he would use any or all to ensure McKinley's election. "A dynamo whirred inside Mark Hanna's head," a contemporary imagined. "This man knew how to carry West Virginia? Send him speakers or money to hire them. Crowds in California liked a lot of music? Give it to 'em!"[18] The Republicans raised uniformed companies of voters and boys, held urban flag-raisings and rural rallies, staged torchlight parades, and marshalled mostly non-uniformed marchers into "sound money" processions.[19] The G.O.P. even introduced some spectacular novelties. Republican parades featured electric-powered torches and searchlights and "Wheelmen's McKinley Clubs," a sign of the bicycling craze.[20] For his part, Hanna promoted a "Flag Day" on which the Republican campaign asked Americans of all parties to display the national colors.[21]

Substantial though they were, the Republicans' spectacular displays did not indicate a rebirth of the old politics. The G.O.P. and the Democracy raised fewer companies than in 1892. The two parties' parades and rallies did not match the glory days of spectacle in the 'seventies and 'eighties. In one respect at least, political display no longer even seemed to serve its old partisan purpose: Hanna's Flag Day, cloaking party in the mantle of patriotism, concealed rather than boosted partisanship. On the whole, the spectacular phase of the campaign appeared not so much innovative as old-fashioned. The Republicans reassembled the Wide Awakes of 1860, a reminder of a political era passing away. Increasingly, spectacle was something recalled from the past, like those aging survivors of the first Lincoln campaign.[22]

The two parties looked forward as well as back in 1896. Each offered the outlines of a new politics rooted in neither the communal activity and partisan display of spectacle nor the sober study of education. At the center of this new approach was a redrawing of the relationship of voter and candidate, a further shift of attention away from communities and voters toward the nominees.

The campaign of 1896 marked the fulfillment of a trend toward greater public activity by the presidential candidates. During the 'eighties, candidates had begun more active campaigning. In 1880, the Republican nominee, James A. Garfield, had experimented a little with a new approach, halfway between seclusion and the stump. Staying at home like most nominees, he greeted delegations of visitors from the front porch of his farm in Mentor, Ohio. Four years later, James G. Blaine had made his disastrous tour, the first significant campaign swing by a presidential nominee since Greeley's twelve years before. In 1888, Benjamin Harrison extended Garfield's front-porch strategy by regularly delivering carefully prepared short speeches to delegations visiting his home in Indianapolis. At the next presidential election, neither Harrison nor Cleveland campaigned actively: the former because of the mortal illness of his wife and his regard for the dignity of the presidency; the latter, by temperament and tradition.[23]

In 1896, for the first time, both major candidates played an active public role in the campaign. Tall, handsome, and only thirty-six, Bryan was a congressman known more for his oratory than for his legislative draftsmanship. He had won sudden fame and the nomination with an extraordinary speech against the gold standard at the Democratic convention in July. Bryan needed to become better known across the country; he also needed to force the Northern press, so largely against him, to carry his silverite message. More desperate and more histrionic than McKinley, Bryan left his front porch in Lincoln, Nebraska, to undertake the most extensive speaking tours yet made by a candidate for president. Accepting the nomination with an oration in New York's Madison Square Garden, he traveled 29,000 miles by rail and carriage to give more than 500 speeches in 29 states across the country. Some observers found Bryan's tours as offensive as his ideas: here was a candidate who paraded his ambition before the public and even referred to himself in his speeches. But Bryan's unprecedented travels did earn him the newspaper space he so desperately needed.[24]

Cautious, dignified, and rather stolid, McKinley knew he could not rival the direct, charismatic appeal of men like Blaine and Bryan. But the Republican nominee was a polished orator, a veteran of the stump and the House of Representatives, ready to exploit the careful strategy of Garfield and Harrison. Almost every day he gave addresses to well-rehearsed delegations at his home in Canton, Ohio. The texts of the speeches were provided to the press, and Heath's Literary Bureau turned them out as pamphlets.[25]

While each campaign revolved around the activity and personality of its candidate, Hanna's efforts especially sharpened the focus on McKinley. A traditional party manager in many respects, Hanna was quite innovative in his handling of the Republican nominee. In addition to educating the electorate with documents, the Republican National Committee tried to present McKinley to the voters in a simple, direct way. Heath's Literary Bureau turned out millions of copies of posters, including innumerable lithographs of McKinley. Hanna, known to associates as a "phrasemaker," liked symbols and pithy slogans. Under his aegis, posters, cartoons, and stickers for envelopes presented McKinley as "The Advance Agent of Prosperity." A "Full Dinner Pail" symbolized the plenty that McKinley's election would surely bring. The emphasis on McKinley was part of an effort to personalize and simplify the Republican message. Posters and cartoons compressed the long arguments of pamphlets into a terse declaration—"The Tariff *is* an Issue"—or a stark choice—"Poverty or Prosperity." Campaigns had used cartoons and illustrated pamphlets before 1896, and the Democrats used them that year as well, but Hanna and the Republicans were pre-eminent in packaging their candidate, simplifying education, and reducing complex ideas to symbols and slogans. Theodore Roosevelt, destined to become one of the great practitioners of this new style, understood what Hanna had done. "He has advertised McKinley," Roosevelt exclaimed, "as if he were a patent medicine!"[26]

As surely as Tilden before them, Hanna, McKinley, and Bryan pointed the way to a new politics. The campaign of 1896 offered the essence of twentieth-century political style: emphasis on the personality of the candidate rather than on his party; concentration on the nominee and national headquarters rather than on events in communities; careful packaging of the candidate, whether on posters or on his front porch; and pictures and slogans—the tools of advertising—to sell him to the voters. Hanna's effort suggested the form of this political style; McKinley's front-porch appearances and, above all, Bryan's tours, the content. If politicians could harness a dynamic personality on a heroic journey, then perhaps they might create a politics whose emotional power would rival spectacular partisanship.

Bound together for a moment in 1896, the three political styles—spectacular, educational, and advertised—met different fates in the twentieth century. Partisan display disappeared swiftly after 1896. Although campaign clubs and marching companies appeared occasionally in the new century, the time was already past when the major parties tried to enroll as many voters and young men as possible in these organizations. By 1908, party leaders made little effort to assemble large campaign clubs.[27] Both Republicans and Democrats raised only a few uniformed companies for token appearances.[28] Theodore Roosevelt, as the Republican candidate for vice president in 1900 and president in 1904, inspired some companies known as "Teddy's Terrors," "Knights of the Big Stick," and, naturally, "Rough Riders."[29] Other companies were simply relics, like the dwindling ranks of original Republican voters reunited in 1900, 1904, and 1908 as "Wide

Awakes," "Pathfinders," "Old Boys," and the "Old Guard."[30] By 1912 the marching company was virtually extinct.

Spectacular parades almost vanished in the first decade of the twentieth century. Processions by daylight and torchlight, not uncommon in 1900 and 1904, were all but gone thereafter—and with them, the banners, transparencies, floats, and fireworks of nineteenth-century display.[31] By 1908 the occasional parade was simply a curiosity, a pale reminder of an earlier time.[32] In the countryside the parties had already apparently abandoned pole-raisings by the turn of the century.[33] Elaborate all-day rallies, with speeches and parades, declined after 1900. Smaller events in schoolhouses or the county seat, once preceded by red fire and a short parade, began to disappear as well.[34] In cities, spectacular rallies featuring both speeches and parades were quite rare by 1908.[35] So, too, were banner-raisings, the urban counterpart of the country pole-raising.[36] People had pretty much given up even the ratification ceremonies that had once kicked off campaigns.[37] In country as well as city, the traditional musical accompaniment of the campaign meeting died away, too. The parties seldom assembled glee clubs or hired brass bands in the new century.[38]

At the same time, political spectators became less demonstrative. Loyal partisans seldom illuminated their homes and businesses after 1900.[39] Election bets with public payoffs were an oddity by 1908; only the occasional unlucky man had to push a penny with his nose after his party lost an election.[40] Northerners still wore campaign buttons—or at least the parties still produced them. Party workers pinned on buttons, and boys collected them, but the mass of voters apparently did not bother with partisan emblems. "Perhaps at one time. . . . voters advertised their preference by openly wearing these buttons," a reporter observed in 1916. "Nobody ever wears a button now, of course, and nobody ever sees one—on a voter. Nobody has worn or seen one since the first McKinley campaign, and it was then regarded as a curiosity."[41] After the turn of the century voters seldom indulged in the traditonal right of triumphant partisans, the victory parade. In 1916 and 1920, processions of victorious Democrats or Republicans were no more than an occasional curiosity.[42]

By the twentieth century, Northerners had lost interest in spectacle. "The people," a reporter wrote from San Francisco in 1900, "have grown tired of the same campaign speeches, a repetition of bonfires, noise of the anvil and fireworks and all that went to awaken enthusiasm." An editor in Connecticut explained the lack of partisan display for the presidential election of 1904: "The truth is that the people did not want it." "The marching clubs will hardly exist as of yore," a politician observed in 1920. "People do not enjoy marching."[43] Spectacular campaigning no longer seemed a vital part of political life. What spectacle there was after the turn of the century observers termed "old-fashioned" and "old-time."[44] Increasingly, they found spectacular partisanship difficult to understand. In 1916 a reporter in Indiana came upon "one of the county's curios," a kerosene torch left over from the campaign of 1892. He wondered why men had once carried torches in parades: "The things spoiled . . . many suits of clothes, for they almost invariably leaked or spilled oil onto the bearers."[45] Drained of meaning as well as oil, torches could not illuminate the political world of the twentieth century.

Spectacular display vanished partly because it no longer reflected the patterns of Northern society. As memories of the Civil War faded, people lost the martial interest that was one facet of campaign spectacle. The Spanish-American War and World War One did not promote the same military fascination evoked by the War Between the States.

The demise of the intimate style of class relations, characteristic of popular politics in the nineteenth century, probably further weakened interest in partisan display. The upper class had long since rejected the ritual of companies and parades for the more detached educational style of the liberal reformers. Too, the wealthy men of Northern cities and towns had less need to give workers uniforms and drinks in the twentieth century. Many of the wealthy had moved from houses near their businesses and their employees to exclusive neighborhoods and suburbs. The well-to-do who remained behind were less inclined to run for local office; in an increasingly centralized nation their political interests often lay outside the community.[46] No one linked the demise of spectacle directly to the class conflicts of the late nineteenth century, but after the Haymarket Massacre of 1886, the Homestead Strike of 1892, the Pullman Boycott of 1894, and countless other confrontations, capitalists and workers probably had little interest in the old political demonstrations of mutual respect.

Fading memories of war and transformed class relations weakened spectacle in particular, but other social change threatened all forms of local electioneering in the twentieth century. In the 1870s and 1880s, presidential campaigns had begun in communities during July and August; in the 1900s, campaigns started in September and October.[47] Rallies, even those without spectacular trappings, became fewer in the early twentieth century. The near disappearance of traditional campaign events was tied to the development of leisure and consumption and to a declining sense of local community.

The emergence of leisure as an ideal and a reality particularly threatened traditional forms of campaigning. By 1900, Northerners, easing their commitment to the work ethic, had begun to proclaim the virtues of play and relaxation.[48] From the late nineteenth century into the twentieth, new entertainments appeared—first vaudeville, amusement parks, baseball, boxing, football, and bicycles, then movies, phonographs, automobiles, and radio.[49] Advertising offered the delights of consumption, which many could not afford but all could savor vicariously.[50]

The implications of leisure and consumption for political campaigning soon became clear. In the nineteenth century the political campaign had challenged theaters and lecture halls for their audiences. In the twentieth century the contest was uneven. The presidential election of 1912 hardly cut into the receipts of Northern theater owners. "There is no doubt that campaigns face a new and enervating competition," a magazine writer asserted in 1924:

> Thirty years ago, when only the larger cities of the country made a specialty of entertainment, a Presidential contest. . . . came along to break a peace that hadn't a fraction of the interruptions life boasts nowadays. In those days the farmer's wife wasn't tuning in on all the Presidents she wanted with a few twists of a gutta-percha knob. The small town merchant hadn't bought a rubber-tired chariot to tour the country, looking for adventure. Main Street hadn't yet begun to blink with bill-boards advertising Broadway stars at cut-

rate moving-picture prices. . . . Those were the days when a campaign burst upon the quiet order of affairs, to touch all the stored-
up thrill that now seeps into twenty different avenues of
entertainment.

Political theater could not compete with these new diversions as a
source of leisure. Neither could politics monopolize the attention
of men and women lured by the pleasures of consumption.[51]

The decline of traditional campaigning was part, too, of a tran-
scendance of community, a shifting of the delicate balance
between local autonomy and national participation that had
allowed spectacular campaigns to flourish in the mid-nineteenth
century. Some sense of community still held Northerners
together, but the communal experience created by the geographical boundaries of cities and towns had begun to wane before
1900. Local autonomy diminished in several ways. Outside trusts
and corporations impinged on localities and determined the economic facts of everyday life. Improved communications—railroads, paved roads, automobiles, newspapers, movies, and
radio—linked towns and cities in more and more centralized
networks.[52]

A process of communal self-revelation, traditional campaigning
lost significance with the eclipse of local community. If outsiders
appeared powerful and intriguing and one's neighbors no longer
seemed so interesting, then watching a local parade or listening to
a hometown speaker became less important. For many Northerners exposed to new fashions and ideas, campaign spectacle was
suddenly unimposing and unsophisticated.

The first hint of such attitudes came as early as the 1860s from
New York City, already proud of its worldly-wise sophistication.
Campaign clubs and companies were popular in New York, but
their members did not like to parade too often and tended to prefer civilian clothes to pseudo-military uniforms. Although the
Democrats and Republicans of New York staged the largest political parades in the country, spectacle did not have quite the same
impact as elsewhere. As the *New York Tribune* cautioned the city's
Wide Awakes in 1860: "[It] is so obvious that a parade of 30,000
similarly accoutered men may be a trifle monotonous before its
end. . . ." Cosmopolitan New Yorkers, "so soon wearied and impa-

tient," the paper explained, would not leave their homes late at night even if "the Prince of Darkness was out on Broadway." A political parade had to offer fancy maneuvers to capture a New York audience. In the late nineteenth century Northern cities seemed to share some of New York's sophistication. Parades in cities featured floats and other horse-drawn displays less frequently than in the Midwestern countryside. Campaign supply houses sold uniforms more readily in rural areas than in the cities.[53]

By the turn of the century even the most isolated Northern communities shared some of the attitudes of New York and experienced, too, a sense of diminished self-importance. In 1892, political audiences in Indiana wanted to hear only national figures, not homegrown orators. In 1916 a reporter in Indiana noted the "Lack of inclination upon the part of country residents, to turn out for local speakers." The same year, another reporter discovered a similar situation in the country towns of Missouri: "The people don't attend meetings as they used to do. They will come for 'headliners,' but that is about all."[54]

As newspapers became more readily available across the North, people became still less likely to attend rallies. "Public speaking is not what it used to be when newspapers were few and when a whole country town would turn out to listen to an argument from either side in a heated campaign," an editor concluded in 1904. "If there is anything worth listening to in the speech the people know that the papers give it what it merits. . . . The morning newspaper at the breakfast table is the orator in these days." Given the availability of newspapers, another editor wrote in 1908, "it is little wonder that the general public is unwilling longer to be jostled by the crowds in ill-smelling halls in order to hear political harangues. . . ." Of course newspaper editors had every reason to exaggerate the triumph of the press over oratory, but the dwindling number of rallies in the 'teens and 'twenties bore them out. Furthermore, rallies seemed to become captives of the press after 1900. The parties often appeared to stage public meetings, not mainly for their effect on the immediate audience as in the past, but in order to get the text of speeches printed in the papers.[55]

Northerners' decreasing physical isolation also contributed to the disappearance of election rallies. In 1916 an Indiana paper attributed "the abandonment of political meetings in the rural communities" to "improved facilities for transportation, enabling rural voters to get to the towns for meetings. Good roads and the automobile have been the big factors. . . ."[56] As Northerners glimpsed the world outside their township or city, they left local campaigning behind.

By the 1920s commentators regarded spectacular politics as part of the lost village life of America. "In more primitive days a torchlight procession marching by houses burning candles in their windows. . .was an epoch, a thrilling event in the drab life of villagers," wrote the *New York Times* in 1924. "There are no villages now. We are all urban, children of the movie and the radio, speeders of the car, 'fed up' with searchlights and colored lights."[57] The *Times* exaggerated the urbanization of America, but it captured precisely the forces transforming political style in the twentieth century.

Although the availability of leisure, the glorification of consumption, and the eclipse of community helped to destroy partisan display, they delivered only the coup de grace to the old politics. Party leaders and publicists had long since attacked and discredited the ideological basis of spectacle. The partisan ideals supporting campaign pageantry had begun to topple in the 1870s and 1880s, well before the social changes wrought by movies and automobiles became important. The immediate financial basis of spectacle also gave way before the twentieth century. By 1892, national and local party leaders had refused to spend significant sums for partisan display. In the early twentieth century, the parties sponsored an occasional marching company, but that was all.[58] Impersonal social change alone did not destroy spectacular campaigning; the Northern upper class had laid the groundwork for that destruction years before in the transformation of partisanship.

In the twentieth century the old party spirit had indeed diminished. Now more than just a handful of Liberal Republicans and Mugwumps criticized parties and rejected passionate, undeviating partisan loyalty. By the 1900s many Northerners, particularly the growing ranks of the middle class, had taken up the liberals' political style. In communities, especially in the cities, groups of citizens rejected the old parties and pursued an issue-oriented, non-partisan local politics. They put pressure on street railway and utility companies with petition campaigns, bi-partisan mass meetings, and newspaper crusades. Around the country, Americans had forged ties that gave them new ways of influencing politics and government. Farmers tested their strength through co-operatives; businessmen formed trade associations; lawyers, doctors, and teachers banded together in professional societies. As the air reverberated with attacks on bosses and machines, Northerners tried to limit the power of parties and politicians with direct primaries, direct election of United States senators, ballot laws, and the initiative, referendum, and recall.[59]

Independence, so long derided, now seemed legitimate and widespread. "In 1884, with the first great bolt from the Republican ranks, independent voting was denounced as little short of treason to the flag," wrote the *Nation* in 1908. "But the change in twenty-four years has been very great. Among intelligent men it is now hard to find one who will vote for a party merely because he or his father has always voted for it." The old prejudices against independence had begun to die. "A few years ago . . . [change] from one party to another involved social, sometimes even business embarrassments," the *Minneapolis Journal* recalled in 1912. "But that has passed. A man may move from one party to the other without in the least losing caste." Split tickets, scratched ballots, and independent candidacies all testified to the ease with which men and women changed parties after 1900. So did the number of states that gave majorities to a presidential candidate of one party and the gubernatorial nominee of another. "The men and women who vote their convictions come from every class," the *New York Times* could observe during the campaign of 1924. "Manufacturers, merchants, bankers, professional men, farmers, all vocations have their quotas, and the women are numerous; and this body of independents will turn the election."[60]

So many people had taken up the independent, secretive style of the nineteenth-century liberals that politicians could no longer fathom the voters' intentions on the eve of an election. "Individuals. . . . are doing their own thinking, and keeping their own counsel," a journalist wrote late in the campaign of 1908. "It is no wonder, therefore, that the politicians who claim the largest degree of actual knowledge are, on the morning after election day, proven to belong to the class of ignorant prophets." In 1912 the "silent vote," descendant of the much smaller "vest-pocket vote" of the 'eighties, upset the calculations of politicians. "The big silent vote is baffling to the prophets. . . ," noted a reporter traveling with Republican candidates through Minnesota's Iron Range. It was the same all across the country. "Notwithstanding the noisiness of the struggle, probably in no campaign in many years have the voters in such large numbers refrained from expressing publicly the man of their choice. . . ," stated the *New York Sun* on the Sunday before the election. "Also in no recent presidential contest has there been so much reticence on the part of regular party voters."[61]

To most observers, the spread of independence meant that the Republicans and Democrats could not rely on hoary partisan appeals. "I believe. . . ," a politician declared in 1908, "that the day of absolute partisan control is gone. . . ." The *Review of Reviews* proclaimed the same year that "old-fashioned party prejudice cannot very successfully be played upon." "Party feeling," a correspondent counselled the Republican presidential nominee, William Howard Taft, in 1908, "is not as intense and therefore not as effective an instrument in vote getting as it was eight or twelve years ago." A congressman from New York City reached the same conclusion in 1924. "There seems to be a drift toward independent voting," he said. "That means that you can't lure them to the polls with the old party loyalty appeal."[62]

Politicians acknowledged the existence of traditional partisans, "people who are easily influenced by bands, banners and a great show," but no major party would use spectacle to capture their votes. Some commentators believed the party vote, however large, did not deserve much attention. "The men who decide elections must be won by superiority of argument and reason," the *New York Times* lectured its readers in 1916. "They must be convinced. The hurrahs of the partisan whose mind is made up don't count."[63]

After 1900 party leaders continued to use educational techniques to catch the independent "silent vote." Education had become orthodoxy, the established style of the Republicans and Democrats. "Fundamentally the method of campaigning in both parties is the same," a reporter wrote in 1908. "There is very much less of the whoopla, red fire, and torchlight parade business now than there used to be. . . . [More] and more the importance of that sort of show has diminished, and the efforts of the National committees have been directed to the straight, hard work of educating the voters and trying to make the individual ballot caster everywhere see the issues of the campaign in the desired light."[64] Still, an evolution, signaled in 1896, was already under way. Without men realizing it, educational campaigns began to change.

In many respects, the presidential election of 1900 was a rerun of 1896. Once again McKinley and Bryan topped the tickets; once again Mark Hanna and James K. Jones managed the national committees. The issues did change somewhat. Although the Democrats endorsed free silver, they stressed their opposition to McKinley's pursuit of colonial possessions after the Spanish-American War of 1898. The issue was new, but the Democratic National Committee ran the same kind of campaign. To get better coverage in the press, the Democrats did seem to take more care to provide advance texts of speeches to newspaper associations. But as four years before, a shortage of money, sympathetic papers, and competent managers plagued the Democratic effort.[65]

Meanwhile, Mark Hanna started up his marvelous campaign machine, slightly less well funded, in praise of gold, prosperity, and overseas acquisitions. Once more Perry Heath oversaw an efficient press service and literary bureau in Chicago. Heath's priorities had changed, however. This time he turned out fewer copies of a smaller variety of documents. The Republicans seemed more concerned with their press operation, which supplied material to over 5000 newspapers. The educational method was different, but the result was the same: McKinley won re-election easily.[66]

The change in education became more apparent in the presidential campaign of 1904. That year the Democrats celebrated a kind of nostalgic return to the Cleveland era. Bryan's followers lost the nomination to Judge Alton B. Parker of New York, a disciple of Cleveland and the gold standard. Naturally enough, the Democratic National Committee took up the old educational style of 1888 and 1892. George F. Parker and Josiah Quincy, veterans of Cleveland's tariff campaigns, came back to the Literary Bureau. Thanks to Alton Parker's wealthy backers, the party had the kind of money—perhaps as much as $1,800,000—needed to run a solid educational campaign. But one thing had not changed: the new national chairman Tom Taggart, an Indiana politico from the Matt Quay school, turned out to be a miserable manager.[67]

While the Democrats looked backward, the Republicans staged a superb, innovative canvass. This time the party ran Theodore Roosevelt, elevated from the vice presidency to the White House by the assassination of William McKinley in 1901. As a youthful member of New York City's elite, Roosevelt had been caught up in municipal and civil service reform. A party man imbued with the reform temper of the age, he despised Mugwumps but adopted much of their political style. Fittingly, he chose George B. Cortelyou, an advocate of education, for national chairman. Private secretary to Cleveland, McKinley, and then Roosevelt, Cortelyou was smooth and meticulous where Mark Hanna had been blunt and aggressive. A contemporary found the new chairman "as smart as lightning, as methodical as a machine, and a gentleman above everything."[68] Only forty-two, Cortelyou, like Roosevelt, represented a new generation of party leaders raised in the atmosphere of a more independent politics.

A tight budget forced Cortelyou to use his resources carefully. With only $1,900,000, slightly more than half of Hanna's war chest in 1896, Cortelyou would not indulge in any spectacular excess. Tightening up the operations of the national committee, he dropped most of the special bureaus that had been hallmarks of Hanna's campaigns. Cortelyou kept the Speakers' Bureau but cut down on the number of hired orators of little repute. Even the director of the bureau downplayed the importance of oratory. "Spellbinding is passing out," he said. "It may last through the next campaign, but not much longer. We are depending more and more on the printed word. . . ."[69]

Despite his tight budget, Cortelyou set aside over half a million dollars to take care of "the printed word." As before, the Literary Bureau cooperated with the Republican Congressional Committee to turn out a textbook. But Cortelyou reined in the production of literature. Following Heath's example in 1900, he cut down still further on the number and variety of pamphlets. "Useless and unnecesary literature was barred," he reported, "and its place taken by what we regarded as strong pamphlets, widely distributed." The bureau stopped distributing pamphlets earlier than usual. In all, the Republican literary operation in Chicago sent out fewer than 23,000,000 copies of only twenty-three different pamphlets.[70]

The Republicans paid more attention to the press. Like past campaigns, party headquarters had to put up with the demands from small foreign-language newspapers for financial support. But Cortelyou spent his money mostly on plate matter and printed supplements for the country and urban press. The Republicans took pains to get the right kind of stories to the right papers. The New York headquarters sent material only to the Eastern press; to soothe Westerners suspicious of the East, the Republicans supplied them with different copy mailed out from Chicago. Cortelyou himself made sure Republican speeches appeared in the press accompanied by "vigorous editorial comment."[71]

Observers quickly noted the shift from documents to papers. "It is but fair to say," the *Kokomo Tribune* declared, "that the campaign . . . has been more distinctly and characteristically a newspaper campaign than any preceding one."[72] James S. Clarkson, now a Republican patronage appointee at the Port of New York, also caught the implications of Cortelyou's canvass. His hopes for power long gone, Clarkson rightly saw the campaign of 1904 as the fulfillment of his educational dream twelve years earlier. "Cortelyou is proving to be a great chairman, a great organizer . . . ," Clarkson exclaimed. "It is the method of the new generation; just as dry goods business and all other kinds of business have been revolutionized and conducted on entirely new methods, so is Cortelyou . . . revolutionizing the system of politics and of campaigning. The red light is no longer a color in politics and the brass band has departed." With Roosevelt's easy victory over Parker, Cortelyou became the model of the modern political manager.[73]

By 1908 Cortelyou's emphasis on the press had caught the attention of Democrats as well as the Republicans. In fact, the Democrats seemed to seize the initiative from the Grand Old Party. To be sure, the Republicans mounted another victorious campaign, this time for Roosevelt's hand-picked successor, William Howard Taft of Ohio. Roosevelt also helped name Cortelyou's replacement as national chairman, Frank Harris Hitchcock. A veteran of the campaign of 1904, Hitchcock was a sleek young public servant in the Cortelyou mold, committed to efficient, businesslike organization.

Amid a rush of worshipful publicity, Hitchcock picked up where Cortelyou had left off. Scaling down the Speakers' Bureau, the new chairman planned to eliminate paid "spellbinders" entirely. The Literary Bureau, co-operating with the Republican Congressional Committee, produced the usual textbook but issued only a dozen different pieces of literature. More than ever, the bureau devoted itself to planting material in the press. To a reporter, the bureau's director seemed like the "managing editor, as it were, of a great newspaper. . . . [He] has surrounded himself with an able corps of paragraphers, copy readers, news editors, exchange editors and the other elements of a newspaper staff." In all, Hitchcock's headquarters in New York reflected the best political wisdom of the day. As the reporter admiringly concluded, "Education, system, business are the watchwords."[74]

Yet Hitchcock's campaign did not work out very well. Education had made Cortelyou's reputation as a manager, but four years later the style seemed to get Hitchcock into trouble. From the start, some party leaders disliked the chairman's manner and resented his methods. Hitchcock quickly had to abandon his plan to drop orators from the payroll. A shortage of funds also limited the campaign. Because of a downturn in business and a new law prohibiting corporate political contributions, the national committee raised just over a million dollars, a paltry sum by Republican standards. Before long, complaints and dissension plagued Hitchcock. William Howard Taft even had to issue a vote of confidence in his manager.[75]

Hitchcock's woes were partly of his own making. His secretive, cold manner alienated party workers. His businesslike methods produced a stolid, uninspired campaign. But much of Hitchcock's difficulties flowed from the educational style itself: what had served eight and four years before now seemed inadequate. One veteran of the national and congressional committees seized on the sober, high-minded tone of education. "The whole trouble," he argued, "is that our chief started out to conduct the national campaign on a plain [sic] above that on which Sunday schools and [churches] are conducted." Theodore Roosevelt also criticized the lack of emotion in Hitchcock's educational canvass. "The campaign," he complained privately, "is being conducted in such a blankety business-like way that all the sentiment which is the very foundation of political enthusiasm and activity has been squeezed out of the canvass." Clearly, Frank Hitchcock's failings were not the only problem in 1908; the campaign of education, even though geared to the press, no longer satisfied the Republican party.[76]

No such discontent appeared among the Democrats. By 1908 they were well used to underfinanced, poorly managed campaigns. The party had given William Jennings Bryan one last, futile nomination for a crusade against the evils of monopoly. Once more, the national committee had little money—only a bit over $600,000. Yet this time, in defeat, the Democrats showed some inventiveness. The national committee, chaired by a New York State newspaperman, concentrated on solving Bryan's longtime problem with the press. One device was an old one: the committee circulated a New York City German paper, owned by the campaign's treasurer, to German voters around the country. More interestingly, at Bryan's urging the Democrats established a Press Committee of leading Democratic newspapermen under the direction of Henry Watterson, editor of the renowned *Louisville Courier-Journal*. Bryan hoped that the committee would counsel the party's regular literary men and improve its relations with the press, especially with those metropolitan journals that had vilified him in 1896 and 1900. As he told Watterson, "You can tone down some of the papers that are against us and tone up some of those that are with us." The Press Committee was not a great success. Despite its counsel, the national committee produced plate matter for country papers too slowly. The urban press remained hostile. To get their message out in the last weeks of the campaign, the Democrats even contemplated issuing their own daily paper. The Press Committee could not compensate for poverty, bad management, and an unpopular cause, but it offered a telling indication of the growing importance of newspapers in campaigns.[77]

The parties' reliance on the press seemed a fulfillment of educational politics. As proponents of education had insisted since the 1880s, independent-minded voters would find newspapers, apparently free of party control, more persuasive than literature obviously turned out by the parties themselves.[78] Yet the transition from pamphlets to papers also signified a retreat from the liberal reformers' educational vision. Party managers no longer thought primarily of educating the people with didactic literature; more and more, these men saw their main function as obtaining as much space for their candidates as possible in the newspapers. The directors of the literary bureaus were becoming political counterparts of Ivy Lee and the other public relations men hired by big business to improve its image in the press shortly after the turn of the century.[79]

The transformation of the bureaus was gradual and involved no change in personnel. As in the nineteenth century, the writers in the literary bureaus were mostly newspapermen; so, for that matter, were the first public relations men. In fact, the parties and the public relations business drew on the same pool of journalists. George F. Parker, a newspaperman and director of the Democrats' educational efforts in 1888 and 1892, employed Ivy Lee, also a newspaperman, in the party's Literary Bureau in 1904; after the election the two men established their own public relations agency. Despite the continuity in personnel, the national committees of the early twentieth century knew they had started something new. The Democrats recognized the change in 1908 when they christened their literary operation first the "Press Bureau" and then the "Publicity Bureau." "More and more," a reporter noted that year, "campaign management has come to follow strictly the lines of publicity adopted in business."[80]

"Publicity" was one new word cropping up in the vocabulary of politicians and newspapermen; another was "advertising." As early as 1904, the *New York Times* could declare that "campaigning is only a political name for advertising. . . ." The *Times* was a bit premature. Despite Mark Hanna's example, party leaders moved slowly to adopt all the techniques of advertising. Elements of old-style education, publicity, and advertising mixed together in the campaigns before the first World War.[81]

When Hanna packaged and sold William McKinley in 1896, advertising was rapidly becoming a highly developed art and a profitable business. Modern advertising began to emerge about 1880, then took off with a rush in the 'nineties. More and more businesses gave up short newspaper advertisements set in small agate type for regular and expensive programs of illustrated display advertisements. Advertisers tested other media as well: magazines, billboards, electric signs, and streetcars. For help, business turned to advertising agencies. Until the 'eighties, advertising firms had done little more for clients than buy newspaper space in bulk. By 1900 such agencies as Lord and Thomas of Chicago planned campaigns, wrote copy, chose illustrations, and selected advertising media for their clients. Between 1880 and 1900, advertising agents pioneered the use of slogans, such as Kodak's "You press the button; we do the rest." The agencies also introduced "human-interest trade-marks" like the "Sozodont Girl" and the boy-in-slicker of Uneeda Biscuit. At the turn of the century, ad men began to talk about the "psychology" of their craft; advertising became more calculating and manipulative. By then, advertising was a well-established arm of American business.[82]

At first, party managers after Hanna were more concerned with gaining space for their candidates in newspapers than in copying ad campaigns. Nonetheless, even the predominantly educational canvasses of 1900, 1904, and 1908 hinted at changes to come. Continuing Hanna's effort to simplify and personalize politics, the Republicans and Democrats widely distributed lithographed portraits of their candidates.[83] The national committees also made more use of cartoons. In 1908 the G.O.P. not only reprinted cartoons from newspapers but hired four cartoonists as well.[84] Campaign managers also began to use the new devices of entertainment during these years. In 1904 the parties showed moving pictures, interspersed with slogans and still photographs of the candidates, to audiences at rallies.[85] In 1908 William Jennings Bryan posed for a movie maker. That year he and William Howard Taft cut phonograph records of their speeches.[86]

The parties were beginning to make use of advertisements, too. As early as 1888 and 1892 the Republican National Committee had placed ads in the streetcars of New York City. In 1904 George Cortelyou and the Republican National Committee "did a great deal" of advertising. In 1908 both national committees and some local committees as well ran ads in newspapers. The investment in advertising was not very large: the Republican Literary Bureau in New York spent only $26,000 on ads that year.[87] These early political advertisements, still far from major orchestrated campaigns, were not a leading feature of the election. But together with records, movies, posters, and cartoons, they suggested the outlines of a new approach to electioneering by the national committees.

That approach became quite clear in the presidential campaign of 1912. For the first time in many years, three major parties fought for the presidency. Theodore Roosevelt, unable to wrest the G.O.P.'s nomination from William Howard Taft, had bolted to form his own Progressive party. Splitting the usual Republican vote, neither Roosevelt nor Taft could overtake the Democratic nominee, Governor Woodrow Wilson of New Jersey. The three parties, divided over the future of industrial America, did generally agree on campaign methods. The Republicans and Progressives copied the Democrats and opened "publicity" bureaus at national headquarters. In all three campaigns, the production of literature took a back seat to cultivation of the press. The publicity bureaus offered stories, advance texts of speeches, editorials, and cartoons to newspapers around the country.[88] More than ever before, party managers advertised in magazines, farm and labor journals, and Sunday papers.[89]

With the spread of theaters around the country, a leading movie-maker had predicted in 1911 "that moving pictures are going to cut a very, very large figure in the coming campaign, and are going to be used by the Chairmen of the Committees, to a far greater extent. . . ." Once again, the candidates appeared on film and made records of their speeches. So that people could see and hear Wilson simultaneously in the era of silent movies, the Democrats played Wilson's records in theaters where his films were shown.[90]

As in 1908, a losing party seemed to be the most innovative. Finishing third, the Republicans, the party of conservatism and solemn Bill Taft, showed the greatest appreciation of advertising. Desperation pushed new party chairman Charles D. Hilles of New York, Taft's personal secretary, to exploit new techniques. The split in the G. O. P. left Hilles without the money and organization necessary for a conventional campaign of education. The Progressive bolt also deprived him of many of the well-known public men needed to boost Taft on the stump. Certain of defeat, party workers were demoralized and the Republican Congressional Committee virtually inactive.[91]

Accordingly, Hilles produced a textbook and some pamphlets but saved his resources for the press and, above all, advertising. The national committee spent an unprecedented sum on ads— apparently in excess of $400,000. Using every medium available, Hilles paid for advertising in streetcars, newspapers, and magazines. The Republicans took out a contract for six weeks of advertisements in weekly magazines, agricultural papers, and Sunday papers. Six different kinds of ads for Taft appeared on 23,000 billboards around the country.[92]

More than other party managers, Hilles appreciated the political possibilities of film. "The moving picture," he told Taft, "has become a tremendous factor in our every-day life. . . . probably . . . the most valuable asset in this campaign." He had Taft, like the other candidates, filmed by a movie company. In 1200 movie theaters, Hilles ran ads whose still pictures offered "a pictorial comparison between the conditions of labor abroad and in this country."[93]

Advertising was the key to the election for Hilles. At a hopeful point in the campaign, when the Republicans still could think of victory, he told Taft: "I think this method of campaigning is in some measure responsible for the turning of the tide, and it was absolutely necessary to put the facts before the people in tabloid form because of the paucity of public speakers." A little ponderously, Taft himself summed up the Republicans' new approach to campaigning. "The press, of course, is the chief source for keeping before the people the controversies of the campaign. . . ," the President declared, "but other methods of advertising are coming into vogue—the use of billboard and electric signs and the advertising panels of the streetcars is a logical outcome of the study of the science of advertising and publicity that so many industrial concerns had occasion to make."[94]

Sketched out in Taft's hopeless campaign in 1912, the advertised style emerged full-blown in the election of 1916. Woodrow Wilson, running for re-election, faced a reunited Republican party and its candidate, Supreme Court Justice Charles Evans Hughes. The campaign turned on the state of the economy and, especially, the question of whether America would stay out of the World War. For the first time, advertising completely overshadowed the oratory and didactic pamphlets of education. Run like modern ad agencies, the national committees shaped the public perception of their candidate-clients through press releases and paid advertisements.

The two parties used similar techniques, but the Democrats carried on the election with greater flair and understanding. Both parties ostentatiously assembled advisory councils of ad men who would, as the Republicans put it, "for the first time apply to politics the same merchandising principles that are applied to successful business enterprises."[95] The councils were window dressing; the national committees, as always, ran the real campaign. Here the Republicans let down. At party headquarters, an inexperienced chairman presided over an uneasy alliance of former Progressives and Taft men. Slow to get down to work, the national committee ran an uninspired campaign.[96]

Since 1896, Republican managers like Hanna, Heath, Cortelyou, and Hilles had led the way in developing the art of electioneering. Now the Democrats took over as the party of innovation. Members of the Democracy discussed advertising much as they had once explored education in the 'seventies and 'eighties. Wilson's men began to think about publicity for his re-election months before the campaign. Already sensitive to the need for a good press, the Democrats had established a publicity group to get out newspaper stories on the achievements of the administration. Late in 1915 and early in 1916, Democratic officeholders considered the need for new campaign methods. "We are not doing politics as they were done twenty years ago, or ten years ago, or five years ago," a Democratic officeholder noted in January. "Today publicity, in all its myriad forms, is ninety per cent of the whole business. . . . this campaign would be won or lost with publicity." "Modern publicity is an advertising art," another officeholder, Frederic C. Howe, observed. "The average man wants material served up to him in a direct way. He has been trained to expect this by the magazines and the press. He expects directness, the dramatic. He is trained to short sentences. . . ." Accordingly, Howe called for men "full of 'pep' and knowledge of things" and "trained in the modern school" to conduct Wilson's publicity. "If I were you," a Democratic leader advised the new national chairman, Vance McCormick, "I would . . . employ three or four of the brightest young advertising experts and enthusiasts in this country and keep them on your staff at headquarters until the campaign closes. Snappy, pungent advertisements, consistently employed throughout the campaign, will have a tremendous effect."[97]

McCormick did not need any prompting. He placed the national committee's Publicity Bureau in the hands of a graduate of the "modern school," Robert W. Woolley. Director of the United States Mint, Woolley had been a newspaperman and chief assistant in the Democrats' Publicity Bureau in 1912. With help from the newspaperman George Creel, he envisioned a campaign of pure publicity and advertisement with almost no educational literature whatsoever.[98]

Woolley was a bit ahead of his time. Local party leaders, not yet attuned to advertised politics, forced him to produce a good deal of literature. The campaign made use of a textbook and documents from the Democratic Congressional Committee. Still, Woolley abandoned old-fashioned, wordy pamphlets for short circulars, preferably no more than three hundred words but "as full of meat as the Sermon on the Mount." In the end, literature, Republican as well as Democratic, played an insignificant part in the campaign.[99]

Woolley's main efforts went elsewhere. Drawing on some of the best journalists in the country, he put together a large staff of writers. Woolley demanded good writing; he made sure that George Creel and the rest of the staff turned out crisp, readable work for the press. A page of plate matter went out every ten days to about 4000 papers. About one cartoon a day went to 1000 dailies. The Publicity Bureau even put out *The Bulletin*, a weekly paper "containing editorials and semi-news and statistical matter for use at any time" by 8500 editors around the country. The New York City dailies and a select list of other papers received special handouts of "strictly news matter." The bureau put out a story each day under Chairman McCormick's name in William Randolph Hearst's chain of papers. There were even special supplements for inclusion in the nation's Sunday papers.

The Publicity Bureau did not simply spew out news willy-nilly. Woolley took great care in placing stories and advance copies in the right papers at the right time. At one point, he laboriously secured testimonials to Wilson from public figures such as Thomas Edison and Henry Ford. Holding back the endorsements for as much as three weeks, Woolley boasted of his ability to release a story to the press at "the psychological moment."[100]

Woolley's press operation was the perfection of a technique already well-established; he broke fresh ground in newer media. Like Charles Hilles, Creel and Woolley appreciated the potential of moving pictures. "We are living in a film age," Creel believed. "The imagination of the hour is impressed almost more by the 'movies' than by the word persuasive in print." Creel looked to "the great cinematograph kings of the country" for "big ideas"; he dreamed of retaining D. W. Griffith as "consulting-architect" for the campaign's films.[101]

That dream did not come to fruition. But Woolley saw to the first production and distribution of films by the party itself. "It was natural," he reported to Vance McCormick, "that in this campaign the moving picture should play a part second only to the newspaper." The Publicity Bureau produced a film of Wilson at work, "The President and His Cabinet in Action." Woolley was especially proud of the film and the way his bureau induced theaterowners to show it. "This was so informative and its propaganda features were so insidious that we were able to have it distributed, without extra cost, through the independent houses and through at least one of the great exchanges," he bragged. A second film, less high-minded, attacked Hughes with a series of comic caricatures; a third dwelled on "the horrors of war, peace in this country, etc." Like the press, most of the nation's movie theaters were owned by Republicans, or so Woolley believed. In any case, he had to overcome some resistance from theater owners unwilling to show his films. Woolley also made his productions available to Democratic committees around the country.[102]

The Democrats did not have the theaters to themselves. The G.O.P. had also gone into the movie business. Hired by the Republican National Committee, a moviemaker shot films of Hughes at home and on a campaign trip. To dramatize the return of the Progressives, the committee produced a movie called "Reunited Party," with a featured appearance by Theodore Roosevelt.[103]

The parties' films encountered some criticism. "It is hard to believe that either democrats or republicans are seriously engaged in an undertaking of this sort and still more difficult to believe that it would be welcomed by the average photo-play manager who knows his business," an editor in Connecticut contended. "People don't go to the movies to get their political opinions or to be instructed as to how to cast their ballots, and a [campaign] play, whatever its 'politics,' would be resented by a large part of any audience. The picture play people would be wise to forbear." But neither national committee had any doubts about the new medium.[104]

Woolley also made innovative use of advertising. The media he chose were not new, but the quality, content, and scale of his ads set a new standard. The Republicans, apparently well supplied with funds, spread advertising lavishly; Woolley and the Democrats employed their smaller ad budget with more thought and effect.

The Democratic ad campaign marked the culmination of the effort to simplify the presentation of politics to the people. George Creel reached back to Mark Hanna for inspiration: "I should attempt to hit upon a phrase to be our trade-mark as the McKinley managers in 1896 made the 'Full Dinner-Pail' theirs, i.e., 'THE ADMINISTRATION THAT'S DONE THINGS' or 'THE "AMERICA FIRST" ADMINISTRATION.'" The Publicity Bureau finally came up with a more memorable slogan, "He Kept Us Out of War." Ad agencies, hired by the Publicity Bureau, ran the slogan in newspapers and magazines, on billboards, streetcars, subway stops, and electric signs. For the last month of the campaign, billboards in the industrial towns of the Northeast and the Midwest paid tribute to Woodrow Wilson with a second slogan. The ad, Woolley wrote enthusiastically, "will depict the war demon held in leash, factories running in full blast, a contented workman with his dinner pail returning to a happy wife and two children who stand greeting him, the dome of the Capitol at Washington in the background, and above it, surrounded by golden clouds, an excellent picture of the President. Underneath on a dark blue background, in big white letters, is the legend: 'He Has Protected Me and Mine.'" The Republican ad men could not match that. Over the course of the campaign, they tried such slogans as "True Americanism," "Lest we forget 1914," and, rather desperately, "Has he kept us out of war?"[105]

The Democrats used advertising more aggressively than ever before. When the Republicans prepared ads publicizing labor leaders' support for Hughes, Woolley learned of the plan in advance and ran his own "complete exposure of the fraud" in ads the same day. Attacking "costly, hypocritical, and absolutely misleading pages of Republican advertisements," the Democratic copy charged that selfish and irresponsible businesmen had paid for them.[106]

Woolley scored his biggest hit with an ad campaign hounding Hughes as the Republican nominee made appearances around the country. This campaign exemplified the way in which publicity techniques were now tied to advertising. Creel enlisted a group of intellectuals to write an open letter asking Hughes ten questions, such as "Would you have filed instant protest against the invasion of Belgium and backed up that protest with the United States Navy?" and "Would you urge universal compulsory military service?" The Publicity Bureau first planted the letter in the press as a news story. Then the questions appeared in newspaper ads and a flyer, both entitled "'YES!' or 'NO!' Mr. Hughes?." When Hughes appeared in a city to speak, the questions greeted him from the local press. As the candidate tried first to avoid and then to answer them, Woolley modified his ads to pose fresh challenges to the Republican candidate. "Make Mr. Hughes Answer!," new copy blared. Hecklers carried the challenge to Hughes at his appearances. By October, the ads linked Hughes to the belligerent stance toward Germany of his supporter Theodore Roosevelt. "War? Mr. Hughes?," asked the ads. *"You would have brought about war!"*

Sure of the effectiveness of his advertisements, Woolley plunged the Democratic National Committee deep into debt for a final flurry of $200,000 worth of ads in the last week of the campaign.[107] After Wilson's convincing victory on election day, observers considered the money well spent. To Roosevelt, Woolley's canvass for the President was "the most brilliant achievement in the history of American politics." Hughes himself blamed his defeat on Woolley's ads. "The Democratic appeal was driven home during the latter part of the campaign by spreading throughout the country enormous picture-posters, giving a lurid display of the carnage of war, while on the side-lines stood a mother and her children looking on,—with the legend underneath—'He has protected me and mine'. . . . I still should have been elected had it not been for the effectiveness, particularly in the Middle West, of the Democratic slogan—'He kept us out of War.'"[108]

Observers saw the power of advertising in another aspect of the campaign. The national committees' ads, they believed, helped to explain the small number of local rallies in 1916. "The old-fashioned political spellbinder, who has made the hustings 'resound' in past campaigns, is being put out of business by the skilled advertising expert," a reporter noted. For proof, he quoted the editor of a small-town paper in Missouri:

> The campaign managers have simply used the skilled advertising expert—the man who is trained in selling merchandise by the power of convincing his readers—to tell in a few sentences or paragraphs what the average orator takes two hours to tell. And the advertising expert tells it much more convincingly and powerfully. He takes the great mass of information, boils it down to concrete issues, and presents it in a manner the average every-day person grasps at a glance.

Advertised politics had triumphed over the remnants of local campaigning left over from the days of spectacle.[109]

The advertised style, simple and direct, had overshadowed education as well. Less didactic and ponderous than the educational campaign, advertising seemed slicker and more manipulative. Political advertisers spoke a new language. Uninterested in educating the people, these men dropped the "highly philosophical" in favor of "double-fisted 'punch' stuff." Exuding a breezy self-confidence, the managers presented political success as a matter of winning enough space in newspapers and magazines. "Given enough lines and any publicity manager will tell you he can make a president," the *Kansas City Star* reported. "And why not? Soaps have been made that way . . . and chewing gum." The era of advertised politics had indeed arrived.[110]

Woodrow Wilson did not keep America out of war, after all. Political advertising shaped his presentation of the First World War to the American people. In 1917 George Creel brought the techniques of the Democratic Publicity Bureau to the government's propaganda agency, the Committee on Public Information. In turn, the wartime experience with Creel's propaganda and with advertising and publicity for war relief, the Red Cross, and the sale of Liberty Bonds spurred the development of advertised politics.[111] But the Republicans, not the Democrats, emerged from the war years with the best advertising machine.

Triumphantly renewed in 1916, Wilson's administration ended in the wreckage of his plans for peace and the League of Nations. The first sign of the Democratic slide came in the Congressional elections of 1918. At the national committee, Robert Woolley, now a member of the Interstate Commerce Commission, and Creel, busy with his propaganda agency, gave way to less talented men. The Republicans, meanwhile, became the first party to put the management of its affairs directly in the hands of a professional advertising man. The new national chairman, Will Hays, brought to his New York headquarters Albert D. Lasker, owner of the pioneer advertising agency Lord and Thomas of Chicago. Together, the two men crafted a campaign that gave the Republicans control of Congress. The election, lamented Robert Woolley, was "a horrible affair."[112]

The presidential election of 1920 continued the Democratic decline. Saddled with Wilson's unpopular legacy, the nominee, Governor James M. Cox of Ohio, faced an uphill battle fought mainly over the League of Nations. Unfortunately, the Democrats conducted a miserable campaign on his behalf. The national committee suffered from a weak new chairman, severe financial difficulties, bad publicity work, and the aura of defeat. Robert Woolley, who had opposed Cox's nomination, refused to run the Democratic Publicity Bureau. Finally, in October, Woolley joined the headquarters and raised money for advertising. With help from George Creel, he tried a reprise of the ten-questions ads that had worked so well in 1916. It was too little, too late.[113]

In the meantime, Will Hays, the Republicans' best manager since Cortelyou, carried political advertising to a new level in the service of handsome and superficial Warren G. Harding. Advertising dominated the campaign, run from elaborate twin headquarters in New York and Chicago. "These are the methods which won the war, put over the liberty loans and raised the vast funds of the Red Cross," exclaimed a reporter. The Republican publicity men were always on the lookout for "a mighty good advertising stunt." They went enthusiastically about what one of them called "the general business of advertising and selling our goods to the public." Hays and Harding consulted chewing gum manufacturer William Wrigley, one of the most successful users of advertising, as if to prove that a president really could be sold like a stick of gum. The campaign even enlisted Arthur Brisbane, William Randolph Hearst's famous editor, to write some ad copy. The Republicans also made heavy use of movies. An "official moving picture staff" filmed Harding's activities at home and on the campaign trail. The publicity men also called on a still photographer to take care of "good intimate detail stuff such as domestic scenes . . . Mrs. Harding dictating her mail . . . and the like. . . ."[114]

Once again, Albert Lasker was on hand to "manufacture the publicity punch." From Chicago, he helped to edit the candidate's speeches and stage-manage the "stunts" at Harding's home in Ohio. With much fanfare, Lasker developed an ad campaign built around the limp slogan "Let's be done with wiggle and wobble"— a reference to the allegedly inconsistent policies of the Wilson administration. Lasker's plan called for Harding to close a speech on August 28 with "wiggle and wobble" and for Republican editors and speakers, warned in advance, to popularize the slogan. "We have prepared billboards which go up October 1st throughout the land, containing the slogan," Lasker told one of Harding's aides. "We want it to appear that when the candidate wrote this sentence in his speech it was merely a passing sentence that he injected, but that it was so forceful that it was spontaneously picked up." Lasker suggested that the aide might call "wiggle and wobble" to the attention of reporters. "But if you do . . . kindly do so in such a way that they won't know that the publicity end of the campaign had anything to do with the expression and the thought appearing in the speech." "Wiggle and wobble" alone did not win the election for Harding, of course, but after 1920 advertising men were in politics to stay.[115]

With the campaign of 1920, the novelty of advertised politics gave way to stultified calculation and artificiality. The transformation of political style was complete. The belief that reasoned appeals should persuade thinking voters—the hallmark of the educational campaign—had disappeared, lost among the billboards decrying "wiggle and wobble." Abandoning education, the political advertisers would manipulate the voter, seize the "psychological moment" to shape his perceptions, and sell him a product. Obviously, politicians had always tried to influence the people, whether with torchlight parades or pamphlets on the tariff. With Hays and Lasker, however, politics entered a new realm of contrived images and salesmanship.

The parties did not forsake the educational style entirely. True to education's ideal of restrained partisanship, politicians had no intention of reviving the emotional party spirit of the nineteenth century. The commodity packaged by political advertisers was not partisanship; the symbol they sold was not the party. Instead, advertised politics offered the candidate. In 1896, McKinley, not the Grand Old Party, became the "Advance Agent of Prosperity." In 1916, Wilson, not the Democracy, "Kept Us Out of War" and "Protected Me and Mine." Here was the influence of sensational journalism and advertising. Like the sensationalist press, the advertised political campaign focused on personality and human interest rather than on partisanship. The candidate became the "human-interest trade-mark" of politics.

The advertising of the candidates completed the transformation of the old relationship of politicians and people. As voters retired to their homes with the death of local spectacular campaigning, the presidential nominees, following Bryan's example in 1896, emerged from hiding to take center stage. Carefully groomed and presented, the candidates struck out on the campaign trail to parade their personality and ambition before an undemonstrative people.

Active campaigning promised great strain on nominees, and many resisted. Incumbent presidents—McKinley in 1900, Roosevelt in 1904, Taft in 1912, Wilson in 1916, Calvin Coolidge in 1924—avoided long speaking tours in favor of a few appearances. The incumbents could claim the dignity of the presidency and the press of the nation's business as excuses to stay at home. They relied on their office to give them enough publicity. In addition, they could use the vice president as a surrogate campaigner. Not all incumbents wanted to avoid the stump. In 1904, an impatient Theodore Roosevelt watched his opponent Alton B. Parker and itched to get out on the trail. "He lays himself wide open and I could cut him into ribbons if I could get at him in the open," Roosevelt told his son. "But of course a President can't go on the stump and can't indulge in personalities, and so I have to sit still and abide the result."[116] Other presidential nominees and the vice-presidential candidates, however reluctant, could not easily resist popular pressure to take to the stump. In 1904 the Democratic presidential candidate, Alton B. Parker, refused long tours to his regret: commentators blamed Parker's defeat in part on his steadfast refusal to show himself to the public on the campaign trail. With Horace Greeley, James G. Blaine, and William Jennings Bryan in mind, politicians had long associated touring with losing. Now Parker offered a cautionary tale with a new moral.[117]

One by one, candidates learned Parker's lesson. In 1908 William Howard Taft, not wanting to become part of a "*rara avis* show," planned a front-porch campaign. But he soon found that people, particularly in the West, "seem to attach little importance to the idea that the candidate should conduct a campaign of dignified silence, and . . . they insist on their right to see and hear the candidate. . . ." Taft abandoned the front porch to tour the country by rail.[118] Four years later, Woodrow Wilson, listening to conflicting advice about the wisdom of touring, declared he would not take the stump. But he, too, had to reverse himself.[119] In 1920, Warren Harding started a front-porch campaign at his house in Marion, Ohio. Criticism soon forced him to leave home for trips out into the country.[120]

Undoubtedly, public opinion flushed Harding and the others out into the open. Americans increasingly sensed that it was proper for men to parade their ambition for the presidency. The republican tradition of the "mute tribune" had died away. "There is certainly nothing un-american or inconsistent with the highest dignity for the candidate for the presidency to campaign the country for the purpose of permitting his fellow citizens to know where he stands on public questions and what his party proposes to do if successful at the polls . . . ," a Republican told Charles Evans Hughes in 1916.[121] Still uncertain that campaign tours meant victory, observers conceded their necessity. The *New York Times* summed up the consensus in 1920. "Of course," the paper pointed out, "there is no way of estimating the value in votes of a candidate's progress through the country, though everybody admits the strong popular desire to see candidates."[122]

Democratic presidential nominees had another compelling reason to campaign. Because so many newspapers opposed the party, candidates from Bryan on used public appearances to win at least some press coverage and to reach the people directly. Franklin Roosevelt, James M. Cox's running mate in 1920, explained their need to tour that year. "The campaign of Governor Cox and myself has been a very strenuous one," he wrote, "because more than three-quarters of the Press is Republican, and we have had to overcome this by personal appeals to the voters."[123]

So, candidates toured across America by rail and automobile. Their ever-larger retinues testified to the nominees' increasingly important role in campaigns. In the mid-nineteenth century a candidate needed only a secretary to handle his correspondence. Harding, on tour in the Middle Western and Border states, traveled on a special train of five cars with more than forty passengers, including party officials, reporters, an "Official Photographer," an "Official Motion Picture Man," a secretary, and a doctor. In 1924, John W. Davis, the Democratic presidential nominee, rode a four-car special train equipped with loudspeakers and broadcasting facilities and carrying, among other people, his personal publicity man, his personal physician, the Democratic publicity manager, the Democratic national chairman, a secret service agent, four stenographers, and at least a dozen newspapermen.[124]

The basic event of a campaign tour was the short speech. The candidate, often standing on the rear platform of his train, delivered as many speeches in as many places as possible in a day. In the 'nineties, the heyday of educational politics, observers measured the strength of a campaign in the number of pamphlets the national committee sent out; now, in the twentieth century, the number of the candidate's speeches, the states he had visited, and the miles he had traveled became the yardstick of a campaign. On a typical day in 1900 Bryan spoke twelve times in Indiana. James M. Cox gave sixteen speeches one day in South Dakota during the election of 1920. Bryan in 1900 and 1908, Roosevelt in 1912, Hughes in 1916, Cox in 1920, and Davis in 1924 each covered thousands of miles to give hundreds of speeches.[125] The vice-presidential nominees followed much the same routine.[126]

On tour, a candidate could not confine himself to speeches. He had to feed a press hungry for "stunts" and "human interest." Partly intended to present the nominee's policies to the public, the tour aimed as much, probably more, simply to show him to the people, to reveal him as a man with the common touch. The presidential nominees tried "stunts" unimaginable in the late nineteenth century. In 1912 Woodrow Wilson reviewed the annual baby parade in Asbury Park, New Jersey. Four years later, Charles Evans Hughes showed off "a good, stout, hearty man's grip" by shaking 10,000 hands one day in Wisconsin. Harding sat at the throttle of his campaign train for a twenty-mile "joy ride" in 1920. His opponent, James M. Cox, "drove a horse around the State Fair track" and had his picture taken with a 120-year-old Indian during an appearance in Minneapolis. One day in 1924, John W. Davis took the mound at the ball park in Omaha to throw a pitch to his running mate, Charles Bryan. A few days later Davis donned a cap and neckerchief to became an honorary member of the Colorado Boy Scouts.[127]

Along with "stunts," candidates did all they could to show themselves and their lives to the people. Accepting much invasion of privacy, nominees gave interviews and let the press trail them to church on Sunday. Candidates allowed photographs and movies of themselves at work and, with their families, at play. If the campaign needed stirring up, they simply took a trip. Asked why he had called on his running mate Calvin Coolidge in Vermont, the Republican vice presidential nominee of 1924 Charles G. Dawes replied, "The publicity department called me up from New York and said they were short on publicity and wanted me to come around this way."[128]

Active campaigning did place great strain on the candidates. An avid public watched them travel from one end of the country to another, their voices worn, their energy gone, pushing themselves to the limit of their endurance. Harding and Davis brought physicians with them for their tours; Roosevelt carried along a tank of oxygen in 1912. Marveling at their exploits, the press compared the presidential candidates to athletes. In 1924, John W. Davis even went into "physical training" before his campaign and traveled with a boxing trainer to keep himself in shape on the road.[129]

Some candidates—Theodore Roosevelt and Bryan, in particular—came naturally to the rigorous discipline of the campaign trail. Some, like Hughes, adapted to it. But most nominees fought the regimen at one time or another. Even Roosevelt objected, in vain, to the demands of the schedule set for him by the Republican National Committee in 1900. Candidates found the invasion of their privacy particularly galling. Running for president in 1924, John W. Davis resigned himself to "about as much privacy as a goldfish." On view to the press day after day in 1904, Alton B. Parker finally lashed out at what he called "promiscuous photographing." Roosevelt and Wilson both tried to avoid having their pictures taken; Wilson would not even allow his managers to release a story on his "home life" to the public. In 1924 Dawes, one of the most outgoing of candidates, refused to have a movie made as he arrived in Grand Central Station. "Hell," he declared, "they're not going to make a damned movie man out of me."[130]

Candidates had to do more than just make themselves available. They had to learn the difficult art of catering to the press. After all, the point was not so much the campaign appearance itself, but the coverage of the event in the newspapers. One candidate after another had to learn to write out his speeches in advance for distribution to the press. "We are not getting the degree of publicity for your speeches that we ought to have, and it is due solely to the fact that you do not give out advance copies," the acting Democratic chairman lectured Woodrow Wilson in 1912. "It is much better to repeat to a large degree former speeches you have made, and to give out advance copies, than to make extemporary speeches and suffer their emasculation in print." "[A]dvance copy is the secret of publicity," another leading Democrat reminded the nominee.

Yet there was a price for sticking to familiar speeches. The press had an unending appetite for novelty. A nominee could not deliver over and over the same set of ideas, written down beforehand or not, and still keep reporters enthusiastic about his candidacy. As a longtime politician told Warren Harding in 1920, "With a number of extemporaneous remarks each day, there must necessarily be constant repetition of ideas and phrases, which soon dull the enthusiasm of the accompanying press correspondents, who complain the candidate has no real issues, and an air of hostility between the candidate and correspondents soon exists that is reflected in the newspaper columns."[131]

Candidates had to offer not only new ideas, but a fresh, pleasing personality as well. Each nominee had to learn to project himself aggressively into the public imagination. John W. Davis, a reserved, scholarly corporation lawyer, learned this lesson painfully over the course of the campaign in 1924. Davis's first appearances were uninspiring. "I know that you dread to do it," his personal manager told him, "but I hope that you will use the word 'I' quite frequently in your New York speech. It gives an address a personal rather than an academic touch." "Inject more human color (heart appeal) into your personality," another aide advised Davis before a campaign swing. "This can be done throughout your trip." As Davis and other candidates well knew, that was a tall order.[132]

Candidates also confronted dangers on the campaign trail. There was still the possibility of a damaging slip. In 1916, for instance, Charles Evans Hughes's efforts to bring the followers of Theodore Roosevelt back into the Republican party suffered from reports that the nominee had snubbed a Progressive leader while on a campaign swing in California. Visiting a state or city, a nominee ran the risk of getting caught in the cross fire between warring factions of his party. He had to avoid appearing to favor one side or the other in some local dispute. There was even physical danger on the campaign trail: campaigning in Milwaukee in 1912, Theodore Roosevelt nearly lost his life to an assassin's bullet.[133]

Candidates had to put up with less violent opposition to their campaigns. Dignified William Howard Taft found himself criticized in 1908 for indulging in a "personal campaign" and "circus" tactics. Men faulted him for making speeches; they faulted him for letting the press cover his rich man's golf games and horseback rides; they faulted him for making records on "a devilish talking machine."[134] After decades of retiring behavior by candidates, the aggressive proclamation of their personality came as a shock to some voters. Not a few, like a Presbyterian minister in New York City, objected to politicians "who use the pronoun 'I' in a brutally egotistic way." But most people welcomed the publicizing of presidential candidates. "It is the business of any man who wishes to be President to see that all the 'human interest' stories about him are told," wrote the *Philadelphia Inquirer* in 1920. "The American people are insatiable upon this point."[135]

By the 'twenties, candidates dominated campaigns as never before. The same innovations that had undermined local campaigning made possible the nominees' prominent role. The trains and automobiles linking towns and cities carried the candidate across the country. The increased circulation of newspapers spread his words and picture; phonograph records captured his voice; movies recorded his activities. In the presidential campaign of 1924, a final innovation, the radio, brought the voices of candidates live to people sitting quietly, privately, at home. All the major nominees made speeches over the air that year. With radio, candidate-dominated politics was complete. The relationship of politician and voter had been transformed.[136]

The candidate's relationship to his party had changed as well. As politicians and journalists quickly understood, personality was overshadowing partisanship. After the turn of the century, they began to interpret elections as personality contests. "As we agreed . . . , this is to be a peculiarly personal campaign," a Republican leader reminded Theodore Roosevelt in 1904. "It is largely to be a campaign of enthusiasm. In no sense is it to be a campaign of education, such for example as the campaign of 1896." Four years later, a Republican leader told William Howard Taft "that this campaign will be run largely on your personality. . . ." "The personal equation," observed the *Review of Reviews* on the eve of the presidential election of 1916, "is even more important nowadays than the party affiliation."[137]

The primary, one of the anti-party reforms of the era, helped promote this politics of personality. By 1912 voters in twelve states could go to the polls to express a preference for a candidate for their party's presidential nomination or choose delegates pledged to vote for him at the party's national convention. Four years later, more than half the states had adopted the presidential primary. To contest the primaries, candidates had to develop their own publicity bureaus. These organizations began to make the candidates less dependent on their party's weakening apparatus. The primary campaigns furthered the public perception of the nominee as an individual rather than the representative of the Republicans or Democrats. The primary, lamented the *Minneapolis Jour-*

nal in 1912, "has made our politics so personal and self-seeking."[138]

In 1916 James Sheffield, a conservative Republican lawyer from New York who had opposed Roosevelt's Progressive bolt four years earlier, realized angrily what had happened to partisan politics. "Men have forgotten," he complained privately to a political ally, "since Theodore Roosevelt became such an interesting and potent figure in our national life, that when we elect a president, we do not elect a personality, but a *party*, a party pledged, through the person of the president, to carry certain fundamentals of party belief into the administrative and legislative features of government. . . . The campaign for the election of a president is a strictly *party* campaign, that is, it is so in principle, even though in practice during the last two or three national elections it has degenerated into a personal campaign." Sheffield went on to enumerate the functions of party in American politics and government. His observations, Sheffield wrote, were "commonplace," but had they been so, he would not have had to make them. As he knew, personality had begun to outweigh party.[139]

By 1920 the pattern was plain. In the nineteenth century, noted the journalist Herbert Adams Gibbons, politicians had been subservient to party. "A candidate for office presented himself to a convention as the exponent of the policies and principles of his party," Gibbons recalled. "When the campaign began, of course, personalities entered in, but the paramount issue of the election was the party, not the man." In the twentieth century, however, a handful of national figures had triumphed over the old partisan politics. "Two decades of Bryan, Roosevelt, and Wilson . . . have changed all that," Gibbons observed. "Instead of choosing candidates to fit in with the exigencies and the strategy of party politics, platforms have been made to suit the candidates. The temptation, to which conventions have succumbed, has been to neglect every condition affecting the party as such, its organization, its strategic interests in the different States, its traditional appeal to and hold upon certain classes of voters, in order to center everything around a particular person. . . . For twenty years both the Republican and Democratic parties have been under the influence of dominant personalities." Bryan, Roosevelt, and Wilson were party candidates, but this was hardly the partisan politics of the nineteenth century.[140]

Slowly, the campaigns of the early twentieth century inaugurated a new politics, a mix of education and advertising. In 1900 education had predominated, with advertising subordinate. The growing emphasis on the press and on "publicity" in the largely educational campaigns of 1904 and 1908 heralded a change in styles. In 1912 Hilles's unsuccessful canvass for Taft offered a politics clearly dominated by advertising. Four years later educational elements remained, but advertising commanded the thinking and the budgets of the party managers. "The last educational campaign was in 1896," a Republican observed that year. He was more or less right.[141]

Party managers and journalists used the term "education" less and less frequently in the new century. The educational style lost its cachet partly because Northern leaders accepted most of its basic principles. In the twentieth century politicians took for granted the importance of system, organization, polls, uncommitted voters, and restrained partisanship. Like the educational campaigners of the 'eighties and 'nineties, 'twentieth-century party leaders placed great emphasis on scientific, businesslike organization. Each campaign rediscovered the wheel, as the new party chairman announced that his would be a truly efficient headquarters run on a business basis.[142] Following the example of Tilden and his disciples, the parties used polls and card indexes to identify uncommitted voters and then concentrated on winning them over.[143]

Education's allure dimmed, too, because some of its grandest aims had not been realized. The campaign of education had never quite lived up to the dreams of its creators. In the 'eighties and 'nineties, W. S. Andrews and James Clarkson envisioned a centrally controlled canvass in which a national committee reached directly to each voter in the land. No campaign came close to realizing that vision. In 1908 Frank Hitchcock evidently hoped to develop a card index recording data on each voter in the country; Republican leaders blanched at the cost of the project— $600,000—and forced him to renounce his plan.[144]

Continuous organization between elections, another of Clarkson's ideas, never quite took hold either. After the campaign of 1904, Republicans considered setting up a "perpetual literary bureau" as "a storehouse of Republican information in the broadest possible sense." Finally established late in 1907, the bureau counted for little and apparently lapsed by 1912. Beginning a few years later, a "Republican Publicity Association" played a modest role in the party.[145]

The Democrats moved about as slowly to meet the need for continuous publicity. Beset by poor chairmen and little money, the national committee lapsed into inactivity after campaigns. After the defeat of 1896, some Democrats tried unsuccessfully to set up a network of itinerant party speakers. Buoyed up by Wilson's election in 1912, the national committee did hold together a small permanent headquarters through the debacle of 1918. Yet by 1920 the national committee had to start up a publicity machine all over again. "I feel very strongly . . . ," Franklin Roosevelt could complain after losing the vice presidency in 1920, "that our weakness in the past has been due largely to the fact that we have conducted our campaigns in most places only during the two or three months before election." The party set up another permanent publicity bureau in 1921. It was not very effective; the same lack of year-round publicity bedeviled the party in 1924 and after.[146]

The National League of Republican Clubs and the National Association of Democratic Clubs, the supposed vanguards of the educational style, never flourished. As chairman of the Republican party, Mark Hanna had no interest in the league of clubs. An anguished James Clarkson watched Hanna let the organization "go to pieces." There were occasional efforts to resuscitate it in the early twentieth century, but the clubs received only perfunctory recognition from party leaders. "There is no use concealing the fact," lamented the league's president in 1904, "that many of the older and regular politicians look with disfavor upon the League work." The organization lasted into the 'twenties, altogether unimportant and ignored.[147]

The National Association of Democratic Clubs had an even swifter decline. Ironically, William Randolph Hearst took over the association in 1900 and turned it into a plaything of his political ambitions. Robbed of its educational purpose and Hearst's support, the organization declined into insignificance after 1904. There was not much need for educational clubs in the world of advertised politics.[148]

During the 1920s education remained a significant yet subordinate part of a politics dominated by advertising. In essence the advertised style emerged as a reaction to the narrow class appeal of education, to the use of advertising by big business, and to the social changes upsetting the older communal politics. Advertised campaigns, like sensational journalism, were a response to liberalism, a challenge to the political style of the reformers. Interestingly, key architects of the new politics rejected liberal reform. William Jennings Bryan, the first great public campaigner, defeated Cleveland and his followers to take power in the Democratic party. McKinley and Hanna, loyal party men, steadfastly opposed independence. Theodore Roosevelt, like Pulitzer, abandoned early liberal associations and became a savage critic of independent reform.[149]

These antipathies were important but they only begin to explain the reaction against liberalism. The educational style was notable for its roots in a single, rather small segment of Northern society; advertised politics, for its emergence simultaneously from different, even conflicting social groups. To be sure, the new style paid tribute to the cultural power of corporate America. Political managers at the turn of the century slavishly copied the techniques of big business. Yet advertised politics cannot simply be seen as a product of the corporations. Neither can it be treated as just one more consequence of the era of Republican domination ushered in by McKinley and Hanna in 1896. Social and political enemies created the advertised style. The advertised politics of personality owed as much to Bryan, the radical-sounding champion of rural America, as it did to McKinley and Hanna, the conservative representatives of Northern big business.

The catholic origins of the advertised campaign suggest that after 1892 politicians of every stripe recognized the need to move beyond the liberals' educational approach. Like the sensational journalists, Republican and Democratic managers sought instinctively to reconstitute a broad, inclusive politics. Their advertised campaigns, by restoring emotion and simplicity to politics, would attract those voters unmoved by the dry appeal of education.

The politicians also turned to advertising to recreate the local intimacy that had supported spectacular campaigns. In 1924 a journalist caught this communal purpose of advertised politics:

> Interpreters of our America tell us we are a lonely nation . . . having lost in our vast distances and the tall tiers of our sky-scraper cities that sense of 'living in a neighborhood' which was true of us in colonial days, and is still true of older nations. . . . Certainly, when it comes to politics, our campaigns reflect this sense of hunting for home ties. It is the business of a campaign manager. . .to create a sense of neighborly affection for his candidate. . . . No other country in the world puts half our emphasis on 'personalities.' Having lost touch in a large measure with our neighborhoods, we insist on recreating contact when we vote.

Projecting the politician's personality through all the devices of modern communication, advertised campaigns attempted to foster a national, extra-local community in the service of politics.[150]

Despite the self-confidence of its creators, advertised politics was an ineffective, defensive effort to make use of the forces threatening political involvement. Advertising offered only a false sense of intimacy, an illusory community. The radio, the railroad, and the automobile did more to weaken the experience of community than to strengthen it. The automobile as a source of leisure did more to cut political involvement than the automobile as a vehicle for candidates did to boost popular interest in politics.

The politicians' dilemma was most apparent in their use of the different mediums of mass communication. In shifting emphasis from the documents of the literary bureaus to the press releases of the publicity men, the party managers revealed a loss of mastery. The parties could not control the twentieth-century press as easily as their own printing presses. By promoting a deliberative, less partisan style, Democrats and Republicans helped to undermine their own cultural authority, their ability to speak directly to the people. As the century wore on they had to communicate through mediums increasingly free from their control. A national committee could use records, billboards, movies, newspaper and magazine ads, and radio to publicize a candidate, but the party was only one of hundreds of advertisers using these mediums. To be sure, such presidents as Theodore Roosevelt and Woodrow Wilson skillfully cultivated the press in order to shape public opinion.[151] Later, Franklin Roosevelt would make inspired use of the radio for his own purposes. But even the most ingenious politicians could not match the parties' easy domination of the press in the mid-nineteenth century.

The innovations of the twentieth century presented other challenges to the parties. Movies, radio, automobiles, newspapers, and advertising diffused the enchantments of leisure and consumption. Each of these mediums helped to overshadow politics as an entertainment. More important, advertising agencies and sensationalist papers directed people's attention to human interest and personalities. From Mark Hanna onward, the parties tried to make use of this development, too. Spectacular campaigns had turned on emotional party spirit; educational campaigns, on the restrained discussion of issues. The focus of the advertised campaign was personality, not partisanship or argument. Politicians made the presidential campaign into a personal appeal. The nominee began to seem larger than his party and his personality more important than his educational pamphlets. In this way, advertised campaigns undercut both the emotional partisanship of spectacle and the rational politics of education. The results were disappointing.

7

"THE VANISHING VOTER"

While Republican and Democratic managers confidently set about perfecting the advertised campaign, more and more Americans turned away from politics. The election of 1896 established a new political style and an era of Republican domination, but the campaign did not foreshadow popular political participation in the new century. In this respect, it was the dull election of 1892, not the excitement of 1896, that marked out the course of early twentieth-century politics. Like the educational campaign in 1892, the new mix of advertising and education failed to stir the people. Indications of their political withdrawal became clearer with each presidential election from 1900 to 1920.

When McKinley and Bryan faced each other again in 1900, there were plentiful signs that people did not find the rematch as exciting as the first confrontation in 1896. Instead of the electricity of the "battle of the standards," there were echoes of 1892.

From around the country came reports of "apathy" and "much less public interest in the canvass than. . .four years ago." "I have never known a National Campaign where there was so little general talk, on the street or in public conveyances, about the result," a man wrote from Cleveland. The apathy told at the polls. Nationwide, 79 percent of the people had voted in 1896; four years later, turnout fell off to 73 percent.[1]

Reports of apathy were more numerous in 1904 when Alton B. Parker unsuccessfully challenged Theodore Roosevelt. Observers described the canvass as "listless" and "exceedingly quiet." "I have never known a Presidential campaign in which the popular interest was so languid. . .," a correspondent told Roosevelt. Charles G. Dawes wrote in his diary, "There is much apathy on the part of the public as regards the campaign—more than I have ever seen before. . . ." On election day, only 65 per cent of the voters cast ballots nationwide.[2]

The election of 1904 set the pattern for the next sixteen years. Each presidential election brought reports of apathy and low turnout. In 1908 the *Review of Reviews* called the race between William Howard Taft and William Jennings Bryan "apathetic beyond all previous experience." "I find little or no enthusiasm anywhere," wrote a traveler in the Midwest. "Never saw as much apathy in a presidential year." There was "apathy," too, in upstate New York and in Maine; out West, one politician discovered "lethargy" in Nevada. Surveying the nation, the *New York Times* described the "DULLEST CAMPAIGN IN QUARTER CENTURY." Still, turnout held steady at the low figure of 1904—65 percent.[3]

In 1912 and 1916, Woodrow Wilson's victories did little to rouse the electorate. Each year, people seemed more apathetic than ever before. "This Presidential campaign bids fair to be famous for general apathy beyond any campaign for forty years. . .," a reader wrote in to the *New York Tribune* in 1916. "No excitement, no interest, no deep concern over what may happen at the polls." "I have never seen a time when the general public was so indifferent to the outcome of a national election," agreed the president of Columbia University, Nicholas Murray Butler. After holding up in 1908, turnout dropped down to 59 percent in 1912 and recovered only slightly to 62 percent in 1916.[4] Four years later, the drop resumed. When Warren G. Harding defeated James M. Cox in 1920, newspaper headlines once again told repeatedly of "APATHY" in this "DEADEST CAMPAIGN."[5] Turnout plunged nationally to just 49 percent.

By the 'twenties, a massive political withdrawal had occurred across the country. Much of it took place in the South, where disfranchisement between 1890 and 1910 had torn the vote away from blacks and many poor whites. Average Southern turnout at presidential elections, 64 percent from 1876 to 1892, fell to 32 percent from 1900 to 1916 and then to just 20 percent in the campaigns of 1920 and 1924. Even in the North, where there was nothing like disfranchisement, people had abandoned the ballot box. After reaching 83 percent in 1896 and 1900, average Northern turnout at presidential elections moved down to 65 percent from 1900 to 1916 and then to only 58 percent in 1900 and 1924. Voting decreased for elections at all levels. Turnout for off-year Congressional contests fell off from 70 percent in 1894 and 1896 down to 42 percent by 1922 and 1926. In the 'twenties, perhaps a fourth of all eligible Northerners never cast a ballot. The non-voters came disproportionately from the ranks of newly enfranchised women, young people, immigrants and their children, and the poor.[6]

As remarkable as the drop in voting was the reluctance of politicians and journalists to acknowledge what was happening. Before 1920 they paid little attention to "apathy" and falling turnout.[7] Dismissing the indifferent mood of the people, party managers and editorial writers pointed to large voter registration figures and the excitement of the last few days of an election as proof of the public's real interest.[8] The politicians and the press saw in quiet elections an indication of the modern code of political conduct introduced by the educational campaign. The lack of public excitement, they argued, meant no lack of interest: the people had simply weighed candidates and issues carefully in private. "People. . . . are not indifferent because they are not shaking their fists in the faces of their neighbors and in other ways showing undue excitement," the *New Haven Journal Courier* wrote in 1908. "If it means anything it means that men have independently thought the situation out . . . and have made up their minds what to do. It is a healthy electorate which acts this way. . . ." Assessing the campaign of 1916, a politician declared, "The day of red fire and shouting is over; the people want to take up the problems in a more serious manner, and when they have reached a conclusion they will cast their ballots."[9]

The apathy and low turnout for the presidential election of 1920 upset these confident assertions. With just half the electorate voting, popular "apathy" could no longer be easily dismissed. A headline in the *Philadelphia Inquirer* told the story: "APATHY OF VOTERS DISMAYS LEADERS."[10]

The low turnout of 1920 started a public debate with an aura of unreality. The political withdrawal of the poor should have pleased the middle and upper classes. Instead, the discovery of "non-voting" touched off a round of lamentation in the 'twenties. Ignoring the poor, well-to-do Americans worried whether enough of the right sort of people cast ballots. The same fears of middle- and upper-class impotence that had animated the liberal disfranchisers of the 1870s now drove the privileged men and women of Calvin Coolidge's America to a new cause. Intent on preserving their power and saving the nation, respectably middle-class and wealthy people used non-partisan educational and advertised campaigns to urge "non-voters" to the polls. Founded on a misperception of the electorate, confined by the limitations of political style, the "Get-Out-the-Vote" movement became an ironic apostrophe to the decline of popular politics.

The debate over non-voting in the 'twenties was largely harmonious. The participants never disagreed fundamentally over the reasons men and women failed to vote, but academic writers on the one hand, and politicians and journalists on the other, drew quite different conclusions from the rise of non-voting. Grounded on some accurate perceptions of the electorate, the discussion ended nevertheless in unwarranted assumptions and apocalyptic warnings.

After 1920, few political observers tried to explain away the decline in mass political interest reflected in non-voting. Unlike some later analysts of political participation, writers in the 'twenties seldom treated diminishing turnout figures as no more than a statistical by-product of the decrease of supposedly massive electoral frauds.[11] Only occasionally did commentators attribute non-

voting principally to the enfranchisement of women and the disfranchisement of Southern blacks.[12] Nearly all of the discoverers
of non-voting recognized that the problem involved white males
as well.

Social scientists and historians produced the most careful studies of falling turnout. In their work they touched on many—but
not all—of the forces affecting popular political participation. In
1924 Charles Merriam and Harold Gosnell, political scientists
at the University of Chicago, published *Non-Voting*, the first
important study of declining turnout. Drawing on interviews
with adults who had not voted in Chicago's mayoral election of
1923, Merriam and Gosnell found that illness or absence from the
city deterred one-quarter of the non-voters, registration difficulties and other administrative obstacles kept another 13 percent
from the polls, and "disbelief in voting," "inertia," or "general
indifference" stopped over half the sample. Women and the
young, Merriam and Gosnell noted, were particularly likely to give
some form of indifference or disbelief as their reason for failing
to vote. Poor people, the political scientists also implied, seemed
less likely to vote than the well-to-do.[13] In 1925 another political
scientist, Ben Arneson, published an article based on data for the
entire electorate of Delaware, Ohio, at the previous year's presidential election. A smaller percentage of the poor and uneducated, Arneson discovered, had voted than of the wealthy and well
educated. Arneson disputed "[t]he prevailing impression that
those living in the less desirable parts of the community are more
likely to exercise their suffrage rights than the residents of other
sections. . . ."[14]

There was more disagreement over the broader causes of non-
voting. In "The Vanishing Voter," an article published in 1924,
the historians Arthur M. Schlesinger and Erik M. Eriksson
attacked the emphasis of advertised politics on personality. They
noted that elections featuring "compelling . . . personalities" such
as Blaine in 1884 and Roosevelt in 1904 and 1912 produced lower
turnouts. In contrast, elections with sharply defined issues as in
1888 and 1896 produced higher turnouts. The turnout data, the
historians argued, ran "counter to the common assumption that
the average American is more interested in magnetic or spectacular personalities than in basic principles." Schlesinger and Eriks-

son also underscored the weakness of the educational style. They observed that turnout continued to fall even though "every presidential canvass since 1896 has involved an elaborate 'campaign of education'. . . ."

Schlesinger and Eriksson were uncertain whether membership in a particular class affected people's decision to vote. "The Vanishing Voter" weighed the Australian ballot, black disfranchisement, and women's suffrage and dismissed them as relatively unimportant factors in the decrease of voting. "It is evident that more powerful forces than any yet mentioned are at work," Schlesinger and Eriksson concluded. "In the judgment of the present writers, these basic influences were, first, the lessening differences between the parties, and second, the increasing complexity of modern life." Nineteenth-century Americans found in politics a diversion to fill their leisure hours; twentieth-century Americans, lured by new recreations and business opportunities and pressed for time in "the frantic, overorganized, spectacular, urbanized machine-driven world," had no place for politics in their lives. Politics, in any case, could not be compelling when the parties no longer differed clearly over important issues.[15]

Schlesinger's and Eriksson's article spurred Harold Gosnell to consider the broader influences on voting. In pieces published in 1924 and 1925, he restated the conclusions of *Non-Voting* and introduced a new consideration—the competitiveness of the party system. Contradicting "The Vanishing Voter," Gosnell argued that "it was not so much a lack of issues as it was a lack of competition between the two major parties that led to a falling off of the vote." Voter turnout reached high levels in the late nineteenth century because the Republican and Democratic parties were so evenly matched. By 1920 and 1924, turnout had dropped off because Republican domination of the North and Democratic domination of the South produced few close contests.[16]

The academic discussions of non-voting that appeared in the mid-'twenties touched on some of the principal findings of later students of electoral behavior. The first writers on declining turnout realized that registration laws, education, class, "the increasing complexity of modern life," party differences, and party competition influenced whether men and women cast ballots. They did not recognize the implications of the changing status of parties and partisanship for political life. Schlesinger and Eriksson, in their comments on educational and advertised politics, seemed to reach toward an understanding of the importance of political style. But they did not carry their analysis back in time to examine the significance of spectacular partisan politics for the voters of the nineteenth century. Still, the academic writers of the 'twenties offered a suggestive, largely accurate picture of the contemporary political world. The public, however, did not see that world quite the same way.

Noted by the press, the academic studies of non-voting influenced popular discussion to some extent.[17] But they did not shape public thinking on several key points. Like the academics, commentators and politicians recognized that difficult registration procedures could cut turnout.[18] Writers and party leaders recognized as well that the world's "complexity" competed with politics, though they often reduced this idea to the distractions of the World Series.[19] Commentators also took note of the lack of party competition but placed greater emphasis on the parties' supposed failure to take clear and different stands on issues. "The people at large," said the Democratic party chairman of New York in 1925, "will take no general interest in an election until they can be convinced that the victory of one party or other means something to the Nation."[20] Some men and women argued that the people failed to vote "because politicians don't fulfill promises."[21]

Schlesinger's and Eriksson's ideas about political style had no impact on the discussion of non-voting. Occasionally someone did suggest that the demise of old-fashioned partisan loyalty had cut into turnout. "My experience has been that loyal party members go to the polls without too much compulsion," observed the chairman of the Republican National Committee, William M. Butler, in 1926. "The man who stays at home is generally the one whose party ties are not very binding."[22]

Unlike the academic writers, journalists and politicians had little uncertainty about the identity of the "Vanishing Voter." Virtually all of them wrongly believed that the upper and middle classes voted less than workers. "The gang wards in any large city always cast the highest percentage of votes," Senator Arthur Capper of Kansas declared in 1926. "It is in the sections where the middle class and wealthy live that votes are scarcest." "While the poor man usually casts his ballot regularly," a Republican leader in New York City insisted in 1924, "the businessman often does not bother to go to the polls." Congressman Bertrand Snell of New York agreed that businessmen, "who have gotten the most out of the country as a class, vote less than the other fellows."

Commentators associated different qualities with non-voters and voters. The former were intelligent, well educated, independent-minded, and conservative; the latter were ignorant, uneducated, boss-dominated, and radical. Arthur Capper said that "citizens who should be best informed to vote intelligently, and best circumstanced to vote unselfishly, are the very ones who abstain from voting." "I believe," former Senator Coleman DuPont of Delaware told a reporter in 1924, "that 50 per cent. of the intelligent voters who would naturally favor a retention of our system of government and oppose all radical innovations never go to the polls, while the radicals not only never fail to vote but give their time as soap box orators trying to influence others to follow them in their attacks upon orderly government." The writer Kenneth Roberts found "the great mass of the people in the United States . . . strongly and determinedly conservative." But he lamented that "the extremists, the radicals, the fanatics, the people who are supporting passionate causes, are always numbered among the voters . . . controlled by the cheap ward politician. . . ." The most powerful public conception about political participation, the image of the wealthy or middle-class non-voter and the poor voter decisively shaped the response to the decline of turnout in the 'twenties.[23]

Journalists and politicians, certain of the identity of the "Vanishing Voter," were equally sure of the meaning of non-voting. They saw the fall in turnout as a threat to democracy and to the nation itself. "Indifferent voters are more dangerous than communists or kings," the *Chicago Tribune* stated in 1924. "They are passive resistance to government." For the *Tribune*, "The Menace of Nonvoters" conjured up visions of "evil and decay," "political sterility," and "race suicide." The same year, the *New York Herald Tribune* called non-voting "a canker. . .eating at the roots of democracy." Should turnout continue to fall, the Democratic presidential nominee, John W. Davis, warned in 1924, "free government is inevitably doomed."[24]

The discoverers of non-voting feared rule by "minorities" or an "oligarchy" as a consequence of popular political withdrawal. "Indifference in the attitude of the American public. . . ," Vice President Charles G. Dawes told the American Legion in 1926, "is tending to substitute government by aggressive and interested minorities for government by the people."[25] Some critics of non-voting believed it would produce rule by party bosses. Ogden L. Mills, the Republican nominee for governor of New York in 1926, warned "that neglect of the ballot led straight to machine control of the Government." Others viewed non-voting as a spur to radicalism of the left—"Bolshevism"—and even of the right—fascism.[26]

For those who spoke and wrote about declining turnout, non-voting was a moral problem, a failure of responsibility by their own class. Over and over, they compared non-voters to "slackers," men who avoided conscription in World War One. Like the draft dodger, the "civic slacker" seemed to be a traitor to class and country.[27]

Delinquent middle and upper classes, a threatened country—these were the perceptions that defined the response to non-voting in the 1920s. For men and women alarmed by falling turnout, the remedy seemed clear: Americans, conservative and respectable, had to return to the polling booth. "The true answer to the question of how to offset the success of minorities in cramming their bogus reforms down America's esophagus," wrote Kenneth Roberts, "lies in bringing enough of America's inarticulate conservatives to the polls to send the radicals back to the tall timbers, whence they could never have emerged if the people of the country had taken the proper interest in the business of government."[28]

To get these conservatives to the polls, the foes of non-voting turned to legislation and exhortation. Some commentators, particularly the academic writers, urged the removal of legal obstacles in order to raise turnout. If people could register and vote easily, more of them would go to the polls. Accordingly, Merriam, Gosnell, and other writers suggested simpler registration procedures, shorter ballots, and voting by mail for residents as well as absentees. Some states and communities did simplify registration and voting and allowed absentees to vote by mail in the 'twenties. But these efforts received little attention. Dry and technical, they did not satisfy the emotional needs of a public stirred by worries over slackers, bosses, and bolsheviks.[29]

Favoring sterner measures, a number of opponents of non-voting turned to the old remedy of compulsory voting. "It is futile to speak of methods of enticing the voter to the polls," one advocate of compulsory voting explained. "The time has come when we must cease indulging in the fond hope that we can educate the public through a sense of patriotism to vote." Instead, government should use the coercive power of the law to force people to the polls. In support of their arguments, proponents of compulsory voting pointed to the example of mandatory suffrage legislation in such countries as Belgium and Czechoslovakia. The draft of World War One also offered a precedent for using the power of the state to deal with civic slackers. "We conscript the citizenry for duty in time of war"; reasoned the author of a compulsory voting bill, "why not conscript them to the duty of citizenship, in time of peace?"[30]

Compulsory voting, its advocates maintained, would cripple bosses and radicals. In New Jersey, Republican legislators proposed a compulsory voting bill during 1926 in order "to weaken the Democratic machine" by forcing Republicans to vote. In Chicago, on the other hand, a writer urged compulsory voting to strike at the left. "Radicalism and every other political folly could be pushed forever into the background if we would wake up and install total-vote government," he promised. "For it is an axiom that there is no more safely conservative force in a country than the voice of the whole people." Throughout the 'twenties, legislators and citizens suggested schemes stipulating taxes, fines, jury duty, and even imprisonment and disfranchisement for adults neglecting to vote. Some people demanded punishment for states as well as individuals through proposals for proportional representation. As in Austria, seats in Congress or the Electoral College would be based on the number of votes cast in a state rather than on its population.[31]

All the proposals for compulsory voting in the 'twenties apparently failed. The plans provoked interest but also an awareness of the incongruity of forcing people to exercise the freedom of choice. "Compulsory civic pride," one critic put it, "is a contradiction in terms." Charles Merriam and others noted the difficulty of enforcing a compulsory voting law. Opponents of compulsion mocked, too, the idea of disfranchising non-voters. "As a punishment," wrote the *New York Times*, "it would be only deprivation of a right for the exercise of which they have little or no inclination." To many commentators, compulsory voting seemed unworkable. "One thing is certain," the *Outlook* declared. "You will never force a man to vote by making a law to punish him if he doesn't—or rather, he will vote once just to overthrow that law." Objections such as this doomed compulsory voting. In the 'twenties Americans would not use the force of law to solve the problem of falling turnout.[32]

Abandoning compulsion, academics and others troubled by non-voting turned to moral suasion. A more popular course, exhortation suited the public temper. But there was disagreement over the proper means of encouraging people to vote.

Merriam, Gosnell, Schlesinger, Eriksson, and some journalists preferred to increase turnout by educating the public. They advocated a dispassionate publicity campaign that would inform voters about registration dates and procedures and perhaps also candidates and issues. To test this idea scientifically, Gosnell studied the effects of mailing registration and voting notices to a sample of Chicago voters before the presidential election in 1924 and a local election in 1925. His sample, Gosnell discovered, had turned out somewhat more fully than a group that had not received reminders to register and vote. Gosnell's study, published in 1927 as *Getting Out the Vote,* commanded little attention; the public had as much interest in controlled mailings as in a shorter ballot, easier registration, and absentee voting. Those alarmed by non-voting wanted something more exciting and dramatic. Merriam and Gosnell feared the results of such an approach. "It is not to be presumed that a series of evangelistic exhortations alone will increase the quantity of voting," they wrote in *Non-Voting.* "The appeal must be made to the intelligence and the interest of the citizen." But "evangelistic exhortations" were just what the foes of non-voting wanted.[33]

While Merriam and Gosnell delivered their warning in 1924, hundreds of thousands of Americans enlisted in the "Get-Out-the-

Vote" movement for the duration of the presidential election. A non-partisan form of advertised politics, the movement expressed more than any other attack on non-voting the tastes and fears of the middle and upper classes. The voting drive of 1924, almost entirely a creation of these groups, became a conservative, patriotic crusade using every publicity device available to encourage the right sort of people to vote. Several organizations started the movement in the summer of 1924. In Washington, D.C., Simon Michelet, a lawyer and veteran of Republican politics, founded the "National Get-Out-the-Vote Club." Michelet planned to sponsor branches of the club in cities and states but made his most significant contribution by publishing articles and pamphlets of statistics on non-voting.[34]

More important, the National Association of Manufacturers (NAM) built a massive publicity campaign around the slogan "Vote as you please, but vote." The NAM printed more than twenty million pamphlets and stickers urging the vote and enlisted the aid of church, civic, and business groups such as the Elks, the Masons, the Rotary Club, the National Association of Credit Men, the American Bankers Association, the American Radio Association, the Motion Picture Producers and Distributors Association, and the Boy Scouts.[35]

The Get-Out-the-Vote movement caught on quickly in the summer and fall of 1924. Party leaders, including the major presidential candidates, endorsed the non-partisan drive.[36] Ministers urged their parishioners to cast ballots.[37] Newspapers asked their readers to register and vote.[38] Boy Scouts, acting as the youthful conscience of the nation, distributed posters and literature from the NAM and implored their elders to go to the polls.[39] The League of Women Voters held conferences, visited voters in their homes, and sent out an "auto caravan" to stimulate political interest.[40] Both the league and *Collier's Weekly* offered awards to the state with the highest turnout. The *Christian Herald* promised a trip to Washington for the minister whose congregation had the highest turnout rate.[41]

Around the country, organizations tried all sorts of publicity stunts to encourage voting. Radio stations broadcast injunctions to vote; movie houses ran slides on voting; and restaurant menus featured voting reminders. Copying a device used in Grand Rapids and other Michigan towns to boost turnout in 1918 and 1919, the Kiwanis Club of Aurora, Illinois, decided to shame non-voters by publicly listing their names, "the same as the names of the slackers . . . during the war." The San Francisco Kiwanis planned to put tags on voters on election day so that the slackers could be recognized and challenged. In Cleveland, a milk company used special bottle caps to remind voters to register. In California and elsewhere people signed pledges as a promise to vote. The Los Angeles Chamber of Commerce founded a "One Hundred Per Cent Register and Vote Club." Hollywood movie actors started chain letters urging recipients to exercise the franchise.[42] In New York City the National Civic Federation (NCF), a meeting ground for the leaders of business, labor, and civic groups, staged a conference on getting out the vote and started the New York Non-Partisan Coordinating Council as an example of how to encourage voting. The council, along with the American Legion, sponsored an "American Patriots Week" in October to help the cause.[43]

Ostensibly impartial, the Get-Out-the-Vote movement seemed to detach the act of voting from considerations of class and party. "Vote as you please. . . ," ran the slogan. But from the start the voting drive of 1924 reflected the values and fears of the middle and upper classes. Although the American Federation of Labor participated in the NCF, workers and working-class organizations never played a visible role in getting out the vote. The movement remained a vehicle for the organizations of the rich and the middle class: the NAM, the American Bankers Association, the Chamber of Commerce, the Kiwanis, and so forth. These groups took the lead because their members feared the loss of political power. "Underlying the movement for getting out the vote is the common belief that precisely the intelligent man, or the man who should be intelligent by reason of economic opportunity and education, refuses to vote," the *New York Times* observed. "The tenement districts turn out on election day, rain or shine. The 'residential' districts play golf. . . ." To encourage the "residential districts" to vote, the movement naturally evoked the favored symbols of those with the largest stake in society: country and commerce. Accordingly, the NCF staged "American Patriots Week" and the NAM and other supporters of the movement likened voters to "stockholders" who should of course attend the "stockholders meeting" of the "corporation" of the United States on election day.[44]

Publicly non-partisan, the Get-Out-the-Vote movement served party as well as class purposes for some of its adherents. Correspondents with the White House assumed that the movement would help defeat the supposedly radical candidacy of the Progressive Robert La Follette and elect Calvin Coolidge, "as it is usually the class who would vote for him that need urging to go to the polls."[45] In membership, language, and aspirations, the Get-Out-the-Vote movement betrayed its roots in conservative America.

In 1924 few people were willing to criticize any effort to increase voter turnout. The *Los Angeles Times* derided the Aurora Kiwanis's plan of publishing the names of non-voters as impractical. More seriously, a reporter for the *New York Times* attacked the National Get-Out-the-Vote Club's approach to the people: "[Its] method is to preach to them about their duty. Talk is useful so far as it goes, but it is no remedy." Another writer deplored the emphasis on "duty." "If ever we have to do politics just out of a sense of duty, we are at the beginning of the end," he observed. "Yet that is the note—the note of a sense of duty—which begins to be stressed in this modernistic decadent campaign. . . .The effectiveness of politics, like the effectiveness of religion or of anything else, is when you just simply cannot help doing it even if all the world tries, not to urge you to do it, but to prevent you from doing it." In a letter to the editor of the *Des Moines Register,* one man questioned the wisdom of increasing turnout. "Would it not be better," he asked, "if only those who are actually sufficiently interested in public affairs to inform themselves regarding the issues of the campaign were to vote?" Such criticism raised important questions but hardly interrupted the campaign to get out the vote.[46]

For all the enthusiasm of its supporters, the voting drive proved a disappointment. To most commentators, the electorate appeared as "apathetic" as ever.[47] On election day, sirens blew, church bells rang, and Boy Scouts bugled the people to the polls. In Newark, New Jersey, telephone operators asked callers, "Have you voted?"[48] Across the country, only 49 percent of the electorate had cast ballots, about the same as four years before. Still, the leaders of the Get-Out-the-Vote movement did not admit failure.

Ralph Easley, chairman of the NCF's executive council, found the results disheartening but promised to continue the movement. More optimistic, the president of the NAM claimed that the voting drive "checked the growing apathy of the voters in national elections and started interest in those quadrennial affairs on an upward curve." Predicting the disappearance of non-voting, Simon Michelet declared, "The start is good, the foundation is solid, and we are equipped for a great future work."[49]

After 1924, Michelet continued to publish his pamphlets and the NAM encouraged better "civic performance" at elections.[50] But the focus of the Get-Out-the-Vote movement shifted to the National Civic Federation. Critical of the voting drive of 1924, the NCF hoped to broaden the popular idea of political participation. "Getting out the vote is a very superficial part of practical citizenship work," Ralph Easley wrote in 1926. The real aim of such work, he maintained, should be the creation of "a more enlightened electorate." "You don't merely want numbers on election day," said Ogden L. Mills, a leader of the NCF. "You want an intelligent vote."

Political participation, according to the NCF, entailed not only intelligent voting but party membership as well. Attributing the "Political chaos" of post-war Europe to the Continent's multiparty governments, the NCF urged citizens to help preserve America's two-party system and thereby the state itself: "[S]ince our Government rests primarily upon the foundation of political parties the duty clearly devolves upon every voter to participate in the maintenance of that Government by enrolling himself with a political party and taking an active part in the framing of its policies and in the selection of its candidates for public office." Party membership, Easley believed, could give the voter better candidates and thus a reason to turn out on election day. "Instead of a 'Get Out the Vote' slogan," Easley concluded, "we ought to have a 'Get Into the Party' slogan."[51]

To foster its broader idea of political participation, the NCF founded a "Department of Political Education" in December 1925. Members of the department's executive council of business, labor, civic, and educational leaders included Elihu Root, Charles Evans Hughes, Alton B. Parker, John W. Davis, General John J. Pershing, Eleanor Roosevelt, and, significantly, Charles Merriam.

The NCF's more restrained approach to politics fit in quite well, after all, with the ideas of Merriam and Gosnell. To head its new department, the NCF chose John Hays Hammond, a millionaire mining engineer who had retired to a life of philanthropy and public service. Beginning in 1908, Hammond had tried unsuccessfully to revive the League of Republican Clubs, once the vanguard of educational politics. As that experience suggested, he was well suited to the NCF's plans for a more educational voting drive. Hammond's selection also emphasized that the NCF, even as it charted a new course, had much in common with other leaders of the Get-Out-the-Vote movement. Like so many of the critics of declining turnout, he believed that non-voters "are generally speaking more upright and better informed as to the true interest of the nation" than many voters. Hammond, too, talked of voters as "shareholders" in the "great corporation" of the United States and blamed non-voting for bossism and party corruption.[52]

In 1926, Hammond and the Department of Political Education resolved to boost turnout for the fall congressional elections. Through speeches and press releases, Hammond stressed the importance of political education and party membership. In cooperation with the American Legion, the department appealed to civic organizations to hold local meetings on party enrollment and voter registration.[53] Calvin Coolidge lent presidential support to the vote drive with several messages, including a well-publicized speech to the Daughters of the American Revolution in April. Rejecting compulsory voting and praising the Get-Out-the-Vote movement, Coolidge called non-voting "our greatest danger," which would replace self-government with rule by the representatives of "selfish interests."[54] Despite the efforts of Coolidge and the NCF, turnout for the election fell below the figure for the congressional contests four years before. Disappointed, Hammond lamented that "there is nothing to show for the work of all our organizations in 1926, although it can safely be assumed that without such an effort the results would have been much more disheartening—a negative consolation at best." He even hinted that compulsory voting might be necessary to ensure high turnout in the future.[55]

Hammond soon set aside his disappointment and helped to lead the NCF in a new effort to stimulate political participation during

1927. In July he released a report on non-voting based on a questionnaire sent to civic leaders around the country. Their suggestions covered the range from disfranchisement of non-voters through easier registration requirements to improved political education. The questionnaire gave hints of the class bias of the Get-Out-the-Vote movement. "The laboring man or mechanic needs no appeal to vote," one of Hammond's correspondents wrote. "It is the 'white collar' citizen whose interest in civic government should be stirred. . . ." Another advised, "Discourage, rather than encourage, voting by those who are uninformed or indifferent." Hammond himself blamed "the 1926 debacle" on "General Apathy." Once more he underscored the importance of educating voters and persuading them to join parties. Criticizing the effort of 1926, he demanded "an entirely different campaign,—not one of platform oratory and publicity stunts alone but one of real, intensive individual service."

Hammond and the Department of Political Education planned to reach this goal "through committees on practical citizenship, to be created in each of the more than 100,000 local bodies . . . composing this movement." The model for these committees was New York's "Committee on Active Citizenship," established in February by the NCF, the American Legion, and civic and business groups to spur registration and voting in the city elections.[56] Each committee, Hammond hoped, would have sub-committees devoted to registering voters, studying issues "in a non-partisan way," discussing "non-political questions" such as primary elections and compulsory voting, and enrolling voters in parties.[57]

During 1927 Hammond's Department of Political Education worked, apparently without much success, to set up local committees on practical citizenship and to plan for the next year's presidential election. Turning again in frustration to compulsory voting, Hammond advocated publicly posting the names of non-voters and temporarily disfranchising them—"a stigma of emasculated citizenship to which no self-respecting man would subject himself." Others involved in the voting movement were frustrated as well.

At the annual convention of the NCF in December, Thomas H. Reed, a political scientist from the University of Michigan, surprised his audience by condemning the drive to get out the vote.

"Nothing, in my opinion, can be accomplished by an indiscriminate ballyhoo to bring out the vote," he declared. "Galvanizing ignorant and careless voters into going to the polls is no cure for the real situation." These remarks seemed aimed as much at the tactics of the NAM as the NCF, but Reed also attacked the civic federation's faith in party membership as a solution to voters' withdrawal from politics. "Political parties must stand for something," he said, "before the people will get interested." Hammond and other NCF leaders at the convention rose quickly to defend the Get-Out-the-Vote movement. But Reed's speech, delivered in the citadel of the voting campaign, revealed how vulnerable the movement had suddenly become.[58]

Reed's speech was part of a wave of criticism that began in 1926 and peaked late in 1927. Emboldened by the voting drive's failures, journalists and academics questioned the aims and assumptions of the Get-Out-the-Vote movement. Coolidge's speech to the Daughters of the American Revolution crystallized opposition. In answer to the president, some newspapers blamed non-voting on politicians who failed to serve the people rather than on the electorate. More blunt, the *Nation* found it "a curious fact that these very leaders of the old school who berate the absentee voters never question our institutions and our political methods." "Voters cannot be driven to the polls nor shamed into going there in appreciable numbers," the journal observed. "The remedy lies elsewhere—in the restoration to the voter of faith in the two political parties and in our politics and government." The *Nation* portrayed non-voting not as apolitical "laziness" but as a political act. "Multitudes . . . deliberately refuse to vote because they feel they have nothing to gain by doing so; that the choice lies between representatives of two parties which are both hopelessly corrupt and outworn, between whom there is no essential difference in principle or program. They feel that this is a rich man's country . . . that our institutions . . . are no longer adapted to a nation . . . under the conditions of extreme capitalism."[59]

In 1927 the criticism became sharper. Writers suggested that the aim of the movement was wrong: society should not encourage non-voters to cast ballots. Attacking the NCF's "moaning . . . about the political evil of the voter's apathy," a reader wrote to the *New York Times:* "We ought not to waste a dollar trying to get people to vote who are so little interested in government that they do not care about exercising their franchise. . . . I think the world will go on just the same, and perhaps a little bit better, if we have more well-informed voting and less number voting."[60]

This position was further developed by William B. Munro, the most prominent and prolific critic of the Get-Out-the-Vote movement. Munro, a professor of government at Harvard and president of the American Political Science Association, attacked the movement in a series of speeches and articles in 1927 and 1928. The voting drive, Munro argued, "is based upon the naive assumption that if you only exhort people with sufficient earnestness they can be induced to accept irrational ideas embalmed in the rhetoric of patriotism." He derided hopes of "improving the quality of our elective officials by the simple device of bawling at the voter to come out and vote." For Munro the Get-Out-the-Vote movement was "not merely unscientific but ridiculous . . . pure waste and futility."[61]

Munro seemed willing to promote higher turnout and, to that end, he favored "easier registration, a simpler ballot, less frequent elections, clearer issues, and less evasive party platforms."[62] But the political scientist wanted turnout of the right kind. "It is hard to see," he wrote, "what real service can ever be rendered to the cause of enlightened government by the mere expedient of herding to the polls, with some sort of militant propaganda, a larger number of uninterested, uninformed, reluctant people. . . ."

Munro did not want to encourage non-voters because, unlike leaders of the voting drive, he did not believe the middle and upper classes voted less readily than the poor. Citing Merriam, Gosnell, Arneson, and his own work, Munro criticized "a common impression that chronic non-voters are to be found chiefly in the ranks of the well-to-do, educated people who ought to know better. . . . On the contrary . . . the best showing at the polls is often made by the best neighborhoods." Munro's data allowed him to turn upside-down the rationale of the Get-Out-the-Vote leaders. "Now if this be true," he insisted, "the so-called slacker vote can hardly be looked upon as a 'menace' to anything except the political machine which depends for success upon herding a high percentage of propertyless, semi-illiterate, uninformed and undiscriminating voters to the ballot box on election day." Munro asked slyly, "May it not be that our uplift organizations, in their rabble-rousing campaigns to 'harry the slackers to the polls,' are merely playing into the hands of the boss and doing some of his work for him?"[63]

Munro's opposition to the Get-Out-the-Vote movement also rested on his reservations about universal suffrage. Criticizing the post-war world's "democracy complex," he doubted whether "universal suffrage will always continue to be interpreted as excluding nobody." For his part, Munro favored "eliminating the least intelligent stratum of the applicants for suffrage," particularly because they reproduced faster than the rest of the population. Given the complexity of modern issues, he explained, "It stands to reason. . . that the art of government will soon outrun the mental competence of the lower ranks in the electorate—if it has not already done so." Munro believed in educating voters to improve them, and he even praised, albeit lukewarmly, the educational efforts of Gosnell and the NCF. But Munro placed greater emphasis on the need for intelligence tests to weed out "about twenty per cent" of the electorate. "There are enough of them to swing an election," he worried. "Can rational men be fairly expected to place unwavering faith in a system of suffrage which commits the destinies of a great nation into such hands as these?"[64]

While Munro attacked the Get-Out-the-Vote movement, other critics defended non-voting as a means of protesting rather than enshrining minority government. In an article published in November 1927, A. K. Laing asserted "The Divine Right Not to Vote." Like Munro, he doubted the capabilities of the electorate. "Complete enfranchisement . . . is merely a degraded survival of the world-old rule of force," Laing wrote; "and when a staggering percentage of qualified voters are admittedly moronic, the tyranny of the majority is tyranny of the most sinister sort." Laing believed that ignorant voters had helped bring about rule by bad leaders, "big business," and "high-pressure lobbying of small groups." He yearned for the day when "the best elements"—"disinterested intellectuals which can deal with sum totals of individuals rather than with sum totals of wealth"—would take power. Until then, Laing refused to vote unless "the definitely moronic class" was disfranchised and the educated—"one in twenty at present"—monopolized the ballot box. For the time being, Laing endorsed the "voters' strike" as "the conscious expression of disapproval of the perversion of a high ideal, the deliberate refusal to be party to what seems a colossal stupidity."[65]

The same month that Laing's article appeared, the *New Republic* printed the anonymous "Confessions of a Non-Voter," for whom "voting is a perfectly foolish and futile thing, a complete waste of time." Party machines ruled the country with the support of the "98 percent" of the electorate "swayed by emotion rather than reason." The small number of "intelligent and independent voters" could make no difference by going to the polling booth. But by refusing to vote, they could undermine the political order. "The more clear-headed professional politicians," observed the author of the "Confessions," "agree that if the non-voting habit gets much more prevalent, the failure of the American political system will be so apparent that something radical may be done about it."[66] Writing in 1928, Charles Merz made the same argument. Voting did not necessarily produce better government; nonvoting could compel America's leaders to offer a meaningful politics. "The only realistic hope of changing the system," Merz insisted, "is to let the politicians know that everyone is not pleased with it." For Merz, non-voting was "a good thing."[67]

The debate over getting out the vote did not go much further because, by 1928, the movement had played itself out. The NCF, the NAM, the League of Women Voters, and the Boy Scouts all worked to stimulate turnout for the presidential election, but their efforts did not match the huge drive four years before.[68] The most publicized aspect of the voting campaign in 1928, typical of the assumptions of the Get-Out-the-Vote movement, was a crusade to close golf courses on election day so the wealthy would have no excuse not to vote. No one suggested closing factories and other workplaces.[69]

The Get-Out-the-Vote movement passed quietly away after the election of 1928, partly from criticism and past failures, partly from intellectual exhaustion, and partly from the reinvigoration of politics. Ironically, the movement collapsed just as commentators began to predict that "our decade of political torpor is over." With the contest between Herbert Hoover and Al Smith, issues seemed to divide the parties again and engage the public. The excitement of the election swept away the talk of non-voting.

Turnout moved up to 56 per cent, a sign of the era of broader political participation that would mature during the New Deal.[70]

The election of 1928 quickly covered over a debate that deserved more careful attention. Critics of the Get-Out-the-Vote movement attacked its goals and techniques. Yet both groups shared a common outlook. They cast their debate over democracy in elitist terms. One side wrung its hands over the supposed political dereliction of the middle and upper classes; the other feared the influence of the allegedly "moronic" lower orders. William B. Munro debunked the illusion of middle- and upper-class non-voting, but he hardly drew more democratic conclusions from his insight.

The Get-Out-the-Vote movement and its critics had real differences of course. In their allusions to rule by "minority" and "oligarchy," there were the outlines of a struggle over the pressure-group, special-interest politics that replaced the party-dominated governance of the nineteenth century. Calvin Coolidge and the other pro-business supporters of the Get-Out-the-Vote movement tended to see special interest rule as a future consequence of non-voting. Opponents of the movement like the Nation and A. K. Laing believed government by business interests already existed; non-voting was the means of protesting, not enhancing, that government.

This was an argument among the comfortable and educated—those privileged men and women with access to the nation's newspaper columns and broadcast booths. Neither side had much interest in the place of workers in this new political system. By and large, the debate over non-voting ignored the working-class withdrawal that was perhaps the chief result of the decline of popular politics in the North.

The debate failed as well to get at the critical sources of declining turnout. Above all, most men and women in the 'twenties never understood the significance of the transformation of political styles. By weakening partisanship, educational and advertised politics tore away the bases of popular political participation. Through newspapers and spectacular campaigns, partisanship had initiated the young into politics, simplified public life, invested the act of voting with multiple significance, and made the vote a reflection of enduring party attachments as much as interest in issues, candidates, or close elections. Education and advertising weakened each one of the partisan linkages between people and politics. Liberal reform, independent journalism, and the educational campaign drained party of its legitimacy and emotional content. The reformers' style weakened the doctrine of party loyalty, made politics more a matter of issues than partisanship, and presented a complex, less accessible political world. The advertised style substituted the personal appeal of the candidate for the broader appeal of his party.

Neither style offered an effective means of socializing the young. Twentieth-century campaigns had nothing comparable to the clubs, companies, and spectacles created for boys like Michael Campbell in the 1870s and 'eighties. Too, the mix of education and advertising helped to strip voting of its extra-electoral significance. Elections lost their role as expressions of martial spirit, leisure, personal identity, communal life, and class theater.

By de-emphasizing partisanship, politicians made turnout more dependent on the allure of issues and candidates. To ensure large votes, managers had to be certain those issues and candidates were interesting and exciting. As the complaints about parties and politicians in the 'twenties made clear, there was no such certainty after 1896. Although the point can be argued, the parties probably differed no less over issues in the early twentieth century than in the nineteenth; politicians were probably about as crooked and unresponsive to the people in the new century as in the old. But the virtue of the politicians and the differences between the parties mattered much more in the era of educational and advertised campaigns.

The transformation of political styles alone cannot explain every aspect of the drop in voting across the North in the early twentieth century. A broad, nationwide change, the rise of educational and advertised politics did not account for variations in turnout from state to state, town to town, and precinct to precinct. The new political styles, powerful influences on the whole society, established the context for declining participation just as spectacular partisanship had provided the setting for the record votes of the late nineteenth century. Within that context, other forces could contribute to the fall in turnout.

As many people recognized at the time, various factors undermined turnout. Dominated by the Republican party, the fourth party system seldom presented close election contests. Turnout tended to drop most in areas—especially the Northeast and Midwest—where Republican control was greatest. Voting dropped off particularly in those regions, too, because the Republicans and Democrats proved unable or unwilling to express the ethno-religious divisions of Northern society as fully as in the past.[71] To a small degree, changes in election laws affected turnout. Cumbersome new registration procedures, literacy tests, and the Australian ballot, more complicated than the old party ticket, may have discouraged some Northerners from voting.[72] In addition, a small percentage of the drop in voting in a few areas may simply have reflected a tightening of election procedures that had allowed men to cast and count fraudulent ballots in the nineteenth century.[73] Some factors probably acted more uniformly across the North. The rise of pressure groups and administrative government decreased the importance of parties and elections. The enfranchisement of women, nationwide after ratification of the Nineteenth Amendment in 1920, intensified the fall in turnout.[74]

The change of political style was related to all these developments. Pressure-group politics, registration laws, the Australian ballot, and educational campaigns each had origins in the liberal reformers' rejection of traditional partisanship. The advertised style owed its ascendancy in part to the Republican hegemony established by Hanna and McKinley in 1896. Changing political style reinforced other factors affecting turnout. By robbing parties of cultural authority, education and advertising made it more difficult for them to serve as vehicles of ethno-religious or any other divisions. By de-emphasizing the vote as an expression of enduring party loyalty, the new style made turnout more dependent on the excitement of close contests—just as elections became uncompetitive in the fourth party system.

The development of educational and advertised politics especially affected those groups receiving the vote in the twentieth cen-

tury: women, young adults, first- and second-generation immigrants, and the poor. None of these people underwent the intense
partisan socialization of older members of the electorate. Brought
up in the political world of party papers and spectacular campaigns, the men who came of age before 1900 still voted regularly;
the newly enfranchised, exposed only to education and advertising, did not.

The low turnout by women offered a certain irony. Denied the
vote in the nineteenth century, they played a limited role in the
man's world of popular politics. Not surprisingly, women prepared the food and decorated the halls for rallies.[75] Girls presented flags and banners to marching companies and dressed as
the "Goddess of Liberty" to salute passing parades.[76] Those
parades often included young women on floats and on horseback.
Most of the women in political processions wore dresses to represent the states or Liberty; some wore military-style uniforms.[77]
Women were denied even this marginal public role in the elections
of the twentieth century. Educational and advertised campaigns
exacerbated women's separation from political life. Like their
brothers, young women had the vote but little socialization into
politics.[78]

Immigrants and the poor suffered particularly from the emergence of new political styles. Independent journalism, pressure
groups, and educational campaigns had only a narrow class
appeal. The liberal style, dispassionate and intellectual, was the
province of the privileged middle and upper classes. Uneducated
men and women, especially those just learning English, were con-
signed to the personalities, slogans, and excitements of advertised
campaigns and sensational newspapers. To be sure, the spectacular partisanship of the nineteenth century had also stirred up emotion and simplified issues. But popular politics tied partisan display to long expositions of public questions in papers and
speeches. Thought and emotion were bound up in a single political style accessible to all. In the twentieth century, the two were
split apart in separate styles. The educated middle and upper
classes, well suited to both, found it relatively easy to comprehend
politics and participate in public life. The poor and uneducated
were mostly restricted to a single mode of political expression, one

that avoided pressure groups and regular voting for intermittent involvement in sensational crusades and exciting elections.

The different styles and turnout rates of the classes were one sign of the decline of popular politics. Northern public life no longer seemed to embrace all classes. In the nineteenth century, rich and poor worked out their relations in the intimate setting of campaign clubs and marching companies. More broadly, ratifications, craft displays, and pole-raisings celebrated popular rights and the power of the people. By the 1920s these rituals had virtually disappeared, and with them the sense that politics entailed the visible assent of the governed and an acknowledgment of their worth as free men. Elections now centered on candidates and their national headquarters rather than on the people of the North's communities. Political style separated rather than drew together different classes. Forsaking clubs and companies, party leaders addressed farmers and workers from a distance, with the help of pamphlets, billboards, and radio broadcasts. Many of the poor, and some of the better-off as well, abandoned the game entirely and stayed home on election day.

The decline of popular politics in the North was not the result of a direct, pre-meditated assault by the wealthy. Despite the liberals' interest in suffrage restriction in the 1870s, Northern leaders never joined the Southern upper class in disfranchising the poor by violence, intimidation, and legislation. To a considerable degree, the gradual drop in turnout across the North reflected the region's capitalist development. Changes in the forms of communication and leisure, in class relations and communal life, and in the practices of business all affected the parties and cut into Northerners' interest in politics and voting. But the decay of political participation was not simply the accidental product of impersonal social forces undirected by human agency. The same class predicament that led the reformers to explore suffrage restriction brought them to attack partisanship and its supporting institutions. From the 1860s to the 1920s, the middle and upper classes of the North diminished the role of parties and party spirit in public life and drew up new rules of political conduct. Partisanship lay at the heart of popular politics; the weakening of the one undermined the other.

Well-to-do Northerners never quite understood what they had done. Popular politics embraced ideas long out of fashion by the 'twenties: partisanship, emotion, simplicity, community, and celebration of the people. The NCF did recognize at least some of the importance of parties in American politics. Still, the organization's effort to boost party membership was more an attempt to make the Republicans and Democrats conform to the liberals' ideal of purified government rather than a restoration of nineteenth-century partisanship. Children of the educational and advertised styles, the men and women of the 'twenties did not accurately perceive the politics of past or present. The failure of the Get-Out-the-Vote movement was testimony to that misperception. Even though most privileged Northerners did not set out to limit political participation, even though they misunderstood the transformation around them, their aspirations and actions destroyed popular politics.

8

CONCLUSION

Foreshadowed in 1928, the renewal of political interest became apparent in the 'thirties. The Depression and the New Deal sent many Northerners back to the polls.[1] Turnout in the North climbed to an average of 70 percent in the presidential elections of 1932, 1936, and 1940; turnout for the off-year congressional elections from 1930 to 1938 moved upward more modestly to 52 percent. Voting increased across the region. The most notable contributions to the growth in turnout came from immigrants, second-generation Americans, and the young.

The revival of voting was an indication of the parties' continuing ability to animate political life. Out of the elections of 1928 and 1932 emerged a new party system, the fifth, composed of new coalitions of Republican and Democratic voters. Elections in the fifth system were more competitive than in the fourth. The parties also articulated social divisions more clearly. In 1928 the contest between the Irish Catholic Al Smith and the Yankee Protestant Herbert Hoover reflected the strong ethnic and religious tensions of twentieth-century America.[2] In the 'thirties the parties split over economic policy, over the impact of the New Deal. The Democrats' strength rested in large measure on their appeal to working-class voters. More than ever, the Republicans had become a party of the wealthy and the comfortable.

Despite the increase in voting and the resurgence of party competition, the New Deal did not mark a return to the popular politics of the nineteenth century. Turnout during the 'thirties never reached the record heights of the 1880s and 1890s. After the stimulus of the Depression, the New Deal, and the creation of the fifth party system, voting leveled off. Sixty-seven percent of eligible Northerners cast ballots in the presidential elections from 1944 to 1960; 49 percent turned out for the off-year congressional contests from 1942 to 1958. After 1960, turnout plunged dramatically. The average vote for president from 1964 to 1980 was 61 percent; off-year congressional turnout fell to an average of 46 percent during the period 1966–78. The votes for the presidential elections of 1976 and 1980—58 and 53 percent respectively— even dropped to the historic lows of the 'twenties.

Electoral politics after 1928 did not draw strongly on all classes. Although turnout increased among the unemployed and those on relief in the 'thirties, there was no sustained mobilization of the poor. During the 'sixties, Southern blacks won back the right to vote. But into the 'eighties, Americans with the smallest incomes and, particularly, those with the least education had the lowest turnout at elections.[3] Neither did the half-century after 1928 resurrect the nineteenth-century style of popular politics. There were no important rituals comparable to the old ratifications, pole-raisings, craft displays, and marching companies. From the 'thirties to the 'eighties politics turned increasingly on leaders and government. The more active the state became, the less conspicuous were the people in communities.

Partisanship, temporarily invigorated in the 'thirties, continued to lose its hold on public life. Fewer and fewer Americans remained loyal to a party; more and more considered themselves independents. The parties played a less significant role in government; party organizations became less powerful. By the 1980s, even the big city machines, the last bastions of traditional party politics, had crumbled. Turning away from old-fashioned partisanship, many Americans practiced the less partisan educational style of politics through pressure groups, lobbyists, and political action committees. Education remained the quintessential expression of the educated middle and upper classes, but beginning in the 'thirties, labor unions, the organized minority of the working class, adopted the style as well.[4]

From the 'thirties to the 'eighties, politicians also refined the advertised politics of personality. Political campaigns focused less and less on party symbols and more on candidates. First radio in the 'twenties and then television in the 'fifties enabled political managers to advertise their candidate and merchandise his personality. The revival of the presidential primary after World War Two furthered the emphasis on the candidate and the importance of his personal organization. The national party committees found their traditional role of campaign management threatened in the 'fifties by outside advertising agencies and virtually usurped in the 'sixties and 'seventies by political consultants. By then, advertised politics, born at the turn of the century, was full-grown.[5]

Of course, politics in the 'eighties did not simply replicate the political style of the early twentieth century. But the logic of our contemporary public life was already apparent by the 1920s. After World War Two, politicians, ad men, and consultants did not inaugurate something fundamentally new; rather, they offered an elaboration, certainly more sophisticated and thorough-going, of a politics already in place for at least fifty years. We cannot fully understand American public life in the 'eighties without recognizing its origins in the decline of popular politics that began in the North before the turn of the century.

Even granting the importance of long-ago campaigns and conflicts in shaping contemporary political style, we still may wonder whether the end, some fifty or sixty years ago, of an electoral politics clearly embracing all classes has deeply affected American society. Why should it matter if millions of people do not vote? The question arises so easily in part because it is a matter of intangibles hardly amenable to empirical testing. No social scientist can declare that for each decrease of x percentage points in turnout there is a corresponding change of y percentage points in the representative or democratic character of society. We can note some telling hints about the value of the vote, particularly in the liberal reformers' hostility to universal suffrage after the Civil War. We note, too, an interesting relationship between turnout and activist government. The more government has intruded in the lives of Americans, the less they have used the vote, one of their principal means of affecting the state. We can wonder whether the waning of political participation was not, in some way, a prerequisite for the active state of the twentieth century, whether politicians did more for the people only when relieved of popular electoral pressure.

Still, there is no satisfying proof here, only supposition and inference. We do not have the violence of disfranchisers and the anguish of their victims, as in the nineteenth-century South, to tell us that the vote means something, that its loss is a tragedy for a people. Accordingly, discussion proceeds in a vacuum. Some scholars, ignoring evidence of corruption, inequality, and repression, romanticize the era of high turnouts in the nineteenth century as a democratic golden age. Others, like the critics of the Get-Out-the-Vote movement sixty years ago, believe it is just as well that the disadvantaged do not cast ballots. Not a few people dismiss voting and elections altogether as an insubstantial political sideshow.

The decline of popular politics did have at least one tangible consequence of enduring importance. As voter turnout fell in the twentieth century, significant challenges to conventional politics diminished. Paradoxically, the era that most celebrated loyalty to the two major parties produced the most serious radical alternatives to them: the Greenbackers, the Knights of Labor, the Populists, and, at the end, the Socialists. There is no coincidence here, but rather a connection, a vital one too often overlooked. Partisanship helped create and sustain radicalism.

Popular politics was both confining and liberating. Obviously, partisanship held men in thrall; party spirit made it difficult for them to break from conventional politics and forge alliances that crossed barriers of class, culture, and race. Yet popular politics also provided the basis of liberation and revolt. In the nineteenth century generations of men grew up habituated to political organization and action. They were not passive observers who watched politics on television and then perhaps cast ballots. Nineteenth-century voters created popular politics in the streets of cities and the fields of the countryside. When these men broke free from the Republican or the Democratic party, they took with them a valuable inheritance: a knowledge of organization and, more important, an understanding that all the people could act politically.

The third-party movements of the late nineteenth century and even the early twentieth century drew freely on this inheritance. To be sure, all were critical of the major parties and traditional partisanship. Partly because they lacked money for uniformed companies and parades, third parties often attacked spectacular display. In 1876 a Greenback editor supporting Peter Cooper for the presidency took note of the Democrats' and Republicans' torchlight parades. "This kind of campaigning the Greenbackers cannot enter into as they have no banks, officeholders or office-seekers to levy upon for the necessary funds," the editor wrote. "Peter Cooper has to depend upon reason, logic and common sense for votes rather than upon display, the tooting of horns and illuminations."[6]

Trying to spread new ideas, third parties naturally relied on pamphlets and literature. But the third parties, middle-class and working-class alike, did not pursue a liberal politics of education. Their political style was based firmly on the tradition of spectacular partisanship, which enfolded literature within the emotional display of communal ritual. In 1884 working-class Anti-Monopolists wore badges and staged banner-raisings to boost Benjamin F. Butler for president. The same year the nativist American Political Alliance, apparently a more middle-class party, outfitted its followers with "campaign equipments" for street parades.[7] For the presidential elections of 1884, 1888, and 1892, the Prohibitionists, also rather middle class, wore uniforms and held banner-raisings.[8]

The use of spectacle by the middle-class third parties perhaps seemed unsurprising; the importance of traditional partisan ritual and organization for the People's party of the 1890s, probably the most broad-based radical movement in the United States, was more arresting. The Populists often drew on the heritage of the major parties. Many a Populist orator supported his unconventional demands for a greenback paper currency or the regulation of railroads by invoking Jefferson, Jackson, or Lincoln. The campaigns of the People's party in the 'nineties also revealed a debt to the old partisan style. Of course, Populists made it clear they were no longer slaves to the major parties. In 1891, a Populist editor in Kansas told the state's dominant Republican party "that noise and smoke, brass bands and 'oratory' have had their day. The people of Kansas now have opinions of their own, which are based upon a careful study of the politics of the past, and the economic questions involving the future welfare of the country; and all the smoke and noise and speeches of the 'big orators' will fail to win them back to the 'grand old party.'"[9]

Defying the Republicans and Democrats, the People's party had every intention of using "smoke and noise and speeches" for its own purposes. In 1892, while the major parties proclaimed the "campaign of education," the Populists tried to elect the presidential ticket of James B. Weaver and James G. Field with a canvass conducted in the tradition of partisan spectacle. The Populists did circulate tracts and pamphlets; the party also benefited from the years of discussion in local branches of the Farmers' Alliance.[10] But literature did not dominate the Populists' campaign as it did the electioneering of the Republicans and Democrats. The tracts and pamphlets of the People's party were balanced by ceremony and display, demonstrations of the collective strength of the people. Wherever the Populists were numerous, they formed campaign clubs and staged parades and rallies with songs, glee clubs, bands, fireworks, and banners. In rural areas, all-day rallies, begun by processions of farmers in their wagons, directly echoed the Republicans' gatherings for Abraham Lincoln in 1860.

The rally of the Populists of Washington, Kansas, in August typified the rituals of the People's party. The affair began with "a long procession . . . from town to the grove, each Alliance and People's party club carrying an appropriate banner, something that reminded the old people of another time when a new party was formed for the purpose of righting great wrongs." For two days, the assemblage heard speeches, listened to band music, and sang songs. The people also declared their loyalties by wearing campaign buttons. "Nearly everybody, men, women and children, wore the same kind of a badge bearing the portraits of Weaver and Field, and 'One Country and one Flag,' also the motto, 'Equal rights to all, special privileges to none,'" wrote an onlooker. "That was the popular badge, and there were thousands of them worn." With such references to Thomas Jefferson and the founding of the Republican party, the Populists used the communal ritual of popular politics to break free from the old parties.[11]

The Populists were almost the last organized, broad-based movement to do so. The Progressive parties of 1912 and 1924 stayed close to the ideas and campaign practices of the major parties.[12] After the turn of the century the Socialist party flourished until World War One. Emerging in the world of educational and advertised politics, much of the Socialist movement had to draw on the experiences immigrant workers brought from their own countries. In the Southwest in particular, Socialism also grew out of Populism and the last vestiges of an indigenous tradition of popular politics. But the party showed as well the marks of the new styles that dominated Republican and Democratic campaigns. In the new century the Socialists seemed to move toward a candidate-centered politics of personality. "The Socialists are doing something they have not been accustomed to do before in their canvass for votes," wrote a visitor to New York City's Lower East Side in 1908. "They are adopting the methods of the established parties and decorating shop windows and fronts of fire escapes and tenement house facades with lithographs of their candidates." Across the state, Socialist candidates for state office campaigned from automobiles, just like the Republican and Democratic nominees. Even the Socialist candidate for president, Eugene V. Debs, toured the country that year in a decorated train called the "Red Special."[13]

After the Socialist party collapsed, Americans generated hardly any significant radical political movements. The Communist Party of America never became a mass organization of importance.[14] In the 'thirties, Huey Long and Father Coughlin led short-lived crusades. But the two men did not represent the popular political style so much as the advertised politics of charismatic leaders and clever media campaigns.[15] By then, Americans had clearly lost touch with a tradition of popular political involvement, organization, and activity.

Historians of protest have tended to deny the importance of this tradition. For them, major-party politics was only repressive and confining, something workers and farmers had to escape for the purer atmosphere of their own organizations. These historians rightly emphasize the importance of the separate collective experience, away from the institutions of the dominant culture, in fostering radicalism. Each movement had to create its own organization in which to nurture a distinctive ideology, a hardy unity, a vital "movement culture." So, in the late nineteenth century, the Populists drew strength from the Farmers' Alliance and local workers' parties grew from assemblies of the Knights of Labor.[16]

There is much that is right in this view. The major parties surely were confining. Certainly, a critical stage in the establishment of a radical political movement was the creation of its own institutions. But why could workers and farmers undertake the difficult task of creating political movements so much more readily in the late nineteenth century? The answer lies not in the alliances and assemblies but in the experiences of these men and women in the two major parties. Recognition of the importance of separate organizations for workers and farmers should not blind us to the radical potential of ideas, institutions, and traditions that were part of the dominant culture. Partisan, popular politics was a broad, rich heritage that could be used by Americans for diverse purposes. So the Populists of Washington, Kansas, took campaign spectacle, a creation of the major parties, and wielded the old ritual against the Republicans in August 1892. It would be wrong simply to dismiss nineteenth-century politics as the "coffin of class consciousness"—purely a middle- and upper-class trap for the unwary poor.[17] This interpretation leads us away from an understanding of the full significance of popular politics in the nineteenth century. Equally important, this view keeps us from recognizing the implications of the demise of that nineteenth-century political world.

Here was the principal consequence of the decline of popular politics: the end of a system that confined people but still gave them a means of political liberation. Partisan politics in the nineteenth century was not necessarily more democratic than the less-partisan politics of this century. It is by no means clear that workers and farmers, through the parties, could make better lives for themselves before 1900 than after. But politics a hundred years ago made it easier for men to envision new alternatives and organize to bring them to life. With the rise of educational and advertised campaigns and the fall of voter turnout, the potential for radical politics seemed to diminish. The transformation of political style entailed more than a change in the superficial aspects of politics. A heritage of popular political action and initiative disappeared along with the record turnouts and torchlight parades.

NOTES

Abbreviations

AS	Ashtabula Sentinel; Semi-Weekly Ashtabula Sentinel
BC	Bangor Daily Commercial
BS	Baltimore Sun
BT	Boston Evening Transcript
BTe	Bridgeport Telegram
CIO	Chicago Daily Inter Ocean
CPD	Cleveland Daily Plain Dealer
CRH	Chicago Record-Herald
CTi	Chicago Times
CTr	Chicago Daily Tribune; Chicago Press and Tribune
DMR	Des Moines Register
DN	Detroit Evening News
EID	Elyria Independent Democrat
GSFP	Granite State Free Press
HC	Hartford Courant
HT	Hartford Times
IFT	Idaho Falls Times
KCS	Kansas City Evening Star
KT	Kokomo Daily Tribune
LAT	Los Angeles Daily Times
MJ	Minneapolis Journal
MT	Minneapolis Tribune
NCF	National Civic Federation
NHJC	New Haven Morning Journal and Courier
NHN	New Haven Morning News
NHP	New Haven Daily Palladium

220

NHR   New Haven Daily Register; New Haven Evening Register
NHU   New Haven Evening Union
NN   Newark Evening News
NYH   New York Herald
NYHT   New York Herald Tribune
NYJA   New York Journal and Advertiser
NYN   New York Daily News
NYP   New York Evening Post
NYS   New York Sun
NYTi   New York Times
NYTr   New York Daily Tribune
NYW   New York World
OSJ   Daily Ohio State Journal
OWH   Omaha World Herald
PI   Philadelphia Inquirer
PPL   Philadelphia Public Ledger and Transcript
RR   Review of Reviews
SFE   San Francisco Examiner
SPPP   St. Paul Pioneer Press
TA   Topeka Advocate
TR   Torrington Register
WA   Waterbury American
WC   Waterloo Courier
WP   Washington Post

1. Popular Politics

1. This account is based on the reports in the NHR, Oct. 10:4, 1876; and the *NHU,* Oct. 10:8, 1876. My conclusions about the fifth, sixth, and eighth wards are drawn from the manuscript population schedules of the Ninth (1870) and Tenth (1880) Censuses of the United States. I have inferred the ethnic make-up of the companies from the list of their officers in *NHR,* Oct. 21:4, 1876.

2. There is still no full account of the emergence of popular politics. For important parts of the story, see John Brewer, *Party Ideology and Popular Politics at the Accession of George III* (London, 1976); Pauline Maier, "The Charleston Mob and the Evolution of Popular Politics in Revolutionary South Carolina 1765–1784," *Perspectives in American History,* IV (1970), 171–96; idem, *From Resistance to Revolution: Colonial Radicals and the Development of American Opposition to Britain, 1765–1776* (New York, 1972); Robert J. Dinkin, *Voting in Provincial America: A Study of Elections in the Thirteen Colonies* (Westport, Conn., 1977); Gary B. Nash, *The Urban Crucible: Social Change, Political Consciousness, and the Origins of the Amer-*

ican Revolution (Cambridge, Mass., 1979); and Stephen E. Patterson, *Political Parties in Revolutionary Massachusetts* (Madison, Wisc., 1973).

3. The turnout figures are rounded from Paul Kleppner's superb statistical study, *Who Voted? The Dynamics of Electoral Turnout, 1870–1980* (New York, 1982), 32. See also the estimates for the period 1840 to 1860 in William E. Gienapp, "'Politics Seem to Enter into Everything': Political Culture in the North, 1840–1860," in Stephen E. Maizlish and John J. Kushma, eds., *Essays in American Antebellum Politics, 1840–1860* (College Station, Tex., 1982), 20–21. The classic examination of the extension of the right to vote is Chilton Williamson, *American Suffrage from Property to Democracy, 1760–1860* (Princeton, 1960).

4. Everett Carll Ladd, Jr., *Where Have All the Voters Gone? The Fracturing of America's Political Parties* (New York, 1978); Arthur T. Hadley, *The Empty Polling Booth* (Englewood Cliffs, N.J., 1978); Richard A. Brody, "The Puzzle of Political Participation in America," in Anthony King, ed., *The New American Political System* (Washington, 1978), 179–212; and Raymond E. Wolfinger and Steven J. Rosenstone, *Who Votes?* (New Haven, 1980).

5. The irony here is that political scientists and not historians were the first to recognize declining voter turnout as an historical issue. See Walter Dean Burnham, *The Current Crisis in American Politics* (New York, 1982); idem, *Critical Elections and the Mainsprings of American Politics* (New York, 1970); Philip E. Converse, "Change in the American Electorate," in Angus Campbell and Philip E. Converse, eds., *The Human Meaning of Social Change* (New York, 1972), 263–337; and idem, "Comment on Burnham's 'Theory and Voting Research,'" *American Political Science Review*, 68 (Sept. 1974), 1024–27. The first comprehensive statistical treatment of declining turnout by an historian is Kleppner, *Who Voted?*. The turnout statistics used here are rounded from those in Burnham, *Current Crisis*, 29. Similar figures appear in Kleppner, *Who Voted?*, 32, 57, 84, and 113.

6. See V. O. Key, Jr., *Southern Politics in State and Nation* (New York, 1949); C. Vann Woodward, *Origins of the New South, 1877–1913* (Baton Rouge, 1951), 321–49; J. Morgan Kousser, *The Shaping of Southern Politics: Suffrage Restriction and the Establishment of the One-Party South, 1880–1910* (New Haven, 1974); and Jerrold G. Rusk and John J. Stucker, "The Effect of the Southern System of Election Laws on Voting Participation: A Reply to V. O. Key, Jr.," in Joel H. Silbey, Allan G. Bogue, and William H. Flanigan, eds., *The History of American Electoral Behavior* (Princeton, 1978), 198–250. The turnout statistics are rounded from Kleppner, *Who Voted?*, 57. See also, Burnham, *Current Crisis*, 30.

7. Figures are rounded from those for "Nonsouth" in Kleppner, *Who Voted?*, 57.

8. Some social scientists have placed great emphasis on registration legislation as a cause of falling turnout. See Converse, "Change"; and Stanley Kelley, Jr., Richard E. Ayres, and William G. Bowen, "Registration and Voting: Putting First Things First," *American Political Science Review*, 61 (June 1967), 359–79. Their arguments are persuasively refuted for the early twentieth century in Paul Kleppner and Stephen C. Baker, "The Impact of Voter Registration Requirements on Electoral Turnout, 1900–1916," *Journal of Political and Military Sociology*, 8 (Fall 1980), 205–26.

9. Most of these insights were first developed in the works of Walter Dean Burnham cited in note 5, above.

10. Kleppner, *Who Voted?*, 55–82.

11. Richard L. McCormick, "The Party Period and Public Policy: An Exploratory Hypothesis," *Journal of American History*, 66 (Sept. 1979), 295–98; and Samuel P. Hays, *American Political History as Social Analysis: Essays by Samuel P. Hays* (Knoxville, Tenn., 1980).

12. Gienapp, "'Politics Seem to Enter into Everything,'" 21; Ronald P. Formisano, *The Transformation of Political Culture: Massachusetts Parties, 1790s–1840s* (New York, 1983), 312.

13. The historian who has paid the most serious attention to political style is Richard J. Jensen, in such works as "Armies, Admen and Crusaders: Types of Presidential Election Campaigns," *History Teacher*, 2 (Jan. 1969), 33–50; *The Winning of the Midwest: Social and Political Conflict, 1888–1896* (Chicago, 1971), 1–33 and 154–77; and, with Steven L. Piott and Christopher C. Gibbs, *Grass Roots Politics: Parties, Issues, and Voters, 1854–1983* (Westport, Conn., 1983). While my analysis diverges at many points from Jensen's interpretation, I have benefited greatly from his pioneering work.

Jean H. Baker offers an important exegesis of Democratic political style in *Affairs of Party: The Political Culture of Northern Democrats in the Mid-Nineteenth Century* (Ithaca, 1983).

14. See the discussion in Sidney Verba and Norman H. Nie, *Participation in America: Political Democracy and Social Equality* (New York, 1972).

2. Partisanship

1. The literature on the rise of parties and turnout is large and growing. Important studies include Richard P. McCormick, "New Perspectives on Jacksonian Politics," *American Historical Review*, 65 (Jan. 1960), 288–301; idem, *The Second American Party System: Party Formation in the Jacksonian Era* (Chapel Hill, 1966); Roy F. Nichols, *The Invention of the American Political Parties: A Study of Political Improvisation* (New York, 1967); Ronald P. Formisano, *The Birth of Mass Political Parties: Michigan, 1827–1861* (Princeton, 1971); idem, *The Transformation of Political Culture: Massachu-*

setts Parties, 1790s–1840s (New York, 1983); William N. Chambers and Philip C. Davis, "Party, Competition, and Mass Participation: The Case of the Democratizing Party System, 1824–1852," in Joel H. Silbey, Allan G. Bogue, and William H. Flanigan, eds., *The History of American Electoral Behavior* (Princeton, 1978), 174–97; William G. Shade, "Political Pluralism and Party Development: The Creation of a Modern Party System, 1815–1852," in Paul Kleppner, ed., *The Evolution of American Electoral Systems* (Westport, Conn., 1981), 77–112.

2. Richard Hofstadter, *The Idea of a Party System: The Rise of Legitimate Opposition in the United States, 1780–1840* (Berkeley, 1972); Michael Wallace, "Changing Concepts of Party in the United States: New York, 1815–1828," *American Historical Review*, 74 (Dec. 1968), 453–91; Richard P. McCormick, *The Presidential Game: The Origins of American Presidential Politics* (New York, 1982), 182–87; Formisano, *Transformation of Political Culture*, 84–106; and Jean H. Baker, *Affairs of Party: The Political Culture of Northern Democrats in the Mid-Nineteenth Century* (Ithaca, 1983), 114–40.

3. Ronald P. Formisano, "Political Character, Antipartyism and the Second Party System," *American Quarterly*, 21 (Winter 1970), 683–709; idem, *Birth of Parties*, 56–80; Michael F. Holt, "The Politics of Impatience: The Origins of Know Nothingism," *Journal of American History*, 60 (Sept. 1973), 309–31; idem, *The Political Crisis of the 1850s* (New York, 1978), 4–5, 130–38, and 175–76; and Paul Kleppner, *The Third Electoral System, 1853–1892: Parties, Voters, and Political Cultures* (Chapel Hill, 1979), 70–86, 293–96, and 331–34. My thinking has been influenced by the de-emphasis on mid-nineteenth-century anti-partyism in Joel H. Silbey, *A Respectable Minority: The Democratic Party in the Civil War Era, 1860–1868* (New York, 1977), 29; and William E. Gienapp, "'Politics Seem to Enter into Everything': Political Culture in the North, 1840–1860," in Stephen E. Maizlish and John J. Kushma, eds., *Essays in American Antebellum Politics, 1840–1860* (College Station, Tex., 1982), 43–46.

4. Thomas B. Alexander, "The Dimensions of Voter Partisan Constancy in Presidential Elections from 1840 to 1860," in Maizlish and Kushma, eds., *Essays in Antebellum Politics*, 70–121; Gienapp, "'Politics,'" 53–59; Walter Dean Burnham, *The Current Crisis in American Politics* (New York, 1982), 27–28, 32–33, and 41–42; and Baker, *Affairs of Party*, 27–70.

5. *PI*, Aug. 14:4, 1884.

6. As James Bryce pointed out in *The American Commonwealth*, 2 vols. (London, 1888), I, 637.

7. See below, Chapter 3.

8. For a fuller discussion of the penny press, see below, Chapter 5.

9. John Lesperance, "American Journalism," *Lippincott's Magazine*, 8 (Aug. 1871), 176. The best general guide to the early history of American newspapers is still Frank Luther Mott, *American Journalism, 1690–1960*,

3d ed. (New York, 1962). See also Culver Haygood Smith, *The Press, Politics, and Patronage: The American Government's Use of Newspapers, 1789–1875* (Athens, Ga., 1977).

10. Melville E. Stone, *Fifty Years a Journalist* (Garden City, N.Y., 1921), 52–53; and also Charles T. Congdon, *Reminiscences of a Journalist* (Boston, 1880), 210–11 and 310–11.

11. Smith, *Press, Politics, and Patronage*, 70–72; and Robert Gray Gunderson, *The Log-Cabin Campaign* (Lexington, Ky., 1957), 156–58. See also the blurb for *The Campaign of Freedom* in the *NYTr*, Sept. 2:2, 1848.

12. E. W. Howe, "Country Newspapers," *Century*, 42 (Sept. 1891), 777; *NHR*, Feb. 11:4, 1881; Mott, *American Journalism*, 205 and 313.

13. Smith, *Press, Politics, and Patronage;* Leonard D. White, *The Jacksonians: A Study in Administrative History, 1829–1861* (New York, 1954), 284–99.

14. Joseph Logsdon, *Horace White, Nineteenth-Century Liberal* (Westport, Conn., 1971), 79 and 101; Bingham Duncan, *Whitelaw Reid: Journalist, Politician, Diplomat* (Athens, Ga., 1975), 23; and Smith, *Press, Politics, and Patronage*, 34–36 and 161–62.

15. For examples of public printing, see *NHP*, Oct. 21:1 and 4, 1856; *CTr*, June 12:2–3, 1860; and *NHR*, May 16:3, 1870.

16. Irving Katz, *August Belmont: A Political Biography* (New York, 1968), 136; *NHR*, Oct. 31:2, 1864, Mar. 10:2, 1869, and Sept. 26:2, 1871; *BC*, Nov. 2:2, 1876.

17. *CTr*, July 2:1, 1860; *CIO*, June 4:3, 1872; *NYW*, Aug. 19:7, 1876; *BC*, July 2:3, 1876; *NYTr*,, Sept. 6:3 and 7:5, 1880, and July 1:4, 1884; Frederic Hudson, *Journalism in the United States* (New York, 1873), 528.

18. Cameron's comment is scrawled on the back of J. R. Schreiner to Cameron, Feb. 9, 1860, Simon Cameron Papers, Library of Congress. See also James Veeck to Cameron, Mar. 10, 1859, R. P. McDowell to Cameron, Mar. 17, 1859, Frey & Foltz to Cameron, Sept. 28, 1859, Cameron to Frey & Foltz, Oct. 11, 1859, and F. Geise & Co. to Cameron, Nov. 4, 1859, Cameron Papers; E. S. Barnard to William E. Chandler, June 14, 1872, J. C. F. Beyland to "Chairman of the National Republican Committee," June 18, 1872, and William S. Jones to William E. Chandler, Aug. 14, 1872, William E. Chandler Papers, Library of Congress; John A. Logan to Zachariah Chandler, Oct. 19, 1876, Zachariah Chandler Papers, Library of Congress; Fred. Wallroth to Samuel J. Tilden, July 19, 1876, and Robert Roth to Tilden, July 24, 1876, Samuel J. Tilden Papers, New York Public Library; James A. Rawley, *Edwin D. Morgan, 1811–1883: Merchant in Politics* (New York, 1955), 69, 241, and 244; and [J. B. Bishop], "An Inside View of Commercial Journalism," *Nation*, 50 (June 12, 1890), 463–64.

19. Mott, *American Journalism*, 205.

20. For some typical glimpses of the editor's political role, see Beman Brockway, *Fifty Years in Journalism: Embracing Recollections and Personal Experiences with an Autobiography* (Watertown, N.Y., 1891), esp. 14–17, 24, 73–74, 233–34, 408, and 414. "American Newspapers," *Chambers's Journal*, 4th series, 1 (June 25, 1870), 408–09, notes the number of former editors in the government of the United States.

21. Brockway, *Fifty Years*, 414.

22. Charles Dudley Warner, *The Complete Writings of Charles Dudley Warner*, ed. Thomas R. Lounsbury, 15 vols. (Hartford, Conn., 1904), XIV, 271; *NHU*, Oct. 28:2, 1884.

23. *CIO*, Mar. 29:2, 1872; *OSJ*, May 21:1, 1864; and *NHR*, Dec. 31:2, 1866, and Jan. 2:2, 1879.

24. Hudson, *Journalism*, 738–39; Mott, *American Journalism*, 463; *EID*, June 6:1, 1860; and *NHR*, Feb. 15:1, 1871.

25. *CPD*, July 1:2, 1856; *AS*, June 20:4, 1860; *CTr*, May 21:2, 1860; *EID*, June 6:2, 1860; *NHJC*, May 19:2, 1860; *NHR*, Mar. 22:2, 1860; *OSJ*, June 9:2, 1864; *GSFP*, May 16:2, 1868; *BC*, July 1:2, 1876; and *WC*, Oct. 4:4, 1876.

26. *NHJC*, Feb. 24:1, 1873.

27. *NYW*, Aug. 17:8, 1868; and *NYTr*, Aug. 6:4, 1884.

28. *AS*, Sept. 26:4, 1860; *EID*, Oct. 3:2, 1860; *NHJC*, Nov. 4:1, 1884; and also *NHP*, Nov. 3:2, 1856; *CPD*, Nov. 3:2, 1856; *CTr*, Apr. 3:2, 1860; *NYTr*, Nov. 3:4–5 and 6:4, 1860; and *NHJC*, Apr. 2:2, 1860, and Oct. 17:1, 1879.

29. *NYTr*, Sept. 28:1, 1880; *NYW*, Sept. 3:1 and 4:8, and Oct. 2:8, 1876.

30. For signs of the friendly relations among newspapermen of different parties, see *NHR*, July 5:5, 1862, and Apr. 23:2, 1880.

31. Brockway, *Fifty Years*, 425; W. D. Howells, "The Country Printer," *Scribner's Monthly*, 13 (May 1893), 546–47; *NHP*, Jan. 4:2, 1870; *NYTr*, Nov. 4:4, 1880. For accusations of lying and treason, see *NHJC*, Aug. 8:2, 1864; *NYW*, Aug. 27:5 and Sept. 4:4, 1868; *NHR*, Mar. 31:2, 1871, and Sept. 22:2, 1879; and *WC*, Sept. 19:5, 1888.

32. Brockway, *Fifty Years*, 423.

33. Franc B. Wilkie, *Personal Reminiscences of Thirty-Five Years of Journalism* (Chicago, 1891), 40; and also Donald W. Curl, *Murat Halstead and the Cincinnati Commercial* (Boca Raton, Fla., 1980), 8.

34. Howells, "Country Printer," 554.

35. *NHJC*, Apr. 2:2, 1872; *CTr*, June 30:2, 1860; Mott, *American Journalism*, 200; and Bryce, *American Commonwealth*, II, 171–72.

36. Mott, *American Journalism*, 153 and 292–96.

37. Congdon, *Reminiscences*, 221–22.

38. *CPD*, Oct. 2:2, 1856; *CTr*, July 21:3, 1860; *NHJC*, Sept. 12:2, 1872, July 31:2, Aug. 16:2, and Oct. 16:2, 1884; *EID*, June 27:2, 1860; *NYTr*, Sept. 24:1, 1880; and *BC*, Aug. 24:1–2, 1876.

39. *NHR*, Aug. 30:4, 1876; *NHJC*, Aug. 31:2, 1876. Note, too, the contrasting accounts of a Republican parade given in *BC*, Aug. 24:1 and 25:2, 1876.

40. *NYTr*, Oct. 10:4, 1860, and Oct. 14:4, 1880; *EID*, Sept. 19:2, 1860. See also *CPD*, Oct. 8:2, 1856; *CTr*, Oct. 10: 1, 1860; *GSFP*, Nov. 14:2, 1868; and *BC*, Sept. 7:2, 1876.

41. *NYW*, Sept. 13:1, 1876; *NHJC*, Apr. 6:1, 1875; and *NHU*, Nov. 3:1, 1880.

42. *BC*, Nov. 8:1, 9:1, and 11:1, 1876. For less splendid victory celebrations, see *CPD*, Oct. 1:2 and Nov. 6:2, 1856; *EID*, Oct. 10:2, 1860; *NHR*, Apr. 2:2 and Nov. 6:2, 1867; *NHJC*, Apr. 2:2, 1872; and *WC*, Nov. 7:1, 1888. On the rarity of illustrations, see Mott, *American Journalism*, 294; and Howells, "Country Printer," 546.

43. See Chapter 5, below, for discussion and documentation of this disparity.

44. "American Newspapers," 406.

45. Richard Watson Gilder, "The Newspaper, the Magazine, and the Public," *Outlook*, 61 (Feb. 4, 1899), 317.

46. Bryce, *American Commonwealth*, II, 204.

47. McCormick, *Second American Party System*, 15–16, 30–31, 49, 54, 69, 75–76, 88, 95, 132, 145, 157–58, 172, 268, 276, 308, and 349–50; idem, *Presidential Game*, 147–54; and Gunderson, *Log-Cabin Campaign*, 1–11, 108–22, 123–47, 201–18, and 232–36.

48. *NYTr*, July 4:7, 1860, July 26:1 and 29:1, 1880, and July 29:2, 1884; *NHR*, Sept. 12:3, 1864, and Aug. 24:4, 1880; *EID*, June 17:3 and July 22:3, 1868; *GSFP*, Sept. 5:2, 1868; *NHJC*, Aug. 9:2, 1872, and June 25:2, 1880; *AS*, June 29:5, 1876, Sept. 22:1, 1880, June 28:1, 1884, and July 5:1, 1888; and *NHU*, July 18:8, 1884. For minors in a campaign club, see *BC*, Aug. 28:1, 1876.

49. *CPD*, Oct. 4:3, 1856; *NHJC*, Sept. 13:2, 1864; *NYTr*, Oct. 16:5, 1860, and Oct. 19:1, 1880; and *NHR*, July 11:2, 1868, June 30:1, 1880, and Oct. 4:3, 1888.

50. *NYW*, Sept. 17:8, 1876. For a comment on the practice, see *NYS*, Sept. 25:3, 1892.

51. *CTr*, June 7:1, 1860; *NYTr*, Oct. 27:3, 1860, and Aug. 11:1, 1884; *NHR*, Sept. 9:2, 1864, and Aug. 21:1, 1880; *NYW*, Aug. 19:1, 1868, and Sept. 16:5, 1876; *NHJC*, Oct. 25:4, 1884; and *PI*, Sept. 29:3, 1884.

52. For workers, see *CTr*, Apr. 16:4, 1860; *NHJC*, Oct. 6:2, 1880; *NHR*, Oct. 4:3, 1880; *NYTr*, Aug. 17:1, 1880; and *NYH*, Sept. 25:3, 1888. For employers, see *NYTr*, Oct. 19:1, 1880.

53. *NHR*, June 30:4 and Aug. 12:3, 1880; and *WC*, Sept. 26:8, 1888.

54. *AS*, July 26:1, 1884; *NYTr*, Mar. 20:7, 1860, and July 8:2, 1884; *NHJC*, June 25:2, 1860, July 16:2, 1880, and July 15:2, 1884; *EID*, June 17:2, 1868; *NYW*, Aug. 19:1, 1868, Sept. 7:7, 1876, and Sept. 4:5, 1884; and *NHR*, Sept. 26:4, 1876.

55. *NHP*, Oct. 14:2, 1856; *NYW*, Aug. 24:1, 1868; *NHJC*, July 2:3, 1880; *BC*, Oct. 18:4, 1876; *NYTr*, Aug. 30:1, 1880; Henry Joslin to Nelson W. Aldrich, Aug. 15, 1884, Nelson W. Aldrich Papers, Library of Congress; James B. Ross to Rutherford B. Hayes, July 17, 1876, Rutherford B. Hayes Papers, Rutherford B. Hayes Library, Fremont, Ohio; *NHR*, Oct. 16:4, 1888; and *WC*, Sept. 19:5, 1888.

56. *NHJC*, Mar. 20:2, 21:2, and 23:2, 1860; *DN*, Aug. 17:4, 1880; *NYTr*, Aug. 30:1 and Sept. 21:2, 1880, and July 26:3, 1884; *NN*, Aug. 26:4, 1884; and *NYH*, Aug. 5:9, 1888.

57. Holt, *Political Crisis*, 176.

58. Julius G. Rathbun, "The 'Wide Awakes': The Great Political Organization of 1860," *Connecticut Quarterly*, 1 (Oct. 1895), 327–35; John G. Nicolay and John Hay, *Abraham Lincoln: A History*, 10 vols. (New York, 1890), II, 284–86; Reinhard H. Luthin, *The First Lincoln Campaign* (Cambridge, Mass., 1944), 173–74; B. F. Thompson, "The Wide Awakes of 1860," *The Magazine of History with Notes and Queries*, 10 (Nov. 1909), 293–96; and Glenn C. Howland, "Organize! Organize! The Lincoln Wide-Awakes in Vermont," *Vermont History*, 48 (Winter 1980), 28–32. For a sense of the activities of the Wide Awakes and the other companies, see *AS*, Nov. 7:4, 1860; *CTr*, Apr. 4:2, May 10:1, 12:1, and 29:1, June 12:1, July 10:1 and 24:1, Aug. 9:1, 10:1, and 24:1, Oct. 4:2, and Nov. 8:1, 1860; *EID*, Sept. 5:3, 12:2, and 26:2, and Oct. 10:2 and 17:3, 1860; *NHJC*, Mar. 19:2, 20:2, and 21:2, May 3:2, and Oct. 5:2, 1860; *NHP*, May 16:2, 1860; and *NYTr*, Mar. 29:6, Sept. 1:5 and 7:8, Oct. 3:4, 4:5, 18:5, and 27:3, and Nov. 3:8 and 12:7, 1860.

59. For Democratic ridicule of the Wide Awakes, see *NHR*, Mar. 23:2, Apr. 25:2, 26:2, and 27:2, July 27:2, Sept. 1:2, and Oct. 30:2, 1860; and *CTr*, July 10:1, 1860. For copies of the Wide Awakes, see Emerson D. Fite, *The Presidential Campaign of 1860* (New York, 1911), 228–29; Luthin, *Lincoln Campaign*, 174; *NHR*, Mar. 27:2, 1860; *NHJC*, Mar. 28:2,1860; *CTr*, Aug. 20:2, Sept. 24:2, and Oct. 5:1, 1860; and *NYTr*, Sept. 18:5 and Oct. 10:9, 1860.

60. *EID*, Sept. 19:3, 1868; *AS*, July 14:1, 1880, and Oct. 11:1, 1884; and *NYTr*, Sept. 18:3, 1880.

61. *NYW*, Aug. 25:1 and Oct. 3:11, 1868; *NHR*, Sept. 12:2, 1868, and Oct. 21:4, 1876; and *NHJC*, Oct. 2:2, 1884.

62. *NYW*, Sept. 14:1 and 30:8, 1876; *NHR*, Oct. 21:4, 1876; *NYTr*, Oct. 11:1, 1880; *NN*, June 11:1 and Aug. 27:4, 1884; and *NHU*, Aug. 2:1, 1884.

63. *NYTr*, Sept. 14:8 and Oct. 9:5, 1860, and Sept. 4:5, 1884; *AS*, Sept. 13:1, 1888; *KCS*, Oct. 7:1 and Nov. 3:1, 1884; *NN*, July 2:1 and Sept. 3:4, 1884; and *NHU*, Oct. 1:8, 1884.

64. *NHJC*, Sept. 10:2, 1872, and July 3:2, 1880; *NYTr*, July 25:1–2, Aug. 30:1, and Sept. 7:1 and 21:1, 1880, and Aug. 3:1–2 and Sept. 11:2, 1884; and *AS*, Aug. 2:1, 1888.

65. *DN*, Aug. 3:4, 1880.

66. *NYW*, Sept. 19:5, 1884 (first quotation); *NYTr*, Aug. 5:1 and Sept. 4:1 (second), 1880, and July 16:1 and 3 (third), 1884; *NHR*, Sept. 30:2, 1868, and Sept. 17:1, 1880; *NHJC*, Sept. 14:2, 18:2, and 24:2, 1872, Aug. 21:2–3, and Sept. 3:2, 4:2, 6:2, and 8:2, 1880, and Sept. 30:2 and Oct. 9:2, 1884; *PI*, July 11:2 and Sept. 8:3, 1884; and *NYH*, Sept. 15:3 and Oct. 25:6, 1888. For the business in the manufacture and sale of uniforms and other campaign paraphernalia, see *NHJC*, Sept. 16:2, 1872, and Sept. 3:2 and Oct. 23:2, 1880; *NHU*, Nov. 10:1, 1880; *NN*, Aug. 16:1, 1884; *NYTr*, Aug. 3:1, 1884, and Aug. 5:9, 1888; *KCS*, Oct. 29:2, 1884; and *NYS*, Sept. 10:5, 1892.

67. *NHJC*, Sept. 25:2, 1872, and Sept. 8:2, 1880; *AS*, July 14:1, 1880, and Sept. 24:1, 1884; *NHR*, Aug. 11:4, 1880; *NHU*, Sept. 19:1, 1884; and Richard T. Lockley to Rutherford B. Hayes, July 20, 1876, Hayes Papers.

68. Note, for instance, the Republican organizations in Binghamton, New York, and Bloomfield, New Jersey, reported in *NYTr*, July 31:2, 1884; and *NN*, Sept. 3:4, 1884.

69. *NHR*, Sept. 29:2 and Oct. 27:2, 1868, and Oct. 11:4, 1876; *NYW*, Aug. 25:1, 1868; *NHJC*, Oct. 1:2 and 19:2, 1872, Aug. 16:2 and 4, and Oct. 4:2, 7:2, and 26:2, 1880; *NYTr*, Sept. 25:1 and Oct. 11:1, 1880; and *NN*, Aug. 8:4 and 22:1, 1884. For a sense of the companies in a city ward, see *PI*, July 11:2 and Sept. 12:2, 1884.

70. Based on a reading of the *NHU, NHR*, and *NHJC* for 1880.

71. *AS*, May 30:4 and June 13:4 and 27:5, 1860; *NHJC*, May 30:2, 1860, June 24:2, 1864, and June 12:2 and July 2:2, 1880; *NYTr*, July 3:5 and 4:5, 1860, and July 16:1 and 3, 1884; *NHR*, July 24:2, 1868; *EID*, July 15:2–3, 1868; *GSFP*, Aug. 29:2, 1868; *NYW*, June 29:5, 1876; U. B. Brewster to Rutherford B. Hayes, July 1, 1876, Hayes Papers; and *NN*, July 23:1, 1884.

72. *NHJC*, Sept. 4:2 and 6:2, 1860, and Sept. 3:2, 1880; *NYTr*, Oct. 17:8, 1860, and Aug. 19:1 and Oct. 19:2, 1880; *NHR*, Sept. 21:3, 1864, and Oct. 5:1, 1876; *GSFP*, Oct. 10:2, 1868; *NYW*, Aug. 24:1 and Sept. 9:1, 1868, and Sept. 30:8, 1876; *AS*, Aug. 17:1, 1876; *WC*, Oct. 25:1,

1876; *NN*, July 10:4 and Aug. 26:4, 1884; and John E. Kendrick to Benjamin Harrison, Oct. 26, 1888, Benjamin Harrison Papers, Library of Congress.

73. *CPD*, Oct. 4:2–3, 1856; *EID*, June 6:6 and 13:2, Aug. 29:2–3, and Sept. 19:2, 1860, and Sept. 9:2, 1868; *NHR*, Sept. 17:2 and 29:3, 1864, and Nov. 1:2, 1872; *NYW*, Oct. 19:6, 1876; *AS*, July 31:1 and Aug. 4:1, 1880, Sept. 17:1, 1884, and Aug. 30:1 (quotation) and Sept. 6:1, 1888; and *NYH*, Sept. 24:4, 1888.

74. *NHR*, Sept. 22:3, 1864, and July 31:4, 1880; *GSFP*, Aug. 29:2, 1868; *NYW*, Aug. 18:5, 1868, and June 30:1, 1876; *NHJC*, Sept. 11:2, 1872, and June 12:3, 1880; *BC*, Aug. 7:2, 1876; Edward E. Brubaker to Rutherford B. Hayes, Sept. 8, 1876, Hayes Papers; *NYTr*, Aug. 17:1, 18:1, and 26:1, 1880, and Aug. 6:2, 1884; *NN*, Aug. 22:1, 1884; *PI*, July 9:2, 1884; and *NYH*, July 20:2, Aug. 7:5, and Sept. 15:3, 1888. For the banner business, see *NYTr*, July 19:2, 1880; *NHJC*, Aug. 4:2, 1884; and F. S. M., "The Making of Campaign Banners," *Harper's Weekly*, 36 (Sept. 10, 1892), 1886.

75. For an amusing competition with banners, see *NN*, Aug. 25:1, 1884.

76. *CTr*, Oct. 16:1, 1860; *NYTr*, Sept. 14:5–8 and 18:5, 1860, and Sept. 18:1–3 and 22:1–2, 1880; *NHR*, Oct. 21:2, 1864; *NHJC*, Oct. 22:2, 1872, and Oct. 26:2, 1880; *NYW*, Sept. 21:8 and 22:1, 1876; and *NN*, Sept. 25:1, 1884.

77. *CPD*, Sept. 30:2 and Oct. 4:2, 1856; *AS*, Nov. 9:5, 1876, Sept. 29:Supplement, 1880, and Nov. 1:1, 1888; *CTr*, July 10:1, 13:2, 23:1, and 25:2, and Aug. 7:2, 14:2, 21:2, and 23:1, 1860; *EID*, Sept. 23:2 and Oct. 14:2, 1868; *NYW*, Aug. 17:8 and 21:1, 1868, and Sept. 29:1, 1876; *NYH*, July 27:5, 1888; and *WC*, Oct. 3:3, 1888. For a rare all-day rally in a city, see *NHR*, Oct. 25:1, 1876.

78. *AS*, Aug. 27:1, 1884; *NHJC*, Sept. 20:2, 1860, Sept. 24:2, 1864, Oct. 11:2 and 21:2, 1872, Sept. 9:2 and 16:2, 1880, and July 22:2, 1884; and *NYTr*, July 27:1 and 28:1, and Sept. 21:2, 1880; and Lew Wallace to Zachariah Chandler, Sept. 26, 1876, Zachariah Chandler Papers. For an earnest discussion of the relative merits of brass bands and glee clubs, see *NYTr*, Sept. 5:5, 1880.

79. Union Republican Congressional Committee, *Hayes & Wheeler Song Book, Series I* (Washington, 1876), 4 and 11. See also *NHJC*, May 25:2 and Aug. 13:2 and 28:2, 1860; William Henry Browne to Rutherford B. Hayes, July 26, 1876, Hayes Papers; *NYTr*, July 30:1, 1880; Frank L. Armstrong to Benjamin Harrison, Sept. 6, 1888, Harrison Papers; Gienapp, "'Politics,'" 33; and Catherine Frances Cavanagh, "Campaign Songs and Ballads," *Bookman*, 20 (Oct. 1904), 115–19.

80. *NHP*, Nov. 3:2 and 4:2, 1856; *CTr*, Oct. 3:1 and 4, 1860; *NHJC*,

Oct. 27:2 and 28:2, 1880; *NYTr*, Oct. 3:4 and 5, 4:5 and 8, 6:10, 9:5, and 24:4 and 8, 1860, and Aug. 27:1, Sept. 4:1, 22:1–2, and 26:1, and Oct. 9:1, 11:1, 12:1–2, and 13:5, 1880; *NHR*, Sept. 23:2 and Oct. 8:2, 1864, Oct. 17:2 and 23:2, 1868, and Oct. 21:1, 1880; *OSJ*, Oct. 10:4, 1864; *GSFP*, Oct. 31:2–3, 1868; *NYW*, Oct. 6:1, 3, 7, and 10, and 30:10, 1868, and Sept. 29:1 and Oct. 6:1 and 27:1 and 12, 1876; *BC*, Sept. 11:1, 1876; *KCS*, Nov. 3:1, 1884; *NN*, Oct. 16:1, 1884; *NYH*, Aug. 5:9 and 10:3, 1888; and *WC*, Oct. 3:3, 1888.

81. *AS*, Aug. 15:4, 1860, and Sept. 29:Supplement, 1880, Oct. 11:1, 1884, and Oct. 18:1 and Nov. 1:1, 1888; *CTr*, July 10:1 and 13:2, and Aug. 1:1, 7:1–2, 10:1, 14:2, 21:2, and 23:1, 1860; *NYW*, Oct. 6:1, 3, 7, and 10, 1868, and Oct. 27:1 and 12, 1876; *PPL*, Oct. 3:1, 1868; *NYH*, July 27:5 and Oct. 22:4, 1888; and *WC*, Oct. 3:3, 1888. For a fuller discussion of women's role in popular politics, see below, Chapter 8.

82. *NYTr*, Sept. 11:2, 1880; *CPD*, Oct. 6:2, 1856. See also *NYW*, Aug. 17:8, 1868.

83. For some Goddesses, see *NHR*, Oct. 17:2 and 23:2, and Nov. 3:2, 1868; and *NHJC*, Oct. 28:2 and Nov. 9:2, 1880. Jane Bushnell Shepherd, *My Old New Haven and Other Memories Briefly Told* (New Haven, 1932), 25, notes the practice of turning off the lights.

84. For buttons and badges, see John Doyle DeWitt, *A Century of Campaign Buttons, 1789–1889* (Hartford, 1959); Edmund B. Sullivan, *American Political Badges and Medalets, 1789–1892* (Lawrence, Mass., 1981); *NHR*, Sept. 3:3, 1864; *AS*, June 11:1, 1884; *NHJC*, June 9:2, 1884; and Leon Burr Richardson, *William E. Chandler, Republican* (New York, 1940), 105. Typical election wagers are noted in *CPD*, Nov. 7:2, 1856; *CTr*, Nov. 8:1 and 16:2, 1860; *NHR*, Nov. 9:2 and 10:2, 1868, and June 9:4, 1880; *NHJC*, Nov. 16:1, 1872, and June 9:2, 1880; *NYTi*, Sept. 14:10, 1872; *NYTr*, Oct. 17:4, 1880; *NN*, Sept. 12:1, 1884; and *PI*, Nov. 2:4, 1892.

85. Bryce, *American Commonwealth*, II, 107–08; Gerson Harry Smoger, "Organizing Political Campaigns: A Survey of 19th and 20th Century Trends" (Ph.D. diss., University of Pennsylvania, 1982), 23–26; Morton Keller, *Affairs of Party: Public Life in Late Nineteenth Century America* (Cambridge, Mass., 1977), 242. For unusual instances of voters—two campaign companies—making their choice plain by marching in a body to the polls, see *EID*, Nov. 7:3, 1860, and *HT*, Nov. 6:8, 1888.

86. *CTr*, July 21:3 and Nov. 8:1, 1860; *EID*, Nov. 28:2, 1860, and Oct. 21:2, 1868; *NHJC*, Apr. 4:2, 1860, Nov. 14:2 and 15:2, 1864, Sept. 15:2, Oct. 14:2, and Nov. 9:2, 1880, and Nov. 13:2, 1884; *NYTr*, Oct. 15:5 and Nov. 9:5, 1860, and Nov. 5:2, 1880; *NHR*, Nov. 15:3, 1864; *BC*, Oct. 18:3, 1876; *AS*, Nov. 6:1, 1880; and *WC*, Nov. 14:1, 1888.

87. Richard J. Jensen, *The Winning of the Midwest: Social and Political Conflict, 1888–1896* (Chicago, 1971), 11; Baker, *Affairs of Party*, 287–91.

88. *NHJC,* Mar. 30:2 and Apr. 2:2, 1860, Oct. 6:2 and 21:2, 1864, Oct. 4:2, 1872, and Oct. 29:2, 1880; *NYTr,* Oct. 6:11, 9:5, 17:4–5, and 22:8, and Nov. 3:8, 5:6, and 7:4, 1860, and Sept. 11:5, 12:7, and 19:1, 1880; *NHR,* Sept. 10:2, 1868; and *NYH,* Aug. 8:4, 1888.

89. *CTr,* Sept. 24:2 and Oct. 30:1, 1860; *NHJC,* Sept. 17:2, 1860. At least one influential Northerner—Horace Greeley—did consider the Wide Awakes the nucleus of a real anti-slavery army: *NYTr,* Sept. 11:8, 1860.

90. *NYTr,* Nov. 12:7, 1860; *NHR,* Oct. 31:1, 1876. See also *KCS,* Nov. 1:1, 1884.

91. *MJ,* Nov. 5:12, 1892.

92. Arthur M. Schlesinger, "Liberty Tree: A Genealogy," *New England Quarterly,* 25 (Dec. 1952), 435–58.

93. For an interpretation of artisanal display, see Sean Wilentz, "Artisan Republican Festivals and the Rise of Class Conflict in New York City, 1788–1837," in Michael H. Frisch and Daniel J. Walkowitz, eds., *Working-Class America: Essays on Labor, Community, and American Society* (Urbana, Ill., 1983), 37–77. Herbert Gutman suggests that artisanal and partisan display may have had common roots in earlier popular entertainments and rituals: *Work, Culture, and Society in Industrial America: Essays in American Working-Class and Social History* (New York, 1976), 56–57. See also Alan Dawley, *Class and Community: The Industrial Revolution in Lynn* (Cambridge, Mass., 1976), 80–81.

94. *CTr,* Aug. 1:1, 1860.

95. Although the distribution of community power in the mid-nineteenth century remains a matter of debate, the critical issue here—upper-class participation in local politics and control of elective offices—appears indisputable. See: David C. Hammack, "Problems in the Historical Study of Power in the Cities and Towns of the United States, 1800–1960," *American Historial Review,* 83 (Apr. 1978), 323–49, and esp. 342; J. Rogers Hollingsworth and Ellen Jane Hollingsworth, *Dimensions in Urban History: Historical and Social Science Perspectives on Middle-Size American Cities* (Madison, Wisc., 1979); Robert A. Dahl, *Who Governs? Democracy and Power in an American City* (New Haven, 1961), 11–31; Michael H. Frisch, *Town into City: Springfield, Massachusetts, and the Meaning of Community, 1840–1880* (Cambridge, Mass., 1972), 39–40 and 142–46; Richard S. Alcorn, "Leadership and Stability in Mid-Nineteenth-Century America: A Case Study of an Illinois Town," *Journal of American History,* 61 (Dec. 1974), 685–702; Estelle Feinstein, *Stamford in the Gilded Age: The Political Life of a Connecticut Town, 1868–1893* (Stamford, Conn., 1973); Stuart M. Blumin, *The Urban Threshold: Growth and Change in a Nineteenth-Century American Community* (Chicago, 1976); and Douglas V. Shaw, *The Making of an Immigrant Community: Ethnic and Cultural Conflict in Jersey City, New*

Jersey, 1850–1877 (New York, 1976), vi and 50–52. In some of the largest cities, upper classes had already begun to withdraw from office-seeking by the 1850s: Sam Bass Warner, Jr., *The Private City: Philadelphia in Three Periods of Its Growth* (Philadelphia, 1968), 79–98. It was in just such cities that the upper-class critique of partisanship and spectacular politics would take shape. See Chapters 3 and 4 below.

96. *CTr*, July 21:3 and 24:1, and Nov. 6:2, 1860; *EID*, Oct. 24:3 and Nov. 28:2, 1860; *NHJC*, Mar. 23:2 and Nov. 6:2, 1860, Nov. 15:2, 1864, and June 12:2 and 25:2, Sept. 30:2, and Oct. 14:2, 1880; *NHR*, Sept. 19:2, 1868, and Oct. 2:1, 1880; *NYW*, Sept. 30:8, 1876; *NYTr*, Aug. 30:1 and Sept. 21:2, 1880; *NN*, July 26:1, 1884.

97. *NYTr*, July 3:5, Sept. 20:6–7, and Nov. 3:8 and 6:5, 1860, Aug. 17:1 and 18:1, Sept. 18:1–3, and Oct. 27:2, 1880, and July 16:1 and 3, 1884; *PPL*, Oct. 1:1, 1868; *NHJC*, Sept. 24:2 and Oct. 6:2, 1864, Oct. 31:2, 1872, and Aug. 18:2, Sept. 15:2 and 28:2, and Oct. 26:2, 1880; *NYW*, Aug. 28:1, 1868, and Sept. 21:8 and Nov. 3:1 and 8, 1876; and *PI*, Oct. 6:2, 1884.

98. The quotation is from the description of the "S. D. Coykendall Gun Squad" in Wm. H. Winton to Benjamin Harrison, Aug. 18, 1888, Harrison Papers.

99. Michael F. Campbell Diary, vols. 21 and 22 of Miscellaneous Diaries Collection, Yale University. The Phalanx is written up in *NHR*, Aug. 21:4 and Oct. 9:1, 1880; and *NHJC*, Oct. 9:2, 1880. Further information on Michael comes from the manuscript schedules of the Ninth Census of the United States (1870), New Haven, Seventh Ward, household 744, and the Tenth Census (1880), District 83, household 25. His obituary is in *NHR*, Aug. 22:3, 1937. On James E. English, see Allen Johnson and Dumas Malone, eds., *Dictionary of American Biography*, 20 vols. (New York, 1928–1936), VI, 165–66; and Edward E. Atwater, ed., *History of the City of New Haven to the Present Time* (New Haven, 1887), 577–80. English's home, which still stands, is described in Elizabeth Mills Brown, *New Haven: A Guide to Architecture and Urban Design* (New Haven, 1976), 183. His views on masters and journeymen are in *NHJC*, Jan. 4:2, 1860. See also *NHR*, Jan. 4:2, 1860, and Oct. 23:2, 1868.

100. Matthew P. Breen, *Thirty Years of New York Politics Up-to-Date* (New York, 1899), 236–38; *DN*, Aug. 6:2 and Sept. 8:4, 1880; and also Eric Falk Petersen, "Prelude to Progressivism: California Election Reform, 1870–1909" (Ph.D. diss., University of California, Los Angeles, 1969), 28 and 34–35.

101. For the different forms of community in American history, see Thomas Bender, *Community and Social Change in America* (New Brunswick, N.J., 1978); Robert H. Wiebe, *The Search for Order, 1877–1920* (New York, 1967), esp. xiii-xiv, 2–4, and 11–43; idem, *The Segmented Society*

(New York, 1975); Rowland Berthoff, *An Unsettled People: Social Order and Disorder in American History* (New York, 1971); Frisch, *Town into City*, 32–49 and 246–47; and John Higham, "Hanging Together: Divergent Unities in American History," *Journal of American History*, 61 (June 1974), 5–28.

102. McCormick, *Presidential Game*, 195 and 216; Katz, *Belmont*, 125 and 277; Rawley, *Morgan*, 49–51, 60–61, 69, 103, and 110–12; Richardson, *Chandler*, 90–91 and 127; and Robert D. Marcus, *Grand Old Party: Political Structure in the Gilded Age, 1880–1896* (New York, 1971), vii–viii, 22–27, and 57–58.

103. Katz, *Belmont*, 136; Rawley, *Morgan*, 67–68, 70–71, 114–16, 199–200, and 242–45; Richardson, *Chandler*, 96–100 and 144–46; and Marcus, *Grand Old Party*, 48–53.

104. E. D. Morgan to William E. Chandler, June 26, 1872, William E. Chandler Papers, Library of Congress.

105. Katz, *Belmont*, 136 and 138–40; Luthin, *Lincoln Campaign*, 171; Alexander C. Flick, *Samuel Jones Tilden: A Study in Political Sagacity* (New York, 1939), 182–83; Rawley, *Morgan*, 61, 66–69, 111–12, 116, 199, and 239–42; Richardson, *Chandler*, 93, 101–06, and 146–49; James E. Edmunds to J. C.F. Heyland, July 17, Edmunds to Blanton Duncan, July 20, J. W. Bassett to William E. Chandler, July 22, Edmunds to R. Buchanan, July 22, John W. Foster to William E. Chandler, Aug. 1, and William E. Chandler to John W. Foster, Aug. 16, all 1872 William E. Chandler Papers.

106. Union Republican Congressional Committee to "Sir," June 1864, Robert C. Schenck et al. to "Sir," Sept. 1868, James G. Blaine Papers, Library of Congress; Thomas L. Tullock to William E. Chandler, Aug. 26, Sept. 7, 15, 17, and 24, and Oct. 9, 13, and 27, 1868, Tullock to William Claflin, Sept. 4, 1868, Tullock to E. B. Washburne, Sept. 11, 1868, Alex. G. Cattell to E. D. Morgan, July 11, 1872, James M. Edmunds to Morgan, July 29, 1872, Edmunds to William E. Chandler, Aug. 1, 3, and 13, 1872, and Edmunds to H. A. Glidden, Aug. 10, 1872, William E. Chandler Papers.

107. *NYTr*, Nov. 8:4, 1860; Charles J. Taylor to Zachariah Chandler, July 16, 1872, William E. Chandler Papers.

108. Luthin, *Lincoln Campaign*, 171; Katz, *Belmont*, 137; *NYTr*, Sept. 26:1, 1880; *PI*, Sept. 8:3, 1884; *NYS*, Oct. 23:9, 1892; William M. Ivins, *Machine Politics and Money in Elections in New York City* (New York, 1887), 61; and A. B. Mason to William Graham Sumner, Sept. 19, 1876, William Graham Sumner Papers, Yale University.

109. M. J. Heale, *The Presidential Quest: Candidates and Images in American Political Culture, 1787–1852* (London, 1982); McCormick, *Presidential Game*; and Gunderson, *Log-Cabin Campaign*, 240–41.

110. Allan Nevins, *Frémont: Pathmarker of the West* (New York, 1939), 450; Philip Shriver Klein, *President James Buchanan: A Biography* (University Park, Penn., 1962), 258; Luthin, *Lincoln Campaign,* 169–71; Nicolay and Hay, *Lincoln,* II, 286–87; Katz, *Belmont,* 137 and 141; Richardson, *Chandler,* 94–95 and 104; Charles H. Coleman, *The Election of 1868: The Democratic Effort to Regain Control* (New York, 1933), 260–61 and 359–62; William S. McFeely, *Grant: A Biography* (New York, 1981), 277–80 and 383–84; Flick, *Tilden,* 315–16; Nevins, *Hewitt,* 312; Keith Ian Polakoff, *The Politics of Inertia: The Election of 1876 and the End of Reconstruction* (Baton Rouge, 1973), 114–16; Allan Peskin, *Garfield: A Biography* (Kent, Ohio, 1978), 482–83 and 498–502; and Allan Nevins, *Grover Cleveland: A Study in Courage* (New York, 1932), 175–84 and 433.

111. Robert W. Johannsen, *Stephen A. Douglas* (New York, 1973), 777–803; Glyndon G. Van Dusen, *Horace Greeley: Nineteenth-Century Crusader* (Philadelphia, 1953), 410, 412, 416, and 418; David Saville Muzzey, *James G. Blaine: A Political Idol of Other Days* (New York, 1934), 311–22; *NYW,* July 15:4, 1884; *NN,* June 23:2 and Sept. 26:2, 1884; John G. Sproat, *"The Best Men": Liberal Reformers in the Gilded Age* (New York, 1968), 84; *KCS,* Sept. 22:2, 1884; *NYH,* Aug. 6:4, 1888; clipping from *Atlanta Constitution,* Aug. 21:?, 1892, William C. Whitney Papers, Library of Congress.

112. *DN,* Aug. 10:2, 1880; "The Etiquette of the Presidential Canvass," *Nation,* 24 (Feb. 1, 1877), 69–70.

113. *PI,* Sept. 16:4 (quotation) and 19:4, 1884; R. W. Patterson to James S. Clarkson, Sept. 20, 1884, James S. Clarkson Papers, Library of Congress; *Atlantic Monthly,* 30 (Nov. 1872), 639–40.

114. For a different view of the importance of national events in the political life of communities, see Wiebe, *Search,* 27–28.

115. James Bryce nicely captured this necessity when he contrasted the behavior of audiences at political rallies and non-political lectures: "In an election campaign it is necessary and expedient to give vent to one's feelings; in listening to a lecture it is not." *American Commonwealth,* II, 657.

116. A point well made in Jensen, *Winning,* 6–11 and 14–15; and Marcus, *Grand Old Party,* 6–7.

117. Horace Greeley, *Recollections of a Busy Life* (New York, 1869), 168; *NYTr,* Oct. 31:4, 1860; and *CTr,* May 31:2, 1860. See also *NHP,* Oct. 23:2, 1856; *CTr,* Aug. 29:2, 1860; *NYTr,* Mar. 16:8 and Oct. 3:4, 1860; *NHJC,* Sept. 21:2, Oct. 27:2, and Nov. 1:2, 1860; and the remark of Thurlow Weed quoted in Gienapp, "'Politics,'" 51–52.

118. *CTr,* July 13:2 (quotation) and 25:2, 1860.

119. Bryce, *American Commonwealth,* II, 175–76; *NYTr,* Oct. 9:1, 1880.

120. *NHJC,* Oct. 29:1, 1880.

3. Partisanship Redefined

1. The concerns of liberal reformers are extensively treated in John G. Sproat, *"The Best Men": Liberal Reformers in the Gilded Age* (New York, 1968); Geoffrey Blodgett, "Reform Thought and the Genteel Tradition," in H. Wayne Morgan, ed., *The Gilded Age,* "revised and enlarged edition" (Syracuse, 1970), 55–76; idem, "The Mugwump Reputation, 1870 to the Present," *Journal of American History,* 66 (Mar. 1980), 867–87; idem, *The Gentle Reformers: Massachusetts Democrats in the Cleveland Era* (Cambridge, Mass., 1966); Gerald W. McFarland, *Mugwumps, Morals, & Politics, 1884–1920* (Amherst, Mass., 1975); Ari Hoogenboom, *Outlawing the Spoils: A History of the Civil Service Reform Movement, 1865–1883* (Urbana, Ill., 1963); Earle Dudley Ross, *The Liberal Republican Movement* (New York, 1919); and Michael E. McGerr, "The Meaning of Liberal Republicanism: The Case of Ohio," *Civil War History,* 28 (Dec. 1982), 307–23.

2. Collective biographies of groups of liberal reformers include McFarland, *Mugwumps,* 17–34; McGerr, "Meaning," 308–12; and Hoogenboom, *Outlawing,* 190–96. On the importance of education for the liberals, see also Blodgett, "Mugwump Reputation," 878–81 and 887; and James Bryce, *The American Commonwealth,* 2 vols. (London, 1888), II, 264–65. For the liberals and social science, see McFarland, *Mugwumps,* 44 and 50; E. McClung Fleming, *R. R. Bowker: Militant Liberal* (Norman, Okla., 1952), 85 and 109; Thomas L. Haskell, The *Emergence of Professional Social Science: The American Social Science Association and the Nineteenth-Century Crisis of Authority* (Urbana, Ill., 1977); and Irwin Unger, *The Greenback Era: A Social and Political History of American Finance, 1865–1879* (Princeton, 1964), 136–39.

3. Geoffrey Blodgett notes this generational change in "Reform Thought," 74–75, and "Mugwump Reputation," 869–70.

4. For a fuller treatment of the liberal journals, see Chapter 5.

5. Fleming, *Bowker,* 129 and 133; and *NHJC,* July 7:1, 1884. See also Blodgett, "Mugwump Reputation," 881–84; Egbert Bartlett to Theodore Dwight Woolsey, May 8, 1876, Woolsey Family Papers, Yale University; William Dudley Foulke, *Fighting the Spoilsmen: Reminscences of the Civil Service Reform Movement* (New York, 1919), 11; Hoogenboom, *Outlawing,* 159–60; James S. Clarkson, "The Politician and the Pharisee," *North American Review,* 152 (May 1891), 613–23; and *NYS,* Sept. 20:1–2, 1892.

6. McFarland, *Mugwumps,* 28–34; McGerr, "Meaning," 308–12.

7. Historians have long divided over the reformers' power and influence. Hoogenboom, *Outlawing,* and Sproat, *"Best Men",* articulate the common view that the liberals were old-fashioned and powerless. In various, even conflicting ways, Blodgett, "Mugwump Reputation," 868–69, 876–78, 881, and 886, Matthew Josephson, *The Politicos, 1869–1896*

(New York, 1938), 141–70 and 341–97, Richard Hofstadter, *The Age of Reform: From Bryan to F.D.R.* (New York, 1955), 136–44,L. E. Fredman, *The Australian Ballot: The Story of an American Reform* (East Lansing, Mich., 1968), idem, "Seth Low: Theorist of Municipal Reform," *Journal of American Studies*, 6 (Apr. 1972), 19–39, McFarland, *Mugwumps*, 50–52, and Christopher Lasch, *The World of Nations: Reflections on American History, Politics, and Culture* (New York, 1973), 80–99, all recognize either reform's place within the late nineteenth-century upper-class or its influence on aspects of twentieth-century politics. Their viewpoint has shaped my understanding of the social and political context of reform.

8. [Jonathan Baxter Harrison], "Limited Sovereignty in the United States," *Atlantic Monthly*, 43 (Feb. 1879), 186. See also idem, "Sincere Demagogy," ibid., 44 (Oct. 1879), 489; [Thomas G. Shearman], "Universal Suffrage," *Nation*, 3 (Nov. 8, 1866), 371–72; George W. Julian, "Suffrage a Birthright," *International Review*, 6 (Jan. 1879), 3; and Cuthbert Mills, "Universal Suffrage in New York," ibid., 8 (Feb. 1880), 199.

9. Francis Parkman, "The Failure of Universal Suffrage," *North American Review*, 127 (July-Aug. 1878), 3–4 and 7.

10. Charles Francis Adams, Jr., "The Protection of the Ballot in National Elections," *Journal of Social Science*, 1 (June 1869), 106; "Majority Government," *Nation*, 24 (Apr. 26, 1877), 245–46. See, in addition, *NHJC*, July 27:2, 1863; Harrison, "Limited Sovereignty," 188–89; and Simon Sterne, *Suffrage in Cities* (New York, 1878), 10–12.

11. Parkman, "Failure," 7; *NHJC*, July 27:2, 1863; and [A. G. Sedgwick], "The Crime Against the Suffrage in Washington," *Nation*, 26 (June 27, 1878), 415.

12. Parkman, "Failure," 5 and 8–10. For earlier arguments against the suffrage, see Chilton Williamson, *American Suffrage from Property to Democracy, 1760–1860* (Princeton, 1960).

13. *NYTi*, Aug. 4:6, 1878; J. Francis Fisher, *Reform in Our Municipal Elections: A Plan Suggested to the Tax Payers of Philadelphia and New York* (Philadelphia, 1866), 16; and Mills, "Universal Suffrage" 200. See also [E. L. Godkin], "The Government of Our Great Cities," *Nation*, 3 (Oct. 18, 1866), 312; ibid., 25 (Nov. 5, 1877), 285; *NYP*, Apr. 18:2, 1877; Parkman, "Failure," 7–8; Theodore Dwight Woolsey, *Political Science, or the State Theoretically and Practically Considered*, 2 vols. (New York, 1878), I, 27–28 and 300; and Matthew P. Deady, *Towns and Cities* (Portland, Ore., 1886), 20–21.

14. "The Latest Bugbear," *Nation*, 1 (July 20, 1865), 69; [Godkin], "'Universal Suffrage and Universal Amnesty,'" ibid., 3 (Nov. 29, 1866), 430–31 (quotation); idem, "Congress and the Educational Test," ibid. (Dec. 20, 1866), 497–98; Adams, "Protection," 109–10; *NHR*, Aug. 8:2, 1881; Charles Dudley Warner, *The Complete Writings of Charles Dudley*

Warner, ed. Thomas R. Lounsbury, (Hartford, Conn., 1904), XIV, 314–15; and Sproat, *"Best Men",* 32.

15. Mills, "Universal Suffrage," 206; Harrison, "Limited Sovereignty," 190. For some later interest in an educational requirement, see *CTi,* July 4:3, 1892; *BC,* Aug. 30:3, 1892; and Chapter 7, below.

16. Harrison, "Limited Sovereignty," 190; Dorman B. Eaton, "Municipal Government," *Journal of Social Science,* 5 (1873), 7.

17. Woolsey, *Political Science,* II, 304–05 and 373–74; Parkman, "Failure," 20; Godkin, "Government," 312; and idem, "The City and the Country," *Nation,* 25 (Nov. 29, 1877), 328. See also Eaton, "Municipal Government," 1–2 and 4; Sterne, *Suffrage,* 31; and Henry C. Lea, "Fetichism in Politics," *Forum,* 9 (June 1890), 430–31.

18. Sterne, *Suffrage,* 16–17 and 19; and also Fisher, *Reform,* 6–8; Mills, "Universal Suffrage," 201–04 and 208–10; and Deady, *Towns,* 22–23.

19. Eaton, "Municipal Government," 7–8; and Van Buren Denslow, "Tammany Hall," *International Review,* 8 (Apr. 1880), 441–42; Deady, *Towns,* 31–32; Fisher, *Reform,* 18–19; Godkin, "Government," 313; idem, "Tweed," *Nation,* 25 (Oct. 18, 1877), 237–38; Mills, "Universal Suffrage," 204–05; Sterne, *Suffrage,* 25; and Woolsey, *Political Science,* II, 301–02, 375–76, 378–80, and 566.

20. Alexander C. Flick, *Samuel Jones Tilden: A Study in Political Sagacity* (New York, 1939), 261–62; *Report of the Commission to Devise a Plan for the Government of Cities in the State of New York. Presented to the Legislature, March 6, 1877 (New York, 1877).*

21. "The Rights of Tax-Payers," *Harper's Weekly,* 21 (Apr. 7, 1877), 263; "Municipal Politics," ibid. (Apr. 28, 1877), 323; "Voting in Cities," ibid. (Sept. 29, 1877), 758–59; "A Mistake," ibid. (Oct. 20, 1877), 819; "The City Amendments," ibid. (Nov. 10, 1877), 879; "Two Questions for the Legislature," ibid. (Nov. 24, 1877), 919; "Distrust of the People," ibid., 22 (Mar. 9, 1878), 187; *NYP,* Mar. 7:2, 17:2, 23:2, and 29:2, Apr. 6:2, 7:2, and 9:2, and Oct. 19:2, 20:2, 22:2, and 24:2, 1877; *Nation,* 25 (Oct. 25, 1877), 248 (quotation); and [Godkin], "The Constitutional Amendment on City Government," ibid., 26 (Feb. 14, 1878), 108–09.

22. *NYP,* Mar. 27:2, 29:3–4, and 31:2, Apr. 3:1–2, 4:1–2, 5:1, 9:1, 13:1, and 25:1, and Nov. 2:1, 1877.

23. Ibid., Mar. 30:4, Apr. 4:1, 10:4, 11:2, and 20:1, and May 18:4, 1877. Tammany's response is in ibid., Apr. 27:1–2 and Oct. 30:1 (quotations), 1877.

24. Julian, "Suffrage,"2–10; *NHR,* Aug. 5:2, 1881.

25. James Russell Lowell, *The Complete Works of James Russell Lowell,* 7 vols. (Boston, 1910), VI, 28–30. See also Fisher, *Reform,* 4.

26. Warner, *Complete Writings,* XV, 201; [A. G. Sedgwick], *Nation,* 27 (July 18, 1878), 42; Shearman, "Universal Suffrage," 372; Lowell, *Com-*

plete Works, VI, 11–12 and 24; Gamaliel Bradford, "Is It the Ballot?," *Nation,* 24 (Jan. 4, 1877), 12. See, too, "The Cities in Politics," *Review of Reviews,* 6 (Nov. 1892), 518–19.

27. Shearman, "Universal Suffrage," 371–72; and also Seth Low, "An American View of Municipal Government in the United States," in Bryce, *American Commonwealth,* I, 634–35; and J. M. L. Babcock, *The Right of the Ballot: A Reply to Francis Parkman and Others Who Have Asserted "The Failure of Universal Suffrage" (Boston, 1879).*

28. Shearman, "Universal Suffrage," 371; Harrison, "Limited Sovereignty," 188–89; and Godkin, "Criminal Politics," *North American Review,* 150 (June 1890), 719. See also [Harrison], "Certain Dangerous Tendencies in American Life," *Atlantic Monthly,* 42 (Oct. 1878), 402; *NYP,* May 9:2, 1877; *NYTi,* July 4:4 and Oct. 20:6, 1878; Woolsey, *Political Science,* II, 565; Godkin, "A Key to Municipal Reform," *North American Review,* 151 (Oct. 1890), 427–28; and Diana Klebanow, "E. L. Godkin, the City, and Civic Responsibility," *New-York Historical Society Quarterly,* 55 (Jan. 1971), 63–65.

29. For evidence of anti-suffrage sentiment and its reception at the turn of the century, see E. L. C. Morse, "The Debasement of the Suffrage," *Nation,* 76 (June 25, 1903), 515; Edwin Burritt Smith, "Debasement of the Suffrage," ibid., 77 (July 9, 1903), 28–29; and Morse, "The Suffrage Again," ibid. (July 30, 1903), 93. For a different view of the liberals' interest in suffrage as the nineteenth century ended, see Sproat, *"Best Men",* 250 and 253.

30. Ibid.; John Higham, *Strangers in the Land: Patterns of American Nativism, 1860–1925* (New York, 1973).

31. *NYTi,* Oct. 20:6, 1878; Henry C. Lea, "The Open Ballot," *Nation,* 24 (Jan. 4, 1877), 11–12; Moorfield Storey, *Politics as a Duty, and as a Career* (New York, 1889), 4–6; and also "The Pennsylvania Constitutional Convention of 1872–73," *Penn Monthly,* 4 (Jan. 1873), 3; Harrison, "Limited Sovereignty," 185; and idem, "Tendencies," 399–402.

32. George William Curtis, *Orations and Addresses of George William Curtis,* ed. Charles Eliot Norton, 3 vols. (New York, 1894), I, 261–85 and 313–37; Storey, *Politics; NYTi,* July 4:4, 1878; Woolsey, *Political Science,* II, 566–67; R. R. Bowker, "Political Responsibility of the Individual," *Atlantic Monthly,* 46 (Sept. 1880), 320; Fleming, *Bowker,* 98–99; Eaton, "Municipal Government," 24; Bryce, *American Commonwealth,* II, 370–71; Godkin, "Criminal Politics," 721; Julian, "The Abuse of the Ballot and Its Remedy," *International Review,* 8 (May 1880), 536–39; and Julian, "Suffrage," 16–17 and 20.

33. F. A. P. Barnard, "The Degradation of Our Politics," *Forum,* 9 (Apr. 1890), 129 (quotation); Curtis, *Orations,* I, 269 and 351; Parkman, "Fail-

ure," 14–19; [Godkin], "Educated Men in Centennial Politics," *Nation*, 23 (July 6, 1876), 5–6; and Harrison, "Limited Sovereignty," 186.

34. Henry Adams, "The 'Independents' and the Canvass," *North American Review*, 123 (Oct. 1876), 463–64; S. Dana Horton, *Proportional Representation. The Election of Party Candidates Under the Free List* (Philadelphia, 1873), 19; and Bowker, "Political Responsibility," 321–22; and also "A True Republic," *Atlantic Monthly*, 46 (Nov. 1880), 716–19; Henry W. Bellows, "Civil-Service Reform," *North American Review*, 130 (Mar. 1880), 250; Dorman B. Eaton, "Parties and Independents," ibid., 144 (June 1887), 549–64; Curtis, *Orations*, I, 45–46, 272, and 309; and McGerr, "Meaning," 316.

35. *NHJC*, Jan. 8:1 and Sept. 25:1, 1873, Oct. 14:1, 1874, and Nov. 28:4, 1881; Curtis, *Orations*, II, 150–52; Barnard, "Degradation," 132; Woolsey, *Political Science*, I, 393; F. W. Whitridge, "A Brake on the Machine," *International Review*, 8 (Mar. 1880), 242–52; "Purifying the Primaries," *Nation*, 22 (May 4, 1876), 288–89; Bowker, "Political Responsibility," 326; Storey, *Politics*, 7–10; and William M. Ivins, *Machine Politics and Money in Elections in New York City* (New York, 1887), 19–22.

36. Brooks Adams, "The Platform of the New Party," *North American Review*, 119 (July 1874), 42; Herbert Tuttle, "The Despotism of Party," *Atlantic Monthly*, 54 (Sept. 1884), 378; and Bowker, "Political Responsibility," 323. See in addition, Frank J. Goodnow, "The Tweed Ring in New York City," in Bryce, *American Commonwealth*, II, 353; Curtis, *Orations*, I, 272 and 305, and II, 145–46; Wayne MacVeagh, "The Next Presidency," *Century*, 27 (Mar. 1884), 672; Woolsey, *Political Science*, II, 557–58; Lea, "Fetichism," 432–33; and Sproat, *"Best Men"*, 60–61.

37. David Montgomery, *Beyond Equality: Labor and the Radical Republicans, 1862–1872* (New York, 1967), 360–68; and Sproat, *"Best Men"*, 48–49.

38. Alexander P. Callow, Jr., *The Tweed Ring* (New York, 1966).

39. Ross, *Liberal Republican Movement;* Sproat, *"Best Men"*, 48–49; and McGerr, "Meaning."

40. Henry C. Lea, "Can Nothing Be Done?," *Nation*, 22 (Mar. 16, 1876), 177–78; Bowker, "Political Responsibility," 322; Woolsey, *Political Science*, II, 566–67; Barnard, "Degradation," 126–27; and Fred B. Joyner, *David Ames Wells, Champion of Free Trade* (Cedar Rapids, 1939), 147–49.

41. Woolsey, *Political Science*, II, 389–93.

42. Sproat, *"Best Men"*, 9; and Leonard W. Bacon, "A Political Paradox," *Forum*, 8 (Feb. 1890), 681–82.

43. Bowker, "Political Responsibility," 320–28 (quotations on 324 and 326); and Lowell, *Complete Works*, VI, 200–01. See also *NHJC*, May 9:2, 1872; *NYH*, Oct. 15:9, 1888; Curtis, *Orations*, I, 278–80; Henry Adams,

"Independents," 460–61 and 466; Eaton, "Parties and Independents"; Curtis Guild, Jr., "A Requisite of Reform," *North American Review*, 152 (Apr. 1891), 506–08; and Bryce, *American Commonwealth*, II, 19–20.

44. Hoogenboom, *Outlawing*, 136–41; Sproat, *"Best Men"*, 89–92; and Fleming, *Bowker*, 103–08.

45. Whitridge, "Brake," 248–52; Fleming, *Bowker*, 114–33 and 198; Sproat, *"Best Men"*, 104–06; *NHJC*, Mar. 25:1, 1880; and Bowker, "Political Responsibility," 327.

46. Curtis, *Orations*, II, 159.

47. Sproat, *"Best Men"*, 112–41; McFarland, *Mugwumps*, 53; and Fleming, *Bowker*, 202–10. For a sense of the Mugwumps' antipathy to Blaine, see *NN*, Sept. 4:1, 1884; and *NHJC*, June 24:3, 1884.

48. "Senator Hill and the Independents," *Harper's Weekly*, 36 (Oct. 1, 1892), 938. The independents' confidence in their power appears in George Walker to Rutherford B. Hayes, July 3, 1876, B. F. Peel to Hayes, July 8, 1876, Rutherford B. Hayes Papers, Rutherford B. Hayes Library, Fremont, Ohio; Dorman B. Eaton, "The Public Service and the Public," *Atlantic Monthly*, 41 (Feb. 1878), 241–52; Julian, "Abuse," 544; J. Laurence Laughlin, "The New Party," *Atlantic Monthly*, 53 (June 1884), 837–40; Curtis, *Orations*, I, 335–36, and II, 158; E. L. Godkin, "The Political Outlook," *Scribner's Monthly*, 19 (Feb. 1880), 613–20; MacVeagh, "Next Presidency," 676; "The Independent Voter in the Next Campaign," *Century*, 27 (Mar. 1884), 786; "A Hurra Campaign," *Harper's Weekly*, 28 (Feb. 2, 1884), 70; "'The Old Guard,'" ibid., 71; "'Here We Go Again!,'" ibid. (Feb. 16, 1884), 103; George Walton Green, "The Shifting Vote. I," ibid. (May 24, 1884), 321; idem, "The Shifting Vote. II," ibid. (May 31, 1884), 347; Lea, "Fetichism," 434; Bryce, *American Commonwealth*, II, 296; Barnard, "Degradation," 127; and "Partisan Recognition of the Independent Voter," *Century*, 40 (Oct. 1890), 950–53.

49. Storey, *Politics*, 14–28 and 31 (quotations from 15–16 and 31).

50. Harrison, "Tendencies," 399–402.

51. Storey, *Politics*, 28; A. B. Mason to William Graham Sumner, Mar. 25, 1877, William Graham Sumner Papers, Yale University; and Joyner, *Wells*, 139–40.

52. Harrison, "Tendencies," 400; "Civil Service Clubs," *Harper's Weekly*, 21 (Nov. 3, 1877), 858; Joyner, *Wells*, 139–40; Flick, Tilden, 120–21; George Haven Putnam, *George Palmer Putnam, A Memoir* (New York, 1912), 280–85; Unger, *Greenback Era*, 141–42; Frank Freidel, "The Loyal Publication Society: A Pro-Union Propaganda Agency," *Mississippi Valley Historical Review*, 26 (Dec. 1939), 359–75; Joel H. Silbey, *A Respectable Minority: The Democratic Party in the Civil War Era, 1860–1868* (New York, 1977), 64 and 137; and George Fredrickson, *The Inner Civil War: Northern Intellectuals and the Crisis of the Union* (New York, 1965), 98–112.

53. Joseph Logsdon, *Horace White, Nineteenth-Century Liberal* (Westport, Conn., 1971), 78–80 and 118; Fleming, *Bowker*, 90–92 and 199–200; Sproat, *"Best Men"*, 78 and 195; and Joyner, *Wells*, 142–45.

54. Abraham L. Earle to Sumner, Oct. 14 and 16, Nov. 1 and 11, 1875, Jan. 18, 1876, and ensuing letters in Sumner Papers; Fleming, *Bowker*, 93–96.

55. Alfred B. Mason to Sumner, Sept. 2, 13, 15, 29, and 30, 1876, and following letters in Sumner Papers.

56. Josiah Quincy to Sumner, Mar. 11, 1885, Emerson W. Judd to Sumner, Sept. 16, 1886, and May 3, 1890, ibid.

57. Samuel W. Mendum, "The Question Clubs and the Tariff," *North American Review*, 150 (Mar. 1890), 301–09.

58. "Civil Service Clubs," 858; Sproat, *"Best Men"*, 262–64; Hoogenboom, *Outlawing*, 186–97; *NHR*, Oct. 11:4 and 26:1 and 4, and Dec. 10:4, 1881, and Dec. 9:4, 1882; and Frank Mann Stewart, *The National Civil Service Reform League: History, Activities, and Problems* (Austin, Tex., 1929).

59. Robert Muccigrosso, "The City Reform Club: A Study in Late Nineteenth-Century *Reform*," *New York-Historical Society Quarterly*, 52 (July 1968), 235–54; McFarland, *Mugwumps*, 87–90.

60. Sproat, *"Best Men"*, 59–60; William Howe Tolman, *Municipal Reform Movements in the United States* (New York, 1895); *NHJC*, Nov. 17:1 and 3, 1896; Frank Mann Stewart, *A Half Century of Municipal Reform: The History of the National Municipal League* (Berkeley, 1950); and David Paul Nord, *Newspapers and New Politics: Midwestern Municipal Reform*, 1890–1900 (Ann Arbor, Mich., 1979), esp. 1–9, 38–40, 53–58, and 59–82.

61. Unger, *Greenback Era*, 136–39; Hoogenboom, *Outlawing*, 55–56 and 65; and Haskell, *Emergence*.

62. Unger, *Greenback Era*, 139–42; Sproat, *"Best Men"*, 194.

63. McFarland, *Mugwumps*, 14–15; Winslow Warren to Sumner, May 15, 1886, and Charles Warren to Sumner, Feb. 24, 1899, Sumner Papers.

64. Everett P. Wheeler, *Sixty Years of American Life: Taylor to Roosevelt* (New York, 1917), 183ff.; Sproat, *"Best Men"*, 56 and 195; John DeWitt Warner to Sumner, May 23, 1889, Sumner Papers.

65. Fleming, *Bowker*, 84–85, 97–98, 101–03, and 219–20; Joyner, *Wells*, 147–49.

66. Albert Stickney, "Government Machinery," *International Review*, 8 (May 1880), 546–80, as well as numerous other works by Stickney; Woolsey, *Political Science*, II, 305–06, 563–65, and 567; Harrison, "Limited Sovereignty," 191.

67. Simon Sterne, *Report to the Constitutional Convention of the State of New York, on Personal Representation, Prepared at the Request, and Printed Under the Auspices of the Personal Representation Society* (New York, 1867);

idem, *Representative Government: Its Evils and Their Reform* (New York?, 1869); *Atlantic Monthly*, 24 (Feb. 1872), 255–56; "Pennsylvania Constitutional Convention," 2–3 and 14–16; S. Dana Horton, *The Election of Party Candidates Under the Free List* (Cincinnati, 1873); idem, *Proportional Representation*, especially 6–7, 19–21, and 31; *NHJC*, Apr. 8:2, 1875; Woolsey, *Political Science*, II, 293–95; John H. Ward, *Reform Within the Party* (Louisville, Ky., n.d.); and John M. Berry, *Proportional Representation. The Gove System. Notes on the Inequality of Existing Methods of Electing Representatives of the People* (Worcester, Mass., 1892).

68. *KCS*, Oct. 11:4, 1884; Frederick W. Holls, "Compulsory Voting," *Annals of the American Academy of Political and Social Science*, 1 (Apr. 1891), 586–614; Edward M. Shepard, *Compulsory Voting: An Address Before the Brooklyn Democratic Club* (Brooklyn?, 1891); and W. T. Donaldson, "Compulsory Voting: With Bibliographies," *Ohio Legislative Reference Department Bulletin*, 1 (Apr. 9, 1914).

69. Sproat, "Best Men", 257–71; Fleming, *Bowker*, 200–02; Hoogenboom, *Outlawing*; A. Bower Sageser, *The First Two Decades of the Pendleton Act: A Study of Civil Service Reform* (Lincoln, Neb., 1935); Foulke, *Fighting*; Paul P. Van Riper, *The History of the United States Civil Service* (Evanston, Ill., 1958). For the use of "business principles" to justify civil service reform, see *NHR*, Nov. 8:2, 1870; Eaton, "Municipal Government," 14; and Hoogenboom, *Outlawing*, 170–71 and 217–18.

70. Ivins, *Machine Politics;* [R. R. Bowker], *Electoral Reform. With the Massachusetts Ballot Reform Act and New York (Saxton) Bill* (New York, 1889); Bryce, *American Commonwealth*, II, 138–40; Alfred B. Mason to Sumner, Mar. 22, 1879, Sumner Papers. For an amusing demonstration of the uses of the un-secret ballot, see *NHR*, Dec. 7:1, 9:1, 11:2, 22:1, 27:1, and 28:2, 1882.

71. M. C. L. [despite the first initial, Henry C. Lea], "Our Danger, and the Remedy," *Nation*, 23 (Dec. 21, 1876), 367–68; idem, "The Open Ballot," ibid., 24 (Jan. 4, 1877), 11–12; "Viva-Voce Voting," ibid. (Mar. 29, 1877), 192–93; *NYP*, May 19:1, 1877; and "Pennsylvania Constitutional Convention," 14.

72. *NN*, Nov. 4:1, 1884; Bryce, *American Commonwealth*, II, 367; James S. Clarkson to Benjamin Harrison, Nov. 2, 1888, Benjamin Harrison Papers, Library of Congress. For indications of the concern for secrecy, see *NYTr*, Nov. 3:2, 1880; and James Stoddard to Henry W. Farnam, Oct. 21, 1884, Farnam Family Papers, Yale University.

73. Fredman, *Australian Ballot;* Richard P. McCormick, *The History of Voting in New Jersey: A Study of the Development of Election Machinery, 1664–1911* (New Brunswick, N.J., 1953), 173–86; Herbert J. Bass, "The Politics of Ballot Reform in New York State, 1888–1890," *New York History*, 42 (July 1961), 253–71; Eric Falk Petersen, "Prelude to Progressivism: Cal-

ifornia Election Reform, 1870–1909" (Ph.D. diss., University of California, Los Angeles, 1969), 91–132; John H. Wigmore, *The Australian Ballot System as Embodied in the Legislation of Various Countries*, 2nd ed. (Boston, 1889); Eldon Cobb Evans, *A History of the Australian Ballot System in the United States* (Chicago, 1917); Bowker, *Electoral Reform; NYH*, Aug. 5:17, 1888; and Henry George to Grover Cleveland, July 9, 1888, Grover Cleveland Papers, Library of Congress.

74. Martin J. Schiesl, *The Politics of Efficiency: Municipal Administration and Reform in America, 1880–1920* (Berkeley, 1977); Bryce, *American Commonwealth*, II, 362–63; McFarland, *Mugwumps*, 13–14 and 86–106; Blodgett, *Gentle Reformers*, 240–61; and Tolman, *Municipal Reform Movements*.

75. *Report of the Commission*, 13–16; Fisher, *Reform*, 12–13; "Pennsylvania Constitutional Convention," 14; Eaton, "Municipal Government," 10–11; *NHJC*, Sept. 30:2, 1873, Sept. 18:1, 1875, and Nov. 17:1, 1896; "One of the Lessons," *Harper's Weekly*, 28 (Nov. 8, 1884), 732.

76. Eaton, "Municipal Government," 10–11; MacVeagh, "Next Presidency," 671.

77. McFarland, *Mugwumps*, 124–72, discusses the reformers' progressive activities.

78. A point nicely made in Blodgett, "Mugwump Reputation," 882.

4. Educational Politics

1. See Chapter 2 above.

2. Alexander C. Flick, *Samuel Jones Tilden: A Study in Political Sagacity* (New York, 1939), esp. 159, 166, 181–91, 193, 201, and 209; "Samuel Tilden: The Democrat as Social Scientist," in Robert Kelley, *The Transatlantic Persuasion: The Liberal-Democratic Mind in the Age of Gladstone* (New York, 1969), 238–92. For Tilden's interest in social science, see his speech to the American Social Science Assocation in Samuel J. Tilden, *The Writings and Speeches of Samuel J. Tilden*, ed. John Bigelow, 2 vols. (New York, 1885), II, 374–79.

3. *KCS*, Oct. 25:2, 1884; "Running the Political Campaign," *Harper's Weekly*, 36 (July 30, 1892), 726. See also Tilden to "Dear Sir," Sept. 11, 1871, Daniel S. Lamont Papers, Library of Congress; W. P. Bemus to Rutherford B. Hayes, July 1, 1876, Rutherford B. Hayes Papers, Rutherford B. Hayes Library, Fremont, Ohio; Tilden to "Dear Sir," Aug. 29, and Oct. 10 and 17, Daniel S. Lamont to Tilden, Sept. 7, Allen C. Beach to "Dear Sir," Oct. 9, "Mem. of S. J. Tilden's Circular letters," all 1874, Samuel J. Tilden Papers, New York Public Library; Keith Ian Polakoff, "The Disorganized Democracy: An Institutional Study of the Democratic Party, 1872–1880" (Ph.D. diss., Northwestern University, 1968), 178–

205; Flick, *Tilden*, 249–50; William C. Hudson, *Random Recollections of an Old Political Reporter* (New York, 1911), 42–47; and "Cost of National Campaigns," *World's Work*, 1 (Nov. 1900), 77.

4. Allan Nevins, *Abram S. Hewitt: With Some Account of Peter Cooper* (New York, 1935); Abram S. Hewitt, *Selected Writings of Abram S. Hewitt*, ed. Allan Nevins (New York, 1937), 145–54, 209–26, 295–311, and 315–37 (quotations from 309–10). See also Alan Trachtenberg, *Brooklyn Bridge: Fact and Symbol*, 2nd ed. (Chicago, 1979), 7–9, 101–09, and 118–24.

5. Hewitt, *Writings*, 159–61; Hewitt to Tilden, Aug. 6 (quotation) and Sept. 2, 1876, Tilden Papers, New York Public Library; Nevins, *Hewitt*, 305–19; *1868: Textbook for the Republican Campaign* (New York, 1868); *The Campaign Textbook: Why the People Want a Change: The Republican Party Reviewed: Its Sins of Commission and Omission: A Summary of the Leading Events in Our History Under Republican Administration* (New York, 1876).

6. *NYTr*, Aug. 8:1, 1876 (second quotation); Untitled memorandum (cited hereafter by it opening words, "The work of a Presidential Campaign") by William S. Andrews, Feb. 20, 1888, in Grover Cleveland Papers, Library of Congress; "To the Person in charge of this Election District," "PLAN OF ORGANIZATION FOR Tilden Reform Clubs," *Tilden and Hendricks. REFORM, Economy and Better Times. 1876* (New York?, 1876?), Abram S. Hewitt to "Dear Sir": National Democratic Committee Circular Number 4 (first), Abram S. Hewitt to "Dear Sir": National Democatic Committee Circular Number 5, Samuel J. Tilden Papers, Columbia University; Hewitt, *Writings*, 160–61; Flick, Tilden, 281–82; *KCS*, Oct. 25:2, 1884; "Cost of Campaigns," 80.

7. *REFORM. FOR PRESIDENT, SAMUEL J. TILDEN. FOR VICE-PRESIDENT, THOMAS A HENDRICKS. WHAT TILDEN HAS DONE IN BREAKING RINGS. THE TWEED RING* (New York?, 1876?); *REFORM. FACTS FOR Independent Voters* (New York?, 1876?); and other leaflets in Tilden Papers, Columbia University.

8. Andrews, "The Work of a Presidential Campaign."

9. *NYTi*, July 10:4, 1888 (first quotation); *NYTr*, Aug. 8:1, 1876; Daniel S. Lamont to George W. Smith, Aug. 18, 1876, E. Casserly to Tilden, Aug. 29, 1876, and Thomas Ewing to Tilden (second), Sept. 25, 1876, Tilden Papers, New York Public Library; Whitelaw Reid to S. J. Bowen, Oct. 17, 1876, Whitelaw Reid Papers, Library of Congress; Andrews, "The work of a Presidential Campaign," Cleveland Papers; and Flick, *Tilden*, 307–08. For some local support for Tilden's approach, see J. M. Goodwin to Edward L. Parris, Aug. 11, 1876, Tilden Papers, Columbia University.

10. Note, for instance, the Republican canvasses in New Jersey and Indiana described in Charles P. Smith to William E. Chandler, Oct. 1, 1868, and O. P. Morton to E. D. Morgan, Aug. 11, 1872, William E.

Chandler Papers, Library of Congress. See also Jno. D. Defrees to Whitelaw Reid, Oct. 23, 1874, Reid Papers.

11. *BS,* July 17:1, 1888. For indications of Tilden's influence on politicians and campaign styles, see *KCS,* Oct. 25:2, 1884; *NYTi,* Sept. 10:4, 1890; *PI,* July 10:9, 1892; *HT,* Aug. 20:2, 1892; *BC,* Oct. 1:9, 1892; R. B. McCrory to William C. Whitney, June 25, 1892, William C. Whitney Papers, Library of Congress; Hudson, *Random Recollections,* 42–47; Hewitt, *Writings,* 162; "Running the Political Campaign," 726; "Cost of Campaigns," 77; and William R. Browne to Warren G. Harding, July 7, 1920, box 166, Warren G. Harding Papers, Ohio Historical Society, Columbus.

12. For the outlines of these two Democratic campaigns, see: Andrews, "The work of a Presidential Campaign," Cleveland Papers; Polakoff, "Disorganized Democracy," 284–330; *NYTr,* July 13:1 and 24:1, and Aug. 16:1, 1880; *KCS,* Oct. 25:2, 1884; Allan Nevins, *Grover Cleveland: A Study in Courage* (New York, 1932), 159–60 and 180–81; and Hudson, *Random Recollections,* 151, 177, and 192.

13. John Sherman to Rutherford B. Hayes, Aug. 1, W. K. Rogers to Hayes, Aug. 16 and 19, R. C. McCormick to Hayes, Aug. 25, 28, and 29 (quotation), and Sept. 3, 11, and 14, J. W. Cracraft to Hayes, Aug. 26, Edward F. Noyes to Hayes, Aug. 27 and 30, all 1876, Hayes Papers; William S. Dodge to William E. Chandler, Aug. 21 and 26, and Sept. 18, R. C. McCormick to Chandler, Aug. 21 and 27, all 1876, William E. Chandler Papers; Zachariah Chandler to Hayes, Sept. 12, 1876, Zachariah Chandler Papers, Library of Congress.

14. C. Dyer to John Sherman, July 27, 1880, John Sherman Papers, Library of Congress; G. W. Hooker to William E. Chandler, July 23, 1880, William E. Chandler Papers; James A. Garfield to Edward McPherson, Aug. 19 and Nov. 8, 1880, and Joseph R. Hawley to McPherson, Aug. 21, 1880, Edward McPherson Papers, Library of Congress; Marshall Jewell to Nelson W. Aldrich, Oct. 11, 1880, and McPherson to Aldrich, Aug. 23, 1884, Nelson W. Aldrich Papers, Library of Congress; campaign documents in box 36, James G. Blaine Papers, Library of Congress; Robert D. Marcus, *Grand Old Party: Political Structure in the Gilded Age, 1880–1896* (New York, 1971), 39–58 and 85–100; *NYTr,* July 7:1, 9:1, 23:1, and 31:5, and Aug. 8:1, 20:1, 24:1, and 31:1, 1880, and July 1:5, 17:1, 30:2, and 31:2, 1884.

15. *PI,* Aug. 1:3, 19:2, and 30:2 (quotation), 1884.

16. Ibid., July 16:2 and Aug. 5:3, 6:2, and 13:2, 1884. For signs of educational campaigning in other states, see *NYW,* Aug. 12:8 and Oct. 29:1, 1884; *NHU,* Sept. 4:8, 1884; and Ballard Smith, "The Political Effect of the Message," *North American Review,* 146 (Feb. 1888), 215–16.

17. Quoted in *NHU,* Aug. 11:8, 1884. For McClure's career, see his *Recollections of a Half Century* (Salem, Mass., 1902).

18. Whitelaw Reid to Rutherford B. Hayes, July 21, 1876, Hayes Papers; Reid to S. J. Bowen, Oct. 17, 1876, Reid Papers; *NYTr*, Aug. 8:1, 1876, Oct. 2:4, 1880, July 1:4 and Aug. 13:4, 1884, and June 28:4, 1888 (quotation).

19. *PI*, Oct. 2:4 and 9:4, 1884; *NHU*, July 21:4, 1884.

20. For Cleveland's relationship with the reformers, see Nevins, *Cleveland*, 280–98 and 367–403; Gerald W. McFarland, *Mugwumps, Morals, & Politics, 1884–1920* (Amherst, Mass., 1975), 55–68; and E. McClung Fleming, *R. R. Bowker: Militant Liberal* (Norman, Okla., 1952), 213–18.

21. *NYTr*, July 22:13, 1888; *NYTi*, Apr. 24:1, 1891, and June 1:11, 1918; *WP*, June 1:4, 1918; Clarkson to William Loeb, Jr., Sept. 15, 1904, Theodore Roosevelt Papers, Library of Congress; and David Crosson, "James S. Clarkson and Theodore Roosevelt, 1901–1904: A Study in Contrasting Political Traditions," *Annals of Iowa*, 42 (Summer, 1974), 344–60. Unfortunately, there is no full-scale biography of Clarkson.

22. Quotation from the draft of a speech delivered to the Sixth Annual Convention of the Republican League of Clubs, Louisville, Kentucky, May 10, 1893, James S. Clarkson Papers, Library of Congress. These and other remarks were apparently deleted from the final text of the speech because they were too long and praised James G. Blaine too much. See also "Permanent Republican Clubs," *North American Review*, 146 (Mar. 1888), 260–61; and Clarkson, "The Politician and the Pharisee,"*North American Review*, 152 (May 1891), 613–23.

23. *NYTi*, Sept. 20:1 and Dec. 13:1, 15:2, 16:1, 17:1–2, 18:1–2, and 19:4–5, 1887; and *NYTr*, Dec. 14:2, 1887, and July 3:1, 1888.

24. *NYTi*, Dec. 19:4, 1887; "Permanent Republican Clubs," 249; Daniel J. Ryan, "Clubs in Politics," *North American Review*, 146 (Feb. 1888), 176. See also "Permanent Republican Clubs," 256 and 264, and the praise for clubs from a leading liberal reformer in Dorman B. Eaton, "Parties and Independents," *North American Review*, 144 (June 1887), 559.

25. "Permanent Republican Clubs," 258 and 263.

26. Ibid., 243 and 257–58.

27. Ryan, "Clubs," 174–76; "Permanent Republican Clubs," 249–50 and 257–58, and also 255 and 263.

28. *NYTi*, Apr. 22:5, 23:5, May 25:5, and June 11:8 and 17:16, 1888, Dec. 3:4, 1904; *BS*, July 4:1 and 4, 5:1, and 6:1, 1888; *NYH*, July 5:3, and 6:2, 1888; Chauncey F. Black to Daniel Lamont, Aug. 18, 1888, Cleveland Papers (quotation).

29. The Quay family believed Clarkson had been offered the chairmanship and turned the post down. It is difficult to imagine that Clarkson would have given up such an opportunity, but he was in poor health during the campaign and may also have had to make time for his business

affairs. See Richard R. Quay to Isaac R. Pennypacker, Mar. 9, 1927, Matthew S. Quay Papers, Library of Congress.

30. *NYTi*, Aug. 19:9, 1891; Clarkson to William Loeb, Jr., Aug. 19, 1906, Theodore Roosevelt Papers; James A. Kehl, *Boss Rule in the Gilded Age: Matt Quay of Pennsylvania* (Pittsburgh, 1981), 93–114.

31. *NYTr*, July 17:6, 1888.

32. William McKinley to Levi P. Morton, July 19, 1888, Levi P. Morton Papers, New York Public Library; *NYTr*, July 13:5, 14:7, and 20:5, and Aug. 4:2, 1888; *BS*, July 23:1, 1888; *HT*, Aug. 3:5, 1888.

33. William B. Allison to Benjamin Harrison, Oct. 13, 1888, Benjamin Harrison Papers, Library of Congress; *NYTr*, July 26:3 and Aug. 3:2 and 17:2, 1888; Nevins, *Cleveland*, 418–20; A. T. Volwiler, "Tariff Strategy and Propaganda in the United States, 1887–1888," *American Historical Review*, 36 (Oct. 1930), 76–96.

34. *NYH*, July 13:2 and 14:2, 1888; *NYTr*, July 4:2, 12:1, and 13:2, Aug. 17:2, and Sept. 2:9, 1888; Marcus, *Grand Old Party*, 158.

35. *NYTr*, Aug. 16:2, 1888.

36. For Lamont's career, see Allen Johnson and Dumas Malone, eds., *The Dictionary of American Biography*, 20 vols. (New York, 1928–1936), X, 563–64; and Anne Marie Fitzsimmons, "The Political Career of Daniel S. Lamont, 1870–1897" (Ph.D. diss., Catholic University of America, 1965).

37. Andrews to Daniel S. Lamont, Feb. 3 and 19, 1888, and "The work of a Presidential Campaign," Cleveland Papers.

38. *BS*, June 27:4, July 24:1 (quotation) and 31:1, 1888; *NYTi*, June 27:1, 30:4, and July 10:4, 1888; *HT*, Aug. 1:4, 1888; *NYTr*, Sept. 2:9, 1888; Nevins, *Cleveland*, 415–17; and F. W. Dawson to Cleveland, July 12 and 20, 1888, Cleveland Papers.

39. *NYTi*, Aug. 5:2, 1888; Calvin S. Brice to Lamont, letter and telegram, Aug. 4, 1888, Cleveland Papers.

40. *BS*, June 19:4, 20:2, and July 27:1, 28:1, and 31:1, 1888; *NYH*, July 14:4, 16:4, Aug. 7:5, 8:4, 18:2, and Oct. 12:5, 1888; *NYTi*, July 10:4 and 12:4, 1888, and June 8:9, 1892; *NYTr*, Aug. 7:2, 10:3, 18:5, and 19:1, 1888; D. James McCutcheon to Lamont, July 9, Eugene T. Chamberlain to Lamont, ca. July 24, P. A. Collins to Cleveland, Aug. 2, George F. Parker to Lamont, Aug. 18, 23, and Sept. 2, Brice to Lamont, Sept. 11, S. P. Sheerin to Lamont, Sept. 12, W. L. Scott to Lamont, Sept. 14, William Foyle to Lamont, Sept. 15, and Wilson S. Bissell to Lamont, Oct. 3, all 1888, Cleveland Papers.

41. Brice to Lamont, Aug. 18 and Sept. 11, Parker to Lamont, Aug. 18, 23, Sept. 2, 6, Oct. 2, and undated fragment, all 1888, Cleveland Papers; George F. Parker, *Recollections of Grover Cleveland* (New York, 1904), 106–10 and 119–22; *National Cyclopaedia of American Biography*, 74 vols. (New

York and Clifton, N.J., 1898-   ), XXIV, 49; *NYH,* Oct. 12:5, 1888; and Nevins, *Cleveland,* 422.

42. *NYH,* Aug. 4:5 and Sept. 17:5, 1888; James E. Graybill to Lamont, July 24 and Oct. 24, Black to Lamont, Aug. 18 and Sept. 4, 1888, Cleveland Papers.

43. Nevins, *Cleveland,* 420–21; Everett P. Wheeler, *Sixty Years of American Life: Taylor to Roosevelt, 1850–1910* (New York, 1917), 183–93; Wheeler to Cleveland, Aug. 14, William M. Ivins to Lamont, Aug. 22, Wilson S. Bissell to Lamont, Aug. 29, 1888, Cleveland Papers; *NHJC,* July 10:2 and 11:2, 1888.

44. *NHU,* Aug. 21:8, 1888; *BS,* July 11:Supplement/2, 1888; and also *NHR,* Oct. 2:4 and 17:2, 1888; *NYH,* July 10:5, Oct. 14:10 and 20:5, 1888; George P. Edwards to Brice, Sept. 29, 1888, Cleveland Papers.

45. *NHJC,* July 23:2, 1888; G. Duff Nichols to Lamont, Aug. 8, George G. McNall to Lamont, Sept. 14, and Solomon Lucas to Lamont, Oct. 15, 1888, Cleveland Papers.

46. Parker to W. U. Hensel, June 26, and W. C. Tarkington to Cleveland, Sept. 21, 1888, ibid.

47. *NYTi,* Oct. 3:4, 1888, and June 8:9, 1892; *NYH,* Oct. 18:13 and 22:4, 1888; Eugene T. Chamberlain to Lamont, June, Ward Gregory to Lamont, July 25, D. Cady Herrick to Lamont, July, William M. Ivins to Lamont, Aug. 10 and 11, Myron H. Peck to Lamont, Aug. 18, Edward Murphy, Jr., to Lamont, Oct. 4, Walter N. Thayer to Lamont, Oct. 15, William C. Hudson to Lamont, Oct. 16, George S. Weed to Lamont, Oct. 19, and Charles S. Fairchild to Lamont, Oct. 21, all 1888, Cleveland Papers.

48. Myron H. Peck to Lamont, July 5 and Aug. 18 (first quotation), Parker to Lamont, Sept. 2 and undated fragment, and Eugene T. Chamberlain to Lamont, July 11 (second), 1888, ibid.

49. P. D. Estue to Lamont, June 26, and William M. Ivins to Lamont, Aug. 10, 1888, ibid.

50. Findlay Harris to R. H. Townshend, June 26, and Myron A. Cooney to Lamont, June 26, 1888, ibid.

51. John Cochrane to Cleveland, Aug. 25, 1888, ibid.

52. *NYTi,* Nov. 6:4, 1888; clipping from *York Gazette,* Nov. 1:?, 1888, enclosed with Black to Cleveland, Nov. 1, 1888, Cleveland Papers.

53. Clarkson, "Politician and Pharisee"; H.Wayne Morgan, *From Hayes to McKinley: National Party Politics, 1877–1896* (Syracuse, 1969), 331.

54. *NYTi,* July 2:8, Aug. 15:1, and Sept. 22:1, 1890.

55. Ibid., Oct. 3:1, 7:1 (quotation), and 12:2, 1890; Clarkson to Benjamin Harrison, Sept. 19 and 26, 1890, Harrison Papers.

56. For the Republicans' undoing, see Morgan, *From Hayes to McKinley,* 320–91; R. Hal Williams, *Years of Decision: American Politics in the 1890s*

(New York, 1978), 19–70; Richard J. Jensen, *The Winning of the Midwest: Social and Political Conflict, 1888–1896* (Chicago, 1971), 58–208; and Paul Kleppner, *The Third Electoral System, 1853–1892: Parties, Voters, and Political Cultures* (Chapel Hill, 1979), 298–356.

57. Clarkson to E. W. Halford, Nov. 20, 1890, Clarkson to Harrison, Nov. 26, 1890, Harrison Papers; *NYTi*, June 11:1, 1891.

58. Clarkson to E. W. Halford, Nov. 20, 1890, and Dec. 5, 1891, Clarkson to Harrison, Aug. 7, 1891, Harrison Papers; Clarkson to Welker Given, Aug. 13, 1894, Clarkson Papers.

59. Clarkson to Harrison, Nov. 26, 1890, Harrison Papers.

60. Harrison to Clarkson, Dec. 2, 1890, Clarkson to Harrison, Nov. 26 and Dec. 3, 1890, ibid.

61. M. M. Copeland to Clarkson, Nov. 21, 1890, Clarkson to Harrison, Dec. 11, 1890, and Aug. 7, 1891, Clarkson to E. W. Halford, Feb. 6, 1891, ibid.

62. Clarkson to Harrison, Aug. 7, 1891, ibid.

63. Clipping, *Iowa State Register*, July 22:?, 1891, Clarkson Papers; Clarkson to Harrison, Nov. 26, 1890, and May 5, 1891, Clarkson to G. M. Dodge, July 20, 1891, ibid.; *NYTi*, May 1:2, June 11:1, and July 28:3, 1891. The Farmers' Alliance understood quite clearly that Clarkson intended the Republican league as a rival to their own organization: *TA*, May 13:9, 1891. For discussion of the political style of the alliance and the People's party, see Chapter 8 below.

64. Clarkson to E. W. Halford, Jan. 24 and Feb. 6, 1891, Harrison Papers; *NYTi*, Apr. 22:5, 23:1, 24:1, and 30:3, May 1:2 and 7:8, and July 28:3, 1891.

65. *NYTi*, July 16:4, 18:1, 19:5, 20:1, 21:1, 30:1, and 31:1, 1891; Clarkson to Harrison, July 22, 1891, Harrison to Clarkson, July 27, 1891, Harrison Papers.

66. Clarkson to Harrison, Feb. 7 and Aug. 7, 1891, Clarkson to E. W. Halford, Sept. 24, 1891, Harrison Papers; *NYTi*, Apr. 13:1, July 2:1, and Aug. 12:8, 1891; Jensen, *Winning of the Midwest*, 154–77.

67. Clarkson to G. M. Dodge, Nov. 9, 1891, Clarkson to E. W. Halford, Nov. 17 and Dec. 5, 1891, Clarkson to Harrison, Jan. 9 and 13, 1892, Harrison Papers; Clarkson to Welker Given, Aug. 13, 1894, Clarkson Papers (quotations).

68. *NYTi*, Apr. 24:1 and Dec. 20:8, 1891; undated clipping, "The Work of the Republican National Committee," Clarkson to Welker Given, Aug. 13, 1894 (quotations), Clarkson Papers; Clarkson to Harrison, Nov. 21, 1890, Clarkson to E. W. Halford, Apr. 23 and 30, and May 13, 1892, Harrison Papers.

69. *PI*, Aug. 17:1 (first and second quotations), Sept. 18:9 and 26:4, 1892; *NYS*, Oct. 9:3, 1892 (third); *HT*, Aug. 20:2, 1892; Thomas H.

McKee to L. E. McComas, Sept. 26, 1892, Harrison Papers; Charles A. Gorman to William C. Whitney, Aug. 4, 1892, Whitney Papers; *BC*, Oct. 1:9, 1892; *RR*, 6 (Nov. 1892), 387–89; *TA*, Aug. 3:5, 1892. For a copy of *Protection and Reciprocity* and a sample of the stereotyped stories, see *AS*, Sept. 15:Supplement and 22:6, 1892. Despite using some of Clarkson's early work, the committee did not start the educational campaign soon enough to please all Republicans: N. Woodhale to William E. Chandler, July 28, 1892, William E. Chandler Papers.

70. Wheeler, *Sixty Years*, 144–48 (first quotation); Parker, *Recollections*, 138–39 (second), 148–50, 154–55, and 167–68; Mark D. Hirsch, *William C. Whitney, Modern Warwick* (New York, 1948), 400–01 and 407–08; Whitney to Cleveland, July 29 and Aug. 11, 1892, Cleveland Papers; William F. Harrity to Whitney, July 2, 1892, Josiah Quincy to Whitney, Oct. 13 and Nov. 3, 1892, Whitney Papers; *HT*, Aug. 9:2, 20:2, and 27:2, and Sept. 3:2, 1892; *PI*, Sept. 18:9 and 26:4, 1892; *BC*, Oct. 1:9, 1892; *NYS*, Oct. 9:3, 1892; *RR*, 6 (Nov. 1892), 387–89.

71. *NYS*, Oct. 9:3, 1892. See also the journals listed in the preceding note.

72. *RR*, 6 (Nov. 1892), 388; *PI*, July 10:9, 1892; *CPD*, Oct. 5:4, 1892; *MJ*, Sept. 12:4, 1892; and also *HT*, Oct. 4:6, 1892.

73. *PI*, July 10:9 and Sept. 18:9, 1892.

74. Ibid., Sept. 23:3 and Oct. 3:1 and 4:2 (quotation), 1892.

75. *NHP*, July 7:1 (quotation), Oct. 19:3, and Nov. 7:3, 1892; *NHU*, Aug. 10:1, 1892; *HT*, Aug. 5:6 and 12:3, and Sept. 20:1, 1892; *HC*, Aug. 12:1, 1892.

76. *OWH*, Oct. 7:1, 1892; *NYS*, Oct. 18:1, 1892; *MJ*, Oct. 29:12, 1892; M. C. Garber to E. W. Halford, Oct. 12, 1892, Harrison Papers. For more signs of depression in the campaign paraphernalia business, see *MJ*, Oct. 20:4 and Nov. 5:12, 1892.

77. For instance, *INSTRUCTIONS AND SUGGESTIONS TO CANVAS-SERS*, enclosed with Charles A. Gorman to William C. Whitney, Aug. 4, 1892, and F. M. D. Guise to Whitney, Sept. 9, 1892, Whitney Papers; *IFT*, Aug. 11:4, 1892; *MJ*, Sept. 29:2, Oct. 3:6 and 4:6, and Nov. 4:1, 1892; and *NYTr*, June 29:5, 1892.

78. Ibid. June 30:1, 1892; *MJ*, Aug. 15:1, 16:4 and 6, 18:1, and 22:4, 1892.

79. *HT*, Aug. 24:1, 1892; John Tracey to "Dear Sir," June 29, 1892, and E. Ellery Anderson to Whitney, Oct. 6, 1892, Whitney Papers.

80. *New York Commercial*, Oct. 22:?, 1892, quoted in *PI*, Oct. 23:1, 1892; *NYS*, Oct. 10:6, 1892. See also *NYTi*, July 3:2 and 5, 1892.

81. G. A. Martin to William C. Whitney, July 12, 1892, Whitney Papers (first quotation); *NYS*, Oct. 3:1 (second) and 26:6, 1892; *PI*, Oct. 24:4,

1892; Robert J. Loveland to E. W. Halford, Oct. 12, 1892, Harrison Papers (third).

82. *BC*, Aug. 26:1 and Sept. 17:2, 1892; *CTi*, July 2:3, 1892; *NHP*, Sept. 20:1 and Oct. 1:1, 1892; *MJ*, Aug. 6:1 and Nov. 7:7, 1892; *NYS*, Aug. 17:7, Sept. 28:2 (quotation), and Oct. 6:2 and 23:8, 1892; *PI*, Aug. 6:2 and 13:4, Sept. 28:5, and Oct. 2:5 and 23:2, 1892; *CPD*, Oct. 12:8, 1892.

83. Compiled from the *NHR*, *NHJC*, and *NHU* for 1880, and the *NHP* and *NHU* for 1892.

84. *PI*, Sept. 25:2, 1892.

85. *OWH*, Oct. 29:4, 1892.

86. *NYS*, Sept. 27:3 and Oct. 9:6, 1892; *NHP*, July 14:5, 1892; Isaac Jenkinson to E. W. Halford, Oct. 1, William H. Trammel to Halford, Oct. 2, Levi N. Brown to Halford, Oct. 4, and James A. Waymire to Halford, Oct. 17, 1892, Harrison Papers.

87. William J. Arkell to Harrison, Sept. 27, C. B. Landis to Halford, Sept. 30, and W. K. Sullivan to Halford, Oct. 8, 1892, ibid.; *OWH*, Sept. 24:1, 1892; *PI*, Oct. 27:1–2, 1892; *MJ*, Aug. 8:6 and Oct. 12:1, 1892; and *CPD*, Oct. 13:1, 1892; and Henry E. Tiepke to William E. Chandler, Oct. 15, 1892, William E. Chandler Papers.

88. *NYS*, Sept. 5:3 and Oct. 9:6, 1892; *PI*, Sept. 24:3, 1892; William H. Trammel to Halford, Oct. 2, 1892, Harrison Papers. See also *BC*, Sept. 10:4 and 12:2, and Oct. 8:10, 1892; *NHP*, Aug. 9:4, 1892; *NYS*, Oct. 4:2, 11:6, and 24:2, 1892; John W. Vrooman to Halford, Sept. 8, John K. Gowdy to Halford, Sept. 29, R. R. Shiel to Halford, Sept. 30, William H. Trammel to Halford, Oct. 7, James A. Waymire to Halford, Oct. 12, Levi N. Brown to Halford, Oct. 18, Daniel M. Ransdell to Harrison, Oct. 18, M. C. Garber to Halford, Oct. 19, and L. D. Guffin to E. Frank Tibbott, Nov. 2, all 1892, Harrison Papers.

89. *NYS*, Sept. 27:3, 1892; *PI*, Sept. 24:3, 1892; William H. Trammel to Halford, Oct. 7, Levi N. Brown to Halford, Oct. 18, and L. D. Guffin to E. Frank Tibbott, Nov. 2, 1892, Harrison Papers.

90. Wayne MacVeagh, "The Next Presidency," *Century Illustrated Monthly Magazine*, 27 (Mar. 1884), 670 (quotation); *DN*, Aug. 21:2, 1880; Charles T. Congdon, *Reminiscences of a Journalist* (Boston, 1880), 25; *PI*, Aug. 29:4, 1884; "Voting Habits, Past and Present," *Nation*, 41 (Dec. 17, 1885), 504–05. For a different view, see Marcus, *Grand Old Party*, 5–6 and 61.

91. *AS*, Oct. 13:1, 1892; *CPD*, Oct. 17:1 and 21:4, 1892; *OWH*, Oct. 14:4, 1892.

92. *BC*, Sept. 28:4, 1892; *NHU*, Aug. 30:4, 1892; *NYS*, Sept. 4:6 and Oct. 10:3, 1892; *PI*, Sept. 25:1, 1892. See Chapter 6 for a fuller treat-

ment of the effect of spectator sports and other diversions on political interest.

93. *BC*, Sept. 12:2, 1892; *NYS*, Sept. 27:3, 1892; *PI*, Sept. 24:3 and 25:1, 1892; Isaac Jenkinson to Halford, Oct. 1, 1892, Harrison Papers.

94. Hugh Beekman to William C. Whitney, Oct. 8, 1892, Whitney Papers; *NYS*, Oct. 4:2, 1892; and also *NHP*, Aug. 9:1 and Sept. 23:4, 1892; and *PI*, Sept. 25:1 and Oct. 31:1–2, 1892.

95. *MJ*, Oct. 4:4 and 22:1 (first quotation), and Nov. 3:2 (third) and 5:2, 1892; *OWH*, Sept. 26:4 and Oct. 11:4 and 14:4, 1892; *HT*, Oct. 15:3, 1892; *BC*, Oct. 8:10, 1892 (second); *CPD*, Oct. 21:4, 1892; William M. Hahn to Harrison, Oct. 6, L. T. Michener to Halford, Oct. 11, William M. Marine to Halford, Oct. 17, Daniel M. Ransdell to Harrison, Oct. 18, and L. D. Guffin to E. Frank Tibbott, Nov. 2, 1892, Harrison Papers; John C. Spooner to G. W. Hazleton, Sept. 26, 1892, John C. Spooner Papers, Library of Congress.

96. *NYS*, Sept. 4:6, 7:6, and 9:6, 1892.

97. *HT*, Nov. 10: 1892. Turnout figure rounded from United States Bureau of the Census, *Historical Statistics of the United States, Colonial Times to 1970, Bicenntenial Edition*, 2 vols. (Washington, D.C., 1975), I, 1072.

98. *HT*, Aug. 27:2, 1892.

99. James A. Rawley, *Edwin D. Morgan, 1811–1883: Merchant in Politics* (New York, 1955), 70–71 and 114–16; Richardson, *Chandler*, 98 and 144–46; Flick, *Tilden*, 303–04; Nevins, *Cleveland*, 180–81; Hirsch, *Whitney*, 408–09; Marcus, *Grand Old Party*, 178 and 243–49; *NHU*, Aug. 11:8, 1884; *PI*, July 10:9 and Sept. 19:4, 1892; *Campaign Contributions. Testimony Before a Subcommittee of the Committee on Privileges and Elections, United States Senate*, 62nd Cong., 2nd sess., 2 vols. (Washington, D.C., 1913), I, 199–202; James S. Clarkson to Wm. Loeb, Jr., Aug. 19, 1906, Theodore Roosevelt Papers; United States Bureau of the Census, *Historical Statistics of the United States*, I, 1081. Figures on national committees' funds must be treated with caution, not only because politicians and journalists lied or exaggerated—they often did—but because they were talking about different things. James Clarkson listed the Republican campaign fund of 1892 as "nearly $6,000,000"; the party treasurer for that year, Cornelius N. Bliss, Sr., a man noted for his probity, gave the amount handled by the committee as $1,160,000. Clarkson's figure, surely inflated, apparently includes money not spent on the national committee's headquarters operation and not disbursed directly by the committee. Bliss's figure refers to money handled and disbursed by the committee.

100. *NYTr*, Oct. 2:4, 1880; Rossiter Johnson, "A Perilous Balance," *North American Review*, 146 (Apr. 1888), 426–27; *NHP*, Aug. 12:1, 1892.

101. "A Retrospect," *Harper's Weekly*, 36 (Nov. 12, 1892), 1082.

5. The Press Transformed

1. Frank Luther Mott, *American Journalism: A History, 1690–1960*, 3d ed. (New York, 1962), esp. 316, 402, 503, 506–09, 546–60, and 635–50; Alfred McClung Lee, *The Daily Newspaper in America* (New York, 1937), 728–29; and Whitelaw Reid, *Some Newspaper Tendencies: An Address Delivered Before the Editorial Associations of New-York and Ohio* (New York, 1879), 6.

2. Eugene M. Camp, "Conscience in Journalism," *Century*, 42 (July 1891), 472; Will Irwin, "The American Newspaper, IV. The Spread and Decline of Yellow Journalism," *Collier's*, 46 (Mar. 4, 1911), 18. See also Charles Dudley Warner, *The Complete Writings of Charles Dudley Warner*, ed. Thomas R. Lounsbury, 15 vols. (Hartford, Conn., 1904), XIV, 266; and J. Lincoln Steffens, "The Business of a Newspaper," *Scribner's Monthly*, 22 (Oct. 1897), 447–67, esp. 460.

3. Rollo Ogden, "Some Aspects of Journalism," *Atlantic Monthly*, 98 (July 1906), 13; Elizabeth L. Banks, "American 'Yellow Journalism,'" *Living Age*, 218 (Sept. 3, 1898), 640–48. See in addition F. B. Sanborn, "Journalism and Journalists," *Atlantic Monthly*, 34 (July 1874), 64–65; James Melvin Lee, *History of American Journalism* (Boston, 1917), 352–53; Bernard Weisberger, *The American Newspaperman* (Chicago, 1961), 118–20; and Mott, *American Journalism*, 312.

4. Sanborn, "Journalism," 60–61; Mott, *American Journalism*, 311–12 and 405–06; and Michael Schudson, *Discovering the News: A Social History of American Newspapers* (New York, 1978), 61–87. For the "professionalization" of America, see, among other studies, Robert H. Wiebe, *The Search for Order, 1877–1920* (New York, 1967); and Burton J. Bledstein, *The Culture of Professionalism: The Middle Class and the Development of Higher Education in America* (New York, 1976).

5. Culver Haygood Smith, *The Press, Politics, and Patronage: The American Government's Use of Newspapers, 1789–1875* (Athens, Ga., 1977), 230–31 and 245–47.

6. *DN*, Aug. 25:2, 1880; *NN*, June 7:1, 1884; *CTi*, July 15:2, 1892; *PI*, July 1:1, 1892: and *SFE*, Sept. 1:1 and 6, 1896.

7. Mott, *American Journalism*, 414–19 and 573–76; Weisberger, *American Newspaperman*, 134–36.

8. Will Irwin, "The American Newspaper, II. The Dim Beginnings," *Collier's*, 46 (Feb. 4, 1911), 14–17; Irwin, "The American Newspaper, V. What Is News?," ibid. (Mar. 18, 1911), 16 (quotation); Oliver Gramling, *AP: The Story of News* (New York, 1940); Victor Rosewater, *History of Cooperative News-Gathering in the United States* (New York, 1930); and Steffens, "Business," 454–55 (quotation) and 467.

9. Mott, *American Journalism*, 384–85; Richard Watson Gilder, "The

Newspaper, the Magazine, and the Public," *Outlook*, 51 (Feb. 4, 1899), 317 and 319.

10. Beman Brockway, *Fifty Years in Journalism, Embracing Recollections and Personal Experiences with an Autobiography* (Watertown, N.Y., 1891), 89 (quotation) and 426.

11. John Lesperance, "American Journalism," *Lippincott's Magazine*, 8 (Aug. 1871), 179–80; Warner, *Complete Writings*, XIV, 288–89.

12. For claims of the impartiality of the Associated Press, see Steffens, "Business," 458; Charles Edward Kloeber, Jr., "The Press Association," *Bookman*, 20 (Nov. 1904), 198; Melville E. Stone, *Fifty Years a Journalist* (Garden City, N.Y., 1921), 223. Charges of bias include Grenville M. Dodge to E. D. Morgan, Aug. 15, 1872, William E. Chandler Papers, Library of Congress; *BC*, Aug. 25:2 and Oct. 9:2, 1876; E. Casserly to Samuel J. Tilden, July 15, 1876, Samuel J. Tilden Papers, New York Public Library; *NYW*, Oct. 24:6, 1876, and Oct. 22:4 and Nov. 12:4, 1884; Lafayette Young to Associated Press, Aug. 11, 1908, William Howard Taft Papers, Library of Congress; J. L. Sturtevant to Melville E. Stone, Oct. 17, 1912, and Stone to Charles D. Hilles, Oct. 19, 1912, Charles D. Hilles Papers, Yale University.

13. Steffens, "Business," 461.

14. Warner, *Complete Writings*, XIV, 293.

15. *NHJC*, May 24:2, 1869.

16. Harry W. Baehr, Jr., *The New York Tribune Since the Civil War* (New York, 1936); Bingham Duncan, *Whitelaw Reid: Journalist, Politician, Diplomat* (Athens, Ga., 1975); Allan Nevins, *The Evening Post: A Century of Journalism* (New York, 1922), 338–495; Richard Hooker, *The Story of an Independent Newspaper: One Hundred Years of the Springfield Republican, 1824–1924* (New York, 1924), 99–167; Joseph Logsdon, *Horace White, Nineteenth-Century Liberal* (Westport, Conn., 1971); Donald W. Curl, *Murat Halstead and the Cincinnati Commercial* (Boca Raton, Fla., 1980).

17. Logsdon, *White*, 267 and 272. For Bryant, Reid, and the Tilden Commission, see above, Chapter 2. The *Springfield Republican* opposed the commission's plan as an effort to shift the blame for the rise of Boss Tweed from the rich to the poor. See *NYP*, Apr. 9:2, 1877.

18. See Chapter 4.

19. Frederic Hudson, *Journalism in the United States* (New York, 1873), 408–90; Mott, *American Journalism*, 215–52; Daniel Schiller, *Objectivity and the News: The Public and the Rise of Commercial Journalism* (Philadelphia, 1981); and Schudson, *Discovering the News*, 12–60. Historians have often overestimated the immediate significance of the *Herald* and the penny press for party journalism. Although Bennett's paper was a great success and influenced later journalists, it hardly swept away the partisan press

before the Civil War. Mott puts the penny papers in proper perspective in *American Journalism*, 215–16 and 253.

20. From "Independent Journalism" in Reid's *American and English Studies*, 2 vols. (New York, 1913), II, 226–27.

21. Charles F. Wingate, *Views and Interviews on Journalism* (New York, 1875), 355–56; George William Curtis, *Orations and Addresses of George William Curtis*, ed. Charles Eliot Norton, 3 vols. (New York, 1894), I, 306.

22. Wingate, *Views*, 24, 53–54, 73–74, 128, and 162.

23. Ibid., 124–25 and 162–63. Liberal reformers outside of journalism also worried over the effect of government advertising on newspapers. See Dorman B. Eaton, "Municipal Government," *Journal of Social Science*, 5 (1873), 27.

24. Wingate, *Views*, 77–78.

25. Horace Greeley, *Recollections of a Busy Life* (New York, 1868), 137. See also Wingate, *Views*, 154; and Curl, Halstead, 43.

26. Wingate, *Views*, 144–45 (quotation); and Curtis, *Orations*, I, 310–11. In addition, see Murat Halstead's interesting contrast of Greeley and James Gordon Bennett, Sr., in Wingate, *Views*, 126–27.

27. Ibid. 49.

28. Logsdon, *White*, 219–33; Matthew T. Downey, "Horace Greeley and the Politicians: The Liberal Republican Convention in 1872," *Journal of American History*, 53 (Mar. 1967), 727–50.

29. Solomon Bulkley Griffin, *People and Politics Observed by a Massachusetts Editor* (Boston, 1923), 130–32 and 136–37; Curl, *Halstead*, 72–90 and 100–01; Duncan, *Reid*, esp. 58–59 and 105; and Logsdon, *White*, 267–69.

30. Stone, *Fifty Years*, 52–60, 107, and 112–13; Icie F. Johnson, *William Rockhill Nelson and the Kansas City Star: Their Relation to the Development of the Beauty and Culture of Kansas City and the Middle West* (Kansas City, 1935); *William Rockhill Nelson: The Story of a Man, a Newspaper, and a City* (Cambridge, Mass., 1915); and David Paul Nord, *Newspapers and New Politics: Midwestern Municipal Reform, 1890–1900* (Ann Arbor, Mich., 1979), esp. 1–9 and 41–44.

31. Reid, *Newspaper Tendencies*, 44–46.

32. *NN*, Sept. 1:2, 1883 (quotation), and July 12:2, 23:2, and 29:2, and Sept. 1:2 and 11:1, 1884; *KCS*, Aug. 1:2 (quotation) and 6:2, Sept. 18:2, and Oct. 18:4, 1884; *NHN*, Dec. 4:2, 1882; Stone, *Fifty Years*, 112–13.

33. Wingate, *Views*, 25, 38, 47–48 (quotations), and 128; Reid, *Newspaper Tendencies*, 53–54; Curl, *Halstead*, 40. See also Warner, *Complete Writings*, XIV, 283.

34. *NN*, Nov. 6:2, 1884; *NHN*, Dec. 6:2, 1882; *KCS*, Oct. 3:4, 1884; and Stone, *Fifty Years*, 52–53 and 107. For the independents' crusades,

see Weisberger, *American Newspaperman*, 32–33; Johnson, *Nelson*, esp. 71–81; *William Rockhill Nelson*, 42–86; and Stone, *Fifty Years*, 157–79.

35. Curl, *Halstead*, 96; Stone, *Fifty Years*, 152; Mott, *American Journalism*, 413–14. For Halstead's campaign paper, see Curl, *Halstead*, 97 and 101; and *NYW*, Aug. 9:4, 10:4, and 12:8, 1884.

36. *KCS*, Aug. 15:2, 1884; Wingate, *Views*, 81–82; Logsdon, *White*, 206–07, 244, and 260; Curl, *Halstead*, 49 and 72–73; Richard W. Kemp, "The Policy of the Paper," *Bookman*, 20 (Dec. 1904), 313; Duncan, *Reid*, 46 and 57–58. The statistics were gathered by counting each paper listed in N. W. Ayer & Son, *American Newspaper Annual, 1891* (Philadelphia, 1891).

37. William Henry Smith, "The Press as a Newsgatherer," *Century*, 42 (Aug. 1891), 528; Brockway, *Fifty Years*, 425–26.

38. Noah Brooks, "The Newspaper of the Future," *Forum*, 9 (July 1890), 570–73; Mott, *American Journalism*, 413–14.

39. Camp, "Conscience," 472.

40. Reid, *American and English Studies*, II, 227.

41. Wingate, *Views*, 48.

42. Julian S. Rammelkamp, *Pulitzer's Post-Dispatch, 1878–1883* (Princeton, 1967), 4–11; Pulitzer to Samuel J. Tilden, Aug. 20, 1876, Samuel J. Tilden Papers, New York Public Library.

43. Rammelkamp, *Pulitzer's Post-Dispatch*, 125–26 and 211–12; Ralph Juergens, *Joseph Pulitzer and the New York World* (Princeton, 1966), 253–54; and Pultizer to Whitelaw Reid, Sept. 28, 1884, Whitelaw Reid Papers, Library of Congress (quotation).

44. Rammelkamp, *Pulitzer's Post-Dispatch*, 41–59, 74–84, 114–62, and 207–83, esp. 114, 125, and 141. Quotation from 41.

45. Juergens, *Pulitzer*, 31; *CTr*, July 12:14, 1896.

46. Juergens, *Pulitzer*, 14 and 355–56; *NYW*, Aug. 18:4 and Nov. 5:1, 1884.

47. *NYW*, Aug. 20:4, Sept. 21:4, 24:5, and 30:4, 1884. The best recent studies of Pulitzer tend to underestimate the complexity of his politics, the importance of his political ambition, and the significance of his Democratic affiliation. George Juergens, denying any link between Pulitzer's tenure with the *Post-Dispatch* and the *World*, overlooks the publisher's continuing drive for political influence and also his intense campaign for Cleveland (Juergens, *Pulitzer*, xiii). Julian Rammelkamp rightly notes the continuity between the *Post-Dispatch* and the *World*, but he sees Pulitzer primarily as a businessman who had renounced political ambition and party journalism after his disappointment at the hands of St. Louis Democratic leaders in 1880 (Rammelkamp, *Pulitzer's Post-Dispatch*, vi and 298).

48. The following account draws on Juergens, *Pulitzer;* Mott, *American Journalism,* 430–45; and Schudson, *Discovering the News,* 91–106.

49. Juergens, *Pulitzer,* 95–117.

50. Ibid., viii-xii, 33–36, 43–92, 118–31, and 132–74.

51. Ibid., 28–29 and 234–330; Will Irwin, "The American Newspaper, III. The Fourth Current," *Collier's,* 46 (Feb. 18, 1911), 14 (quotation).

52. Juergens, *Pulitzer,* 332–43.

53. My thinking on this point has been stimulated by Michael Schudson's contrast of "Two Journalisms in the 1890s"—the working-class sensationalism of the *World* and the middle-class informational style of the *New York Times.* Schudson does not discuss independent journalism, but the factual *Times,* a Mugwump bolter in 1884, obviously grew out of the independent press of the 'seventies. See Schudson, *Discovering the News,* 88–120.

54. Juergens, *Pulitzer,* 32 (quotation), and 175–236, esp. 175–76, 212–13, 228–29, 233–37, and 287.

55. Ibid., 66–69 and 120–21.

56. *NYW,* Aug. 23:1, 24:1, and 31:1, and Oct. 8:1, 11:1, and 30:1, 1884.

57. Ibid., July 17:4 and Nov. 15:4, 1884.

58. Irwin, "American Newspaper, III," 27 (quotation); and idem, "American Newspaper, IV." For a good, brief summary of the yellow press, see Mott, *American Journalism,* 519–45. On Hearst himself, see W. A. Swanberg, *Citizen Hearst: A Biography of William Randolph Hearst* (New York, 1961).

59. Arthur Brisbane, "Yellow Journalism," *Bookman,* 19 (June 1904), 402 and 404. Not a few observers considered the yellow press a radical threat to the country. See, for instance, "A Danger to Democracy," *Century,* 72 (June 1906), 317–18. Roy Everett Littlefield, III, *William Randolph Hearst: His Role in American Progressivism* (Lanham, Md., 1980) treats Hearst's political career.

60. Quotations from Irwin, "American Newspaper, IV," 18. See, too, Aline Gorren, "The Ethics of Modern Journalism," *Scribner's Monthly,* 19 (Apr. 1896), 507–13, and L. White Busbey, *Uncle Joe Cannon: The Story of a Pioneer American* (New York, 1927), 295. For instances of the interest of the *Journal* in personalities, see the pieces on Republican leaders in *NYJA,* Oct. 1:1 and 8:4, 1900.

61. *NYJA,* Oct. 21:36–39; Steffens, "Business," 462.

62. Note Irwin's interesting comments in "American Newspaper, IV," 20.

63. Mott, *American Journalism,* 666–73. Quotations from *NYN,* Oct. 27:1 and 28:1, and Nov. 1:1 and 3:1, 1924. For the paper's endorsements in the campaign of 1924, see Oct. 30:15 and Nov. 2:11, 1924. For an

interesting discussion of the tabloids' appeal to immigrants unfamiliar with English, see "THE NEWS AS A TEACHER" in Nov. 5:15, 1924.

64. Irwin, "The American Newspaper, VI. The Editor and the News," *Collier's*, 47 (Apr. 1, 1911), 19.

65. Mott, *American Journalism*, 589–90; Edmund Ryan and Firmin Dredd, "Country and Non-Metropolitan Journalism," *Bookman*, 20 (Oct. 1904), 120–38.

66. Statistics based on counts of Northern papers listed in N. W. Ayer & Son, *Directory of Newspapers and Periodicals, 1931* (Philadelphia, 1931).

67. S. Gordon to Thomas H. Carter, Oct. 29, 1908, and also John H. Raferty to Carter, Nov. 13, 1908, Thomas H. Carter Papers, Library of Congress; and George M. Smith to Francis G. Newlands, Nov. 12, 1900, Francis G. Newlands Papers, Yale University.

68. *KT*, Nov. 6:4, 1900. For more of the woes of the small-town party editor, see E. W. Lanier to Robert W. Woolley, Oct. 25, 1916, box 11, Robert W. Woolley Papers, Library of Congress.

69. Ibid., Nov. 10:4, 1904.

70. *DMR*, Aug. 26:6, 1924; *NYHT*, Oct. 5:II/6, 1924.

71. *NHR*, Jan. 3:2, 1871; Franc B. Wilkie, *Personal Reminiscences of Thirty-Five Years of Journalism* (Chicago, 1891), 320; Ryan and Dredd, "Country Journalism," 130.

72. Quotation from *NHP*, Oct. 21:4, 1892. *HT*, Aug. 3:5, 1888, notes the passing of the masthead ticket in New York City. For late examples of the masthead ticket, see *KT*, Sept. 1:4, 1900; *NHJC*, Aug. 1:4, 1900; *LAT*, Oct. 1:8, 1900; and Charles D. Hilles to William Howard Taft, Sept. 15, 1912, William Howard Taft Papers, Library of Congress.

73. *NHJC*, Sept. 1:1, 1920; *NYHT*, Oct. 1:14, 1924; *DMR*, Aug. 1:1, 1924; *CTr*, Oct. 1:1, 1924. For an exception, see *LAT*, Sept. 1:1, 1924: "Liberty Under Law—Equal Rights—True Industrial Freedom."

74. See above, Chapter 4.

75. *NHP*, Nov. 9:5, 1892; *PI*, Nov. 10:4, 1892, and Sept. 22:12, 1920. See also *HC*, Oct. 28:4, 1892; *HT*, Oct. 4:1–2, 1920; and *MJ*, Sept. 16:4 and Oct. 5:4, 1892.

76. McAdoo to Byron R. Newton, July 4, 1923, Byron R. Newton Papers, Yale University. In addition, see *PI*, Sept. 22:12, 1920, and *DMR*, Sept. 4:3, 1924. In 1891, the ratio of Republican to Democratic papers was 1.6 to 1. In 1931, just after the Republican-dominated fourth party system, Republican weeklies outnumbered Democratic weeklies 3.3 to 1; Republican dailies outnumbered their Democratic counterparts by 3.8 to 1. These figures were derived from counting the papers listed in Ayer, *Annual, 1891;* and idem, *Directory, 1931*. The Democrats were painfully aware of the shortage of loyal papers: Key Pittman to Fremont Older, Aug. 8, 1916, and Pittman to Warren Gard, Aug. 24, 1916, box 8, Key

Pittman Papers, Library of Congress; Fred Biermann to Thomas J. Walsh, Sept. 9, 1920, box 373, Thomas J. Walsh Papers, Library of Congress; Rossyln M. Cox to Franklin D. Roosevelt, July 15, 1920, box 13, Group 15, W. U. Goodman to Roosevelt, Dec. 20, 1924, Isaac S. Giles to Roosevelt, Dec. 13, 1924, box 8, and numerous other letters in boxes 8 and 9, Group 11, Franklin D. Roosevelt Papers, Franklin D. Roosevelt Library, Hyde Park, New York.

77. *NYHT,* Oct. 29:14, 1924.

78. *LAT,* Sept. 13:3, and Oct. 12:1 and 15:1, 1924; *CPD,* Oct. 6:1, 1924. See, too, *CTr,* Oct. 2:4 and 11:1, 1924; and *NYHT,* Oct. 3:1, 1924.

79. Frank Luther Mott, *A History of American Magazines,* 5 vols. (New York and Cambridge, Mass., 1930–68).

80. Here again I have profited from Michael Schudson's contrast of the *New York World* and the *New York Times* in *Discovering the News,* 88–120.

6. Advertised Politics

1. For the Cleveland Democrats' disasters, see H. Wayne Morgan, *From Hayes to McKinley: National Party Politics, 1877–1896* (Syracuse, 1969), 440–81, 493–97, and 502–05; J. Rogers Hollingsworth, *The Whirligig of Politics: The Democracy of Cleveland and Bryan* (Chicago, 1963), 1–68; Richard J. Jensen, *The Winning of the Midwest: Social and Political Conflict, 1888–1896* (Chicago, 1971), 209–308; Paul Kleppner, *The Cross of Culture: A Social Analysis of Midwestern Politics, 1850–1900* (New York, 1970), 179–375; idem, "Coalitional and Party Transformations in the 1890s," in Seymour Martin Lipset, ed., *Party Coalitions in the 1980s* (San Francisco, 1981), 89–105; and Samuel T. McSeveney, *The Politics of Depression: Political Behavior in the Northeast, 1893–1896* (New York, 1972), 32–221.

2. *SFE,* Sept. 6:7, 1896; *CTr,* July 4:4, 18:2, and 22:3, and Aug. 14:9, 1896; Charles G. Dawes to M. A. Hanna, July 30, 1896, and William M. Osborne to William McKinley, Aug. 11, 1896, William McKinley Papers, Library of Congress; Allan W. Paige to Ebenezer J. Hill, July 20, 1896, Ebenezer J. Hill Papers, Yale University.

3. Interview with Charles Dick, Feb. 10, 1906, Hanna-McCormick Family Papers, Library of Congress.

4. *CTr,* July 12:2 and 21:1, and Aug. 29:2 and 30:11, 1896; *RR,* 14 (Sept. 1896), 264; Newell Dwight Hillis, "An Outlook Upon the Agrarian Propaganda in the West," ibid., 304–05; ibid. (Oct. 1896), 397–98; W. B. Shaw, "Methods and Tactics of the Campaign," ibid., 554 and 557; *NN,* Sept. 26:7, 1896; Joseph C. Sibley to William Jennings Bryan, July 16, 1896, W. J. Stone to James K. Jones, July 31, 1896, William Jennings Bryan Papers, Library of Congress; and Paolo E. Coletta, *William Jennings*

Bryan, I. Political Evangelist, 1860–1908 (Lincoln, Neb., 1964), 204, 198–200.

5. Two older works—Herbert Croly, *Marcus Alonzo Hanna: His Life and Work* (New York, 1912); and Thomas Beer, *Hanna* (New York, 1929)—still give the clearest insight into the Republican chairman. The best general account of his campaign is in Robert D. Marcus, *Grand Old Party: Political Structure in the Gilded Age, 1880–1896* (New York, 1971), 195–250. For Hanna's educational plans, see *CTr*, July 3:4, 4:4, 18:2, 20:3, 21:1, and 22:3, and Aug. 14:9 and 16:16, 1896; and Beer, *Hanna*, 160.

6. Charles G. Dawes, *A Journal of the McKinley Years*, ed. Bascom N. Timmons (Chicago, 1950), 106; Marcus, *Grand Old Party*, 243–50; interview with Cornelius N. Bliss, Oct. 1905, Hanna-McCormick Family Papers.

7. Typical interviews are in *CTr*, Aug. 12:12, 13:12, 14:9, and 22:1, 1896.

8. Garret A. Hobart to McKinley, Aug. 20, 1896, McKinley Papers; *CTr*, July 16:4, 17:4, 21:1, 29:1, and 30:3, and Aug. 3:2, 1896.

9. For the operations of the Speakers' Bureau, see *CTr*, July 30:4 and Aug. 16:25–26, 1896; Shaw, "Methods," 558–59; and W. M. Hahn to John C. Spooner, Aug. 10, 1896, John C. Spooner Papers, Library of Congress. The New York headquarters had its own Speakers' Bureau as well: Powell Clayton to Ebenezer J. Hill, Aug. 26 and 28, 1896, Hill Papers. On the departments, see *CTr*, July 16:4, 18:2, 22:3, and 29:4, and Aug. 9:11, 16:16, 18:2, and 22:1, 1896.

10. Dawes to Hanna, July 30, 1896, Dawes to McKinley, Aug. 1, 1896, McKinley Papers; *CTr*, Aug. 16:25–26, 1896; Dawes, *Journal*, 88–106. Note also, Bliss interview, Hanna-McCormick Family Papers.

11. *CTr*, July 17:4, 21:1, 23:10, 24:4, 25:4, 26:7, 28:2, and 31:5, and Aug. 2:3 and 6, 4:4, 14:9, and 16:25–26, 1896; Dawes to McKinley, Aug. 1, 1896, McKinley Papers; Shaw, "Methods," 554–55; Dawes, *Journal*, 106; Dick interview, Hanna-McCormick Family Papers; Allen Johnson and Dumas Malone, eds., *Dictionary of American Biography*, 20 vols. (New York, 1928–1936), VIII, 489–90; *National Cyclopaedia of American Biography*, 74 vols. (New York and Clifton, N.J., 1898–   ), XVI, 204–05. A selection of the Literary Bureau's pamphlets, including several editions of Heath's catalog, is bound in the Yale University Library as Republican National Committee, Bureau of Publication and Printing, *Pamphlets, 1896* (Chicago?, 1896?).

12. *CTr*, July 28:21, 1896. In the same vein, see E. V. Smalley to Albert Shaw, Aug. 28, 1896, Albert Shaw Papers, New York Public Library.

13. H. G. McMillan to James S. Clarkson, Sept. 5, 1896, James S. Clarkson Papers, Library of Congress; *CTr*, Aug. 14:9 and 16:25–26, 1896; William M. Osborne to McKinley, Aug. 11 and Sept. 1, 1896, McKinley

Papers; Shaw, "Methods," 556–57; Chester Griswold to John C. Spooner, Aug. 6, 1896, Spooner Papers.

14. *NN*, Sept. 26:7, 1896; *CTr*, July 25:4, Aug. 17:3 and 25:3, and Sept. 12:2, 1896; Shaw, "Methods," 555–56; Warner P. Sutton to Ebenezer J. Hill, June 30, Lewis D. Apsley to Hill, July 25, T. E. Spencer to Hill, July 25, Joseph W. Babcock to Hill, Aug. 6 and 23, Spencer to Hill, Sept. 26 and Oct. 3 and 10, all 1896, Hill Papers.

15. *CTr*, Aug. 16:2, 1896; W. A. Calderhead to Hill, July 28, 1896, Hill Papers.

16. *NN*, Nov. 3:4, 1896; and James W. Gleed to Albert Shaw, Oct. 19, 1896, Shaw Papers. A sense of the local educational campaign emerges from *NN*, Aug. 21:1 and Sept. 2:1, 9:2, and 16:1, 1896; *NHR*, Sept. 16:1, 1896; *CTr*, Aug. 1:2, 9:3, 14:1–2, 15:1, 17:1, 20:2, 23:25, 28:2, 31:1, and Sept. 7:3, 1896; *NHJC*, Oct. 20:2, 1896; Horace Cole to Ebenezer J. Hill, July 16 and Aug. 15, O. F. Fyler to Hill, July 22, James W. Hague to Hill, July 28, and James Joyce to Hill, Sept. 28, all 1896, Hill Papers; E. K. Webb to Bryan, Oct. 30, 1896, Bryan Papers; and H. G. McMillan to James S. Clarkson, Sept. 5, 1896, Clarkson Papers. Observations on the educational character of the election are in *AS*, July 23:1, 1896; *NN*, Oct. 24:4, 1896; Shelby M. Cullom, *Fifty Years of Public Service* (Chicago, 1911), 274; Shaw, "Methods," 553; and *RR*, 14 (Oct. 1896), 397–98.

17. For instance, *NN*, Sept. 22:4, 1896; *NHJC*, Oct. 31:1, 1896.

18. Beer, *Hanna*, 162.

19. For some companies, see *CTr*, July 18:2, 19:4, 21:3, and 26:4, Aug. 16:2, 18:1–2, and 30:11, and Sept. 6:12 and 14:2, 1896; *NN*, Sept. 26:1 and Oct. 22:1, 1896; *NHR*, Sept. 1:1, 5:5, 8:8, 22:9, and 30:8, 1896; *NHJC*, Oct. 1:5, 1896. For examples of rallies, see *CTr*, Aug. 5:4, 8:2, 16:2, 18:1, 19:1, 3, and 4, and 25:2, and Sept. 3:1 and 4, 1896; *NN*, Aug. 19:1, Sept. 16:7 and 18:1, and Oct. 23:1 and 28:1, 1896; *NHR*, Sept. 5:5, 1896; *NHJC*, Oct. 2:7 and 16:1, 1896. Parades include *CTr*, Aug. 16:2 and Sept. 4:3 and 16:2, 1896; *NN*, Oct. 10:1, 24:1, and 29:1, 1896; *NHJC*, Oct. 8:1, 24:3, and 29:1, 1896.

20. For electric parades, see *CTr*, Sept. 13:8, 1896; *NHJC*, Oct. 28:3, 1896. For the "Wheelmen," see *CTr*, Aug. 5:4, 9:30, 21:5, and Sept. 3:4 and 13:8, 1896; *NN*, Aug. 1:7, 7:1, and 14:1, Sept. 10:2, and Oct. 3:5 and 27:2, 1896; *NHR*, Sept. 5:5, 1896.

21. *NYTi*, Oct. 18:5 and 31:8, and Nov. 1:1–3, 1896.

22. *NHR*, Sept. 28:10 and 29:4, 1896; *NHJC*, Oct. 2:7, 1896. For treatment of spectacle as old-fashioned, see *NHR*, Sept. 7:1 and 24:4, 1896.

23. Allan Peskin, *Garfield: A Biography* (Kent State, 1978), 498–500; Jensen, *Winning*, 13–14; Allan Nevins, *Grover Cleveland: A Study in Courage* (New York, 1932), 503; Harry J. Sievers, *Benjamin Harrison: Hoosier President* (Indianapolis, 1968), 241–45; Harrison to Henry Cabot Lodge,

July 30, 1892, and Harrison to Whitelaw Reid, Aug. 15, 1892, Benjamin Harrison Papers, Library of Congress.

24. *CTr*, Aug. 9:1–2, 11:1 and 3–4, 13:1–3, 23:2, 25:4, 26:3, 27:4, 28:4, and 29:3, and Sept. 24:5 and 29:1, 1896; *NN*, Aug. 12:1 and Sept. 24:5 and 29:1, 1896; *NHR*, Sept. 24:1–2, 1896; Shaw, "Methods," 558; Joseph C. Sibley to Bryan, July 16, 1896, Bryan Papers; and Coletta, *William Jennings Bryan, I.*, 161–69 and 174–89.

25. *CTr*, July 2:3, 1896; Dick interview, Hanna-McCormick Family Papers; Charles G. Dawes to Harding, Aug. 30, 1920, box 116, Warren G. Harding Papers, Ohio Historical Society, Columbus. Typical front-porch appearances by the candidate are reported in *CTr*, July 26:4, 28:2, 30:1, and 31:4, Aug. 13:4, 14:3, and 30:1–2, and Sept. 6:3, 1896; and Joseph P. Smith, ed., *McKinley's Speeches in September* (Canton, Ohio, 1896?). The best biography of the Republican nominee is H. Wayne Morgan, *William McKinley and His America* (Syracuse, 1963).

26. Interview with Elmer Dover, Sept. 1905, Hanna-McCormick Family Papers; Shaw, "Methods," 555 and 557–58; *RR*, 14 (Sept. 1896), 264; Hillis, "Outlook," 304–05; *CTr*, July 24:4, 26:7, and 30:4, and Aug. 16:25–26, 1896; Lewis D. Apsley to Ebenezer J. Hill, Aug. 4, 1896, Hill Papers; Beer, *Hanna*, 165–66 (quotation).

27. *KT*, Aug. 21:5 and 31:5, Sept. 28:5, and Oct. 2:8, 4:5, and 10:4, 1900; *LAT*, Oct. 6:12 and 7:II/1, 1900; *NHJC*, Aug. 29:2, Sept. 22:2 and 22:7, Oct. 1:8, 4:5, 9:3, 10:3, 11:4, 15:6, 24:3, and 31:4 and 6, and Nov. 1:6, 1900, and Oct. 5:2, 6:1, and 28:5, 1908; *NYW*, Sept. 27:7 and Oct. 20:2, 1900; and Samuel J. Graham to Woodrow Wilson, Aug. 12, 1912, Woodrow Wilson Papers, Library of Congress.

28. *LAT*, Oct. 3:4 and 13, 14:7, and 24:12, 1900; *NHJC*, Oct. 16:3, 17:5, 19:6, 22:8, and 25:5, 1900; *NHR*, Oct. 7:1–2 and 11:2, 1904; *PI*, Sept. 11:9, 13:4, 15:4, and 28:16, 1904; and D. E. Moore to Alton B. Parker, Sept. 8, 1904, box 11, Alton B. Parker Papers, Library of Congress.

29. *KT*, Aug. 17:8, 18:8, 21:5, and 24:8, Sept. 14:5 and 18:5, and Oct. 3:5, 1900; *NHJC*, Sept. 10:3 and 29:9, and Oct. 5:7 and 6:7, 1900; *LAT*, Oct. 19:II/1 and 25:9, and Nov. 3:II/1–2, 1900; *PI*, Sept. 4:9 and 7:4, and Oct. 9:9, 1904.

30. *KT*, Sept. 1:4, 4:8, and 5:5, 1900; *NHJC*, Sept. 10:3, 11:8, and 19:3, 1900, and Oct. 3:1 and 15:1 and 3, 1908; *NHR*, Oct. 1:3, 1904; *PI*, Sept. 28:1 and 16, and Oct. 8:4, 12:16, and 23:9, 1904; and Thomas H. McKee to George B. Cortelyou, Sept. 23, 1904, Robert Reyburn to Cortelyou, Sept. 29, 1904, and Cortelyou to McKee, Oct. 1, 1904, George B. Cortelyou Papers, Library of Congress.

31. *LAT*, Oct. 17:7 and 28:III/10, and Nov. 4:7 and IV/1, 1900; *NHJC*, Oct. 1:2, 3:7, 6:7, 17:6, and 30:7, 1900; *NYW*, Sept. 15:7 and Oct. 13:2,

1900; *PI,* Oct. 15:4, 16:9, 19:16, 23:1 and 16, and 26:1 and 4, and Nov. 4:2 and 6:1, 1904; *NHR,* Oct. 15:3, 1904; *MJ,* Nov. 3:II/1, 1912; and John Francis Reynolds, "Testing Democracy: Electoral Participation and Progressive Reform in New Jersey, 1888–1919" (Ph.D. diss., Rutgers University, The State University in New Jersey, 1980), 134, 136–37, and 265–66. Some final banners, transparencies, and floats include *KT,* Oct. 27:5 and 8, 1900; and *PI,* Oct. 2:1 and 9 and 30:6, 1904. For comment on the rarity of parades, see *MJ,* Oct. 20:Comic Weekly/4, 1912.

32. *NYTr,* Sept. 28:2 and Oct. 12:4, 1908; *WA,* Oct. 29:8 and 16, 1920; Myrtle N. Halterman to Warren G. Harding, Oct. 29, 1920, box 171, Harding Papers.

33. Arthur M. Schlesinger, "Liberty Tree: A Genealogy," *New England Quarterly,* 25 (Dec. 1952), 458. A rare pole-raising is in *KT,* Aug. 17:7, 1916.

34. *KT,* Sept. 3:8, 5:5, 13:4, 19:6, 22:5, 24:5, 25:3, and 26:5, and Oct. 5:5, 8:3 and 5, 9:4, 12:5, 18:4, 25:5, and 27:5 and 8, 1900.

35. *LAT,* Oct. 19:II/1, 1900; *NHJC,* Oct. 3:5 and 16:1, 1900, and Oct. 15:1 and 3 and 30:7, 1908; *PI,* Oct. 2:1 and 9, 1904; *NYTi,* Aug. 26:3, 1904.

36. *NHJC,* Oct. 2:3 and 26:6, 1900, and Oct. 13:1, 1908; *NYW,* Sept. 25:7, 1900; *NHR,* Oct. 5:2, 1904; *PI,* Sept. 13:4 and 25:9, 1904; and *HT,* Oct. 14:23, 1920.

37. Note the suggestion to stimulate ratifications in W. G. McAdoo to Woodrow Wilson, Aug. 15, 1912, Wilson Papers.

38. *KT,* Sept. 14:5 and 19:6, and Oct. 5:5, 8:5, and 12:5, 1900; *LAT,* Oct. 3:4 and 13, 19:II/1, and 20:II/1, 1900; *NHJC,* Oct. 16:6, 1900; *PI,* Sept. 4:II/2, 1904; *NYW,* Sept. 15:7 and 30:5, and Oct. 13:2, 1900; Henry G. Hogan to William Howard Taft, Aug. 7, 1908, William Howard Taft Papers, Library of Congress.

39. *KT,* Oct. 9:4 and 12:5, 1900; *NHJC,* Oct. 6:7, 13:7, and 16:6, 1900.

40. *NHJC,* Nov. 9:5, 1900, and Nov. 5:1, 1908.

41. *KCS,* Oct. 23:16, 1916; and *NYTr,* Oct. 12:4, 1908. But see also *NYTi,* Sept. 4:III/5, 1904; *PI,* Aug. 22:14 and Oct. 18:4, 1904; Elmer Dover to George B. Cortelyou, Oct. 5, 1904, Cortelyou Papers; Bernard Korbly to Thomas J. Walsh, Oct. 14, 1916, box 171, Robert W. Woolley to Walsh, Aug. 31, 1916, and "Secretary to the Manager" to Woolley, Aug. 31, 1916, box 176, Thomas J. Walsh Papers, Library of Congress.

42. *PI,* Nov. 9:3, 1904, and Nov. 3:2, 1920; *KT,* Nov. 16:1, 1916.

43. *NYW,* Aug. 2:6, 1900; *NHR,* Oct. 13:6, 1904; Joseph C. Bonner to Warren G. Harding, July 20, 1920, box 165, Harding Papers.

44. For these expressions and variations on them, see *NHJC,* Oct. 6:1, 1900; *PI,* Oct. 2:1 and 9 and 23:1 and 6, 1904; *NHP,* Oct. 13:1 and 29:1,

1910; *MJ*, Nov. 3:II/1, 1912; *KT*, Sept. 21:12, Oct. 7:1, and Nov. 7:1, 1916; *NYTi*, Aug. 27:VII/3 and Sept. 7:6, 1916, and Sept. 10:1, 1924.

45. *KT*, Aug. 14:4, 1916.

46. Sam Bass Warner, Jr., *Streetcar Suburbs: The Process of Growth in Boston (1870–1920)*, 2nd ed. (Cambridge, Mass., 1978); idem, *The Private City: Philadelphia in Three Periods of Its Growth* (Philadelphia, 1968); Zane Miller, *Boss Cox's Cincinnati: Urban Politics in the Progressive Era* (New York, 1968); Robert A. Dahl, *Who Governs? Democracy and Power in an American City* (New Haven, 1961), 11–31; J. Rogers Hollingsworth and Ellen Jane Hollingsworth, *Dimensions in Urban History: Historical and Sociological Perspectives on Middle-Size American Cities* (Madison, Wisc., 1979); David C. Hammack, "Problems in the Historical Study of Power in the Cities and Towns of the United States, 1800–1960," *American Historical Review*, 83 (Apr. 1978), 323–49.

47. For the parties' tendency to put off the start of campaigns, see George T. Pettengill to Albert Shaw, Sept. 13, 1900, Shaw Papers; *KT*, Aug. 17:1, 1904; and *MJ*, Oct. 15:6 and 20:9, 1912.

48. Daniel T. Rodgers, *The Work Ethic in Industrial America* (Chicago, 1978); Francis G. Couvares, "The Triumph of Commerce: Class Culture and Mass Culture in Pittsburgh," in Michael H. Frisch and Daniel J. Walkowitz, eds., *Working-Class America: Essays on Labor, Community, and American Society* (Urbana, Ill., 1983), 123–52; John F. Kasson, *Amusing the Million: Coney Island at the Turn of the Century* (New York, 1978); "The Reorientation of American Culture in the 1890's," in John Higham, *Writing American History: Essays on Modern Scholarship* (Bloomington, Ind., 1970), 73 102.

49. Gunther Barth, *City People: The Rise of Modern City-Culture in America* (New York, 1980), 148–228; Robert C. Toll, *On With the Show: The First Century of Show Business in America* (New York, 1976); Kasson, *Amusing the Million;* Foster Rhea Dulles, *America Learns to Play: A History of Popular Recreation, 1607–1940* (New York, 1940), 182–376; Steven A. Riess, *Touching Base: Professional Baseball and American Culture in the Progressive Era* (Westport, Conn., 1980); Robert Sklar, *Movie-Made America: A Social History of American Movies* (New York, 1975), 3–157; Robert S. Lynd and Helen Merrell Lynd, *Middletown: A Study in Modern American Culture* (New York, 1929), 225–312.

50. Stuart Ewen, *Captains of Consciousness: Advertising and the Social Roots of the Consumer Culture* (New York, 1976); Daniel J. Boorstin, *The Americans: The Democratic Experience* (New York, 1973), 137–48.

51. Charles Merz, "The Campaign Opens: The Great American Game of Presidential Elections," *Century*, 108 (July 1924), 307. See also *NYH*, Aug. 19:10, 1888; *RR*, 30 (Oct. 1904), 388; and *MJ*, Oct. 27:VIII/8, 1912.

52. Thomas Bender, *Community and Social Change in America* (New Brunswick, N.J., 1978); Robert H. Wiebe, *The Search for Order, 1877–1920* (New York, 1967); idem, *The Segmented Society* (New York, 1975); Rowland Berthoff, *An Unsettled People: Social Order and Disorder in American History* (New York, 1971); Michael H. Frisch, *Town into City: Springfield, Massachusetts, and the Meaning of Community, 1840–1880* (Cambridge, Mass., 1972); John Higham, "Hanging Together: Divergent Unities in American History," *Journal of American History*, 61 (June 1974), 5–28.

53. *NYTr*, Sept. 20:4 and Nov. 2:8, 1860; and *NYS*, Sept. 10:5, 1892. See, also, the interesting observation on the relative weakness of Chicago's Wide Awake movement in *CTr*, Sept. 19:1, 1860.

54. John K. Gowdy to E. W. Halford, Sept. 29, 1892, Harrison Papers; *KT*, Oct. 19:1, 1916; *KCS*, Nov. 2:6, 1916. See also J. R. Currens to John C. Spooner, Oct. 23, 1900, Spooner Papers; *NHR*, Oct. 13:6, 1904; *BT*, Oct. 7:3, 1920; *NYTi*, Aug. 29:III/11,1920.

55. *PI*, Aug. 4:8, 1904; *NHJC*, Oct. 30:6, 1908.

56. *KT*, Oct. 19:1, 1916.

57. *NYTi*, July 17:14, 1924. See also ibid., July 28:12, 1920; and *MJ*, Nov. 3:II/1, 1912.

58. *LAT*, Oct. 24:12, 1900; *PI*, Sept. 7:4, 1904; *RR*, 38 (Nov. 1908), 525; Charles D. Hilles to George R. Sheldon, Oct. 16, 1912, Charles D. Hilles Papers, Yale University.

59. Among the most important works that chart these political transformations are Samuel P. Hays, *The Response to Industrialism 1885–1914* (Chicago, 1957), 48–70 and 154–56; Wiebe, *Search for Order*, 111–223; Richard L. McCormick, "The Party Period and Public Policy: An Exploratory Hypothesis," *Journal of American History*, 66 (Sept. 1979), 279–98; idem, *From Realignment to Reform: Political Change in New York State, 1893–1910* (Ithaca, 1981); Reynolds, "Testing Democracy"; David P. Thelen, *The New Citizenship: Origins of Progressivism in Wisconsin, 1885–1900* (Columbia, Mo., 1972); Mansel G. Blackford, *The Politics of Business in California, 1890–1920* (Columbus, Ohio, 1977); and David Paul Nord, *Newspapers and New Politics: Midwestern Municipal Reform, 1890–1900* (Ann Arbor, Mich., 1979).

60. *Nation*, 87 (Oct. 1, 1908), 302; *MJ*, Oct. 6:4, 1912; *NYTi*, July 20:VIII/1, 1924; and also *WP*, Sept. 21:3, 1900; *RR*, 30 (Dec. 1904), 646 and 648–50; ibid., 37 (Oct. 1908), 398; ibid., (Nov. 1908), 555 and 651; [Oswald Garrison Villard], "A Triumph of Independence," *Nation*, 87 (Nov. 12, 1908), 454; *KT*, Oct. 18:1, 1916; Marion Wilson to Francis G. Newlands, Aug. 1, 1900, Francis G. Newlands Papers, Yale University; and Key Pittman to Warren Gard, Aug. 24, 1916, box 8, Key Pittman Papers, Library of Congress.

61. Henry Litchfield West, "The President and the Campaign," *Forum*, 40 (Nov. 1908), 421; *MJ*, Oct. 27:4 and Nov. 3:1 and IX/12, 1912. See also ibid., Oct. 24:4, and Nov. 2:1, 1912; and Reynolds, "Testing Democracy," 112–15.

62. Fay N. Seaton to Joseph L. Bristow, Nov. 6, 1908, Joseph L. Bristow Papers, Kansas State Historical Society, Topeka; *RR*, 38 (Aug. 1908), 131; Francis B. Loomis to William Howard Taft, Sept. 5, 1908, Taft Papers; Boyden Sparkes, "How Can We Make 'Em Vote?" *Collier's*, 174 (Sept. 20, 1924), 38.

63. Merrill Moores to William Howard Taft, Oct. 29, 1912, Hilles Papers; *NYTi*, Sept. 21:10, 1916; and also Harry Thurston Peck, "The Presidential Campaign," *Bookman*, 20 (Oct. 1904), 138–44; *KCS*, Nov. 11:10, 1916; and L. Ames Brown, "The President on the Independent Voter: An Authoritative Statement of Mr. Wilson's Attitude Toward His Campaign for Reelection," *World's Work*, 32 (Sept. 1916), 494–98.

64. *NYTi*, Aug. 9:V/2, 1908.

65. J. G. Johnson to Bryan, July 20, C. A. Walsh to Bryan, July 24, W. S. Hutchins to Bryan, July 25, James K. McGuire to Bryan, Aug. 3, James K. Jones to Bryan, Aug. 4, and O. J. Smith to Bryan, all 1900, Bryan Papers; and *KT*, Oct. 1:6, 1900.

66. George W. Rouzer to John C. Spooner, Aug. 14, 1900, Perry Heath to Spooner, Sept. 7, 1900, and Elmer Dover to Spooner, Aug. 18, 1904, Spooner Papers; Charles R. Buckland to Albert Shaw, Nov. 2, 1900, Shaw Papers; Henry C. Payne to Knute Nelson, Aug. 13, 1900, Knute Nelson Papers, Minnesota Historical Society, St. Paul; Henry C. Hedges to Ebenezer J. Hill, Aug. 2, 1900, Hill Papers; Charles G. Dawes to McKinley, July 29, 1900, and Perry Heath to George B. Cortelyou, Aug. 20, 1900, McKinley Papers; *KT*, Oct. 1:6, 1900; and *NHJC*, Sept. 10:4, 1900.

67. James Otis Wheaton, "The Genius and the Jurist: A Study of the Presidential Campaign of 1904" (Ph.D. diss., Stanford University, 1964), 359–78; *Campaign Contributions. Testimony Before a Subcommittee of the Committee on Privileges and Elections, United States Senate*, 62nd Cong., 2nd sess., 2 vols. (Washington, D.C., 1913), 38–39 and 55–56; Daniel S. Lamont to Richard Olney, Oct. 6, 1904, Daniel S. Lamont Papers, Library of Congress; James P. Hornaday, "Chairman Taggart and the Democratic Campaign," *RR*, 30 (Sept. 1904), 289–93; and *NYTi*, Aug. 17:7 and 26:3, and Sept. 4:3, 1904.

68. Wheaton, "Genius and the Jurist," 266; Albert Halstead, "Chairman Cortelyou and the Republican Campaign," *RR*, 30 (Sept. 1904), 294–98.

69. *Campaign Contributions*, 24 and 31; *NYTr*, Aug. 2:2 and 3:1, 1904, Sept. 2:2, 1908; *NYTi*, Aug. 2:3 and 7:3, 1904, and Aug. 29:III/11, 1920 (quotation); and Dawes, *Journal*, 383.

70. *Campaign Contributions*, 25 and 32 (quotation); *NYTr*, July 31:2 and Aug. 2:2, 1904; O. P. Austin to Cortelyou, June 7, 1904, and ensuing letters, James W. Babcock to Cortelyou, Aug. 23, 1904, Elmer Dover to Cortelyou, Sept. 27 and Oct. 5, 1904, with enclosed "Literature Distribution Statement - to October 3rd 1904," N. B. Scott to Cortelyou, Sept. 27, 1904, Cortelyou Papers; O. P. Austin to John C. Spooner, July 6, 1904, Elmer Dover to Spooner, Aug. 18, 1904, Spooner Papers; *RR*, 30 (Aug. 1904), 146; ibid. (Nov. 1904), 528–29.

71. Harry S. New to Cortelyou, Aug. 9, 16, and 29, 1904, Charles Dick to Cortelyou, Aug. 20, 1904, and Cortelyou to Dick, Aug. 21, 1904, Cortelyou Papers; Cortelyou to Theodore Roosevelt, Oct. 2, 1904 (quotation), Theodore Roosevelt Papers, Library of Congress.

72. *KT*, Nov. 10:4, 1904.

73. Clarkson to Leigh Hunt, Oct. 1, 1904, Clarkson Papers; Clarkson to Cortelyou, Nov. 11, 1904, Cortelyou Papers; Clarkson to William Loeb, Jr., Sept. 15, 1904, Theodore Roosevelt Papers. Note, in the same tenor, *NYTr*, July 9:6, 1908.

74. Snell Smith, "Chairman Frank Harris Hitchcock," *RR*, 38 (Oct. 1908), 439–42; Walter Wellman, "The Management of the Taft Campaign," ibid., 432–38; *NYTr*, July 9:6, 18:2, 30:2, and 31:2, and Aug. 3:2, 4:2, 9:1, 16:2, 19:2, and 23:2, and Sept. 27:IV/8 (quotation), 1908; *NYTi*, Nov. 1:II/10, 1908; "*LIST OF LITERATURE ISSUED BY REPUBLICAN NATIONAL COMMITTEE,*" ca. Aug. 1908, Richard V. Oulahan to Taft, Sept. 1 and 10, 1908, and Victor L. Mason to Taft, Oct. 8, 1908, Taft Papers; O. P. Austin to James S. Sherman, July 1, Sherman to H. C. Loudenslager, July 25 and Aug. 3, Francis Curtis to Sherman, July 29 and Aug. 7, and Sherman to Theodore Roosevelt, Sept. 6, all 1908, James S. Sherman Papers, New York Public Library.

75. *Campaign Contributions*, 46 and 81–83; *NYTi*, Nov. 1:II/10, 1908; *NYTr*, Sept. 2:2, 4:2, and 22:2, 1908; James S. Sherman to Joseph G. Cannon, July 4 and 29, Sherman to James A. Tawney, Aug. 24 and Sept. 4, Sherman to S. W. Smith, Sept. 3, and Thomas H. Carter to Theodore Roosevelt, Sept. 29, all 1908, James S. Sherman Papers; R. A. Ballinger to James R. Garfield, Sept. 27, 1908, B. B. Ray to Garfield, Oct. 6, 1908, James R. Garfield Papers, Library of Congress; Theodore L. Weed to Oscar S. Straus, Sept. 28, 1908, Oscar S. Straus Papers, Library of Congress.

76. James A. Tawney to Sherman, Sept. 2, 1908, and Theodore Roosevelt to Sherman, Sept. 5, 1908, James S. Sherman Papers.

77. *Campaign Contributions*, 63, 83–84, and 102–04; Josephus Daniels, "Mr. Bryan's Third Campaign," *Review of Reviews*, 38 (Oct. 1908), 423–31; *NYTi*, Oct. 18:V/1 and Nov. 1:II/10, 1908; *NYTr*, July 26:2 and 27:2, and Aug. 3:2, 1908; F. M. Dyer to "National Com.," Oct. 15, T. J. Pence to Josephus Daniels, Oct. 15, 24, and 27, Herman Ridder to F. M. Dyer,

Oct. 19, Daniels to "the Editor," Oct. 21, Ridder to Daniels, Oct. 26, all 1908, box 669, Josephus Daniels Papers, Library of Congress; William Jennings Bryan to Henry Watterson, July 15, and Aug. 4 (quotation), 8, and 22, 1908, Daniels to Watterson, Sept. 30, 1908, Henry Watterson Papers, Library of Congress.

78. Bingham Duncan, *Whitelaw Reid: Journalist, Politician, Diplomat* (Athens, Ga., 1975), 101; *MJ*, Sept. 17:4, 1892; *Review of Reviews*, 6 (Nov. 1892), 519.

79. For the early history of public relations, see Ray E. Hiebert, *Courtier to the Crowd: The Story of Ivy Lee and the Development of Public Relations* (Ames, Iowa, 1966); Alan R. Raucher, *Public Relations and Business, 1900–1929*, (Baltimore, 1968).

80. *NYTi*, Aug. 9:V/2, 1908. For the Democrats' changing self-conception, see the different letterheads of Josephus Daniels to Henry Watterson, Sept. 30, 1908, and Daniels to William Jennings Bryan, Oct. 6, 1908, Watterson Papers. New Jersey Democrats used the term "publicity" as early as the campaign of 1907: Reynolds, "Testing Democracy," 134. See also, Francis G. Newlands to H. A. Dunn, Sept. 19, 1908, Newlands Papers.

81. *NYTi*, Sept. 4:III/5, 1904.

82. Frank Presbrey, *The History and Development of Advertising* (Garden City, N.Y., 1929), 302–564; Ewen, *Captains*.

83. Elmer Dover to Cortelyou, Sept. 15 and Oct. 5, 1904, with enclosed "Literature Distribution Statement - to October 3rd 1904," Harry S. New to Cortelyou, Sept. 22, 1904, Cortelyou Papers; Josephus Daniels to Consolidated Lithograph Co., Oct. 26, 1908, box 669, Daniels Papers; Victor L. Mason to James S. Sherman, Sept. 18, 1908, James S. Sherman Papers; *PI*, Oct. 17:3, 1904; and Hitchcock to Taft, July 26, 1908, and William Hayward to Taft, Sept. 7, 1908, Taft Papers.

84. Halstead, "Chairman Cortelyou," 298; *NYTi*, Sept. 4:III/5, 1904.

85. *PI*, Oct. 3:2 and Nov. 1:2, 1904.

86. *NYTi*, Sept. 8:1, 1908; Daniels, "Bryan's Third Campaign," 429; *NHJC*, Oct. 28:5, 1908; Richard V. Oulahan to Fred W. Carpenter, Aug. 10, 1908, Taft Papers.

87. *NYTr*, Sept. 5:2, 1888; *OWH*, Oct. 28:4, 1892; *Campaign Contributions*, 25 (quotation) and 81–83; Charles W. Bryan to Norman E. Mack, Oct. 16, 1908, box 669, Daniels Papers; Richard V. Oulahan to Taft, Sept. 1, 1908, Taft Papers; *NHJC*, Oct. 31:7 and 11, and Nov. 2:5, 7, and 10, 1908.

88. *MJ*, Oct. 23:5, 1912, gives a good introduction to the three campaigns but overemphasizes the differences among them. See also George Kibbe Turner, "Manufacturing Public Opinion: The New Art of Making Presidents by Press Bureau," *McClure's Magazine*, 39 (July 1912), 316–

27. For the Democrats' press operation, see J. C. Hammond to Josephus Daniels, [ca. Sept.-Oct., 1912], Robert W. Woolley to Daniels, Oct. 3 and 21, 1912, and Daniels to "Brother Editor," Oct. 19, 1912, box 670, Daniels Papers; Woolley to William G. McAdoo, Oct. 23, 1912, William G. McAdoo Papers, Library of Congress; Josephus Daniels to Alton B. Parker, Aug. 5 and 19, 1912, Parker Papers; *Farmers' National Campaign Page No. 1, Woodrow Wilson's Speeches, Advance Copy of Governor Wilson's Address to Voters, to Be Read at Democratic Rally, on Saturday, November 2, 1912,* all box 34, *Campaign Cartoons Issued by DEMOCRATIC NATIONAL COMMITTEE Presented to ROBERT W. WOOLLEY by C. R. MACAULEY 1912,* bound volume, box 35, Robert W. Woolley Papers, Library of Congress. For the Republican press effort, see Charles D. Hilles to William Howard Taft, Aug. 17, 18, and 22, 1912, M. K. Yoakum to Rudolph Forster, Sept. 24, 1912, Louis N. McGuerin to Hilles, Oct. 1, 1912, Taft Papers; *Open Letter to the Hon. Woodrow Wilson, Candidate of the Democratic Party for President, from Charles D. Hilles, Chairman of the Republican National Committee,* Oct. 22, 1912, David S. Barry to Carmi A. Thompson, Oct. 26, 1912, Hilles Papers.

89. Charles D. Hilles to William Howard Taft, Aug. 22, 1912, Taft Papers; J. C. Hammond to Josephus Daniels, [ca. Sept.-Oct., 1912], Robert W. Woolley to Daniels, Oct. 3 and 21, 1912, and M. J. Wade to Daniels, Nov. 4, 1912, box 670, Daniels Papers; Joseph R. Davies to Thomas J. Walsh, July 28, 1916, Walsh Papers.

90. Hal Reid to William Howard Taft, Oct. 17, 1911 and [Aug. 1912] (quotation), Taft Papers; *NYTi,* Aug. 9:1, 1912; and *MJ,* Oct. 20:Comic Weekly/4, 1912.

91. *RR,* 46 (Aug. 1912), 149–50; Charles D. Hilles to William Howard Taft, Aug. 16 and 19, Sept. 27, and Oct. 4 and 11, 1912, William Tyler Page to T. W. Brahany, Sept. 27, 1912, Walter H. Wilson to Hilles, Oct. 11, 1912, Taft Papers; *CIO,* Sept. 10:5, 1912; G. J. Diekema to Elihu Root, Sept. 6, 1912, John W. Hutchinson, Jr., to Root, Oct. 5 and 29, 1912, Elihu Root Papers, Library of Congress.

92. *MJ,* Oct. 23:5, 1912; *NYTi,* Sept. 1:3, 1912; Hilles to Taft, Sept. 11, and Oct. 2, 3 and 4, 1912, William Tyler Page to Rudolph Forster, Oct. 12, 1912, Taft Papers; Frank C. Williams to Hilles, Oct. 11, 1912, Hilles Papers.

93. Hilles to Taft, Aug. 17, 1912 (quotations), Rudolph Forster to Hal Reid, Aug. 31 and Sept. 10, 1912, Taft Papers; *MJ,* Oct. 23:5, 1912; *NYTi,* Sept. 1:3, 1912; *CIO,* Sept. 1:4, 1912; *CRH,* Sept. 1:5, 1912.

94. Hilles to Taft, Oct. 3, 1912, Taft Papers; *MJ,* Oct. 21:1, 1912.

95. *NYTi,* July 23:14 (quotation), and Sept. 4:7, 1916; *NYTr,* July 23:5, 1916.

96. *NYTi*, July 26:20 and 29:3, and Aug. 8:4, 1916; E. C. McKay to F. M. Crossett, Nov. 10, 1916, Charles Evans Hughes Papers, Library of Congress; F. P. Corrick to Harold Ickes, Oct. 5, 1916, Ickes to Will H. Hays, Dec. 12, 1916, Harold Ickes Papers, Library of Congress; S. A. Perkins to C. D. Hilles, July 26, and Aug. 18 and 28, 1916, William H. Taft to Hilles, July 27, 1916, Winfield T. Durbin to Hilles, Aug. 10, 1916, Hilles to Perkins, Sept. 5, 1916, and Hilles to C. N. McArthur, Nov. 6, 1916, Hilles Papers; Theodore H. Price and Richard Spillane, "Stalking for Nine Million Votes," *World's Work*, 22 (Oct. 1916), 666–69.

97. John B. Elliott to Robert W. Woolley, Jan. 25, 1916, Woolley Papers; Frederic C. Howe to William G. McAdoo, June 13, 1916, McAdoo to Vance McCormick, July 10, 1916, McAdoo Papers. Note also D. H. MacAdam to Woolley, Feb. 25, 1916, enclosing MacAdam to Otto Praeger, Feb. 25, 1916, and Woolley to Charles R. Crane, Mar. 1, 1916, Woolley Papers.

98. See Woolley's manuscript autobiography, "Politics Is Hell," especially chapter 24, box 44, and the memorandum, *"BUREAU OF PUBLICITY.,"* box 34, in ibid. For Creel's approach to the campaign see two outlines in ibid., one that begins *"As to the general issue,"* in the Creel file, box 4, the other entitled "A PUBLICITY CAMPAIGN ABOUT THE CONSTRUCTIVE WORK OF THE WILSON ADMINISTRATION.," in the "McAdoo, 1915" file, box 27, ibid. The second outline has no attribution but is clearly Creel's work: note the similarities in prose and typing style between the two outlines. S. D. Lovell attributes the outline to William G. McAdoo in *The Presidential Election of 1916* (Carbondale, Ill., 1980), 92.

The following paragraphs draw on Woolley to Vance McCormick, Mar. 1, 1917, a seventeen-page final report on the publicity bureau in the Woolley Papers.

99. *"BUREAU OF PUBLICITY.,"* ibid. There is a good selection of the Democrats' literature in box 35, ibid. Many of the documents are bound as *Campaign Literature Issued by The Democratic National Committee, 1916* (New York, 1917?). See also: Publicity Bureau, Western Democratic Headquarters, memorandum to "ALL BUREAUS," Sept. 18, 1916, box 168, John F. McCarron to Thomas J. Walsh, Sept. 13, 19, and 25, box 172, Walsh Papers; D. H. MacAdam to Woolley, July 10, 1916, Woolley Papers; *NYTi*, July 23:14, Sept. 10:4, and Oct. 1:2, 1916; Price and Spillane, "Stalking," 667 and 674.

100. Quotations from Woolley to Vance McCormick, Mar. 1, 1917, Woolley Papers; and Woolley to Edward M. House, Sept. 6, 1916, Edward M. House Papers, Yale University. See also: Woolley to Joseph P. Tumulty, Aug. 24, 1916, and Frank H. Gould to Woolley, Feb. 7, 1917, with enclosures, Woolley Papers; Woolley to House, July 26 and Aug. 5, 1916, House Papers; Thomas J. Walsh to *Fulton Leader*, Sept. 1, 1916, box

168, and press releases, "The Federal Reserve Act and the Farmer" and "CASH FOR THE FARMER," box 176, Walsh Papers; Henry F. Hollis to William G. McAdoo, Aug. 24, 1916, McAdoo Papers; Homer S. Cummings to Josephus Daniels, Aug. 15, 1916, Daniels Papers; Key Pittman to Woolley, Aug. 8 and 11, 1916, Woolley to Pittman, Aug. 10, 1916, box 8, Pittman Papers; Arthur B. Krock to Henry Watterson, Aug. 16, 1916, Watterson Papers.

A copy of *The Bulletin* is in box 27 and a scrapbook of praise for Woolley's work in box 28 of the Woolley Papers. Woolley also underscores the importance of "the psychological moment" in Woolley to House, May 16, 1916, ibid. For some rare criticism of Woolley's press operation, see F. S. Bonfils to McAdoo, Aug. 22, 1916, McAdoo Papers.

101. "A PUBLICITY CAMPAIGN ABOUT THE CONSTRUCTIVE WORK OF THE WILSON ADMINISTRATION.," Woolley Papers.

102. Woolley to Vance McCormick, Mar. 1, 1917, ibid.; Woolley to House, Sept. 6, 1916, House Papers. See also: C. R. Macauley to Woolley, June 24, 1916, Vance McCormick to Woolley, Sept. 28, 1916, Woolley Papers; and Woolley to Thomas J. Walsh, Oct. 2, 1916, box 176, Walsh Papers.

103. Price and Spillane, "Stalking," 667 and 671; *NYTi*, Aug. 26:4, 1916; *KT*, Oct. 25:1, 1916; *TR*, Oct. 24:5, 1916; and Hays, *Memoirs*, 107.

104. *TR*, Oct. 3:4, 1916.

105. "A PUBLICITY CAMPAIGN ABOUT THE CONSTRUCTIVE WORK OF THE WILSON ADMINISTRATION.," Woolley Papers; Woolley to House, Sept. 6, 1916, House Papers. Actually, the bureau's original slogan was "With honor he *has* kept us out of war"; Democratic speakers and writers quickly shortened it to the more effective, and famous, version. See Woolley to Carter Glass, Jan. 16, 1936, ibid. For aspects of the parties' use of advertising, see D. H. MacAdam to Woolley, no date, Woolley to Alfred Lucking, Oct. 25, 1916, and Woolley to James M. Cox, Aug. 21, 1920, ibid; *KCS*, Oct. 29:10A, 1916; Woolley to House, Aug. 5 and Sept. 6, 1916, House Papers; Price and Spillane, "Stalking," 667; and Will H. Hays, *Memoirs* (New York, 1955), 105. Samples of Republican and Democratic ads are in *TR*, Nov. 6:4, 5 and 8, 1916; *KCS*, Oct. 29:13A, 30:11, and 31:10, and Nov. 1:11, 2:8 and 9, 3:10A and 2B, 4:7, 5:13A, and 6:8–10, 1916; and *KT*, Oct. 31:9, and Nov. 1:7, 2:2, and 4:7, 1916. For interesting comment on the parties' use of slogans, see *BT*, Oct. 7:16, 1920.

106. Woolley to Thomas B. Love, Sept. 10, 1920, Woolley Papers; *KCS*, Nov. 6:13, 1916.

107. Woolley to Vance McCormick, Mar. 1, 1917, Woolley, "Politics Is Hell," chapter 29, Maylin Hamburger to E. M. Scholz, Jan. 23, 1917, with

other letters in David Lawrence file, box 11, and copy of the ten-questions pamphlet, box 35, all in Woolley Papers.

108. Lovell, *Presidential Election of 1916*, 179; Autobiographical Notes, "XII–1916," 14–15, box 181, Hughes Papers. See also Birch Helme to Warren G. Harding, Aug. 9, 1920, box 172, Harding Papers.

109. *KCS*, Nov. 2:6, 1916.

110. Woolley to House, Sept. 6, 1916, House Papers; Price and Spillane, "Stalking," 671; and *KCS*, Oct. 23:16, 1916.

111. *RR*, 62 (Oct. 1920), 346; Presbrey, *History of Advertising*, 565–70; David M. Kennedy, *Over Here: The First World War and American Society* (New York, 1980), 45–92 and 105.

112. John B. Elliot to Woolley, Dec. 9, 1918, Woolley to Elliott, Jan. 17, 1919, Woolley Papers; Albert Lasker Oral History, 115–22, Columbia University; Seward W. Livermore, *Politics Is Adjourned: Woodrow Wilson and the War Congress, 1916–1918* (Middletown, Conn., 1966), esp. 105–11. For Lasker, see John Gunther, *Taken at the Flood: The Story of Albert D. Lasker* (New York, 1960); and Albert D. Lasker, *The Lasker Story, As He Told It* (Chicago, 1963).

113. Woolley to James M. Cox, Aug. 5 and Sept. 14, 1920, Woolley to Daniel Roper, July 22, Aug. 16, 17, and 19, and Oct. 6, 1920, Thomas M. Alexander to George White, July 21, 1920, Woolley Papers; Gordon Auchincloss to Edward M. House, Sept. 14, 1920, Woolley to House, Sept. 14 and 29, 1920, House Papers; James M. Cox to T. T. Ansberry, Oct. 9, 1924, John W. Davis Papers, Yale University; George White to Thomas J. Walsh, Aug. 16, 1920, Walsh to Key Pittman, Sept. 16, 1920, and Walsh to White, Sept. 24, 1920, box 373, Walsh Papers; Harold Ickes to Hiram Johnson, Sept. 11, 1920, Ickes Papers; Key Pittman to John Sharp Williams, July 28, 1924, Pittman Papers; and *WP*, Oct. 11:5, 1920.

114. Quotations from Ibid. Oct. 4:2 and 10:5, 1920; W. A. Grant to Howard Mannington, Aug. 27, 1920, box 171, Judson C. Welliver to Scott Bone, July 19 and 31, 1920, box 165, Harding Papers. See also Will Hays to Harding, Sept. 18, 1920, box 97, Richard Barry to Harding, Aug. 20, 1920, Hubert Work to Harding, Oct. 3, 1920, box 163, Paul M. Bone to George B. Christian, July 26, 1920, Judson C. Welliver to Scott Bone, July 31, 1920, box 165, Arthur Brisbane to Harding, Aug. 3 and Oct. 5, 1920, Harding to Brisbane, Aug. 6, 1920, box 166, Welliver to W. A. Grant, July 30 and Aug. 6, 1920, Grant to Christian, Aug. 5, 1920, Grant to Welliver, Aug. 20, box 171, ibid. For a good account of the Harding campaign, see Randolph C. Downes, *The Rise of Warren Gamaliel Harding, 1865–1920* (Columbus, Ohio, 1970), 452–631.

115. Lasker Oral History, 131–35, Columbia University; *NYTi*, July 28:1 and 4, 1920; Will H. Hays to George B. Christian, July 15, 1920, box 97, Lord and Thomas to *Marion Daily Star*, July 12, Christian to A. D.

Lasker, July 26 and Aug. 21, Lasker to Christian, July 28, Aug. 19, 20, 23, and 24, and telegram, Aug. 24, Lasker to Scott Bone, Aug. 18, Lasker to Judson Welliver, Aug. 20 (second quotation), Welliver to Lasker, Aug. 23, box 120, Christian to William Wrigley, July 26, Wrigley to Christian, July 28 (first), box 126, all 1920, in Harding Papers.

116. Theodore Roosevelt to Kermit Roosevelt, Oct. 26, 1904, Theodore Roosevelt Papers. See also *NYW*, Aug. 16:2, Sept. 18:7, and Oct. 16:3, 1900, and Aug. 29:2, 1912; *NYTi*, July 13:2, 1904, Aug. 13:1, 1912, Sept. 20:1 and 21:16, 1916, and July 15:3, 22:1 and 3, and 23:1, Aug. 2:2, and Sept. 3:3, 1924; *LAT*, Oct. 15:3, 20:2, and 22:2, 1924; George B. Cortelyou to William Loeb, Jr., July 19, 1904, and Theodore Roosevelt to Cortelyou, Oct. 1, 1904, Theodore Roosevelt Papers; Vance McCormick to Thomas J. Walsh, Sept. 30 and Oct. 3, 1916, box 172, Walsh Papers.

117. *NYTi*, July 30:1, Aug. 9:1, 19:3, 23:3, Sept. 3:3, and Oct. 19:1 and 21:6, 1904; *RR*, 30 (Nov. 1904), 522–24 and 528.

118. Taft to James S. Sherman, July 18, 1908 (first quotation), and Sherman to Taft, Oct. 8, 1908, James S. Sherman Papers; *NYTr*, Aug. 13:1 and 21:1, and Sept. 4:2, 6:1 (second), 14:3, and 26:1–2, 1908.

119. *NYTi*, Aug. 4:5 and Sept. 15:1, 1912; *NYW*, Aug. 25:4 and 27:4, 1912; William F. Sapp to Wilson, Aug. 10, 1912, John J. Treacy to Wilson, Aug. 17, 1912, Wilson Papers.

120. Charles G. Dawes to Harding, Aug. 30, 1920, box 116, Victor Heintz to Howard Mannington, July 21, 1920, box 118, Harding to Albert J. Beveridge, July 8, 1920, James P. Goodrich to Harding, Sept. 14, 1920, P. E. Goodrich to Harding, June 14, 1920, box 127, D. M. Kitselman to Harding, July 13, 1920, box 128, Harry S. New to Harding, June 18, 1920, box 129, Henry Cabot Lodge to Harding, July 8, 1920, box 144, Thomas O. Marvin to Harding, June 18, 1920, box 145, Albert Shaw to Harding, Sept. 23, 1920, box 180, Harding Papers; *NYTi*, July 8:2, 9:1, 12:1, 16:4, and 29:1, Aug. 6:3, and Sept. 12:1, 1920; *PI*, Sept. 3:4, 13:12, 19:1, 23:4, and 28:1, and Oct. 8:1 and 22:1, 1920.

121. James E. Watson to Hughes, June 13, 1916, Hughes Papers.

122. *NYTi*, Sept. 8:10, 1920.

123. Franklin Roosevelt to Ronald Campbell, Oct. 9, 1920, box 13, Group 15, Franklin D. Roosevelt Papers, Franklin D. Roosevelt Library, Hyde Park, New York; and also Key Pittman to John W. Davis, Sept. 28, 1924, box 12, Pittman Papers.

124. "*ITINERARY* SENATOR HARDING'S SPEAKING TOUR," Oct. 6, 1920, *Memorandum to Mr. George Christian*, Oct. 12, 1920, and A. H. Shaw, memorandum, Oct. 8, 1920, box 122, Harding Papers; *NYTi*, Aug. 9:2 and 31:VIII/1, and Sept. 1:3, 1924. See, also, Edward G. Riggs, "The Newspaper and Politics," *Bookman*, 19 (July 1904), 492.

125. For candidates on the road, see *NYW*, Oct. 2:1, 6:7, 10:3, and 17:1–4, 1900, and Aug. 30:4, and Sept. 3:4, 4:3, 5:5, 26:4, and 27:4, 1912; *NHJC*, Oct. 27:1, 1908; *KT*, Sept. 19:1, 20:2 and 4, 21:1–2, and 22:1–2, 1916; *PI*, Sept. 3:4, 4:4, 9:1, and 29:4, and Oct. 8:5, 1920; *SPPP*, Sept. 9:1 and 3, 1920; *NYTi*, Sept. 6:1, 1924; and *CTr*, Oct. 7:1 and 10:14, 1924.

126. *NYW*, Sept. 8:7, and Oct. 2:7 and 7:1, 1900, Aug. 27:4 and 29:3, and Sept. 3:10, 1912; *PI*, Sept. 2:3 and 4:4, 1904, and Sept. 9:4 and 29:4, and Oct. 8:5, 1920; *CTr*, Oct. 3:2, 1924; and *NYTi*, Sept. 2:3, 1924.

127. *NYTi*, Sept. 1:3, 1904, and Sept. 7:27 and 11:3, 1924; *NYW*, Aug. 22:18, 1912; *KT*, Sept. 21:12, 1916; *PI*, Oct. 11:4 and 12:12, 1920; *SPPP*, Sept. 7:1 and 4, 1920; *LAT*, Oct. 23:3, 1924; *NYN*, Oct. 18:25, 1924; and *DMR*, Aug. 12:2 and 24:M–12, 1924.

128. George B. Cortelyou to William Loeb, Jr., July 8, 1904, and John A. Sleicher to Loeb, July 12, 1904, Theodore Roosevelt Papers; *NYTi*, July 11:7, and Aug. 15:7 and 22:7, 1904, and Aug. 1:1 and 26:1 and 3 (quotation), 1924; *NYW*, Sept. 26:5, 1912; and *KT*, Oct. 25:1, 1916.

129. *LAT*, Oct. 6:3, 1900; *NYW*, Sept. 15:1 and Oct. 2:1, 1900, and Sept. 4:3, 1912; *NHJC,*, Oct. 29:3 and 30:6, and Nov. 4:1, 1908; *MJ*, Oct. 12:4, 1912; *KT*, Aug. 11:5 and 23:2, 1916; *TR*, Nov. 4:4, 1916; *NYTi*, Aug. 15:III/11, 1920; *PI*, Sept. 14:12, 1920; *CPD*, Oct. 13:7, 1924; *DMR*, Oct. 6:2 and 7:1, 1924; and John W. Davis to Mrs. Andrew J. Peters, July 21, 1924 (quotation), and Davis to Dr. J. J. Richardson, Aug. 4, 1924, Davis Papers.

130. *NYTi*, July 16:2, 1904 (second quotation), July 13:2 (first), and Aug. 22:1 and 3 (fourth), 1924; John A. Sleicher to William Loeb, Jr., July 18, 1904, Theodore Roosevelt Papers; Loeb to George Cortelyou, Aug. 11, 1904, Cortelyou Papers; undated clipping in scrapbook, 32, box 28, and Joseph P. Tumulty to Woolley, Aug. 12, 1916 (third), Woolley Papers; Riggs, "Newspaper and Politics," 492–93; *WP*, Oct. 24:Magazine/1, 1920.

131. William G. McAdoo to Wilson, Sept. 5, 1912, and Atlee Pomerene to McAdoo, Sept. 18, 1912, Wilson Papers; Birch Helme to Warren G. Harding, July 3, 1920, box 172, Harding Papers; and also Medill McCormick to Charles Evans Hughes, Aug. 25, George W. Perkins to Hughes, Sept. 6, Robert R. McCormick to Hughes, Oct. 2, and Frank A. Vanderlip to Hughes, Oct. 18, all 1916, Hughes Papers; Key Pittman to John W. Davis, Sept. 28, 1924, box 12, Pittman Papers; *NYTr*, July 4:5, 1916.

132. Key Pittman to John W. Davis, Sept. 28, 1924, box 12, Pittman Papers; Gordon Auchincloss to Davis, memorandum, with Auchincloss to E. M. House, Aug. 8, 1924, House Papers.

133. George Cortelyou to Theodore Roosevelt, Sept. 16, 1904, Theodore Roosevelt Papers; Birch Helme to Warren Harding, July 3, 1920, box 172, and John W. Vrooman to Harding, July 28, 1920, box 182, Harding Papers.

134. Travis W. Benjamin to Taft, July 9 (first quotation), W. Jones to Taft, Aug. 4 (third), W. R. Mandigo (?) to Taft, Aug. 6 (second), J. A. Greene to Taft, Aug. 6, and M. C. Garber to Fred W. Carpenter, Sept. 3, all 1908, Taft Papers; Harry A. Walters to James S. Sherman, Sept. 3, 1908, James S. Sherman Papers; *NYTr*, Aug. 9:II/1, 1908; Henry Litchfield West, "Unforeseen Factors of the Current Campaign," *Forum*, 40 (Sept. 1908), 201. Warren Harding got into similar trouble for smoking cigarettes: Winfield T. Durbin to Harding, Aug. 12, 1920, box 127, and L. G. Higley to Harding, Sept. 27, 1920, box 128, Harding Papers.

135. *NYW*, Sept. 3:4, 1912; *PI*, Oct. 12:12, 1920.

136. For the impact of the radio on the campaign of 1924, see *NYTi*, July 18:3, 19:1–2, 20:1, 21:1 and 10, 23:3, 24:1, 25:1, 27:VIII/15, 29:4, 30:2, and Aug. 1:2 and 10, 3:3, 7:1, 10:1, 12:3, and 15:2, 1924; Helen Bullitt Lowry, "Political Revolution by Radio," in ibid., July 20:IV/1 and 14, 1924; *LAT*, Sept. 7:II/10, and Oct. 21:1, 23:1, and 24:1, 1924; *DMR*, Aug. 31:M/8, 1924; *RR*, 70 (Sept. 1924), 237; Merz, "Campaign Opens," 307; Bruce Bliven, "How Radio Is Remaking Our World," *Century*, 108 (June 1924), 147–54; William D. Nicholas to KFKX, Sept. 6, 1924, Hugh A. Wilson to KFKX, Sept. 6, 1924, Mr. and Mrs. John Berger to KFKX, Sept. 7, 1924, and other letters to KFKX in box 33, Davis Papers.

137. Albert J. Beveridge to Theodore Roosevelt, Aug. 9, 1904, enclosed with William Loeb, Jr., to George Cortelyou, Aug. 12, 1904, and also Beveridge to Cortelyou, Aug. 9, 1904, Cortelyou Papers; Charles E. Magoon to Taft, Aug. 26, 1908, Taft Papers; *RR*, 44 (Oct. 1916), 355; and also ibid., 30 (Nov. 1904), 522–24 and 528; and ibid., 46 (July 1912), 3.

138. *MJ*, Oct. 20:II/4, 1912. For the impact of primaries on party organization, see Morton Albaugh to Chester I. Long, Nov. 17, 1916, Chester I. Long Papers, Kansas Historical Society; Chester B. Horn to Franklin Roosevelt, Dec. 29, 1924, box 8, Lee B. Ewing to Roosevelt, Dec. 22, 1924, Henry Hunter to Roosevelt, Dec. 26, 1924, John F. Doherty to Roosevelt, Jan. 2, 1925, and John I. Williamson to Roosevelt, Mar. 9, 1925, box 9, Group 11, Franklin D. Roosevelt Papers; Turner, "Manufacturing"; and James W. Davis, *Presidential Primaries: Road to the White House* (Westport, Conn., 1980).

139. Sheffield to Charles D. Hilles, Dec. 15, 1916, Hilles Papers.

140. Herbert Adams Gibbons, "The Presidential Campaign," *Century*, 100 (Oct. 1920), 832–40.

141. Leslie M. Shaw to J. Hampton Moore, May 15, 1916 (quotation), and Shaw to "Dear Sir," May 18, 1916, J. Hampton Moore Papers, Philadelphia Historical Society.

142. Walter Wellman, "The Management of the Taft Campaign," *RR*, 38 (Oct. 1908), 432; Snell Smith, "Chairman Frank Harris Hitchcock," ibid., 440–42; Josephus Daniels, "Bryan's Third Campaign," ibid., 424; ibid., 46 (Aug. 1912), 150; *CIO*, Sept. 16:4, 1912; *NYTi*, Aug. 17:3, 1912, July 16:1 and 3, 1912, and July 2:9, 1916.

143. *AS*, July 5:1, 1900; *KT*, Aug. 26:7 and Oct. 7:6 and 8:1, 1904; *NYTi*, Sept. 4:III/5, 1904; W. S. Rodie to Alton B. Parker, Aug. 18, 1904, with enclosed poll blanks and instructions, box 11, Parker Papers; Wellman, "Taft Campaign," 434–35; Walter S. Dickey to William Howard Taft, Aug. 11, 1908, Taft Papers; Daniel C. Roper to Edward M. House, Aug. 5, 1916, and House to Woodrow Wilson, Sept. 30, 1916, House Papers; and *Worker's Manual* (New York?, 1916?), box 35, Woolley Papers. The parties' polling arrangements, however, were not always perfect: Charles D. Hilles to C. N. McArthur, Nov. 6, 1916, Hilles Papers.

144. *NYTi*, Aug. 27:1, 1908; *NYTr*, Oct. 3:2, 1908.

145. Francis Curtis to L. A. Coolidge, Nov. 3, 1904 (quotations), and Francis Curtis to George Cortelyou, Dec. 12, 1904, Cortelyou Papers; Curtis to James S. Clarkson, Jan. 2, 1908, Clarkson Papers; Curtis to Oscar S. Straus, Feb. 15, 1908, Straus Papers; Charles F. Scott to Charles D. Hilles, Dec. 14, 1912, enclosed with Hilles to Elihu Root, Dec. 19, 1912, Root Papers; Anson W. Prescott to Charles Evans Hughes, July 3, 1916, Hughes Papers; and *Presidential Campaign Expenses: Hearings Before a Subcommittee of the Committee on Privileges and Elections, United States Senate*, 66th Cong., 2nd sess., 2 vols. (Washington, D.C., 1920), II, 1134–35.

146. Walter Vrooman, *The New Democracy: A Handbook for Democratic Speakers and Workers* (St. Louis, 1897); A. Mitchell Palmer to Robert W. Woolley, March 30, 1915, box 34, Joseph P. Tumulty to Woolley, and W. D. Jamieson to Woolley, Jan. 8, 1920, Woolley Papers; Gerson Harry Smoger, "Organizing Political Campaigns: A Survey of 19th and 20th Century Trends" (Ph.D. diss., University of Penslyvania, 1982), 98–100; Franklin Roosevelt to John P. Hume, Nov. 8, 1920, box 16 (quotation), and Roosevelt to A. R. Titlow, Nov. 16, 1920, box 22, Group 15, Homer Cummings to Franklin Roosevelt, Dec. 12, 1924, Edward E. Leake to Roosevelt, Dec. 13, 1924, with clipping, box 8, Roosevelt to Atlee Pomerene, Dec. 6, 1924, box 9, Group 11, Franklin Roosevelt Papers; and George White to Thomas J. Walsh, Apr. 9, 1921, and Richard Linthicum to Walsh, May 5, 1921, box 373, Walsh Papers.

147. James S. Clarkson to William Loeb, Jr., Aug. 19, 1906, Theodore Roosevelt Papers (first quotation); Clarkson to Leigh Hunt, Nov. 17,

1903, Clarkson Papers; J. Hampton Moore to George Cortelyou, June 28, July 23 (second quotation), Aug. 10, and Dec. 1, 1904, Cortelyou to Moore, Sept. 1, 1904, and John A. Stewart to Cortelyou, July 23, 1904, and other letters, Cortelyou Papers; J. Hampton Moore to Theodore Roosevelt, June 28, 1904, Theodore Roosevelt Papers; John Hays Hammond to W. H. Taft, Aug. 1, 20, and 27, and Oct. 9, 1908, Charles D. Hilles to Taft, Aug. 16, 1912, Taft Papers; John Hays Hammond, *The Autobiography of John Hays Hammond*, 2 vols. (New York, 1935), II, 538–39 and 585; *NYTi*, Aug. 27:2, 1904; and *NYTr*, Aug. 15:1 and Sept. 2:2 and 13:3, 1908.

148. Max F. Ihmsen to William Jennings Bryan, July 24, 1900, Bryan Papers; *NYJA*, Oct. 1:2, 4:1–2, 5:1–2, 7:63, and 8:7, 1900; *NYTi*, Sept. 3:3, 1904; Josephus Daniels to Alton B. Parker, Sept. 21, 1904, Parker Papers; William C. Liller to Thomas J. Walsh, Nov. 10, 1916, Walsh Papers.

149. John G. Sproat, *"The Best Men": Liberal Reformers in the Gilded Age* (New York, 1968), 133–37 and 327.

150. Merz, "Campaign Opens," 309.

151. George Juergens, *News from the White House: The Presidential-Press Relationship in the Progressive Era* (Chicago, 1981).

7. "The Vanishing Voter"

1. *NHJC*, Oct. 31:4 (first quotation) and Nov. 5:4, 1900; *NYW*, Sept. 3:3, 9:3, 16:4E (second), and 19:7, 1900; B. F. Miles to Albert Shaw, Oct. 6, 1900, Albert Shaw Papers, New York Public Library (third); *Des Moines Leader*, Oct. 28:?, 1900; and *LAT*, Oct. 25:5 and 26:5, 1900. The national turnout figures here and in the following paragraphs are drawn from United States Bureau of the Census, *Historical Statistics of the United States, Colonial Times to 1970, Bicenntenial Edition*, 2 vols. (Washington, D.C., 1975), I, 1071–72.

2. *PI*, Aug. 21:8, Sept. 12:3, 18:8, and 25:18, and Oct. 2:8–9 (first quotation) and 3:4 (second), 1904; *RR*, 30 (Nov. 1904), 519; William E. Chandler to Theodore Roosevelt, Sept. 10, 1904, and Lyman Abbott to Roosevelt, Oct. 3, 1904 (third), Theodore Roosevelt Papers, Library of Congress; Charles G. Dawes, *A Journal of the McKinley Years*, ed. Bascom N. Timmons (Chicago, 1950), 384 (fourth); G. A. Knapp to John C. Spooner, Sept. 20, 1904, John C. Spooner Papers, Library of Congress; B. F. Spaulding to George B. Cortelyou, Oct. 15, 1904, and L. T. Michener to Cortelyou, Oct. 17, 1904, George B. Cortelyou Papers, Library of Congress; "Apathy," *Nation*, 79 (Nov. 17, 1904), 388; James Otis Wheaton, "The Genius and the Jurist: A Study of the Presidential Cam-

paign of 1904" (Ph.D. diss., Stanford University, 1964), 410–13; and *KT*, Oct. 3:7, 1904.

3. *RR*, 38 (Oct. 1908), 387; Henry Dennis to James S. Sherman, Aug. 21, 1908, S. Sheldon Johnson to "Dick," Sept. 12, 1908, and M. P. Cook to Sam. W. Smith, Sept. 19, 1908, James S. Sherman Papers, New York Public Library; Frank L. Reber to Francis G. Newlands, Aug. 24, 1908, Francis G. Newlands Papers, Yale University; *NYTi*, Oct. 12:4, 1908. See also James S. Clarkson to Albert W. Swalm, Aug. 17, 1908, James S. Clarkson Papers, University of Iowa, Des Moines; *NHJC*, Oct. 12:5 and 13:6, 1908; *NYTi*, Sept. 8:1 and Oct. 13:2 and 18:VII/10, 1908; Henry Litchfield West, "Business Depression and the Popular Mind," *Forum*, 40 (Oct. 1908), 304; idem, "The President and the Campaign," ibid. (Nov. 1908), 413; and "An Era of No Feeling," *Nation*, 88 (July 9, 1908), 26.

4. Charles E. Townsend to William H. Taft, Oct. 13, 1912, and P. J. McCumber to Charles D. Hilles, Oct. 27, 1912, Charles D. Hilles Papers, Yale University; *MJ*, Oct. 22:4, 1912; *NYTr*, Aug. 1:10, 1916 (first quotation); Nicholas Murray Butler to Francis B. Loomis, Oct. 23, 1916, Francis B. Loomis Papers, Stanford University (second); *KCS*, Oct. 8:1 and 11:2, 1916; *KT*, Oct. 30:1 and Nov. 1:1, 1916; and *NYTi*, Sept. 10:V/3, 1916.

5. *BT*, Oct. 8:3 and 14:3, 1920; *PI*, Sept. 2:12, 5:9, 7:12, 19:II/8, 20:7 and 12, 23:5, 26:5 (first quotation), and 30:11, and Oct. 3:1, 5 (second), and 12, 11:12, 22:14, 24:II/8, 25:12, and 31:II/8, 1920; *SPPP*, Sept. 5:5, 6:4, and 14:1, and Oct. 26:10, 1920. See also Hilles to Nicholas Murray Butler, Aug. 26, 1920, Hilles Papers; Elmer Dover to Warren G. Harding, July 30 and Sept. 3, 1920, box 101, Birch Helme to Harding, Sept. 14, 1920, box 172, Albert Shaw to Harding, Sept. 23, 1920, box 180, and Albert J. Beveridge to Harding, July 6, 1920, box 127, Warren G. Harding Papers, Ohio Historical Society, Columbus; *BTe*, Oct. 18:8, 1920; *NYTi*, Aug. 30:3, 1920; *HT*, Oct. 2:6 and 4:1–2, 1920; and *WA*, Nov. 2:7, 1920.

6. Paul Kleppner, *Who Voted? The Dynamics of Electoral Turnout, 1870–1980* (New York, 1982), 55–82. Turnout figures rounded from those for "Nonsouth" in tables on 22 and 57. Kleppner's regional estimates seem comparable with the national statistics presented in United States Bureau of the Census, *Historical Statistics of the United States*, I, 1071–72.

7. *NYTi*, Aug. 20:V/8, 1916; and John Francis Reynolds, "Testing Democracy: Electoral Participation and Progressive Reform in New Jersey, 1888–1919" (Ph.D. diss., Rutgers University, The State University in New Jersey, 1980), 247–49.

8. *LAT*, Oct. 26:5, 1900; *NHJC*, Oct. 31:4 and Nov. 5:4, 1900; *KT*, Nov. 1:1, 1916; *BT*, Oct. 8:3, 1920; *PI*, Oct. 24:II/8, 1920; *SPPP*, Oct. 26:10, 1920; and *HT*, Oct. 12:20, 1920.

9. *NHJC*, Oct. 13:6, 1908; and *NYTi*, Sept. 10:V/3, 1916. See also *LAT*, Oct. 25:5, 1900; Dawes, *Journal*, 384; George E. Taylor to George B. Cortelyou, Oct. 7, 1904, Cortelyou Papers; James S. Clarkson to Leigh Hunt, Oct. 1, 1904, James S. Clarkson Papers, Library of Congress; *NYTi*, Oct. 12:4 and 18:VII/10, 1908; *BT*, Oct. 14:13, 1920; *PI*, Sept. 2:12 and 20:12, and Oct. 3:1, 11:12, 22:14, and 25:12, 1920; *SPPP*, Sept. 14:1, 1920; Albert Shaw to Harding, Sept. 23, 1920, box 180, Albert J. Beveridge to Harding, July 6, 1920, box 127, Harding Papers; and Reynolds, "Testing Democracy," 166–67.

10. *PI*, Sept. 26:5, 1920.

11. *NYTi*, May 12:26, 1926. For a rejection of the fraud argument, see William B. Munro, "Is the Slacker Vote a Menace?," *National Municipal Review*, 17 (Feb. 1928), 80.

12. *NYTi*, Oct. 7:22, 1924 and Oct. 18:II/4, 1925.

13. Charles E. Merriam and Harold F. Gosnell, *Non-Voting: Causes and Methods of Control* (Chicago, 1924), esp. 14, 34, 50–51, 160–63, and 251–52.

14. Ben A. Arneson, "Non-Voting in a Typical Ohio Community," *American Political Science Review*, 19 (Nov. 1925), 816–25. Quotation from 819.

15. Arthur M. Schlesinger and Erik McKinley Eriksson, "The Vanishing Voter," *New Republic*, 40 (Oct. 15, 1924), 162–67.

16. Gosnell, "The Vanishing Voter," ibid. (Nov. 5, 1924), 253; and idem, "The Voter Resigns," ibid., 44 (Oct. 21, 1925), 224–25. See also Eriksson's response in "Party Competition and Voting," ibid., 45 (Dec. 2, 1925), 50.

17. For instance, Boyden Sparkes, "Are You an Election Day Alien?," *Collier's*, 74 (Aug. 16, 1924), 12–13; idem, "Why Don't They Vote?,'" ibid. (Aug. 30, 1924), 6–7; idem, "How Can We Make 'Em Vote?," ibid. (Sept. 20, 1924), 11, 12, and 38; *DMR*, Aug. 24:M/9 and 29:4, 1924; *NYTi*, Oct. 14:22, 1924.

18. Silas Bent, "Is the Ballot a Blessing," *Century*, 116 (Sept. 1928), 626–27; Victor Rosewater, "A Proposal to Cure Vote-Shirking," *National Municipal Review*, 17 (Feb. 1928), 78–79.

19. Samuel Spring, "The Voter Who Will Not Vote," *Harper's Magazine*, 145 (Nov. 1922), 748; *CTr*, Oct. 5:1, 1924; *LAT*, Sept. 25:II/4 and Oct. 6:II/4 and 7:1, 1924; *NYTi*, Sept. 13:23, 1924; Bent, "Is the Ballot a Blessing," 632; Rosewater, "A Proposal," 78; and Herbert C. Pell, Jr., to Alton B. Parker, Sept. 10, 1925, and Clem Shaver to J. H. Hammond, Sept. 15, 1926, box 91, NCF Papers, New York Public Library.

20. On party competition, see George Wheeler Hinman, Jr., "Getting Out the Vote," *Review of Reviews*, 70 (Oct. 1924), 409–12; *NYTi*, Sept. 14:28, 1924; Walter Lippmann, "Birds of a Feather," *Harper's Magazine*,

150 (Mar. 1925), 408–09; and Benjamin F. Worcester to Alton B. Parker, Aug. 19, 1925, and Hannah M. Durham to Parker, Aug. 24, 1925, box 91, NCF Papers. For party differences, see *CTr*, Oct. 4:6, 1924; *DMR*, Aug. 29:4, 1924; *NYTi*, Aug. 17:VIII/12 and Sept. 7:II/4 and 12:20, 1924, and Oct. 23:III/4, 1927; Bent, "Is the Ballot a Blessing," 632; and L. E. Dillingham to Parker, Aug. 15, 1925, T. E. Dye to Parker, Aug. 20, 1925, and Herbert C. Pell, Jr., to Parker, Sept. 10, 1925 (quotation), box 91, NCF Papers.

21. Milton Carmichael to Alton B. Parker, Aug. 17, 1925, Francis Prescott to Parker, Aug. 17, 1925, and Mary C. Franzman to Parker, Jan. 30, 1926 (quotation), box 91, ibid.

22. William M. Butler to Alton B. Parker, Aug. 15, 1925, box 91, ibid.

23. *NYTi*, Sept. 12:3 and Oct. 21:7, 1924, and Dec. 19:IV/23, 1926; Sparkes, "How Can We Make 'Em Vote?," 38; and Kenneth L. Roberts, "The Inarticulate Conservatives," *Saturday Evening Post*, 196 (July 21, 1923), 44. See also *CTr*, Oct. 4:6, 1924; *NYHT*, Nov. 4:18, 1924; and *NYTi*, Aug. 18:15, 1924. For earlier assertions about middle- and upper-class non-voting, see *MJ*, Oct. 8:16 and 20:Comic Weekly/4, 1912.

24. *CTr*, Oct. 4:6, 1924 (first quotation); *NYHT*, Oct. 4:10 and Nov. 4:18 (second), 1924; *NYTi*, Sept. 11:3, 1924 (third), Oct. 9:24, 1925, and Sept. 25:7 and Oct. 21:4, 1927; *CPD*, Oct. 4:8, 1924; Rosewater, "A Proposal," 77.

25. *LAT*, Oct. 3:II/4–5, 1924 (first quotation); *NYTi*, Sept. 16:22 (second) and Oct. 6:5 and 14:22, 1924, and Feb. 11:10 and Oct. 13:4 (third), 1926; Roberts, "Inarticulate Conservatives," 44.

26. Spring, "Voter Who Will Not Vote," 744–46; *NYTi*, Nov. 1:2, 1926 (first quotation), and Apr. 1:V/2 and Aug. 16:8, 1928; *New York Commercial*, July 24:1, 1924 (second), in file 473, Calvin Coolidge Papers, Library of Congress.

27. For examples of the use of the term "slacker," see *PI*, Sept. 19:II/8 and Oct. 3:12, 1920; *SPPP*, Oct. 15:10, 1920; *CTr*, Nov. 9:2, 1924; *LAT*, Sept. 28:II/4, 1924; *NYTi*, Aug. 9:8, 1926, and May 13:6, 1927; Charles H. Sherrill, "Voting and Vote-Slacking," *North American Review*, 220 (Mar. 1925), 401–04.

28. Roberts, "Inarticulate Conservatives," 48.

29. Merriam and Gosnell, *Non-Voting*, 77, 233–35, and 237–41; Rosewater, "A Proposal," 79–80; *NYTi*, Nov. 30:28, 1926; and W. E. Hamilton to Ralph M. Easley, Mar. 21, 1925, box 91, NCF Papers.

30. Spring, "Voter Who Will Not Vote," 747; Lincoln C. Cummings to E. T. Clark, June 24, 1924, and Cummings to Calvin Coolidge, June 27, 1924, file 473, Coolidge Papers.

31. *NYTi*, Aug. 4:12 and Sept. 9:VIII/3, 1923, and also Aug. 31:VIII/10 and Sept. 10:1, 1924, Nov. 8:II/4, 1925, Jan. 17:22, Feb. 4:2, 5:9, and

8:18, May 15:20, Nov. 10:3 and 16:26, and Dec. 19:IV/1 and 23, 1926; *DMR*, Sept. 18:1, 1924; *LAT*, Oct. 2:II/4 and 25:II/4, 1924; *NYHT*, Oct. 14:14, 1924; Sherrill, "Voting and Vote-Slacking,"403–04; Wilbur F. Wakeman to William A. Prendergast, June 11, 1926, and Charles R. Parmele to Coolidge, Oct. 21, 1926, file 473, Coolidge Papers.

32. *NYTi*, Sept. 11:22, Oct. 22:1, and Dec. 4:20 (second quotation) and 25:16, 1924, Nov. 15:20, 1926 (first), Jan. 22:14 and July 10:II/3, 1927; Merriam and Gosnell, *Non-Voting*, 241–43 and 257–58; *DMR*, Oct. 11:4, 1924; "Selling Democracy to the Voter," *Outlook*, 146 (July 27, 1927), 402 (third); Rosewater, "A Proposal," 77; Edward M. House, "The Problem of the Vote," *McCall's Magazine*, 54 (Aug. 1927), 67.

33. Merriam and Gosnell, *Non-Voting*, 168, 235–37, and 243–46 (quotation); Gosnell, *Getting Out the Vote: An Experiment in the Stimulation of Voting* (Chicago, 1927), esp. 111; Schlesinger and Eriksson, "Vanishing Voter," 166–67; *NYTi*, Oct. 22:1, 1924, and Jan. 22:14, 1927; *DMR*, Oct. 11:4, 1924.

34. *NYTi*, July 7:4, 27:VIII/1, and 31:3, Aug. 10:2 and 17:7, and Sept. 2:1, 1924, and Apr. 26:5, 1926; *DMR*, Sept. 2:7, 1924; Michelet, "The Millions of Americans Who Fail to Vote," *Current History Magazine of the New York Times*, 21 (Nov. 1924), 247–49; Michelet to C. B. Slemp, July 12, 1924, with pamphlets and press releases, in files 1832 and 1832A, Coolidge Papers. See also Michelet's correspondence with Walter Lippmann in folder 817, box 20, series one, Walter Lippmann Papers, Yale University.

35. John E. Edgerton to Coolidge, Sept. 5, 1924, with enclosed pamphlet, *STOCKHOLDERS MEETING OF THE U.S.A.* (n.p., 1924?), and NAM press release of Sept. 2, 1924, and Edgerton to Coolidge, Apr. 20, 1926, file 473, Coolidge Papers; *NYTi*, July 7:4 and Sept. 2:4, 1924; *DMR*, Sept. 3:1, 1924.

36. *LAT*, Sept. 3:12 and 12:II/1 and 8, 1924; *NYTi*, Aug. 20:3 and 25:3, Sept. 8:3, 11:3, and 14:2, and Oct. 3:2 and 28:3, 1924; C. B. Slemp to Russell R. Whitman, July 28, 1924, Slemp to John E. Edgerton, Sept. 9, 1924, Slemp to Michelet, Sept. 19, 1924, Slemp to Mrs. Aaron Schloos, Sept. 22, 1924, and Frederick C. Hicks to E. T. Clark, Oct. 27, 1924, file 473, Coolidge Papers.

37. *CPD*, Oct. 1:1, 1924; *DMR*, Sept. 19:3 and 21:M/8, 1924; *NYTi*, Aug. 1:13, Sept. 5:19, 6:11, and 13:12, and Oct. 13:3, 1924; C. A. McPheeters to Coolidge, Sept. 16, 1924, and Frank Hampton Fox to Coolidge, Sept. 24, 1924, file 473, Coolidge Papers.

38. *CPD*, Oct. 9:3–4, 1924; *LAT*, Sept. 30:1 and Oct. 21:1 and II/4, 26:II/4, and 28:1, 1924; *NYHT*, Oct. 7:16 and 8:12, 1924; and *NYTi*, Nov. 4:20, 1924.

39. *CPD,* Oct. 1:1 and 12:II/1, 1924; *LAT,* Sept. 14:II/12, 1924; *NYTi,* Aug. 24:II/5, 1924.

40. *NYTi,* July 16:3 and Aug. 17:II/2 and 18:15, 1924.

41. Ibid., Jan. 26:3, Feb. 4:4, and Apr. 18:17, 1925.

42. *CTr,* Oct. 7:5 and 9:2 (quotation), 1924; *CPD,* Oct. 2:4, 9:7, 10:1, 15:8, and 18:5, 1924; *DMR,* Sept. 14:E/1–2, 25:4, and 30:7, and Oct. 3:2 and 7:2, 1924; *LAT,* Sept. 25:3, 26:II/10, 28:II/5, and 29:2, and Oct. 1:II/11, 3:2, 4:3, 8:II/13, and 11:4, 1924; *NHJC,* Nov. 3:3, 1924; *NYTi,* Sept. 7:II/29 and 21:II/3, Oct. 8:30, 14:34, and 19:II/2, and Nov. 4:31, 1924; Russell R. Whitman to Coolidge, July 24, 1924, R. A. Grady to C. B. Slemp, Aug. 30, 1924, Frank H. Cole to Coolidge, Sept. 14, 1924, A. U. Quint to Slemp, Sept. 29, 1924, William F. Garcelon to Slemp, Sept. 29, 1924, with clipping from *Metuchen Record,* Sept. 26:1, 1924, and William E. Hasseltine to Coolidge, May 12, 1925, with clipping, "Little Ripon Gets Out Big Vote," from *Kiwanis Magazine* (May 1925), file 473, Coolidge Papers. For the voting drive in Michigan during 1918 and 1919, see John Palmer Gavit, *Americans By Choice* (New York, 1922), 330–34 and 369.

43. *NYTi,* Sept. 7:II/5 and 12:3, and Oct. 5:7, 7:4, 10:7, 12:3, 27:5, and 31:3, 1924.

44. Ibid., Nov. 14:20, 1927; and also NAM, *STOCKHOLDERS MEETING OF THE U.S.A.; NYTi,* Oct. 3:2, 1924; and *NYHT,* Oct. 7:16, 1924.

45. Frederic Zeigen to Coolidge, Sept. 12, 1924, Thomas L. Elder to Slemp, Sept. 2, 1924, and H. A. Hope to "Secretary of the President," Oct. 21, 1924 (quotation), file 473, Coolidge Papers.

46. *LAT,* Oct. 13:II/4, 1924; *NYTi,* Aug. 13:14, 1924; William Hard, "'Politics Ain't What It Was,'" *Nation,* 119 (Oct. 22, 1924), 441–42; and *DMR,* Nov. 2:E/6, 1924. See also *NYTi,* Aug. 14:14, 1924.

47. *CPD,* Oct. 12:II/4, 1924; *DMR,* Sept. 14:L/4 and 28:M/6, and Oct. 13:4, 1924; *LAT,* Oct. 10:4, 1924; *NHJC,* Oct. 1:6 and 4:8, and Nov. 4:11, 1924; *NYTi,* Nov. 3:1–2, 1924; and Harold Ickes to H. W. Johnson, Sept. 9, 1924, Harold Ickes Papers, Library of Congress.

48. *NYTi,* Aug. 17:II/2 and Nov. 2:8 and 9:22, 1924.

49. Ibid., Nov. 9:22 (second quotation), 16:II/2 (first), and 19:2, 1924, and Sept. 20:6, 1926; "The Banner States in Civic Duty: Indiana and Kansas," *World's Work,* 40 (Jan. 1925), 238–39; "No Longer a Minority Election," *Outlook,* 139 (Feb. 11, 1925), 206 and 208; *NYHT,* Oct. 13:12, 1924; and James E. West to J. H. Hammond, Nov. 11, 1924, box 91, NCF Papers.

50. *NYTi,* May 31:II/1, 1925, and Aug. 2:19 (quotation), 1926; E. T. Clark to Michelet, Apr. 3 and 6, 1926, Michelet to Clark, Apr. 5, 1926, and various pamphlets, file 473, Coolidge Papers.

51. *NYTi*, Dec. 14:16, 1925, and June 29:22 and Sept. 19:X/14 and 22:12, 1926; and Ralph M. Easley to W. B. Munro, Nov. 17, 1924, box 63, NCF Papers. The full history of the NCF's role in the Get-Out-the-Vote movement has yet to be written from the voluminous papers of the organization in the New York Public Library.

52. *NYTi*, Oct. 30:23 and Dec. 14:16, 1925, and June 21:7, 1926; "*GET OUT THE VOTE*, Broadcast by Mr. Hammond November 1st, 1926, over W.R.C. Station Washington, D. C.," box 9, John Hays Hammond, Sr., Papers, Yale University; Hammond, *The Autobiography of John Hays Hammond*, 2 vols. (New York, 1935), II, 538–39 and 585; Hammond form letter, May 19, 1927, box 91, NCF Papers. Charles Merriam was not in favor of urging men and women to join parties: Merriam to Ralph M. Easley, Feb. 12, 1925, box 64, ibid.

53. *NYTi*, Jan. 30:32, Feb. 3:27, June 21:7, Sept. 5:II/1, 19:13, and 22:12, Oct. 3:II/1, and Nov. 2:3, 1926; "*GET OUT THE VOTE*," box 9, Hammond Papers.

54. *NYTi*, Apr. 20:1–2 (quotation) and 26:5, Oct. 12:29, and Nov. 1:1, 1926.

55. Ibid., Jan. 3:2, 1927.

56. Ibid., Feb. 3:II/1, May 12:16, and July 4:17, 1927. Quotations from Hammond, *SHALL WE WIPE OUT IN '28 THE SHAMEFUL RECORD OF '26 OR SHALL WE BOW TO MINORITY RULE?* (n.p., 1927), enclosed with Ralph M. Easley to E. T. Clark, July 18, 1927, file 473, Coolidge Papers.

57. "*GET OUT THE VOTE*," speech by Hammond to Massachusetts Committee on Active Citizenship, Boston, Oct. 4, 1927, in box 11, Hammond Papers.

58. Ibid.; *NYTi*, Nov. 4:15 and 20:II/4, and Dec. 16:24 (Reed speech), 1927.

59. *Literary Digest*, 89 (May 1, 1926), 12; "How to Make Americans Vote," *Nation*, 122 (May 5, 1926), 492.

60. *NYTi*, July 9:12, 1927.

61. Munro, "Physics and Politics—An Old Analogy Revised," *American Political Science Review*, 22 (Feb. 1928), 1–11. See also *NYTi*, Nov. 12:18 and Dec. 29:13, 1927.

62. Ibid., Nov. 12:18, 1927.

63. Munro, "Is the Slacker Vote a Menace?," 80–85.

64. Munro, "Intelligence Tests For Voters: A Plan to Make Democracy Foolproof," *Forum*, 80 (Dec. 1928), 823–30; idem, "Is the Slacker Vote a Menace?," 86. For attention to Munro's ideas, see *NYTi*, Nov. 14:20, 1927; "Is the Slacker Vote a Menace?," *RR*, 78 (Mar. 1928), 309–10; and "Let the Vote Alone!," *Independent*, 120 (June 2, 1928), 521–22 and 536.

65. A. K. Laing, "The Divine Right Not to Vote," *Independent*, 119 (Nov. 26, 1927), 521–22 and 536.

66. "Confessions of a Non-Voter," *New Republic*, 52 (Nov. 9, 1927), 307–09.See the response from Roy V. Peel in "A Voter Objects," ibid. (Dec. 14, 1927), 103–04.

67. Charles Merz, "Baiting the Ballot Box," *Forum*, 80 (Nov. 1928), 641–46.

68. *NYTi*, Mar. 3:3, Apr. 6:3, May 7:6, July 23:5, Aug. 20:3, Sept. 17:4, and 26:20, Oct. 31:18, and Nov. 4:IX/22 and 5:25, 1928; Katharine Ludington to Coolidge, Nov. 26, 1927, Ludington to Everett Sanders, Jan. 9, 1928, and C. S. Hutson to Coolidge, Sept. 24, 1928, file 473, Coolidge Papers.

69. *NYTi*, July 16:1 and 28:2, Aug. 15:10, Sept. 20:28, and Oct. 19:3 and 24:8, 1928.

70. Ibid., May 27:III/4,and Nov. 4:V/1 and 11:11, 1928. For further discussion of the election of 1928 and the revival of voting, see Chapter 8.

71. Kleppner, *Who Voted?*, 55–58 and 70–82, and also Chapter 1, above.

72. For hints that registration and the Australian ballot cut into turnout, see *NYH*, Oct. 17:4, 1888; *NYS*, Sept. 30:6, 1892; and Redfield Proctor to Benjamin Harrison, Sept. 7, 1892, Benjamin Harrison Papers, Library of Congress. Some political scientists have advanced changes in election laws as a primary cause of falling turnouts in the North: Philip E. Converse, "Change in the American Electorate," in Angus Campbell and Philip E. Converse, eds., *The Human Meaning of Social Change* (New York, 1972), 276–95; Stanley Kelley, Jr., Richard E. Ayres, and William G. Bowen, "Registration and Voting: Putting First Things First," *American Political Science Review*, 61 (June 1967), 359–77; Jerrold G. Rusk, "The Effect of the Australian Ballot on Split Ticket Voting: 1876–1908," ibid., 64 (Dec. 1970), 1220–38; and idem, "Comment: The American Electoral Universe: Speculation and Evidence," ibid., 68 (Sept. 1974), 1028–49. Walter Dean Burnham and Paul Kleppner have demonstrated that election laws had far less impact on Northern voting in the early twentieth century than first assumed: Burnham, *The Current Crisis in American Politics* (New York, 1982), 60–72; Kleppner, *Who Voted?*, 9–10 and 60–62; and Kleppner and Stephen C. Baker, "The Impact of Voter Registration Requirements on Election Turnout, 1900–16," *Journal of Political and Military Sociology*, 8 (Fall 1980), 205–26. See also Richard P. McCormick, *The History of Voting in New Jersey: A Study of the Development of Election Machinery, 1664–1911* (New Brunswick, N.J., 1953), 185–86.

73. With little evidence, Converse dismisses the decline of turnout as simply a statistical artifact of the end of supposedly widespread corrupt

practices after 1900: Converse, "Change," 281–95; idem, "Comment on Burnham's 'Theory and Voting Research,'" *American Political Science Review*, 68 (Sept. 1974), 1024–26. In the late nineteenth century, many commentators, including some sympathetic to liberal anti-partyism, believed reports of corruption were exaggerated. See James Bryce, *The American Commonwealth*, 2 vols. (London, 1888), II, 109 and 121–33; *NHP*, Sept. 2:4, 1892; *NYS*, Sept. 1:6 and Oct. 10:10, 1892; *Review of Reviews*, 6 (Nov. 1892), 387–88; and *NHJC*, Oct. 16:5, 1896. Converse's argument is countered with statistics in William E. Gienapp, "'Politics Seem to Enter into Everything': Political Culture in the North, 1840–1860," in Stephen E. Maizlish and John J. Kushma, eds., *Essays in American Antebellum Politics, 1840–1860* (College Station, Tex., 1982), 22–32. See also Richard J. Jensen, *The Winning of the Midwest: Social and Political Conflict, 1888–1896* (Chicago, 1971), 34–57. Converse, one might add, does not take account of the abundant literary evidence that legally qualified Northern voters were losing interest in politics and neglecting to turn out for elections after 1900.

74. Burnham, *Current Crisis*, 35, 60, 72–75, and 139–42; Kleppner, *Who Voted?*, 9 and 60–63; and idem, "Were Women to Blame? Female Suffrage and Voter Turnout," *Journal of Interdisciplinary History*, 12 (Spring 1982), 621–43.

75. *EID*, Nov. 7:2, 1860, and Sept. 9:2, 1868; *NHJC*, May 1:2 and Aug. 27:2, 1860, Oct. 6:2 and 15:2, 1864, and Oct. 23:2, 1880; *NHR*, Oct. 17:2, 1868; *AS*, Oct. 18:1 and Nov. 5:1, 1888.

76. *NYTr*, Oct. 1:5, 1860; *NHJC*, Oct. 28:2, 1880; *NHR*, Oct. 17:2 and 23:2, and Nov. 3:2, 1868.

77. *NHP*, Nov. 4:2, 1856; *CTr*, July 10:1 and 13:2, and Aug. 1:1, 7:2, 10:1, 14:2, 21:2, and 23:1, 1860; *NYW*, Oct. 6:1, 3, 7, and 10, 1868, and Oct. 6:1, 1876; *AS*, Sept. 29:Supplement, 1880, and Oct. 18:1 and Nov. 1:1, 1888; *NHJC*, Nov. 9:2, 1880; *NYH*, Oct. 16:6 and 21:11, and Nov. 3:5 and 4:1, 1888; and *MJ*, Aug. 23:7, 1892.

78. *NYTi*, May 1:26, 1927. For a trenchant critique of the parties' approach to enfranchised women, see Ruth McCormick to Will Hays, Aug. 2, 1920, enclosing "GENERAL CAMPAIGN SUGGESTIONS for Mr. Will H. Hays and Mrs. Harriet Taylor Upton from Mrs. John G. South and Mrs. Medill McCormick," box 120, Harding Papers.

8. Conclusion

1. The following paragraphs draw on Paul Kleppner, *Who Voted? The Dynamics of Electoral Turnout, 1870–1980* (New York, 1982), 83–141.

2. For the role of ethnic, religious and other factors in the election of '28, see Allan J. Lichtman, *Prejudice and the Old Politics: The Presidential Election of 1928* (Chapel Hill, 1979).

3. In addition to Kleppner, *Who Voted?*, see especially Raymond E. Wolfinger and Steven J. Rosenstone, *Who Votes?* (New Haven, 1980).

4. David S. Broder, *The Party's Over: The Failure of Politics in America* (New York, 1972); Walter Dean Burnham, *The Current Crisis in American Politics* (New York, 1982); William J. Crotty and Gary C. Jacobson, *American Parties in Decline* (Boston, 1980); Everett Carll Ladd, Jr., with Charles D. Hadley, *Transformations of the American Party System: Party Coalitions from the New Deal to the 1970s*, 2nd ed. (New York, 1978); Samuel Lubell, *The Hidden Crisis in American Politics* (New York, 1971); Austin Ranney, "The Political Parties: Reform and Decline," in Anthony King, ed., *The New American Political System* (Washington, 1979), 213–48; and Richard Jensen, "The Last Party System: Decay of Consensus, 1932–1980," in Paul Kleppner, ed., *The Evolution of American Electoral Systems* (Westport, Conn., 1981), 203–42.

5. Stanley Kelley, Jr., *Professional Public Relations and Political Power* (Baltimore, 1956); Dan Nimmo, *The Political Persuaders* (Englewood Cliffs, N.J., 1970); Melvyn H. Bloom, *Public Relations and Presidential Campaigns: A Crisis in Democracy* (New York, 1973); Robert Agranoff, ed., *The New Style in Election Campaigns*, 2nd ed. (Boston, 1976); Larry J. Sabato, *The Rise of Political Consultants: New Ways of Winning Elections* (New York, 1981); Sidney Blumenthal, *The Permanent Campaign*, rev. ed. (New York, 1982); Robert Westbrook, "Politics as Consumption: Managing the Modern American Election," in Richard Wightman Fox and T. J. Jackson Lears, eds., *The Culture of Consumption: Critical Essays in American History, 1880–1980* (New York, 1983), 143–73; and Kathleen Hall Jamieson, *Packaging the Presidency: A History and Criticism of Presidential Campaign Advertising* (New York, 1984).

6. *NHU*, Oct. 21:4, 1876.

7. *NN*, Aug. 26:1, Sept. 11:1 and 19:1, and Oct. 14:1, 1884; *NHJC*, June 11:2, 1884; *PI*, Oct. 2:3, 1884. See also Leon Fink, *Workingmen's Democracy: The Knights of Labor and American Politics* (Urbana, Ill., 1983).

8. *NN*, Aug. 28:1 and Oct. 2:4, 1884; *NHJC*, Sept. 2:2, 1884, and July 26:3 and Aug. 3:8, 1888; *NHR*, Oct. 13:1, 1888; and *BC*, Aug. 11:2, 1892.

9. *TA*, May 13:4, 1891.

10. *DN*, Oct. 1:2, 1892; *TA*, Aug. 10:13, 1892.

11. *TA*, May 13:10, 1891, and Aug. 10:1, 2, and 9 (quotations) and 24:10, Sept. 21:5, and Oct. 19:8 and 12, 1892. For a tantalizing reference to the party's deliberations about uniforms, see *MJ*, Aug. 11:1, 1892. For Populist political style, see also Lawrence Goodwyn, *Democratic Promise:*

The Populist Moment in America (New York, 1976), particularly 194–95, 311, and 384–85.

12. For La Follette's campaign in 1924, see *NYTi,* July 24:1 and 28:1, and Aug. 3:3 and 25:3, 1924; *CTr,* Oct. 7:1, 1924; and *DMR,* Aug. 17:M/ 10 and Oct. 6:M/2, 1924. For the Progressive campaign of 1912, see above, Chapter 6.

13. *NYTi,* Aug. 18:4, and Oct. 5:1–2 and 19:3 (quotation), 1908; *NYTr,* Aug. 18:4, 1908; Garrin Burbank, *When Farmers Voted Red: The Gospel of Socialism in the Oklahoma Countryside, 1910–1924* (Westport, Conn., 1976); James R. Green, *Grass-Roots Socialism: Radical Movements in the Southwest, 1895–1943* (Baton Rouge, 1978).

14. Theodore Draper, *The Roots of American Communism* (New York, 1957).

15. Alan Brinkley, *Voices of Protest: Huey Long, Father Coughlin, and the Great Depression* (New York, 1982).

16. The quoted phrase and the notion are from Goodwyn, *Democratic Promise.*

17. Alan Dawley, *Class and Community: The Industrial Revolution in Lynn* (Cambridge, Mass., 1976), 70 and 219.

SELECTED BIBLIOGRAPHY

As the notes include the major sources used in writing this study, all those materials need not be cited again here. It does seem worthwhile to list the manuscript collections and newspapers consulted and to comment on the most important of them.

Manuscript Collections

Nelson Aldrich Papers, Library of Congress
Gordon Auchincloss Papers, Yale University
James G. Blaine Papers, Library of Congress
William Jennings Bryan Papers, Library of Congress
Simon Cameron Papers, Library of Congress
Michael F. Campbell Diary, Yale University
Thomas H. Carter Papers, Library of Congress
William E. Chandler Papers, Library of Congress
Zachariah Chandler Papers, Library of Congress
James S. Clarkson Papers, Library of Congress
Grover Cleveland Papers, Library of Congress
Calvin Coolidge Papers, Library of Congress
George B. Cortelyou Papers, Library of Congress
Josephus Daniels Papers, Library of Congress
John W. Davis Papers, Yale University
Farnam Family Papers, Yale University
James A. Garfield Papers, Library of Congress

James R. Garfield Papers, Library of Congress
John Hays Hammond, Sr., Papers, Yale University
Hanna-McCormick Family Papers, Library of Congress
Warren G. Harding Papers, Ohio Historical Society
Benjamin Harrison Papers, Library of Congress
Rutherford B. Hayes Paper, Rutherford B. Hayes Library
Ebenezer J. Hill Papers, Yale University
Charles D. Hilles Papers, Yale University
Edward M. House Papers, Yale University
Charles Evans Hughes Papers, Library of Congress
Harold Ickes Papers, Library of Congress
Daniel S. Lamont Papers, Library of Congress
Albert D. Lasker Oral History, Columbia University
Walter Lippmann Papers, Yale University
William G. McAdoo Papers, Library of Congress
William McKinley Papers, Library of Congress
Edward McPherson Papers, Library of Congress
Levi P. Morton Papers, New York Public Library
National Civic Federation Papers, New York Public Library
Francis G. Newlands Papers, Yale University
Byron R. Newton Papers, Yale University
Alton B. Parker Papers, Library of Congress
Key Pittman Papers, Library of Congress
Frank L. Polk Papers, Yale University
Matthew S. Quay Papers, Library of Congress
Whitelaw Reid Papers, Library of Congress
Franklin D. Roosevelt Papers, Franklin D. Roosevelt Library
Theodore Roosevelt Papers, Library of Congress
Elihu Root Papers, Library of Congress
Albert Shaw Papers, New York Public Library
James S. Sherman Papers, New York Public Library
John Sherman Papers, Library of Congress
John C. Spooner Papers, Library of Congress
Oscar S. Straus Papers, Library of Congress
William Graham Sumner Papers, Yale University
William Howard Taft Papers, Library of Congress
Samuel J. Tilden Papers, Columbia University
Samuel J. Tilden Papers, New York Public Library
Thomas J. Walsh Papers, Library of Congress
Henry Watterson Papers, Library of Congress
William C. Whitney Papers, Library of Congress
Woodrow Wilson Papers, Library of Congress
Robert W. Woolley Papers, Library of Congress
Woolsey Family Papers, Yale University

Most of these collections contain at least a few items of importance. Several are indispensable for tracing the decline of popular politics. The William E. Chandler Papers offer a clear picture of the role of national party committees in spectacular campaigns during the mid-nineteenth century. Michael Campbell's diary gives a fascinating picture of the impact of partisan spectacle on a young worker. The two Tilden collections, fragmentary though they are, provide necessary detail on the origin of the educational campaign. The Cleveland Papers are essential for the campaign of 1888; the Harrison Papers, for the apathetic election of 1892. For James Clarkson's ideas and projects, his few papers in the Library of Congress must be supplemented by the Harrison Papers.

The evolution of the educational campaign after 1900 cannot be followed without the Cortelyou and Taft Papers. The superb collection of Woolley Papers documents the Democrats' advertised campaign of 1916. The Davis, House, Pittman, Walsh, and Franklin D. Roosevelt Papers detail the Democrats' decline from the triumph of 1916 to the defeats of 1920 and 1924. Albert Lasker's schemes emerge from the Harding Papers. For the Get-Out-the-Vote movement, the Coolidge and National Civic Federation collections are irreplaceable.

Newspapers

Ashtabula Sentinel; Semi-Weekly Ashtabula Sentinel
Baltimore Sun
Bangor Daily Commercial
Boston Evening Transcript
Bridgeport Telegram
Chicago Daily Inter Ocean
Chicago Daily Tribune; Chicago Press and Tribune
Chicago Record-Herald
Chicago Times
Cleveland Daily Plain Dealer
Daily Ohio State Journal
Des Moines Register
Detroit Evening News
Elyria Independent Democrat
Granite State Free Press
Hartford Courant
Hartford Times
Idaho Falls Times
Kansas City Evening Star
Kokomo Daily Tribune
Los Angeles Daily Times

Minneapolis Journal
Minneapolis Tribune
New Haven Daily Palladium
New Haven Daily Register; New Haven Evening Register
New Haven Evening Union
New Haven Morning Journal and Courier
New Haven Morning News
Newark Evening News
New York Evening Post
New York Daily News
New York Daily Tribune
New York Herald
New York Herald Tribune
New York Journal and Advertiser
New York Sun
New York Times
New York World
Omaha World Herald
Philadelphia Inquirer
Philadelphia Public Ledger and Transcript
St. Paul Pioneer Press
San Francisco Examiner
Topeka Advocate
Torrington Register
Washington Post
Waterbury American
Waterloo Courier

Good examples of urban Republican dailies in the heyday of party journalism include that stalwart sheet the *Chicago Inter Ocean* and also the *New Haven Palladium* and the *Philadelphia Inquirer*. The *Chicago Tribune*, the *New Haven Journal Courier*, and the *New York Tribune* illustrate Republican journalism tinged on occasion with independence. Representative Republican papers of the period of watered-down partisanship from the 1890s to the 1920s include the *Des Moines Register*, the *Minneapolis Journal*, the *Minneapolis Tribune*, and the *New York Herald Tribune*. The *Baltimore Sun*, the *Chicago Times*, and the *Cleveland Plain Dealer* exemplify the evolution of Democratic urban papers over the period of this study.

Liberal, independent journalism emerges from the pages of the *Kansas City Star*, the *Newark Evening News*, and the *New Haven Morning News*. For sensational journalism, one must begin with the *New York World* under Joseph Pulitzer. The yellow press is best represented by Hearst's *New York*

Journal and Advertiser. The *New York Daily News* typifies the tabloids of the 'twenties.

Several urban dailies have special strengths. The *New York Post* is essential for the fate of the Tilden Commission's amendments in 1877 and 1878; the *Baltimore Sun,* for the Democratic educational campaign of 1888; the *Chicago Tribune,* for the Republican canvass of 1896; the *New York Times,* for the activities of the national committees at each presidential election and for the Get-Out-the-Vote movement. The usefulness of great New York papers like the *Times* and the *Tribune* is to be expected; the excellent reporting in such fine Midwestern papers as the *Cleveland Plain Dealer,* the *Des Moines Register,* the *Kansas City Star,* the *Minneapolis Journal,* and the *Minneapolis Tribune* is an unexpected resource.

The Democratic *Daily Commercial* of Bangor, Maine, and the wonderful Republican *Tribune* of Kokomo, Indiana, give a good idea of partisan daily journalism in small towns from the end of the Civil War to the early twentieth century. Weekly "country" journalism throughout the period of this study is well illustrated by the Democratic *Idaho Falls Times* and three Republican sheets: the *Ashtabula Sentinel* of Jefferson, Ohio; the *Granite State Free Press* of Lebanon, New Hampshire; and Iowa's *Waterloo Courier.*

For a glimpse into Populism, I turned to the *Topeka Advocate,* the leading weekly of the People's party in Kansas. Before its conversion to the Democratic party in the late 'seventies, the *New Haven Union* offered insights into the Greenback movement.

INDEX